CORRECTION SYMBOLS

(**Boldface** numbers refer to sections in the *Handbook*.)

ab	abbreviation **39**	**mood**	error in mood **2b, 12b**
ack	acknowledging sources	**num**	number **40**
	MLA style **46**		**27–38**
	APA style **47**		
adj/adv	adjective/adverb **16a–d**		**28e**
agr	agreement **13, 14**		dash **31**
appr	inappropriate language **24, 25, 26**	**. . .**	ellipsis points **35**
art	article **20a**	**.?!**	end punctuation **27**
awk	awkward construction **17**	**( )**	parentheses **32**
bias	biased language **25b**	**" "**	quotation marks **34**
cap	capital letter **41**	**;**	semicolon **29**
case	error in case **15**	**par, ¶**	start new paragraph **4d**
cl	cliché **24, 26**	**//**	faulty parallelism **21c**
coh	coherence **4**	**pass**	passive voice **12b, 22c**
comp	comparison **19b–d**	**ref**	pronoun reference **14b**
con	connotation **26c**	**rep**	repetition **22a**
coord	coordination **9e, 21a**	**rev**	revise **3**
cs	comma splice **11a**	**sexist**	sexist language **25a**
ct	critical thinking **5**	**shift**	unnecessary shift **17a–h**
dev	inadequate development **2, 3a**	**sl**	slang **24a**
div	faulty word division **38e**	**sp**	misspelled word **42**
dm	dangling modifier **18a**	**ss**	faulty sentence structure **7, 9, 10, 11, 17i, 19**
exact	exactness **24, 26**		
fl	flowery language **22b, 24**	**sub**	subordination **9d, 21b**
frag	sentence fragment **10**	**t**	verb tense **12b**
fs	fused sentence **11b**	**trans**	transition needed **4d**
gr	grammatical error **7, 8, 9, 20**	**var**	lack of variety in sentence structure **23**
hyph	incorrect use of hyphen **38**	**vag**	vague word **26a, b**
		vb	verb form **8b, 12**
inc	incomplete construction **7, 19, 20**	**w**	wordy **22**
		ww	wrong word **24, 26**
ital	italics (underlining) **36**	⌒	close up space
jg	jargon **22, 24c, 26**	⸜	delete
lc	lowercase **41**	**x**	error
log	faulty logic **6c, d**	∧	insert
mixed	mixed construction **17i**	**#**	insert space
mm	misplaced modifier **18b**	⌣	transpose

The Modern Writer's Handbook

FIFTH EDITION

Frank O'Hare

THE OHIO STATE UNIVERSITY

Robert Funk

EASTERN ILLINOIS UNIVERSITY

Allyn and Bacon

BOSTON   LONDON   TORONTO   SYDNEY   TOKYO   SINGAPORE

Vice President: Eben W. Ludlow
Editorial Assistant: Grace Trudo
Executive Marketing Manager: Lisa Kimball
Production Administrator: Susan Brown
Composition Buyer: Linda Cox
Manufacturing Buyer: Suzanne Lareau
Cover Administrator: Linda Knowles
Editorial-Production Services: Omegatype Typography, Inc.

Library of Congress Cataloging-in-Publication Data
O'Hare, Frank.
    The modern writer's handbook / Frank O'Hare, Robert Funk. — 5th
ed.
        p.   cm.
    Includes index.
    ISBN 0-205-29900-8 (alk. paper). — ISBN 0-205-29899-0 (case). —
ISBN 0-205-30923-2 (instructor's annotated ed.)
    1. English language—Rhetoric Handbooks, manuals, etc.   2. English
language—Grammar Handbooks, manuals, etc.   3. Report writing
Handbooks, manuals, etc.   I. Funk, Robert.   II. Title.
PE1408.037   2000
808'.042—dc21   99-25711
                                                            CIP

Acknowledgments appear on page 618, which constitutes a continuation of
the copyright page.

Printed in the United States of America
10 9 8 7 6 5 4 3 2 1   03 02 01 00 99

Contents

PART II
READING CRITICALLY
AND WRITING LOGICALLY

PART III
GRAMMAR

PART IV
SENTENCE FORM

PART V
CLEAR SENTENCES

PART VI
DICTION AND STYLE

PART VIII
THE RESEARCH PAPER

PART IX
ACADEMIC AND BUSINESS WRITING

Preface

To the Instructor

The fifth edition of *The Modern Writer's Handbook* remains up to date, complete, and user friendly. Although deliberately compact and concise, it is complete and comprehensive enough to provide students with the advice and information they might need in a composition course, in a writing-across-the-curriculum class, or in the writing center. In preparing the revisions for this latest edition, we have added several new features that build on the pedagogical strengths of the successful fourth edition.

Concise, Comprehensive Coverage

The fourth edition provided a large number of compact-book users with some remarkable features that are usually found only in the giant handbooks, and these have been retained:

- Strong units on writing across the curriculum, including full-length and fully annotated MLA and APA papers.
- A student's essay in multiple drafts, with commentary and annotations that illustrate the process of developing and revising a paper.
- The User's Self-Help section that allows students to self-test and is also useful in writing centers.
- Efficient, accessible units on composing clear sentences and correcting problems in syntax and usage.
- Checklists to summarize key operations that students need to remember.

- A full system of cross-referencing, which helps students to find information quickly and work with the handbook on their own.
- A comprehensive, up-to-date glossary of usage.
- A comprehensive index.

New and Revised Sections

The fifth edition includes several important revisions and additions:

- Part I, The Process of Writing, has been revised, reorganized, and updated, bringing it in line with current composition theory and practice.
- Part II, Reading Critically and Writing Logically, is a new, separate section that focuses on critical reading and writing arguments.
- In place of an isolated chapter on writing with a computer, the handbook now contains a series of "tips" that give specific, practical information and advice for using a word processor at all stages of the writing process, including revising and editing.
- The instruction for doing research (Chapter 44) includes detailed information for using online catalogs, databases, and the Internet to locate and retrieve sources. This section also contains advice and warnings about the use of Internet materials.
- The MLA and APA documentation chapters now include the most recent guidelines and samples for citing electronic sources.
- An updated discussion of the parts of speech (Chapter 8) acknowledges the distinction between form-class words and structure-class words and includes brief discussions of determiners, qualifiers, and expletives.
- The discussion of paragraphs (Chapter 4) includes revised instruction on writing introductions and conclusions along with several new approaches and examples.

■ The material on English as a Second Language (Chapter 20) has been revised and improved; the section on determiners, in particular, has been clarified and reorganized.

■ The commentary on avoiding biased language (Chapter 25) has been expanded to provide specific, up-to-date guidelines about acceptable and unacceptable usage.

■ The section on writing about literature (Chapter 49) contains a new student paper, one that focuses on literary analysis, cites quotations from the primary text, and uses secondary sources for support.

■ Other sections have been freshened, amplified, and refocused.

Improved Pedagogy

Updated Instruction in Prewriting.   Directions for finding and developing a topic now include suggestions for using the Internet. There are new and additional examples of freewriting and brainstorming, a new checklist for analyzing audience and purpose, a new discussion about the writer's role, and a new checklist for planning the first draft.

Expanded Advice on Revising.   New sections include Revising from the Top Down, Revising for Style, and Getting Feedback: Peer Review. There are new checklists for revising content and organization, for preparing peer critiques, and for editing and proofreading.

Added Instruction on Critical Reading.   The new material on Being a Critical Reader includes specific suggestions for active reading, making inferences, and evaluating texts; it also provides sets of useful questions for reading more carefully and critically.

Revised Approach to Argument.   The chapter on writing arguments has been refocused and expanded in several ways: it now presents a clear, straightforward procedure for constructing an argumentative essay; explains how and when to use refutation; and contains a sample published essay, which is annotated to point out the main strategies for developing an argument.

Models and Examples. This edition contains a new sample of student writing and retains all but one of the previous ones, including a student's essay in multiple drafts and two sample research papers. Each of these models is annotated to help the student understand how a piece of writing develops and what decisions a writer needs to make. Also retained in this edition are excerpts of student papers from courses in the social, natural, and applied sciences.

In addition, literally hundreds of examples appear throughout the text to illustrate the various principles of sentence style, grammar, and usage. Nearly fifty paragraphs by student and professional writers serve as examples of writing or appear in exercises.

Checklists. Eleven checklists appear at critical points in the text to serve as efficient summary references for student writers. A listing of these checklists appears on the inside front cover of the handbook.

Word-Processing Tips. Thirty-nine suggestions for using the word processor are distributed throughout the text, placed where they are most directly helpful. These include warnings about the limitations of spell checkers and grammar checkers—encouraging students to edit their writing carefully in the context of their own meanings.

Exercises. The exercises in this edition are varied in content and reflect the diversified makeup of today's student body. Many of the exercises consist of related sentences to simulate proofreading and editing in paragraph form.

English as a Second Language.   The revised chapter on ESL presents the most common difficulties encountered by student writers whose first language is not English; comprehensive exercises reinforce the instructional units in the chapter.

Self-Diagnostic Section.   The User's Self-Help section at the end of the handbook features a set of self-administering diagnostic tests on grammar, punctuation, mechanics, syntax, and diction. The answer key identifies the topic at issue in an incorrect sentence; it then refers the student to the appropriate section of the handbook where a detailed explanation of the feature may be found and exercises can be worked to improve skills in selected areas.

Organizational Improvements

The basic organization of the fifth edition retains and improves on the successful organization of the previous edition. The handbook begins with the stages in the writing process from prewriting through planning, drafting, revising, and editing of the final product. It also treats writing coherent paragraphs. The book then reviews the key issues in critical thinking, active reading, and writing arguments. Then follows a description of English grammar and several related sections on sentence form and sentence clarity. The book also includes units on punctuation, mechanics, and spelling. The handbook concludes with complete coverage of the research paper, followed by concise discussions of academic and business writing. Each of the handbook's nine parts subdivides into chapters and then further subdivides into sections that contain a rule followed by examples, cross-referenced to appropriate sections in the handbook. Exercises that allow for practical applications of the subject matter appear throughout.

Supplements for the Instructor

- The casebound *Instructor's Annotated Edition to Accompany The Modern Writer's Handbook* provides overprinted answers and suggested responses to all of the exercises.
- *An Introduction to Teaching Composition in an Electronic Environment,* developed by Eric Hoffman and Carol Scheidenhelm, both of Northern Illinois University, offers a wealth of computer-related classroom activities. It also provides detailed guidance for both experienced and inexperienced instructors who wish to make creative use of technology in a composition environment.
- *The Allyn & Bacon Sourcebook for College Writing Teachers,* second edition, compiled by James C. McDonald of the University of Southwestern Louisiana, provides instructors with a varied selection of readings written by composition and rhetoric scholars on both theoretical and practical subjects.
- *Teaching College Writing,* an invaluable instructor's resource guide developed by Maggy Smith of the University of Texas at El Paso, is available to adopters who wish to explore additional teaching tips and resources.
- *Diagnostic Test Bank and Test Bank, 2000* includes tests, keyed to the relevant handbook sections, for analyzing common errors. The additional exercise sets on grammar, punctuation, and mechanics topics supplement those found in the handbook. (It is also available in computerized Windows and Macintosh formats.)

Supplements for the Student

- *Writer's Toolkit CD-ROM* offers a complete writing environment for planning, drafting, and revising and presents a wealth of heuristic devices to assist students with a variety of computer activities. (It works on both Macintosh and IBM platforms.)
- *GrammarCoach Software* provides ten interactive modules, each containing sixty separate exercise items, on each of the

ten most common student grammar, punctuation, and mechanics trouble spots.

■ *CompSite Website* offers resources and instructional material for students, including helpful information on using computers for writing, techniques for using the Internet for research, and a forum for exchanging papers and writing ideas.

Acknowledgments

We appreciate the assistance given for the fifth edition by reviewers who helped us to focus on constructive revisions of the fourth edition and to refine manuscript drafts for the new edition. Thanks for special help goes to Michal Brody, University of Texas at Austin, for help with the improvements and revisions of the ESL chapter.

For reviewing help with this and previous editions, we are most grateful to John M. Adair, Cumberland County College; Larry Beason, University of South Alabama; Niki E. Black, Red Rocks Community College; Michal Brody, University of Texas at Austin; Susan Chin, DeVry Institute of Technology; Walter H. Johnson, Cumberland County College; Robert Lamm, Arkansas State University; Joe Law, Wright State University; Karen Peterson Welch, University of Wisconsin–Eau Claire; and Joan Worley, University of Alaska, Fairbanks.

We remain particularly indebted to Eben Ludlow, Vice President at Allyn and Bacon, for his advice and leadership throughout this project. Thanks are also due to Grace Trudo, Editorial Assistant at Allyn and Bacon, for her help with many of the editorial and production details, to Fred Courtright for securing the permissions, and to Bonny Graham for her invaluable assistance in guiding the book through its final production.

Frank O'Hare
The Ohio State University

Robert Funk
Eastern Illinois University

To the Student

This book will help you develop and refine your writing skills with guidance from your instructor. It does not provide you with a foolproof formula for writing an essay or for avoiding all errors. No such shortcuts exist. *The Modern Writer's Handbook* does provide you with a plan for good writing that begins by illustrating general writing strategies and proceeds to help you work through prewriting, planning, drafting, revising, and editing. The book offers you options, not laws. It is not wrong, for example, to compose a first draft without writing a formal outline first, but because some people find outlining helpful, we describe strategies for outlining in Section 2b.

How to Find the Information You Need

This handbook has been designed to help you locate information quickly. It is a good idea to spend a few minutes familiarizing yourself with how the book works, especially with the devices that will help you find the information you need.

Blue Tabs at the top of each page in the handbook contain particular chapter numbers, section letters, and chapter symbols (these symbols are shorthand for the chapter title and correspond to the correction symbols listed on the front endpapers). The tabs can help you find information by thumbing through the book. Note also that at the top of every page, **chapter titles** appear in full on left-hand pages and **section titles** appear on right-hand pages to give you more specific guidance.

Checklists (boxed and tinted blue) appear throughout the handbook and provide you with convenient summaries of the handbook's guidelines on writing and revising. A list of all the handbook's checklists appears on the inside cover of the text. **Numerous lists** appear throughout the text to assist you with your writing.

Endpapers (the inside front and back covers and facing pages) contain important information:

1. A list of all the handbook's checklists appears on the inside front cover.

2. A list of correction symbols, which your instructor may use in correcting your essays and papers, appears on the end-paper facing the inside front cover. For example, if your instructor marks the symbol *dm* in the margin of your paper, you can consult the correction symbol list and note that the abbreviation means *dangling modifier*—a topic covered in section number **18a.** You can then consult the section number indicated (**18a**) for more information.

3. On the back endpapers, you will find an overview of the handbook's contents. Glance at it to get a sense of how the handbook is structured.

The **User's Self-Help** section at the end of the book contains a set of self-administering "diagnostic tests." Your teacher may require you to complete them, or you can do them on your own initiative. The tests concern grammar, syntax, diction, and punctuation/mechanics. Each is followed by an answer key that identifies for you the topic at issue in an incorrect sentence and leads you to the section of the handbook where the issue is presented in detail. There you can work on the designated exercises that will help you improve your skill on those topics.

The **Glossary of Usage** and the **Glossary of Grammatical Terms** provide you with accessible and brief explanations of which words to use in certain situations. For example, use the Glossary of Usage to determine whether the word *who* or *whom* is appropriate. Use the Glossary of Grammatical Terms to find the definitions of basic grammatical terms such as *case* or *pronoun*. Entries are arranged alphabetically in both glossaries.

The general **Index** contains a complete listing of all topics covered in the handbook along with page references and is designed for easy access.

Organization

This book first presents a general view of the writing process: planning, drafting, and revising your essay. It then considers the surface features of the language, emphasizing the important conventions that educated readers expect to encounter when they read your writing. The handbook concludes by introducing you to the specialized writing tasks you will encounter in your various college courses and in the business world.

Part I offers advice about the writing process: preparation for writing, planning and producing the first draft, revising (reseeing) the draft, and proofreading and editing it. Next, paragraph development is discussed, including organizational and developmental strategies as well as transitions within and between paragraphs.

Part II focuses on the importance of critical reading and writing arguments. It contains guidelines for active reading, making inferences, and evaluating texts. It also includes specific suggestions for building an effective argument.

Parts III through VII examine the principles of grammar, sentence form, clear sentences, diction and style, punctuation and mechanics, and spelling. You will use these parts of the book for reference if you are already familiar with grammatical principles and the terms and conventions of usage. If your understanding of these concepts is shaky, you can use these sections to help you master the conventions of grammar and usage.

Part VIII explains and illustrates how to write a research paper: how to select and limit a topic; how to plan, research, and write the paper; and then how to document it according to the styles recommended by the Modern Language Association (MLA) and the American Psychological Association (APA). A complete annotated sample research paper demonstrates each style. Refer to these samples for guidance as you write your own papers.

Part IX explains and illustrates the types of writing you will be called on to do in your different college courses—whether in literature classes or the social, natural, and applied sciences—

and in the business world (with examples of each type of writing). You may also find the chapter on preparing for writing essay examinations (Chapter 51) useful.

The handbook is divided into parts, then into chapters and sections. Each chapter contains sections that explore in detail the subject matter at hand. For instance, Part VI, Diction and Style, contains the following subdivisions: Chapter 24, Appropriate Word Choice; Chapter 25, Sexist and Biased Language; and Chapter 26, Exact Word Choice. Each of these chapters is further subdivided into sections. Thus, Chapter 24 covers the following: **24a** slang, **24b** colloquialisms, **24c** jargon, and **24d** gobbledygook. Each of these sections provides you with advice to follow, examples for clarification, and practice exercises.

You learn to write better only by writing often. *The Modern Writer's Handbook* serves as a guide to all steps in the writing process and with continued use will help you grow in competence and confidence. Paradoxically, the more diligently you use this handbook, the less you will need it.

Frank O'Hare
The Ohio State University

Robert Funk
Eastern Illinois University

User's Guide to Locating Information

Use the *back endpapers* for a *compact contents* if you know which topic might give you the right information. The *main contents* will show you further detail.

Use the *index* to find the word or term that will lead you to the right information.

Use the *correction symbol chart* on the *front endpaper* to interpret an instructor's mark and follow it to the appropriate information in this book.

Use the "*Helpful Checklists*" inventory in the *front endpaper* to locate useful checklist procedures for writing and research processes.

Use *section numbers* to follow cross-references within the text that may lead you to more precise information.

Here are the location features and reference features available on a typical page:

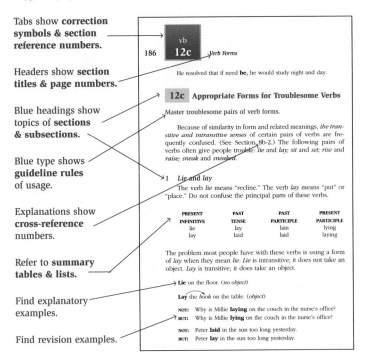

Tabs show **correction symbols & section reference numbers.**

Headers show **section titles & page numbers.**

Blue headings show topics of **sections & subsections.**

Blue type shows **guideline rules** of usage.

Explanations show **cross-reference** numbers.

Refer to **summary tables & lists.**

Find explanatory examples.

Find revision examples.

---

vb
186 **12c** Verb Forms

He resolved that if need **be,** he would study night and day.

12c **Appropriate Forms for Troublesome Verbs**

Master troublesome pairs of verb forms.

Because of similarity in form and related meanings, *the transitive and intransitive senses* of certain pairs of verbs are frequently confused. (See Section 8b-2.) The following pairs of verbs often give people trouble: *lie* and *lay; sit* and *set; rise* and *raise; sneak* and *sneaked.*

1 *Lie* and *lay*

The verb *lie* means "recline." The verb *lay* means "put" or "place." Do not confuse the principal parts of these verbs.

PRESENT INFINITIVE	PAST TENSE	PAST PARTICIPLE	PRESENT PARTICIPLE
lie	lay	lain	lying
lay	laid	laid	laying

The problem most people have with these verbs is using a form of *lay* when they mean *lie*. *Lie* is intransitive; it does not take an object. *Lay* is transitive; it does take an object.

Lie on the floor. (*no object*)

Lay the *book* on the table. (*object*)

NOT: Why is Millie **laying** on the couch in the nurse's office?
BUT: Why is Millie **lying** on the couch in the nurse's office?

NOT: Peter **laid** in the sun too long yesterday.
BUT: Peter **lay** in the sun too long yesterday.

THE MODERN WRITER'S HANDBOOK

Part

I

THE PROCESS
OF WRITING

The finished essay is the product of the writer's work, but it is a product that results from a series of interrelated and interwoven actions known collectively as a *process*. This process is complex and unpredictable, and writers develop their own distinct processes as they grow in experience. The process also shapes itself as it goes.

When you decide to write an essay, your image of the final product is often vague or ill-defined. You might, for example, begin with an idea of writing about air pollution but find yourself discussing alternative forms of energy, only to discover that what you really feel strongly about is the possible danger of nuclear reactors. The process of writing often produces such discoveries.

In addition, the process may loop back on itself or even change direction altogether. It is somewhat misleading, then, to describe writing as a series of steps that one completes in a fixed and uniform order. But familiarity with the sequence of steps in the writing process will help you to understand the process as a whole and give you freedom to apply it as you find best in your case. The actions most writers find necessary in the process of writing are *prewriting, drafting, revising,* and *editing.*

1 Preparing to Write: Prewriting

When people think about writing a paper, they usually think about the finished product. They envision a paper that is correct in both *form* and *content*. In truth, however, a successful draft stems from planning and preparation, which in the writing process is called **prewriting.** This stage of the process involves various activities that enable you to focus on a specific subject and generate examples, illustrations, and details to support and explain that subject. This stage also includes identifying and addressing two elements of writing that affect the effectiveness of your paper: its **purpose** and **audience.** But the emphasis at this point in the writing process is on content—on finding and developing ideas—rather than on form.

1a Finding a Topic

One of the first things you have to decide is what to write about. In many writing situations, the topic is decided for you. Your employer asks for a memo or report; you need to write for information or request an action; you feel compelled to express your opinion on a given issue. You have more leeway when your history professor asks for a paper on the Great Depression or your economics teacher assigns an essay on the national debt.

1 Start with a general subject

If allowed to select your own topic, you might begin by identifying a general subject that appeals to you, one that you can refine and narrow as you work through the process. Also consider the sources of information available to you. Will you be relying on personal experiences and observations? Or will you be expected to gather information through interviews, reading, or the Internet? Here is a list of general subjects that you might find useful as a starting point in your search for a topic:

PERSONAL INTERESTS	GENERAL TOPICS
Hobbies and leisure activities	Health and nutrition
Careers and work experiences	Social problems
Families	Education
Life changes	Nature and the environment
Places you have visited	Science and technology
Likes and dislikes	Crime and justice
Special interests	Sports and entertainment

2   Use the Internet

If you have access to the Internet, you can use its many resources to look for a topic. You might join a chat group, subscribe to a newsgroup, surf the Web, or look through online periodicals. Using a browser, you can check out listings and sites in a range of subject areas: arts and humanities, business and the economy, computers, education, entertainment, government, health, news and media, recreation and sports, science, and society and culture. A quick look under entertainment, for instance, reveals a long list of specific topics—everything from "amusement and theme parks" to "comics and animation," "performing arts," and "television." If you want to write about something about television, you can look under that heading to lead you to more specific ideas, such as amateur television, ratings, TV violence, the V-chip.

As you can see, the Internet contains an overwhelming array of resources. That's why you need to use it carefully: you can consume a lot of valuable time, and the sources you find there are not always reliable. For advice on evaluating and documenting online sources, see Sections 44b-3, 46b-4, and 47b-4.

3   Try other methods

Here are some other ways to find a suitable topic for an unspecified essay:

- Open a newspaper or magazine at random and read the first piece or article you see. Keep trying until something inspires you to state an opinion about it.
- Open a magazine and look only at the ads until you find one that leads you to generate a topic.
- Walk through a crowded area (the mall, the student union) or sit in a busy place (the cafeteria, the library), anyplace where many people congregate. Then, with notepad in hand, simply observe and take notes on what you see. Chances

are that you will see something that will interest you enough for you to explore it through writing.

- Go through your class notes and see whether they will jog your memory or imagination.
- Leaf through the last book you read and look for any marginal notes you might have made. Do any of these lead you toward a topic?

1b Generating Content

There are a number of ways to explore a subject and generate ideas: *freewriting, journal writing, brainstorming, clustering, questioning,* and *interviewing.*

If you are still not sure what to write about, these prewriting activities can help you to decide. If you have an assigned topic or have picked one of your own, these techniques will help you to clarify your thinking and develop your ideas. Experiment with these suggestions until you find the practices that work for you. If some do not help, don't frustrate yourself by following them.

1 Freewriting

Freewriting means just what it sounds like: you write with complete freedom, not bothering about correctness or style or punctuation or anything else. You just record whatever comes to your mind as you think about the topic. Usually, you set a timer and try to write for five or ten minutes straight, without stopping.

You can use unfocused freewriting to search for a topic, as the student does in this example:

So I have to write 3 to 4 pages on anything I want. What am I interested in these days? Well, always in sports, since I was a kid. I like the competition. Get a high from all the work and exercise involve, there's a lot in the sports that I do. Makes me feel good all over. And healthy. A lot of students do sports, but some don't. More and more girls are involved. I really like to swim. Everything in swimming is individual even though I'm part of a team. Basketball's different, have to think of all the plays and patterns we learned and be a real team player. Wonder which sport is better for me all around. Both are fun in different ways.

As you can see, not all of the material that is produced in this process will be useful. But sometimes a random observation will lead to specific focus. With freewriting, as you will discover, almost any subject will take you in some direction. By the end of this freewriting, one or two specific ideas for an essay have surfaced: the contrast between the individuality of swimming and the teamwork of basketball and the question of which sport is best.

You can also focus your freewriting on a topic that you want to explore and develop, as in this example:

The Great Depression of the 1930s. My grandparents' time. I think of listening to my parents talk about how my grandparents talked about the Depression, then hearing my grandparents at Thanksgiving worrying about my uncle changing careers. Mom says they can't stand the idea of someone giving up a good job to go back to school because the Depression still influences their thinking. They'll always be more security conscious than their kids. Wonder if she's right. They don't like the idea of my choice of a history major without a teaching minor. Not enough jobs there. Nothing to fall back on. That goes along with Mom's thinking, too. Also they never want to owe any money, don't use credit cards, save until they can buy their car with cash instead of payments. They feel the really own it then. That may be related.

2   Journal writing

Like freewriting, **journal writing** provides an opportunity to record thoughts and observations for later use. Many professional writers keep journals or notebooks in which they jot down impressions, reactions, descriptions, the germs of ideas—anything that might contribute to a piece of writing.

You can also reflect on a specific topic in journal writing. If you decide to keep a journal in which you record more than brief notes, try to make the entries involve you in thinking, preferably in analysis. Instead of merely recording "I went to a movie tonight," take the time to examine your responses to it. How did you feel when you saw it? Why did you feel this way? What incidents or characters in the movie provoked your responses? This approach will develop your thinking on a topic and generate details and examples to use in your writing.

3   Brainstorming

Freewriting will help you to discover a specific focus in the random material that you generate, but **brainstorming** is a far more deliberate, purposeful attempt to develop a specific list of information. You can brainstorm alone or in a group. Obviously, the results of a group's brainstorming will be more diverse than the products of a single imagination. But the object in either case is the same: to write down as much as you can about the topic selected. In the following example, a student wanted to write about donating body organs; she began by jotting down a series of questions she had about the topic:

Donor banks—how do they work?

Expense?

How is the donating done?

Any restrictions on who can donate? Any laws about it?

Technical aspects?

Who donates and why?

Why don't more people do it?

With that last question, the student hit on a specific idea that captured her interest: the need to change the attitudes of people who are unwilling to donate organs. She directed her thinking toward this point and did some more brainstorming:

Why are people opposed?

Religious attitudes—the body is sacred—"temple of God"

May be uninformed, don't know how to go about it.

Self-concepts tied in with our physical bodies.

Could be afraid of mutilation. Or that they might not be really dead.

Procrastination—people put off the decision. But that could be economically caused.

Reasons to donate: helping other people to live, alleviating suffering.

How many people donate?

Case histories and examples—children, blind people, heart victims, kidney failure.

Note that this example of brainstorming includes a mixture of questions and fragments—that's all right for now. The goal is to generate as much writing as you can about the topic. If your brainstorming does not result in an adequate range of thoughts or does not seem to be leading toward a useful topic, try it again in ten or fifteen minutes, or try another topic.

4 Clustering

A variation of brainstorming is **clustering.** Write your topic in the middle of a piece of paper or on your computer monitor. As ideas that relate to the topic occur to you, place them randomly around the topic. Let one point lead you to another. Try to visualize your ideas as rays of light streaming out from the central topic. Then examine the related ideas and see what kinds of connections you can find among them. Draw lines between the connected ideas. If some of the satellite ideas lead to more specific clusters, write those down as well. You might want to expand to a new page, clustering around an idea that one of your first clusters suggested.

Clustering is a flexible, nonlinear way of examining a topic. Its purpose is not only to generate more ideas about your topic but also to help you discover relationships that exist between ideas. Look at the following example of clustering around the topic of favorite sports:

5 Questioning

A somewhat more structured way to explore a topic is to use the traditional **journalists' questions.** Reporters gather information for news stories by asking *who?, what?, when?, where?, how?,* and *why?* This set of questions will not only help you to generate ideas but will also ensure that you don't overlook any important aspects of the topic. Not all of these questions might be relevant to your essay topic, so try modifying them to suit your needs:

> *What* makes it important?
> *What* are the consequences of it?
> *What* can be done about it?
> *What* changes can be made to it?
> *What* point can I make about it?
> *How* has it affected people?
> *How* is it managed?
> *Where* did it originate?
> *Where* does it have the most impact?
> *Where* should changes be made?
> *Why* am I interested in it?
> *Why* are other people interested in it?
> *Who* is the most interested in this topic?
> *Who* has some power in this area?

Some of the questions will yield more ideas than others. Use the ones that provide the most details and point you to an interesting, focused topic.

6 Interviewing

Almost any subject can be profitably developed by talking to people who have special knowledge on the topic. The student who did some freewriting on the Great Depression can verify and expand her thinking by talking to her grandparents and parents about how their lives and attitudes were affected.

Exploring Ideas
ON A WORD PROCESSOR

Most of the prewriting techniques discussed in this chapter can be done on the computer. When you work through with these activities, concentrate on entering your ideas without concern for spelling, grammar, or punctuation. For example, when you do freewriting, type words and ideas as fast as you are able. If you can, turn down the contrast on the monitor to write without seeing the screen, or turn the monitor off. It's important to generate as much writing as possible. When you're finished, you can view the freewriting or brainstorming electronically, using the boldface or italic codes to highlight the points and details that seem most valuable. Or you can print out the copy and use it to rough out your ideas.

You can also use e-mail to help develop a topic. Send a message to someone in your class or to a friend. Try out your ideas as you would in a conversation or with a tutor. Ask the person receiving your e-mail to ask questions and offer suggestions.

If you have a draw or paint program, use it to do some visual planning such as clustering. For journal writing, start a file for each assignment, and type in thoughts and questions that occur to you as you work. As you develop more material, review it periodically and highlight the important points; then transfer these highlighted items to a separate file for later use.

If you do interview someone about a topic, tell the person what your purpose is and indicate approximately how long the interview will take. Plan your questions ahead of time, and avoid asking questions that can be answered with a simple yes or no.

If you can, tape record the interview to ensure accuracy. Try to get as many facts and details as you can. You can eliminate any material that proves to be irrelevant, and you might end up refining your topic to fit the information you have gathered.

EXERCISE 1-1

Select two of the following general topics (or come up with a couple of your own). Using prewriting techniques of your choice, explore each topic until you have an idea suitable for a 500- to 700-word essay. Then generate a list of ten specific topics for each of your two choices.

recycling household wastes	smoking cigarettes
verbal harassment	rock groups
keeping in shape	saving money
late-night television programs	keeping a pet
drinking and driving	caring for others
space travel	preparing meals
advances in technology	parental obligations
the joys of giving	a favorite hobby
doing household repairs	women in politics
homeless people	children's literature

1c Determining the Purpose

As you search for a topic to write about, you also have to decide what you want to accomplish in your paper. The **purpose** for writing is not the same as the reason for writing. An error in your telephone bill gives you a reason, or motivation, to write to the telephone company, but the purpose of your letter is to *inform* the company that it has made a mistake and to *persuade* it to make a correction in your favor. This distinction also applies to academic situations. The reason for writing an essay is that your teacher assigned it, but your purpose in writing the essay goes beyond that limited motive.

1   The primary purposes

In determining your purpose for writing, you may choose to do any of the following:

- **To inform:** sharing facts, explanations, and ideas—in articles, reports, memos, and research papers.
- **To instruct:** telling someone how to perform some task—for example, connecting a printer to a computer.
- **To analyze:** examining a topic, such as an economic theory or a work of literature, and pointing out how its various parts work together.
- **To persuade:** trying to change someone's mind or behavior.
- **To argue:** presenting your opinion on an issue that has differing viewpoints, supporting your position with reasoning and information, and urging acceptance of your view.
- **To evaluate:** criticizing a performance, an experience, or a work of art.

This list is not exhaustive, but it includes the primary purposes. Two or more purposes may characterize the same essay; for example, an argumentative essay may be analytical, and an evaluation paper may include an expression of the writer's opinion. You will probably find it most helpful to select a single purpose and let it serve as the primary goal while you work on developing your first draft.

2   The basic purpose statement

You might be able to establish a preliminary purpose by filling out the following statement:

In this essay I will _____.

Fill in the blank with statements such as

record my impressions of (the topic);
express my opinion that (the topic)
is or is not _____;

> *argue that* (the topic) *should or should not be approved;*
> *analyze* (the topic) *to show that* _____;
> *instruct my readers how to* _____.

You need not use exactly these phrases, but do give yourself something specific to accomplish in your paper.

1d   Identifying an Audience

One of the best ways to help you establish a purpose in your writing is to consider your readers' needs and interests. Successful writing involves providing a focus and supporting information that will communicate your ideas to those for whom you are writing.

1   Your teacher as audience

The first step in communicating your ideas is to identify your audience. Sometimes doing so seems too simple; if you are writing a paper for a class, then the audience would logically seem to be your instructor. But it isn't always that simple. If you write your paper with the idea that only your teacher will read it, then you are preparing the paper to fit the special, idiosyncratic needs of a single person whom you have gradually come to know better day by day in class. As a result, you begin to get a sense of what that instructor knows and does not know, and you begin to make subtle adjustments in your presentation. In other words, as you develop a sense of your shared knowledge, you leave out material that you feel reasonably sure your instructor already knows.

Yet the writing that you do in class should prepare you for writing that you will be doing later in life. On the job and in your community, you will be writing for readers who have different expectations and who will not be pleased if your writing doesn't meet those expectations. You need to get beyond the captive and limited audience of an instructor and learn how to write for an audience of general readers.

2 Focus on the general reader

Successful newspaper columnists such as Ellen Goodman and Dave Barry, along with thousands of their colleagues nationwide, reach millions of readers every day. They do so by providing information that most people would need to understand the points they are presenting. In writing terms, they focus on the general reader, the average individual who knows a little about many things but lacks the specific information on the topic the writer wants to present. The general reader knows what an opera generally is but not the specific details about a specific opera; the general reader knows that blood carries nourishment throughout the body but not the specific role that red blood cells, white blood cells, and platelets play in this process. And the general reader might know that the increase in the number of working mothers means a greater need for child care but not that there are not nearly enough reliable, inexpensive child care centers available.

Likewise, the general reader has a variety of interests. This variety works to your benefit as the writer. As you assess the material you have produced through your prewriting and try to decide on a focus, consider the interests of the average person. Think, for example, of specific subjects that you like and of how your interests developed. Certainly, you did not awaken one day with the level of enthusiasm you have today about any subject—and you cannot expect that your reader is automatically going to have such a deep interest either. Therefore focus on some aspect that you believe will lead the average reader to develop an interest, much as it gradually led to a greater interest on your own part. Considering the needs of the general reader will ease your job of choosing a focus for your writing.

Of course, you will occasionally want to write for a more expert audience. If you are preparing a lab report for chemistry,

ANALYZING AUDIENCE AND PURPOSE

To increase your abilities to identify your audience and your purpose, ask yourself the following questions about your readers during the process of planning your writing:

1. How much do my readers know about the topic?

2. What new or additional information will I need to supply? What questions will they have? What terms will I have to define and explain?

3. Will my readers be interested in the topic? If not, how can I get them interested?

4. Will they be in agreement with my ideas? Do I have to be careful not to offend them?

5. How do I want my readers to respond? Do I want to inform, persuade, entertain, or move to action?

6. What do I want my readers to get from my paper? Do I expect them to change or take an action?

7. What are their age, class, education, and gender? How important are these factors to my purpose and presentation?

you will probably be writing for readers who are at least as knowledgeable about chemistry as you. If you are writing an article for a running magazine, you will be writing for a group of running enthusiasts who share a great amount of technical information about running. You will not need to gear down your presentation for these audiences. On the other hand, if you are preparing a pamphlet on human conception for an elementary school student audience, you will adjust your presentation, this time to a far simpler level than you would for the general reader.

As with any writing assignment, the whole context—the subject, reader, and purpose—must be considered. If you take some time to consider these elements, especially the most important element in the writing process—your reader—you will be more likely to develop an effective focus. That is the first step toward writing a successful paper.

1e Considering the Writer's Role

As you analyze your purpose and audience, you should also think about what role you play in the presentation. How do you want to come across to your readers? Are you writing as an expert, an unbiased observer, an interested nonspecialist, a passionate advocate? Even if you don't consciously choose a role, some sense of you as the writer will come across in your writing.

You can control the extent to which your audience is aware of your personality. In personal writing, for example, you might want to use *I* frequently and choose familiar language and personal details that will make your readers feel close to you. In other kinds of writing, such as a scientific report or a business memo, you might want to maintain some distance by writing in the third person and using abstract or technical language that reveals little of your personal feelings. The following questions will help you to think more specifically about the role you want to project in a particular piece of writing:

- What is my relationship to my readers? Am I writing to equals? To experts? To beginners?
- What is my attitude toward my topic? Am I enthusiastic? Bitter? Cynical? Concerned? How much do I want my audience to perceive this attitude?

- How closely do I want my readers to feel my presence as a writer? Do I want to address them directly, individual to individual? Or do I want to write to them from a distance?
- What response do I want from my audience? Amusement? Agreement? Action?
- What can I do to get my readers' attention and respect?

2   Planning and Drafting

You have chosen a topic, gathered material, identified your audience and purpose; now it's time to think about the form your writing will take. You can shape your thoughts and ideas by settling on a tentative focus, developing a preliminary outline, and writing a first draft.

2a   Focusing the Topic: A Working Thesis

At this stage in the writing process, you will want to come up with a **working thesis,** which will give direction to your thinking and help you to organize the materials you've generated in the prewriting. A working thesis, however, should evolve from your writing and not serve as a mold into which your writing must be forced.

1   Stating the thesis

The thesis for your paper should be a complete sentence that encapsulates the point you want your essay to make. As you devise your working thesis, keep two things in mind:

1. Do not worry at this time about the exact wording of your thesis. Good writing does not happen on the first try. Make the plainest possible declaration of what you want to accomplish. A thesis almost always includes a value judgment. One good way to begin is to formulate a tentative thesis, like this:

I think <u>(topic)</u> is_____

shows_____

should or should not_____

because_____.

2. Do not assume that your thesis statement is a fixture. If work on your essay proves that the thesis statement is indefensible or that some other aspect of the topic is more appealing, more interesting, or more controversial, restate your thesis to meet the new developments. Remember that you are experimenting with an idea in the rough. You have several drafts in which to test the central idea for validity.

If you use a tentative thesis, take the product another step before beginning to write. *Make sure that your thesis statement does more than merely announce your topic.*

TOPIC:	A Brooklyn neighborhood
TENTATIVE THESIS:	I think my Brooklyn neighborhood is unique because diverse cultures form a unique identity.
WORKING THESIS:	My own neighborhood, Bay Ridge, shows how diverse ethnic cultures combine to give the area a unique identity.

This working thesis not only announces the topic but also restricts it, moving from the general concept *a Brooklyn neighborhood* to a specific one, *Bay Ridge*.

Build on the tentative thesis to include specific words. The more precise you are, the more guidance you will have in writing your draft.

TOPIC:	Drivers' responsibilities
TENTATIVE THESIS:	I think young drivers are unaware of the responsibilities involved in driving.
WORKING THESIS:	A person of seventeen seldom appreciates all the responsibilities of driving.

Be certain that your working thesis is *unified*—that is, concerned with one idea. Ideas of secondary importance may appear in a subordinate clause, but your main point should be expressed in the main clause:

TOPIC:	Underage drinking
TENTATIVE THESIS:	I think teenage drinking is a real problem in our school.
WORKING THESIS:	Many teenagers begin drinking because of peer pressure, although anxiety and parental example play a role as well.

Most often, the first attempt to produce a working thesis results in a statement that is too broad to suit the writing situation, such as

Agricultural subsidies have major disadvantages.

This thesis is so broad that a book could be written about it. You will want either to limit the topic to fit the expected length or to abandon it and search for a new topic.

Less often, the first attempt at a working thesis will produce a statement that is too narrow, one that cannot be developed sufficiently to meet the needs of the assignment, such as

Reading history books is boring.

This thesis is such a vague and limited generality that developing it into an essay would be difficult. Sometimes you don't know whether your thesis statement is too broad or too narrow until you begin to develop it. If you discover it to be either of these, do some more prewriting (e.g., brainstorming, clustering) on the topic again to discover a remedy, or try some priming writing (see Section 2b-2).

A working thesis should make a *vigorous* statement; it should assert the topic in a context that demands explanation, expansion, analysis, or defense.

BLAND: Sending children to day care has positive benefits.

VIGOROUS: Good day-care centers teach children to share with others, to build immunity to diseases, to develop communications skills, and to become self-sufficient.

The thesis statement will usually appear in the opening paragraph of your finished essay, but let the essay's development determine its final wording and placement.

EXERCISE 2-1

Comment on the usefulness on each thesis, and explain what content you would expect to find in the essay.

1. Our student council has major organizational flaws and can't seem to succeed in planning successful events.

2. The interesting and colorful professor of economics succeeds in making us want to study the subject.

3. At least five important reasons exist to convince students to pursue a liberal arts major in college.

4. Fast-food restaurants no longer provide fast food.

5. The campus bookstore charges too much money for everything in an attempt to exploit a captive market.

EXERCISE 2-2

Write thesis sentences for the topics that you developed in Exercise 1-1.

2   Priming writing

Sometimes you can think and think, but you simply cannot come up with an acceptable working thesis statement. If this happens, try **priming writing.** This technique is a more structured version of freewriting or brainstorming. First, set a goal of 150 to 200 words, and start writing sentences about the topic. But try to produce connected sentences with details or subordinate points to support generalizations without worrying about style. The purpose of this writing is to prime the pump, to get your mind and fingers working with your topic and in the mood to write.

The following is an example of priming writing on the topic of sports and health:

Lots of kids participate in sports these days, especially as youngsters. But we constantly hear how out of shape American youth are. And physically unfit. Basketball is called American's favorite sport these days, especially in late winter—I guess it's because so many kids play it and watch the games. Almost everyone has a hoop in the driveway or can get to a playground hoop. It is good exercise and fun. Swimming is good exercise and fun, too, but much harder to do because you have to find a pool or a lake. Maybe that's why fewer kids swim. But swimmers do their thing all their lives, if they want to. But basketball players in grade school seldom continue beyond high school. The competition is tough. You need the skills. But is it whole-body exercise or confined to legs and arms? There are lots of injuries in basketball but fewer in swimming. Swimming is often the exercise to heal basketball injuries.

Although the writing resulting from the priming contains no specific thesis yet, it does express some of the writer's feelings and attitudes about the relative merits of swimming and playing basketball: more people swim as adults than play basketball. As a result, the writer has a more definite direction and can develop a tentative thesis statement.

I think swimming is a healthier participation sport than playing basketball is.

A more explicit statement derived from the tentative thesis might be the following:

Swimming could replace basketball as the favorite participation sport of American youth because people can do it regardless of age, it puts less stress on the body, and it involves a better-rounded workout.

2b Planning the Paper

Once you have generated some ideas and formulated a working thesis, you may want to pull your preliminary decisions together in some fashion.

1 Making preliminary decisions

The checklist on the following page will help to direct your thinking as you begin to transform your prewriting materials into an organized essay.

2 Outlining

An outline provides a framework or model for a first draft. It can help you shape and organize your thoughts and keep you from making organizational blunders. An **informal outline** is especially practical for those times when you are struggling to

PLANNING THE FIRST DRAFT

Write out your responses to each question.

1. What is my topic?

2. What is the main point I want to make about the topic?

3. Who is my audience? That is, what group(s) of readers do I want to reach?

4. What is my specific purpose in regard to these readers?

5. What kinds of evidence am I going to use?

6. What role am I playing as the writer? What image do I want to project?

Your responses will probably turn out something like these:

1. *Topic:* needle exchange programs to reduce the spread of AIDS

2. *Main point:* Needle exchange programs are an effective and relatively inexpensive means of reducing the spread of HIV among drug users.

3. *Audience:* general public but especially readers who doubt or are unsure about the value and usefulness of needle exchanges

4. *Specific purpose:* to get doubters to reconsider their opinions—to understand why needle exchanges are effective, not detrimental

5. *Evidence:* mainly reasons and explanations, but also summaries of several studies I've read about needle exchanges and a couple of quotations from columnist Clarence Page, who has written on this issue recently

6. *Role:* I want to come across as informed and interested but not as an expert. I want my readers to feel that I'm sharing knowledge and information with them, not preaching or talking down to them. I want to seem reasonable and logical.

establish a preliminary thesis, plan your first draft, and organize your ideas. An informal outline can take the form of a **scratch outline,** in which you use words and phrases and sometimes even symbols to sketch out your ideas either on paper or on the computer. Because this type of outline is primarily for your own use, you do not need to be overly concerned with format. The following example illustrates a typical scratch outline:

Swimming vs. basketball

Alone vs. team

All ages; younger kids

Pool; gyms

Fewer injuries; more injuries

More active; less active

Formal outlines, as you might guess, have more structure and detail than informal outlines. Formal outlines are especially valuable for keeping your thoughts on a topic organized, and some instructors require the submission of formal outlines along with the essay. If a formal outline is required, you might opt for the **sentence outline,** in which each subordinate topic of the thesis appears as a sentence and the sentences follow the order of development that the essay will follow. Usually, but not always, each sentence in the outline serves as a topic sentence for a paragraph in the essay. Consider the following example of a sentence outline:

SENTENCE OUTLINE

Thesis: Because it provides competition for people of all ages and skill levels, puts less stress on the human body, and results in a more well-rounded workout, swimming could replace basketball as the favorite participation sport of America's youth.

1. With the fitness level of American children at its current state, it would be logical to assume that children do not play sports.
2. Basketball remains one of the most intensely played games in the country, but it involves a relatively small number of participants.
3. Swimming provides a means of lifelong competition for athletes of all ages.
4. The game of basketball puts much stress on the human body.
5. Basketball provides a limited workout for the athletes who play it.
6. Swimming involves a workout for the entire body.
7. Once people know all the facts, swimming could become the favorite participation sport of both youth and adults.

Another type of formal outline is the **topic outline.** This kind of outline lists topics, rather than complete sentences, and usually includes the details that will appear within each paragraph. When the topic outline is completed, the first draft is not far off. The most common type of formal topic outline uses a combination of Roman numerals, capital letters, Arabic numbers, lowercase letters, and lowercase Roman numerals to indicate the various divisions of a subject. The largest divisions are indicated by Roman numerals, each of which is subdivided into sections signified by capital letters. If further subdivision of these sections is required, it is signified by Arabic numbers, and so on. One traditional rule to remember with the formal outline is that any topic you divide must be separated into at least two portions; logically, one apple cannot be divided into one piece. In other words, there must be a subtopic B if there is a subtopic A, a subtopic 2 if there is a subtopic 1, and so on. The following example shows the arrangement of part of a typical formal topic outline:

FORMAL TOPIC OUTLINE

Thesis: Because it provides competition for people of all ages and skill levels, puts less stress on the human body, and results in a more well-rounded workout, swimming could replace basketball as the favorite participation sport of America's youth.

Roman numeral	I.	Poor physical condition of youth
Capital letter	A.	Basketball
Arabic number	1.	At home
	2.	At school
	B.	Swimming
	C.	Fewer health problems
	II.	Basketball
	A.	Spectator sport
	B.	School sport
	1.	Participation
	2.	Really talented
Lowercase letter	a.	College teams
	b.	Pro teams

As you can see, the writer who chooses a formal topic outline as a start must think the topic through completely and develop working notes *before* trying to write a formal outline. (The scratch outline can usually serve this purpose.) The formal topic outline is equally effective for short essays and research papers. In addition, it can be valuable in *revising* papers. Once you have a suitable draft, you can plot your ideas into the framework of an outline and be certain that every part of your draft is relevant and connected.

Outlining
ON A WORD PROCESSOR

If you did your prewriting on the computer, you can use the cut and paste functions of your word-processing program to move key phrases and sentences from your freewriting or brainstorming into an informal outline. Some programs let you go back and forth between screens or windows, a feature that makes it easier to turn prewriting into an outline. You can also use the word processor to revise an informal outline into a formal one by inserting Roman numerals and uppercase letters to mark the major divisions. It also helps to put the main headings in large, bold letters; they keep the larger structure of your paper in view as you fill in subheadings and subpoints.

2c Writing the First Draft

At this point, you are ready to write a first draft. But take a breather for a moment. All those prewriting and planning steps will help you get started, but there is such a thing as getting bogged down in the preliminaries. Another way of getting started

DRAFTING STRATEGIES

1. Write the first draft well before the finished essay is due. A week in advance is desirable; a twenty-four-hour lead is essential. *Don't wait until the last minute.*

2. Write the first draft as rapidly as possible. You want to capture ideas rather than form.

3. Put off making corrections in spelling and mechanics until you are ready to produce the final copy. If you worry too much about mechanics too soon, you can suppress your creativity and divert your attention from more important issues.

4. Write double or triple space. Leave room to insert.

5. Cross out; do not erase. And when you cross out, let what you have crossed out show through. You might want to go back to that wording later.

6. Be sloppy. Discourage yourself from even thinking of the draft as finished work.

7. Write the draft in a place where you are comfortable. You want a free flow of ideas.

8. Do not worry too much about the opening and conclusion. Many writers just get something down and fix it later. Keep your mind on your thesis, the main supporting ideas, and the details that support these ideas.

9. If your first draft wanders from your thesis or suggests more interesting developments, stop. Weigh the merits of getting back to the original thesis against the possible value of letting the writing lead you to a new thesis. At this stage nothing is permanent.

is to plunge right in and see what happens. This approach works for some writers. But to plunge in under the impression that the first draft will become the final draft with only a bit of light tinkering is foolhardy.

Whether you make careful preparations or let the essay happen as you write, you must regard the first draft as tentative and temporary. Often, a first draft is an exploration, a place where you test your ideas, work out your organization, and discover your voice. You can develop and refine it later.

Keeping in mind that the first draft is only a discovery draft, use the strategies outlined in the checklist on page 29 to guide you in composing your first draft.

EXERCISE 2-3

From the list of topics in Exercise 1-1, select a topic that you have not written about, or work with topics provided by your instructor. Using prewriting techniques, generate content, arrive at a working thesis, and then construct a scratch outline. Develop the scratch outline into a formal outline, and write a first draft of the essay. When you submit this paper, also submit your prewriting and outlines.

2d   Sample First Draft

Kit Hoffman began writing his first draft of "swimming vs. basketball" as most of us do, without an idea for a topic. As shown in Chapter 1, he used the various prewriting strategies to arrive at the possible topic of which sport—basketball or swimming—is healthier for its participants. He explored and developed the topic through clustering, identified a purpose and audience, and, after additional prewriting and critical analysis, arrived at a working thesis: "I think swimming is a healthier participation sport than playing basketball is." Outlining helped Kit to structure and organize his ideas. He then produced the first draft that begins on page 32.

Drafting
ON A WORD PROCESSOR

With a computer you can write a draft of your paper, save it or delete it, quickly devise another draft, compare different versions, and make changes to words or to entire blocks of the draft with ease. Some word-processing programs will let you look at more than one draft of your paper simultaneously. The computer also adapts to the nonlinear workings of the mind during the writing process. If you think of a new detail or a whole sentence that belongs in an earlier section, you can move the cursor back to that point with a click of your mouse and add the material.

Because you can easily rearrange material and make changes, you should produce the draft freely. Don't concern yourself with grammar, punctuation, and format at this stage; think, instead, of your thesis, purpose, and audience. Repeat prewriting techniques, if you need to, right at the terminal. Here are other suggestions to keep in mind when drafting on a computer:

- Keep a file for material that you delete—words, sentences, and paragraphs that you discard as you draft. You might want to return to these scraps later in the process and even restore some of them to the paper. This scrap file can also be a very useful source of material for later assignments.
- Use symbols or bold letters to mark places that you want to return to in your draft. Or put notes to yourself in brackets. You can locate these reminders by using the search function, but be sure to delete them before you submit a final draft.
- Save your work frequently. You might also use different file names for each draft that you write (such as *draft 1, draft 2,* and so on). You can read over these drafts and evaluate them later.
- Print out your drafts for review. How sentences and paragraphs fit together is easier to see on paper than on the computer screen. You will also have a copy of your work in case your hard drive crashes or you misplace your disk.

SWIMMING VS. BASKETBALL

1   All the kids I knew in grammar school arid junior high school were involved in sports, especially basketball, baseball, track, and swimming. But when I got into high school, fewer students were involved, especially in basketball and baseball. Few were involved in football mostly, I guess, for fear of becoming injured. Few of us made it onto our school teams. We (my friends and I) had basketball hoops in our driveways. You could always get nine kids together to play ball. Racing lost its appeal during the junior high years. You had to get a ride to go swimming at the YMCA pool or at the city park. Our school didn't have a pool. My parents took turns driving me to the pool. I think swimming is a healthier participation sport than playing basketball is.

2   People in our country worry about the physical health of our teens. Even though we do sports, we keep hearing and reading about how out of shape the average teen is. Maybe its the kind of sports we do. That's odd when you consider how many sports opportunities we have as youngsters. Maybe its the attitude we have doing these sports. Basketball is surly the most popular sport we do. You can find hoops everywhere: at school, playgrounds, driveways. We all love to crowd around the basket, bang into each other, and get all the rebounds.

3   As kids we played basketball all year round. And in the spring we all got involved in the tournaments and watched, especially those in high school, called "March Madness" in Illinois. I know two of our varsity players in high school who played on our junior high team. No one from our grade school team even made it in junior high. And the two in high school didn't make it on a college team. I stopped playing while in junior high.

4   I've been a swimmer for a longer time than I've been a basketball player. I began at age seven and still swim. Lots of older people swim even in competitions. They'd probably have heart attacks playing basketball.

5   Lots of basketball players get hurt. It must be due to playing on that hardwood floor. There's a lot of running in playing basketball, from one end of the floor to the other and then a lot of jumping when you get there. It's hard on the legs, especially the knees. Fewer injuries in swimming. After all, the water is soft.

6   Strong legs are important in both sports. Swimming requires strong arms too. And coordination of limbs with breathing is important too. But basketball players need to coordinate their arms in a different way. Dribbling the hall has no counterpart in swimming. Maybe swimming involves more body coordination: strong heart and lungs, especially when you go underwater.

7   Swimming, I think, involves more physical action. A college coach once said that swimming is good therapy for basketball injuries. No one suggests playing basketball as a remedy for sore legs, arms, or back from swimming. Maybe if swimming was our most popular participation sport, we would all be healthier adults.

---

3   Improving the First Draft: Revision

A common myth about writing is that good writers get it right the first time. The truth is that good writers almost never say what they want to on the first try; they nearly always plan on revising. Every piece of writing should go through at least three drafts: the first (or rough) draft, the revision draft, and the editing draft. If you don't work through those last two, you won't achieve the best results, no matter how good you think your first draft is.

Revision involves more than just tidying up your prose. The process of correcting your spelling, punctuation, and mechanics is called *editing,* but your paper is not ready for that yet. First you need *re-vision*—seeing again—to discover ways of making your writing more effective.

3a   Revising from the Top Down

Not all revising is the same. One kind of revision involves large-scale changes, ones that significantly affect the content and structure of your paper. Such changes might include enlarging or narrowing your thesis, adding more examples or cutting irrelevant ones, and reorganizing points to improve logic or gain emphasis. A second kind of revision focuses on improving style: checking paragraph unity, strengthening transitions, combining and refining sentences, finding more effective words, adjusting tone. Most teachers and writers recommend a top-down approach to revising—that is, starting with the large-scale issues and working down to the smaller elements. If you try to do the fine-tuning and polishing first, you will use up valuable time and energy and might never get around to the main problems.

1   Outline the first draft

To revise effectively, you must probe to discover possible new insights and overlooked opportunities. You must also examine what you have written to be sure that it properly communicates what you want to say. One way to focus on content and organization is to make a brief outline of your first draft. This kind of after-the-fact outlining is not a waste of time, as it allows you to detect flaws in your organization and to review the development of your main ideas at the same time. First, write down your thesis statement; then add the topic sentence of each paragraph along with your important supporting ideas. Don't bother with complete sentences; short phrases are easier to check and evaluate.

After completing this brief outline, you should use it to check your paper for unity and completeness by using the questions in the following checklist:

REVISING CONTENT AND ORGANIZATION

1. Who are my readers? How will they respond to my points?

2. Do the thesis and the conclusion match? If they do not, which should I choose to guide my revision?

3. Does every topic sentence relate to my thesis and my conclusion? Is each point a development toward the conclusion?

4. Is each topic sentence developed with adequate specific facts, illustrations, or examples?

5. Is every point or detail relevant? Do any overlap and need to be cut?

6. Do the sentences and paragraphs follow one another with no breaks and no confusion? Are there any points I have left out or failed to explain adequately?

7. Are the sentences and paragraphs clearly tied together?

(See Chapter 4 for detailed advice about building unified, well-developed paragraphs.)

2   Analysis of the first draft

Returning to his draft after a few days had passed, Kit looked carefully at what he had written. He outlined his draft and used the questions in the checklist above to analyze his paper. He realized that coherence, completeness, and audience considerations would require some degree of change. Here is how he reacted to each of the paragraphs of his first draft:

Paragraph 1. Perhaps my opening sentence is a generality. I should limit the mention to four short examples and maybe develop two of them. I think my preliminary thesis fits nicely at the end of the paragraph, but maybe I could place it at the beginning. I'm not sure that the thesis provides enough information. Lots of passive constructions, but I'll take care of those later.

Paragraph 2. Again, my topic sentence is a generality. I must be sure that I'm communicating clearly to my audience. I really like basketball, but I really think that swimming is a better all-around sport. Maybe I need to mention swimming in this paragraph.

Paragraph 3. Maybe I don't make my point in this paragraph too clear. What I want to communicate is that lots of kids begin playing basketball in grade school but even by junior and senior high school, the numbers have thinned out greatly. The former active athletes now become spectators. Not much experience involved in that.

Paragraph 4. This paragraph on swimming needs more development. I need to brainstorm it some more. As it is, it is too "me" centered.

Paragraph 5. This paragraph also needs more development. I want to show that swimming is such good exercise that it is sometimes recommended for healing basketball injuries.

Paragraph 6. I bring the two sports together in this paragraph for the first time. Does each get equal treatment? Do I want each to get equal treatment? Think this through some more.

Paragraph 7. I'd better check the source of the coach information. Does this paragraph ramble as a conclusion? I need to get it in harmony with my introductory paragraph.

3b Revising for Style

Once you are satisfied that your ideas are fully developed and effectively organized, you need to consider the shape of each sentence. Consider these points:

Do the sentences clearly and concisely express my meaning?
Is any phrasing wordy or repetitious?
Does the writing sound natural and interesting?
Are the sentences forceful and varied?
Are there some short, choppy sentences that need to be combined? Are there some long ones that need to be broken up?

Rewrite those sentences that carry key ideas to make them elegant and emphatic. Work particularly hard on the opening and closing sentences—especially that last one. Don't let an otherwise fine essay trail off limply at the end because you ran out of steam. (See Part V for details about clear, effective sentences.)

Now is also the time to look up word meanings and use your thesaurus, if necessary, to find just the right words. You want to make sure the word choices are vivid, accurate, and appropriate. (See Part VI for information and instruction about language and word choice.)

Revising
ON A WORD PROCESSOR

Since computer programs have virtually eliminated the need for retyping, revision has become an easier task. You can use the word processor's cut and paste functions to shift whole sections and entire paragraphs if you decide to re-arrange your points. On the sentence level, you can go back and change a word, move a phrase, add to a series, or just tinker with the words until you are satisfied. Here are some specific suggestions for revising on your computer:

- Check your sentence length and variety by hitting the return key after each sentence. (You should work with a copy of your main file when doing this procedure.) Each sentence will now look like a separate paragraph. Examine them closely. Do they all appear to be the same length? Do they all begin the same way? Are they all in the same pattern?
- Check for unwanted repetition by using the search function to locate words that you suspect you use too often. Do you use words such as *very, thing, great, nice,* and *this* too much? Do you repeat jargon and technical terms too frequently?
- Print out hard copy to read. Some problems are easier to see on a printed copy than on the computer screen. You see more paragraphs at a time, for example, on the page. On the screen, you might not have noticed that your transitional phrases at the beginning of several paragraphs are exactly the same or that some paragraphs are noticeably shorter (or longer) than the others.

3c   Getting Feedback: Peer Review

Writers routinely seek the help of potential readers to find out what is working and what is not working in their drafts. Even professional writers ask for suggestions from editors, reviewers, teachers, and friends. In college, your composition instructor might divide your class into small groups to review one another's papers and provide suggestions for improvement. In the workplace, much of the writing that you do will be passed around, with various writers adding their sections and making suggestions about yours.

Someone else can often see places where you *thought* you were being clear but were actually filling in details in your head, not on the page. You can help people who are reviewing your paper by assuring them that you want honest critical responses. Here are some guidelines to follow when asking for help with your revision:

1. *Specify the kind of help you want.* If you already know that the spelling needs to be checked, then ask your readers to ignore those errors and focus on other elements in the draft. If you want suggestions about the thesis, the introduction, the tone, the organization, the examples, or the style, then ask questions about those features.

2. *Ask productive questions.* Be sure to pose questions that require more than a yes or no response. Ask readers to tell you in detail what *they* see.

3. *Do not be defensive.* Listen carefully to what your reviewers have to say, and interrupt only when you don't understand their comments. Above all, don't argue with your readers. If something confused them, it confused them. You want to see the writing through *their* eyes, not browbeat them into seeing it the way you do.

4. *Make your own decisions.* Remember that this is your paper; you are responsible for accepting or rejecting the feedback that you get. If you don't agree with the suggestions that are offered, then don't follow them. But also keep in mind that your peer reviewers are likely to be more objective about your writing than you are.

REVIEWING A DRAFT

Use these questions in preparing your responses to someone else's paper:

1. What is especially interesting or effective about this draft?

2. Does the paper have a clear purpose? How well does the draft focus on this purpose?

3. Does the reader have all the necessary information to understand this paper? What additional examples or details might improve the essay?

4. Does the writer give more information than is needed? Are all parts of the paper relevant to the purpose, or could some parts be deleted?

5. Does the title tell what the paper is about? Does it catch the reader's attention?

6. What does the opening accomplish? How else might the writer begin?

7. Is the draft clearly organized? If not, how can the writer make the connections clearer and easier to follow?

> 8. Do mechanical errors (such as misspellings) distract the reader and detract from the quality of the writing? Do the sentences seem clear, or are some hard to untangle?
>
> 9. Does the draft conclude in an effective way, or does it seem to end abruptly or trail off into vagueness? How else might it end?
>
> 10. Give any suggestions or reactions that you think would be valuable to the writer. What did you like best about the draft? What would you like to know more about?

1 Peer responses

Kit submitted his first draft to some classmates for peer review. A sampling of the comments he received follows:

1. You seem to be trying to say that you think swimming is a better sport than basketball.

2. You spend more time writing about basketball than swimming.

3. Is your thesis precise enough? Why not include reasons in your thesis?

4. Your tone is appealing because you sound like a college student. Watch that reference to the coach in the last paragraph. Do you know its source? I'd move it up to an earlier paragraph, maybe the one on basketball injuries.

5. Do you need to mention rides to the swimming pools?

6. Your essay has real possibilities because it's interesting to me. I never thought about these things before. But you need to get

it organized better and make sure you have transitions between your paragraphs to make them flow together.

7. You need to do more with swimming to convince your reader.

8. I'd change the title. Sounds like you dislike basketball because you didn't make it beyond grade school teams.

Peer Review
ON A WORD PROCESSOR

If your personal computer or workstation is networked and your instructor allows it, you can use peer review to help you with revisions. Using e-mail or an electronic bulletin board designated for that purpose, your peer reviewers can access your file, read your draft or revised essay, and leave messages for you about its strengths and weaknesses. You can write some questions at the end of your essay to elicit specific responses about features that you know you need help on: Do you think my thesis works? Is the approach in the second paragraph appropriate? Do you see any ambiguities in my ideas? Some computer programs, such as Daedalus Integrated Writing Environment, permit writers and reviewers to interact simultaneously by means of their interchange function.

EXERCISE 3-1

Select any two adjoining paragraphs in Kit's first draft (or paragraphs designated by your instructor) in Section 2d. How would you revise these two paragraphs? What suggestions would you make to the author?

2   Revising the first draft

Taking into consideration his own analysis of the first draft and the comments from his classmates, Kit was able to see his essay anew. He kept some of his own ideas and those of his peers but rejected some as well. Kit revised the first draft extensively and then proceeded through several additional drafts. Many writers find it useful to produce multiple drafts. Through each one, they can work toward expressing their ideas more clearly and directly.

The excerpt that follows, showing the second paragraph of the first draft, illustrates some of Kit's revisions. In this paragraph, he revises to communicate his ideas with clarity and show greater awareness of his readers.

EXAMPLE OF REVISION

Some p   America
People in ~~our country~~ worry about the physical health of our

                    participate in   constantly
teens. Even though we ~~do~~ sports, we ~~keep~~ hearing and read~~ing~~

                                                    m
about how out of shape the average teen is. Maybe it's the kind of

                              C   ing   participation
sports we do. ~~That's odd when you~~ consider how many sports

                                        as well as
opportunities we have as youngsters. ~~Maybe its~~ the attitude we

                              e one of   s
have doing these sports. Basketball is suly the most popular sport.

      as evidenced by the   in
we do. ~~You can find~~ hoops everywhere: at school, playgrounds,
and on   where
driveways. ~~We~~ all love to crowd around the basket, bang into each

      try to
other, and get all the rebounds.

3d Editing and Proofreading

You edit and proofread your writing to correct errors in spelling, grammar, punctuation, diction, and mechanics. This is the last stage of the writing process. This final check might be noncreative and mechanical, but it is crucial. Spell "receive" as "recieve" and your paper will strike someone as flawed, no matter how ingeniously it is written.

When editing and proofreading, look up in this handbook or a dictionary every point in your essay that you have marked for spelling, punctuation, or grammar. The checklist on the next page will you help you to turn out a finished paper that you can be proud of.

After making all editorial changes, carefully proofread your essay one last time to be certain that you have not inadvertently created new problems while eliminating the older ones. The main point to remember about proofreading is that it is vitally important. Readers generally notice mistakes in form first; therefore if you know that you are weak in punctuation or spelling, proofread with special attention to these issues or persuade someone who is knowledgeable in these areas to proofread with you.

EXERCISE 3-2

Revise and rewrite the following paragraph, which is from the first draft of a student's essay. You might wish to rearrange the order of the sentences or combine sentences to achieve organization, unity, and so on.

I spent much of my childhood doing one of two things. As a young child, solitude was my savior. I would take long walks through nearby woods. I would relax in a swing attached to a tremendous oak tree. This was peaceful. It was also refreshing for me. I enjoyed my solitude. There are other pleasant things I associate with solitude. I connect the word with personal reflection serenity peaceful quietness and reflection. I imagine the warm silence of a monastery. Solitude is growth, also, in a comic way, I pictured the famous Calgon commercial. After a hectic day a woman sits in her bubble bath. She is in her solitude. She is content.

EDITING AND PROOFREADING

1. Read your final draft backward, from last word to first word. You might find errors that you miss in reading from beginning to end.

2. Check each pronoun carefully. Does it have an antecedent? Can it possibly refer to the wrong antecedent?

3. Read each sentence critically. Make sure each one is a full sentence, not a fragment.

4. Read your essay aloud. Where you make pauses in reading to make the sense clear, have you used the appropriate punctuation mark?

5. Be careful about possessives. Have you included all the apostrophes you should?

6. Make sure that all modifiers are clearly placed near the words they modify.

7. Pay particular attention to words that sound alike: *its/it's, to/too/two, there/their/they're, your/you're, then/than.*

8. Check the format of your paper. Have you observed the manuscript format that your teacher expects?

9. If there is time, put your paper aside for twenty-four hours, and return to it for fresh and objective insights.

Editing and Formatting
ON A WORD PROCESSOR

All word-processing programs let you delete and add letters, punctuation marks, and words, making it easy to implement those final corrections in grammar, mechanics, and spelling. Most programs also have a search function that allows you to locate every instance of a given word in your paper and replace or respell it throughout with one simple command. Some programs come with a thesaurus that you can use to look up synonyms for words you've been using too often or for finding more specific words than the ones you have used.

Tools that enable the computer to check spelling and style are also available. Use these spell checkers and grammar checkers if you have them, but be aware of their limitations. They can't distinguish between sound-alike words such as *to* and *too,* and style checkers often offer advice that is not appropriate for your writing situation. It might be easier for you to print out a draft and mark that for editing changes. Errors that you miss on the screen tend to stand out on the printed page.

After you have edited your text, you'll need to format it before printing. Most word-processing programs offer an array of options for formatting the final copy of your essay. Here are some features that you might want to consider:

- *Type font.* Use a font that is a normal size. The most popular is 12-point, the default setting on many computers. Also choose a style that is not too fancy or offbeat. Most teachers will not want you to use a script font, which looks like handwriting and is difficult to read for more than a few words.

- *Margin justification.* You are probably used to producing essays that have left-justified margins (flush left). But word processors give you the option of justifying the right margin as well, creating a page that resembles one from a printed book. Unfortunately, text that has been justified on a computer often contains extra spaces between words in some lines, resulting in gaps that can be quite distracting. If your machine doesn't have the technology to create the real look of a typeset page, you should probably turn off the right-justification command.

- *Paging codes.* You can automatically include your name and the page number on every page of your final copy. Check your word-processing program to see how you can insert a "header" or a "running head" into your essay. Place it in the upper right corner of the pages, one half inch from the top edge of the paper.

- *Headings.* You can use headings to highlight main ideas and to indicate shifts in topics, making the text easier to follow. Word-processing programs make using headings a snap. With a single command, you can center them, or you can set them flush left and boldface them. You can also indent material to set it off and thus call attention to it. If you glance at the formatting of this book, you will see a number of options for breaking up blocks of type, adding emphasis, and thus achieving greater readability. You can perform every one of them with your word processor.

Remember, however, that the essential factor in making a text easy to follow is having it clearly and logically organized. All the formatting in the world is not going to save a paper that is not unified or lacks continuity.

3e   Sample Final Draft

Kit revised his paper extensively and wrote additional drafts before editing and proofreading his work. The result of his endeavors is the final draft reproduced here.

FINAL DRAFT

Title

Swim for Your Life

Thesis with three supporting reasons

1

Because it provides competition for people of all ages and skill levels, puts less stress on the human body, and results in a more well-rounded workout, swimming could replace basketball as the favorite participation sport of America's youth.

Background for the thesis

We constantly hear criticism of the physical fitness level of American youth, who today possess a greater percentage of body fat and score lower on fitness tests than the children of forty years ago. Consequently, one reasons that if people leave childhood unhealthy, they will remain unhealthy as adults. Given America's spiraling health care costs, many people seek ways to make our children more physically fit in the hope that the fitness standard will last throughout a lifetime.

Illustration to support above background

For example, former President Bush appointed one of Hollywood's most popular stars, Arnold Schwarzenegger, to champion the cause of physical fitness in our country.

2

With the fitness level of American children at its current state, it would be logical to assume that they do not play sports. This is not the case.

Support for the topic sentence

Although countless basketball hoops can be seen in driveways and playgrounds across the land, people use these hoops to practice shooting around casually rather than run up and down a court as in an intense game. If Americans found another physically demanding sport to replace basketball, one that would help to improve the health of its

Possible positive results

participants, this sport could greatly help to improve the physical fitness level of American children. Americans, as a result, would no longer have some of the health problems that they have today.

"Selectivity" of participation in basketball

3   Basketball remains one of the most intensely competed games in this country, but it involves a relatively small number of participants. Millions of people tune their television sets to basketball championships on the professional, college, and even high school levels. However, the window of

Example to support topic sentence

competitive opportunity in this sport actually remains quite limited. A junior high school team provides the first organized competition for most basketball players, the majority of whom end their competitive careers sometime between then and their graduation from high school. As a junior high

Additional example

school basketball player in the seventh and eighth grades, I was able to excel as the leading scorer on the team. However, as the rest of my classmates began to mature physically, I became less and less valuable as a team player. My basketball career ended after the ninth grade. If an athlete truly possesses talent, he or she may continue a career on the collegiate or even the professional level. But a professional career in basketball usually ends when the athlete reaches his or her thirties. Thus, even for the most talented basketball player, the competitive life span lasts only about fifteen years. But no assurance exists that the athlete will be allowed to compete from the beginning of that competitive window. Frequently, more youngsters

Reiteration of the topic sentence

get cut from junior and senior high school teams than remain. As a result, only the really talented elite get a chance to experience the thrill of competition on the hardwood.

Transitional phrase

4   On the other hand, swimming provides a means of lifelong competition for athletes of all ages. United States Swimming, the governing body

Support for the "swimming" aspect of the thesis

of competitive swimming in this country, holds competitions for children as young as five years old. In addition, U.S.S. also has established a master's program in which no upper age limit for competition

Supporting example

exists. When I swam for a U.S.S. team during my grade school years, a master's team practiced in the pool before we did. The members of that team included college students, businesspeople, teachers, and retirees. All felt very comfortable despite their varying ages and abilities. Thus, a swimmer can compete throughout her or his lifetime instead of only the fifteen years available to the elite

Additional
example

basketball players. Furthermore, U.S.S. divides the
swimmers into age groups as well as six different
skill levels based on previous performance times to
intensify competition. For each skill level, then,
U.S.S. holds a state meet in which all age groups
can participate. Hence, swimmers of all ages and
skill levels receive the chance to test their abilities

Paraphrase
and elabora-
tion of topic
sentence

against that of other athletes. Such opportunities
can inspire children of all ages to train for and to
stay active in the sport, thus maintaining better
physical conditioning and resultant stamina, which
can lead to a healthier adulthood.

Transitional
word

Disadvantage
of basketball
playing

5   Additionally, the game of basketball puts much
stress on the human body. Sprained ankles, twisted
knees, and tendonitis frequently afflict many
basketball players. Even if no single traumatic event
occurs, the impact of landing on a wooden floor
thousands of times takes its toll. Virtually no
basketball players compete after the age of forty
because their bodies simply cannot take the

Transitional
word

Contrast in
content:
advantage of
swimming

Supporting
example

Connective
phrase

punishment any longer. But the sport of swimming
places very little stress on the bones and joints of
the human body. In fact, trainers often use
swimming to rehabilitate injuries incurred in
playing other sports. The fluid motion in water and
the lack of physical impact involved in swimming
do not lend themselves to injuries. As a result,
swimmers spend more time practicing and
competing and less time in training rooms than

basketball players. In addition, swimmers can swim,
competitively or otherwise, long after basketball
players have hung up their high-tops. For these
reasons, swimming provides better long-term health
benefits than does basketball.

Paragraph
summation

Word   6
repetition for
coherence

Basketball provides a limited workout for the
athletes who play it. The leg muscles become the
focus of most of the actions performed on a
basketball court. At a men's basketball game, one
often hears comments like, "Wow! Look at the
size of his calves." Shooting, rebounding, and
playing defense all require a certain amount of leg
strength. However, few of the muscles in the rest
of the body get exercised. Although running up and
down the court does require some cardiovascular
stamina, depending on the tempo of the game,
players spend much of their time at one or the
other end of the court where mobility becomes
quite limited.

Support for
topic sentence

Transitional   7
phrase

On the contrary, swimming involves a workout
for the entire body. Arm, leg, and abdominal
muscles work together to propel an athlete through
the water. The most valuable benefit in swimming
comes from the cardiovascular conditioning that
a swimmer receives. Because a swimmer must
hold his or her breath while swimming, the lungs
and heart both work much harder together than
they do in basketball, resulting in a healthier
heart and lungs in the long term. Swimming,

Support for
topic sentence

then, provides a workout for the entire body, so it should provide more long-term positive health benefits.

Conclusion 8

Restatement of main clause of thesis statement

Once people know all the factual positive results of the sport, swimming could become the favorite participation sport not only of America's youth but also of adults as well because it provides the opportunities for lifelong participation and enjoyment. If American children and their parents adopted swimming as their sport of choice, it would result in a much healthier nation.

---

4 Building Coherent Paragraphs

A **paragraph** is a group of sentences that develops an idea about a topic. The word *paragraph* comes from an ancient Greek word referring to the short horizontal line that the Greeks placed beneath the start of a line of prose in manuscripts to indicate a break in thought or a change in speaker. This convention of marking the places in a written work where the sense or the speaker changed was followed by medieval monks, who used a red or blue symbol much like our modern paragraph symbol (¶) in their manuscripts. Today, we indicate such a change in thought by indenting the first line of each new paragraph.

Although a paragraph is usually self-contained, at the same time it is usually part of a larger work, such as an essay or a research paper, and depends on the paragraphs before and after it. For example, look at the following four paragraphs:

Modern American Indian women, like their non-Indian sisters, are deeply engaged in the struggle to redefine themselves. In their struggle they must reconcile traditional tribal definitions of women with industrial and postindustrial non-Indian definitions. Yet while these definitions seem to be more or less mutually exclusive, Indian women must somehow harmonize and integrate both in their own lives.

An American Indian woman is primarily defined by her tribal identity. In her eyes, her destiny is necessarily that of her people, and her sense of herself as a woman is first and foremost prescribed by her tribe. The definitions of a woman's roles are as diverse as tribal cultures in the Americas. In some she is devalued, in others she wields considerable power. In some she is a familial/clan adjunct, in some she is as close to autonomous as her economic circumstances and psychological traits permit. But in no tribal definitions is she perceived in the same way as are women in western industrial and postindustrial cultures.

In the west, few images of women form part of the cultural mythos, and these are largely sexually charged. Among Christians, the madonna is the female prototype, and she is portrayed as essentially passive: her contribution is simply that of birthing. Little else is attributed to her and she certainly possesses few of the characteristics that are attributed to mythic figures among Indian tribes. This image is countered (rather than balanced) by the witch-goddess/whore characteristics designed to reinforce cultural beliefs about women, as well as western adversarial and dualistic perceptions of reality.

The tribes see women variously, but they do not question the power of femininity. Sometimes they see women as fearful, sometimes peaceful, sometimes omnipotent and omniscient, but they never portray women as mindless, helpless, simple, or oppressed. And while the women in a given tribe, clan, or band may be all those things, the individual woman is provided with a variety of images of women for the interconnected supernatural, natural, and social worlds she lives in.

Paula Gunn Allen
from *The Sacred Hoop*

Each of these paragraphs develops its own point. This point, which guides the paragraph, is often referred to as the **controlling idea** and is usually expressed in a topic sentence. The controlling idea of the first paragraph is that American Indian women, like other women in our society, are struggling to define their identities. The idea is made more specific by the sentences that follow. The controlling idea of the second paragraph is that the identity of American Indian women is closely allied to tribal customs and beliefs. This idea is supported by examples of such customs and beliefs. The controlling idea of the third paragraph is that, in contrast, the identity of women outside American Indian culture is easier to define and appears more restricted. This idea is supported by showing that such identities can be summarized as the madonna/goddess figure versus the witch/whore figure. The controlling idea of the fourth paragraph is that American Indian cultures view women in a less restrictive way but still acknowledge the power of femininity. This idea is supported by concrete, specific examples.

Although each of the four paragraphs is controlled by its own idea, the four also work together. The first paragraph presents a general controlling idea and makes it narrower. The second paragraph specifically informs the reader of the diverse forms that women's identities assume among various American Indian tribes, which differ greatly from non–American Indian conceptions. The second continues the general subjects discussed in the first paragraph but focuses on American Indian tribal cultures. The third paragraph then discusses the controlling idea in the non–American Indian culture, and the fourth paragraph clarifies how women are viewed in American Indian cultures. Therefore we can say that although a paragraph is largely self-contained, its general subject and controlling idea must conform to the objectives of the larger work of which it is a part.

A paragraph is composed of individual sentences, but these sentences must cohere to result in effective communication.

Paragraphs too must contribute to the coherence of the paper as a whole by providing unity, a consistent recognizable method of development, and clear transition from one idea to another.

4a Unity

Unity in a paragraph results when all the sentences in the paragraph relate to and develop the controlling idea. In other words, no sentences digress, or go off the track. Unity evolves from the uses of a topic sentence and relevant support.

1   The topic sentence

A paragraph develops a controlling, or main, idea, which is stated in a **topic sentence.** Functioning in a paragraph as a thesis statement functions in an essay, a topic sentence establishes the direction for the paragraph, with all the other sentences in the paragraph supporting and developing it.

Although a topic sentence often appears at the beginning of a paragraph, it may also be placed in the middle or at the end. When it is placed at the beginning of the paragraph, the rest of the sentences support the topic sentence, and the paragraph is developed deductively. In other words, the main idea appears first, and then the information supporting this idea follows. For example, the following paragraph concerns the British composer Peter Maxwell Davies. The controlling idea, or the idea to be developed, is that he had a difficult time winning recognition both at home and abroad.

> **For Davies, winning recognition wasn't easy, at home or abroad.** He was born near Manchester, a grim industrial city. The son of working-class parents, he taught himself composition by studying scores in the library. When he asked to study music at his grammar school, in preparation for the O-level exams given all British students, the headmaster scoffed. The faculty at the Royal

Manchester College of Music and at Manchester University, where Davies subsequently studied, proved to be hardly more enlightened. It was the mid-fifties, and the Austrian moderns—Mahler and Bruckner—were still highly suspect. So, in fact, was anyone but such homegrown products as Sir Edward Elgar, Ralph Vaughan Williams, and Charles Villiers Stanford. Davies wanted none of it. Along with a group of other students, including Harrison Birtwistle, who were eager to hear the new European music, he began listening to Stravinsky and Schoenberg.

Annalyn Swan
"A Visionary Composer"

Sometimes the topic sentence appears in the form of a question. When this occurs, the rest of the paragraph answers the question. For example, the following paragraph details, through support of the initial topic sentence, how individuals must be allowed to mature at their own rates and in their own ways:

Why should we be in such desperate haste to succeed and in such desperate enterprises? If a man does not keep pace with his companions, perhaps it is because he hears a different drummer. Let him step to the music which he hears, however measured or far away. It is not important that he should mature as soon as an apple-tree or an oak. Shall he turn his spring into summer? If the condition of things which we were made for is not yet, what were any reality which we can substitute? We will not be shipwrecked on a vain reality. Shall we with pains erect a heaven of blue glass over ourselves, though when it is done we shall be sure to gaze still at the true ethereal heaven far above, as if the former were not?

Henry David Thoreau
Walden

A paragraph that begins with a topic sentence sometimes ends with a concluding statement that restates the controlling idea, or summarizes or comments on the information in the paragraph. For example, the following paragraph is about wolves.

The controlling idea is that they are Holarctic. The topic sentence is printed in **boldface** and the concluding statement is in *italics*.

> **Wolves, twenty or thirty subspecies of them, are Holarctic—that is, they once roamed most of the Northern Hemisphere above thirty degrees north latitude.** They were found throughout Europe, from the Zezere River Valley of Portugal north to Finland and south to the Mediterranean. They roamed eastern Europe, the Balkans, and the Near and Middle East south into Arabia. They were found in Afghanistan and northern India, throughout Russia north into Siberia, south again as far as China, and east into the islands of Japan. In North America the wolf reached a southern limit north of Mexico City and ranged north as far as Cape Morris Jesup, Greenland, less than four hundred miles from the North Pole. *Outside of Iceland and North Africa, and such places as the Gobi Desert, wolves—if you imagine the differences in geography it seems astonishing—had adapted to virtually every habitat available to them.*
>
> Barry Holstun Lopez
> *Of Wolves and Men*

Sometimes the topic sentence occurs at the end of the paragraph. When this is the case, the topic sentence provides the focus for the sentences that lead up to it. The paragraph is developed inductively; that is, the evidence is given first and then the conclusion derived from this evidence is given. For example, the following paragraph is about the Hill Country in Texas. The controlling idea, or the idea that the rest of the sentences lead up to, is that to the early settlers, this country seemed like a paradise.

> And the streams, these men discovered, were full of fish. The hills were full of game. There were, to their experienced eyes, all the signs of bear, and you didn't need signs to know about the deer—they were so numerous that when riders crested a hill, a whole herd might leap away in the valley below, white tails flashing. There were other white tails, too: rabbits in abundance. And

as the men sat their horses, staring, flocks of wild turkeys strutted in silhouette along the ridges. Honeybees buzzed in the glades, and honey hung in the trees for the taking. Wild mustang grapes, plump and purple, hung down for making wine. **Wrote one of the first men to come to the Hill Country: "It is a Paradise."**

Robert A. Caro
The Path to Power

This type of topic sentence often appears in opening paragraphs, where it acts as a lead-in to the body of the paper.

Sometimes the topic sentence is delayed until the middle or near the middle of the paragraph. When this is the case, the topic sentence serves as a bridge, or transition, between the information in the first part of the paragraph and the information in the second. The following paragraph is about King Richard III of England. The controlling idea of this paragraph is that the traditional view of Richard III has been obstinately opposed over the years.

History is always written by the victors. The basic Tudor picture of Richard as a bloodthirsty tyrant was handed down through the standard histories of England and the school textbooks for five centuries. **There has been an obstinate opposition, however.** Beginning with Sir George Buck in the 17th century, a series of writers and historians have insisted that Richard was not getting a fair break, that the Tudor version was largely fabrication: far from being a monster Richard was a noble, upright, courageous, tenderhearted and most conscientious king. This anti-Tudor version reached its definitive statement in the work of Sir Clements Markham, a 19th-century eccentric who spent years of passionate research trying to prove that crimes attributed to Richard were either outright libels by, or the actual work of, a pack of villains, most notably including Cardinal Morton and Henry VII.

Robert Wernick
"After 500 Years, Old Crookback Can Still Kick Up a Fuss"

2 Support

Support your controlling idea with specific information—facts, statistics, details, examples, illustrations, anecdotes—that provides proof for your idea. Consider the following paragraph:

> Oranges and orange blossoms have long been symbols of love. Boccaccio's *Decameron,* written in the fourteenth century, is redolent with the scent of oranges and orange blossoms, with lovers who wash in orange-flower water, a courtesan who sprinkles her sheets with orange perfume, and the mournful Isabella, who cuts off the head of her dead lover, buries it in an ample pot, plants basil above it, and irrigates the herbs exclusively with rosewater, orange-flower water, and tears. In the fifteenth century, the Countess Mathilda of Württemberg received from her impassioned admirer, Dr. Heinrich Steinbowel, a declaration of love in the form of a gift of two dozen oranges. Before long, titled German girls were throwing oranges down from their balconies in the way that girls in Italy or Spain were dropping handkerchiefs. After Francis I dramatically saved Marseilles from a Spanish siege, a great feast was held for him at the city's harborside, and Marseillaise ladies, in token of their love and gratitude, pelted him with oranges. Even Nostradamus was sufficiently impressed with the sensual power of oranges to publish, in 1556, a book on how to prepare various cosmetics from oranges and orange blossoms. Limes were also used cosmetically, by ladies of the French court in the seventeenth century, who kept them on their person and bit into them from time to time in order to redden their lips. In the nineteenth century, orange blossoms were regularly shipped to Paris in salted barrels from Provence, for no French bride wanted to be married without wearing or holding them.

> **John McPhee**
> "Oranges"

The controlling idea of this paragraph is contained in the first sentence. Notice all the details McPhee gives to support his controlling idea. First he tells us about oranges and orange blossoms in Boccaccio's *Decameron.* Then he tells us about Countess Mathilda in the fifteenth century and how the gift of oranges from her admirer led to the custom of German girls throwing oranges from their balconies. Next he tells us how Francis I was pelted with oranges as a token of love and how Nostradamus published a book on how to prepare cosmetics from oranges and orange blossoms. Finally, he tells us that in the nineteenth century a French bride would not want to be married without holding or wearing orange blossoms. Notice how fully he treats these details. He tells you not only that Boccaccio wrote about oranges and orange blossoms in the *Decameron* but also what he said about them—the lovers, the courtesan, the mournful Isabella.

Notice all the supporting details Peter Steinhart uses to develop his controlling idea in the following paragraph:

> Adobe is an ancient material. Peruvians and Mesopotamians knew at least 3,000 years ago how to mix adobe—three parts sandy soil to one part clay soil—and box-mold it into bricks. The Walls of Jericho, the Tower of Babel, Egyptian pyramids, and sections of China's Great Wall are adobes. So are more modern structures like Spain's Alhambra, the great mosques of Fez and Marrakesh, and the royal palace at Riyadh.
>
> Peter Steinhart
> "Dirt Chic"

Not only must a paragraph contain support for its controlling idea, but this support must be relevant. Consider the following paragraph:

> Several writers have used San Francisco as a backdrop for their novels. Kathryn Forbes's novel *Mama's Bank Account,* on which the movie *I Remember Mama* was based, is set in San Francisco. The immigrant family lives on Steiner Street, in a big house in the middle of the city that Mama loved so well. Jack London's novel *The Sea Wolf* is enriched by its vivid depiction of San Francisco, the city in which London grew up. London set what is perhaps his most famous novel, *The Call of the Wild,* in the Klondike, however.

Dashiell Hammett's detective, Sam Spade, lives and works in San Francisco. As he solves his cases, Spade reveals to us the seamy underbelly of the city, which challenges his ideals and forces him to develop a mask of cynicism. Other writers reveal to us the corrupt side of city life, too. For example, in his short novel *Maggie: A Girl of the Streets,* Stephen Crane shows us the lower depths of New York's Bowery and the effects of this environment on the destiny of a young girl, Maggie Johnson.

This paragraph lacks unity. The controlling idea is that several writers have used San Francisco as a backdrop for their novels. However, the paragraph contains three sentences that do not relate to this main idea. The fifth sentence is a digression because it does not develop the idea of novels set in San Francisco. The last two sentences also digress. The next-to-last sentence is not limited to San Francisco, and the last is concerned with New York City.

Digressions weaken your paragraphs. Eliminate or rewrite any sentences that do not develop the controlling idea. Notice how the sample paragraph is improved by removing the digressions:

Several writers have used San Francisco as a backdrop for their novels. Kathryn Forbes's novel *Mama's Bank Account,* on which the movie *I Remember Mama* was based, is set in San Francisco. The immigrant family lives on Steiner Street, in a big house in the middle of the city that Mama loved so well. Jack London's novel *The Sea Wolf* is enriched by its vivid depiction of San Francisco, the city in which London grew up. Dashiell Hammett's detective, Sam Spade, lives and works in San Francisco. As he solves his cases, Spade reveals to us the seamy underbelly of the city, which challenges his ideals and forces him to develop a mask of cynicism.

EXERCISE 4-1

Underline the topic sentence in each of the following paragraphs. Also notice the details, examples, and explanations that are used to support the topic sentence.

1. It took infinite power to produce these little electrons, to raise them from the possible to the actual state, to throw them out of the realm of nothing into the simple, dimensional existence. No matter how insignificant they are in the order of creaturehood— they have neither intelligence, freedom, nor reflection—they are tremendously more wonderful than nothing. And to prove their excitement at the fact of existence, they expand as water, evaporate as air, explode as fire, congeal as rock. In their congealed state (minerals) they are proletarian or aristocratic as the case may be: junk or jewels. I admire them very much massed in the magnificence of a mountain, diffused in the plume of a cloud, banked in the brilliance of a star.

   Leonard Feeney
   "You'd Better Come Quietly"

2. A suburban lady comes staggering out of the cocktail bar of a hotel which is making money, begins to yodel and perform the split in the lobby and is firmly but gently shoved outside by the house detective in the honest performance of his duty. Two weeks later it develops through the affidavits of friends who were lushing with her at the bar, that the plaintiff drank nothing but mild, nutritious stingers, prescribed by her physician as a remedy for anemia, and that she was not plastered but just

suddenly faint, not yodeling but crying for help, not doing the split but swooning. Therefore she has been publicly humiliated to an extent which cannot be compensated for a nickel less than $50,000.

Westbrook Pegler
" 'T Aint Right"

3. In any science, the hardest question to answer is "why?" In many cases, the question is unanswerable. From one point of view, it is strange that human beings speak so many languages and that these languages undergo any changes at all. Other human activities are identical and unchanging everywhere—all human beings smile, cry, scream in terror, sleep, drink, and walk in essentially the same way. Why should they differ in speech, the one aspect of behavior that is uniquely human? The answer is that, whereas the capacity to learn language is innate, the particular language that anyone uses is learned. That is, the ability to learn languages is universal and unchanging, but the languages themselves are diverse and constantly changing.

C. M. Millward
The Biography of the English Language

4. One of the ends of life, and therefore one of the ends of education, is to understand our place in the universe, our relation

to our surroundings, human and physical; and so the relation of our civilization to the factors that have made it what it is. For everything about us has a history, and if we know something of the history, we understand the thing better. He is but ill-educated who cannot read with intelligence the literature of his country, understand broadly how it comes to be clothed in the shapes in which it is expressed, respond to the appeals it makes to ideas and emotions through words which store up literary energy and give it forth, as radium stores and gives out physical energy; who cannot apprehend the terms in which the sciences indispensable for the conduct of his everyday life name their elements and processes; who has no vision of the background of his religious worship, his standards of conduct and taste, and the social and political institutions of the nation to which he belongs.

H. R. James
Our Hellenic Heritage

5. When we read for information, we acquire facts. When we read to understand, we learn not only facts but their significance. Each kind of reading has its virtue, but it must be used in the right place. If a writer does not understand more than we do, or if in a particular passage he makes no effort to explain, we can

only be informed by him, not enlightened. But if an author has insights we do not possess and if, in addition, he has tried to convey them in what he has written, we are neglecting his gift to us if we do not read him differently from the way in which we read newspapers or magazines.

Mortimer J. Adler
How to Read a Book:
The Art of Getting a Liberal Education

4b Organizational Strategies

A paragraph should be developed and organized in a purposeful way to assist the reader in following your argument or line of reasoning. The paragraph's organization should depend on your overall aim in the particular section of your essay. Sometimes, a method of development will come to you naturally, without thought; at other times, you will have to choose deliberately from a variety of options to fulfill your purpose. These options include some organization strategies as well as some more specific techniques commonly called the patterns, or modes, of development.

You have a variety of organization strategies available to arrange your paragraphs. The following represent the most common types:

1 General to specific

Arrange your information from **general to specific** when you want to present a general idea first and then supply specific examples, details, or reasons to support your idea. The following paragraph is organized in a general to specific pattern. Notice how the information in it becomes more and more specific.

As of now, the biological productivity of the lower Hudson is staggering. Fishes are there by the millions, with marine and freshwater species often side by side in the same patch of water. All told, the population of fishes utilizing the lower Hudson for spawning, nursery or feeding grounds comprises the greatest single wildlife resource in New York State. It is also the most neglected resource; at this writing, not one state conservation department biologist is to be found studying it regularly. Besides sea sturgeon, the river is aswarm yearround or seasonally with striped bass, white perch, bluefish, shad, herring, largemouth bass, carp, needlefish, yellow perch, menhaden, golden shiners, darters, tomcod, and sunfish, to cite only some. There is the short-nosed and round-nosed sturgeon, officially classified by the Department of the Interior as "endangered," or close to extinct, in the United States. Perhaps it is extinct elsewhere along the Atlantic Coast, but not only is the fish present in the Hudson, but occasional specimens exceed the published record size in the scientific literature. The lower Hudson also receives an interesting infusion of so-called tropical or subtropic fishes, such as the jack crevalle and the mullet, both originally associated with Florida waters.

Robert H. Boyle
The Hudson River

2   Specific to general

Arrange your information from **specific to general** when you want to present specific details first and then lead up to a generalization about them. The following narrative paragraph uses a specific to general pattern. The paragraph starts with a specific description of the birds' behavior, which leads up to a generalization about their behavior: They were anting, or deliberately covering themselves with ants.

As he walked in an orange grove behind Trinidad's Asa Wright Nature Centre, Ray Mendez noticed a pair of birds that were behaving strangely. The birds—violaceous trogons, judging from the ring of bright orange around their eyes—were preoccupied with something, so preoccupied that they seemed to have lost their usual bird sense. They appeared fascinated, expectant, oblivious. Mendez drew close and watched. Suddenly one of the trogons broke from its perch and flew a hard flat line at an ants' nest hanging from a tree branch. The bird crashed into the nest, held on, and then shoved itself in headfirst, allowing *Azteca* ants to cover its body. It flittered its wings a moment and the *Azteca* boarded them too. Then the trogon flew back to a safe perch, and Mendez, entranced by the mystery of these events, suddenly saw the simple answer. The trogons were anting.

David Weinberg
"Ant Acid Spells Relief"

The following paragraph is also organized in a specific to general pattern. The author first gives evidence supporting his argument and then concludes the paragraph with a general statement of his position.

American workers understand that the manufacturers of arms have been the bulwark of the capitalist system in the United States, as well as of the communist Soviet Union. In their bones these workers sense that what financial security they have—little enough—is tied to the billions of dollars invested in the arms race. Where would America's "free enterprise" be without that ongoing safety net? Some of us—the more privileged—can afford not to wonder. But most cannot. It wouldn't hurt the peace movement if we found a better way to reach out to this less affluent majority, if we coupled our opposition to nuclear weapons with a clear and compelling program for economic reform.

Robert Coles
"The Doomsayers:
Class Politics and the Nuclear Freeze"

3 Climactic order

Arrange your information in **climactic order,** or by order of importance with the most important last, when you want to begin by supporting your generalization with the least important information and build up to the most important. The following paragraph is organized in climactic order. It starts with the least important criterion for judging a behavior as conscious and builds up to the most important.

> What criteria lead us to judge that a particular behavior is conscious? What is the difference between the eight-month baby who clumsily knocks over its milk, and the two-year-old who obviously does it on purpose? Several things incline us to judge that another being is acting consciously: if it studies its goal before acting, if it chooses one of a very flexible set of behaviors, or even a novel behavior with detours to reach the goal. Conscious purpose seems especially likely if some learned symbol like "No! Naughty!" communicates the situation to the aggravated parents. Finally, if there is misdirection—hiding or lying—it seems likely that the creature has formed some conception of other animals' intentions and awareness.
>
> **Alison Jolly**
> **"A New Science That Sees Animals**
> **as Conscious Beings"**

4   Time order

Arrange your information in **time order** when you want to explain a sequence of events or tell a story. The details in the following expository paragraph are organized according to time order:

> Jesuit missionaries stationed in China were probably the first voyagers to bring soybeans to Europe, in the seventeen-thirties, and there, like potatoes before them, the beans were considered a horticultural curiosity. Specimens were planted at the Jardin des Plantes, in Paris, in 1739, and in London's Kew Gardens—these probably from India—in 1790. (As early as 1712, a German botanist, Engelbert Kämpfer, who had visited Japan in the sixteen-nineties, published a recipe for soy sauce; that may have been the first time any Europeans were informed that the bean was in any respect edible.)
>
> **E. J. Kahn, Jr.**
> **"Soybeans"**

5 Spatial order

Arrange your information in **spatial order** when you want to explain or describe the relative physical positions of people or objects. The details in the following descriptive paragraph are organized according to spatial order:

> Greenwich Village is a mass of "little twisted streets that crossed and recrossed each other and never seemed to get anywhere. . . ." In its center is Washington Square, a stretch of green, bordered by a number of park benches, where one can sit and read, talk, or do nothing at all. In the background of Washington Square looms New York University. Before Washington Square became a park in 1827, it had been "in successive decades Potter's Field, parade grounds, place of executions. . . ." During Millay's time, little delicatessens and coffee shops helped to create an old English atmosphere in the Village.

> **Anne Cheney**
> *Millay in Greenwich Village*

4c Patterns of Development

Numerous other techniques are available in addition to the general techniques for arranging your paragraphs. The **patterns of development,** for instance, enable you to explain information in specific ways as dictated by your purpose and can even be used to develop entire essays, not just paragraphs. These patterns can be used alone in a paragraph or essay or can be used together to suit your writing needs. The following represent the most commonly used of the patterns or modes of development:

1 Description

Develop your paragraph through **description** when you wish to provide specific details that accurately paint a picture of your topic in the reader's imagination (objective description) or that re-create an impression you have of your topic (subjective description). Be certain to report your point of view, the real or imaginary point from which you are viewing the thing described. If the point of view changes during the description, indicate that for your reader. Following is an example of a subjective description. Note that not all descriptive details are visual.

> Stand on a hilltop in late September, and you can see October coming. Not October only, but all of autumn, which flows like a tide across this land of ours. It creeps down from the mountaintops in a haze of leaf color. It strides across the meadows in a foam of final blossom. It rustles through the marsh-grass at the foot of the shore's dunes, whispers down the valleys in a southward rush of wings, tangs the evening air with wood smoke. Not only can you see autumn; you can hear it, you can feel it in the air upon your cheek, you can smell its pungence.
>
> Hal Borland
> "Autumn in America"

2 Definition

Develop your paragraph through **definition** when you want to clarify how you are using a term, to assign a particular meaning to a word, or to discuss an abstract concept from a special or unusual point of view. If you think your reader will not know or understand how you are using a term, be safe and define it; however, remember to include in the paragraph *why* a definition is necessary.

> What is war? It is not weapons or warheads or even military force itself; these are only "the *means* of war." According to Clausewitz, war is simply "an act of force to compel our enemy to do our will." That is precisely what the Vietnamese are attempting to do to the Cambodians, what Iraq tried to do to Iran, what Somalia is striving to do with Ethiopia, what Israel attempted to do in Lebanon, and why Soviet troops are in Afghanistan.
>
> Colonel Harry G. Summers, Jr.
> "What Is War?"

3 Classification

Develop your paragraph through **classification** when you wish to group information into types or classes to find or to explain patterns of *similarities*. The following paragraph classifies ranks within a troop of rhesus monkeys:

> The core of the troop's structure is a series of matriarchies. A mother ranks above her own daughters until she becomes very, very old. She supports them in fights, so her offspring rank just below her and thus above all the other matriarchies that she can dominate. Young males commonly migrate to other troops. A male's adult rank depends on his own fighting prowess and on his charm—much of his status depends on whether the females of his new troop back him up. A female, on the other hand, is usually locked for life into the nepotistic matrix of her kin. Her adult rank is roughly predictable the day she is born. But female status changes do occasionally happen, and it is worth a young female's while to test the system. In the wild, predation and disease knock out relatives at random, so there is more flexibility than we see in our well-tended captive colonies. Wild or captive, kinship is still the major fact of female social life. A baby learns early those situations when its relatives will come and help—and when they won't.
>
> Alison Jolly
> "A New Science That Sees Animals
> as Conscious Beings"

4 Comparison and contrast

Develop your paragraph through **comparison and contrast** when you want to show the similarities and/or differences between two or more things. You have several options in presenting the information. One way is to present the items being compared and contrasted one at a time; the result is called the **block pattern,** exemplified in the following excerpt:

> Villamuelas, Spain—Soldiers don't start out as generals nor politicians as presidents. In business, managers work their way up.

Except for a lucky few, the realization slowly and steadily comes to just about everyone that the top is out of reach.

But bullfighting works the other way around. A bullfighter rockets to the top. From first blush, he is a matador—that bold and arrogant swordsman who artfully entices the bull to its moment of truth. A matador monopolizes the spotlight long enough to convince the world of his incompetence. Then his own moment of truth arrives: the shock of failure and the dawning knowledge that he will never be on top again.

Barry Newman
"Banderillo"

Another option is to alternate points of the comparison or contrast, called the **alternating pattern,** which is illustrated in the following paragraph:

Twenty-four-year-old Clark Wolfsberger, a native of St. Louis, and Kim Wright, twenty-five, who is from Chicago, live in Dallas. They've been going together since they met as students at Southern Methodist University three years ago. They are an attractive pair, trim and athletic, she dark and lissome, he broad-shouldered and square-jawed. They have jobs they took immediately after graduating—Clark works at Talent Sports International, a sports marketing and management company; Kim is an assistant account executive at Tracy-Locke, a large advertising agency—and they are in love.

Bruce Weber
"The Unromantic Generation"

A third option is to mix the two types of presentations: You present most of the comparison/contrast in the block pattern and then present the key points in the alternating pattern to highlight and emphasize significant similarities or differences.

5 Analogy

Develop your paragraph with **analogy** when you wish to stress comparisons between things that are unlike. In the following paragraph, the author presents an analogy comparing the crowd on the boardwalk in Atlantic City to a nest of social insects:

> Viewed from a suitable height, the aggregating clusters of medical scientists in the bright sunlight of the boardwalk at Atlantic City, swarmed there from everywhere for the annual meetings, have the assemblages of social insects. There is the same vibrating, ironic movement, interrupted by the darting back and forth of jerky individuals to touch antennae and exchange small bits of information; periodically, the mass casts out, like a troutline, a long single file unerringly towards Childs's. If the boards were not fastened down, it would not be a surprise to see them put together as a nest of sorts.
>
> **Lewis Thomas**
> *On Societies as Organisms*

6   Example and illustration

Develop your paragraph by **example,** one or more short instances, or by **illustration,** a longer, sustained example that usually appears in the form of a story, when you want to make your ideas specific by supporting them with evidence. Examples work best when you use two or three that are truly representative. Because illustration consists of one sustained example of several sentences, its use is not as frequent but can be equally effective in relating to and supporting your topic sentence. In the following paragraph, the author uses illustrations as a lead-in to the topic (last) sentence:

> I have seen many students read a difficult book just as if they were reading the sports page. Sometimes I would ask at the beginning of a class if they had any questions about the text, if there was anything they did not understand. Their silence answered in the negative. At the end of two hours, during which they could not answer the simplest questions leading to an interpretation of the book, they would admit their deficiency in a puzzled way. They were puzzled because they were quite honest in

their belief that they had read the text. They had, indeed, but not in the right way.

Mortimer J. Adler
How to Read a Book:
The Art of Getting a Liberal Education

See also paragraphs 3, 4, and 5 of the student's sample essay in Section 3e for samples of short example.

7   Process

Develop your paragraph through explanation of a **process** when you wish to show how something is done or how something works. The following paragraph explains how we listen to music:

> We all listen to music according to our separate capacities. But, for the sake of analysis, the whole listening process may become clearer if we break it up into its component parts, so to speak. In a certain sense we all listen to music on three separate planes. For lack of a better terminology, one might name these: (1) the sensuous plane, (2) the expressive plane, (3) the sheerly musical plane. The only advantage to be gained from mechanically splitting up the listening process into these hypothetical planes is the clearer view to be had of the way in which we listen.

Aaron Copland
"How We Listen to Music"

8   Cause and effect

Arrange your information through **cause and effect** when you want to discuss the causes behind certain effects or the reasons for certain results or consequences. Be certain that you have carefully thought out all the implications of your cause and effect statements. For example, one can write that candidate X lost the election because she did not get enough votes. Although this is true, a full treatment would include the reasons why enough people did not vote for candidate X. (See Section 6d on logical fallacies.) The following paragraph gives the result first—the transformation of the tartan into an instrument of Scottish nationalistic ideology. It then provides the reasons or causes that brought about this result.

> A cluster of events transformed the tartan into an instrument of nationalist ideology. In the wake of the great defeat of Bonnie Prince Charlie in 1745, the British banned Highland wear, including tartans and the kilt, under penalty of six months in prison for a first offense and seven years' transportation for a second. The elder Pitt simultaneously formed the Highland regiments for service abroad. They alone were permitted to wear the plaid and the kilt, both for reasons of esprit de corps and, no doubt, to impede desertion: a man running about in a skirt south of the border or in France was a conspicuous object. This is, most likely, when tartans peculiar to certain regiments became established. Finally, Scottish nationalism, seeking to extirpate both Irish and Lowland roots of the culture, turned to the literal invention of an ancient Highland culture, kilt and all. The final triumph came when Lowland Scotland, offered this bogus tradition, eagerly accepted it.

> **Alexander Cockburn**
> **"The Origin of the Kilt"**

EXERCISE 4-2

Compose one paragraph on a suggested topic using any three of the following patterns of development.

Description: the face of an older person you know; a building you pass daily; a car you would like to own; a busy place—the cafeteria, library, student union, dorm lobby.

Definition: what you mean by *beauty;* how the dictionary distinguishes between a *statesman* and a *politician;* how the etymology of the word *umpire* is informative; a current slang term

Classification:	varieties of students in your composition class; types of housing; current popular music; kinds of cars you have owned
Comparison and contrast:	two people you like very much; attitudes toward smoking; two classes you enjoy for different reasons
Example and illustration:	attitudes toward birth control; underage drinking; qualities for success; activities that require teamwork
Process:	tying a bow in your shoelace; shampooing your hair; starting a car; heating soup; how you begin writing a paper
Cause and effect:	why some of your peers don't vote; why a runner loses a race; something done carelessly; what caused an automobile accident

EXERCISE 4-3

Describe the method of development used for each of the following paragraphs. Some of the paragraphs might use more than one method. Underline the topic sentence in each paragraph. Why has the author placed it in that position? Does it indicate the type of development in the paragraph?

1. A shoe is a form of clothing, a covering for the foot. Designed to fit about the foot in a snug but comfortable fashion, it often makes the foot feel as if it has incorporated the shoe as part of its being. Modern shoes usually have some strong agent such as rubber or leather on the bottom, called the sole, which proves helpful in protecting the foot from uncomfortable walking surfaces. The top half of the shoe that crosses over the foot, attached to the sole, is generally made of a more flexible material, in order to take on the shape of one's foot. Some shoes simply slip onto the foot, whereas others have tightening devices such as shoestrings, buckles, or velcro to prevent the shoe from falling off the foot.

From a student's essay

2. They tumble down mountain sides; they meander through flat farm lands. Valleys trail them; cities ride them; farms cling to them; roads and railroad tracks run after them—and they remain, permanent, possessive. Next to them, man's gleaming cement roads which he has built with such care look fragile as paper streamers thrown over the hills, easily blown away. Even the railroads seem only scratched in with a penknife. But rivers have carved their way over the earth's face for centuries and they will stay.

> **Anne Morrow Lindbergh**
> *North to the Orient*

3. It might be well to take a brief look at the ends which are in fact being aimed at in this country. There are four of these; they are the same life objectives which inexperienced adolescents usually think supremely worth while. Two of them—the quest for money and the quest for pleasure—are the goals which increasingly, for a half century at least, have determined the cultural pattern of America. The other two—the quest for power and the quest for erudition—are equally inadequate, but to the pursuit of them more than a few are already turning as they find themselves increasingly bored by what has become the American way of life.

> **Bernard Iddings Bell**
> *Crisis in Education*

4. By literature, then, is meant the expression of thought in language; where, by "thought" I mean ideas, feelings, views, reasoning, and other operations of the human mind. And the art of letters is the method by which a speaker or writer brings out in words, worthy of his subject, and sufficient for his audience or readers, the thoughts which impress him. Literature, then, is of a personal character; it consists in the enunciations and teachings of those who have a right to speak as representatives of their kind, and in whose words their brethren find an interpretation of their sentiments, a record of their own experience, and a suggestion for their own judgments.

> **John Henry Newman**
> *The Idea of a University*

5. While many writers, and among them not a few men of science, are convinced that we live at a crisis in western civilization, opinions are divided about the nature of the crisis and the role which science has to play in helping to resolve it. According to some, science will be responsible for our ruin, because it has given mankind the power to destroy itself. According to others, science will work our salvation, because it is only another name for reason, and if we drop our outworn modes of thought we can use it to build a new metaphysic, a new ethic, and a new religion. According to others again, science can put an end to want, and if we abolish want we shall abolish also hatred, envy and avarice; therefore we need science for both the physical and the moral health of society.

> E. F. Caldin
> *The Wind and the Rain*

4d Transition

Even if all the sentences in a paragraph relate to a controlling idea and follow an organized method of development, it is still helpful to the reader's understanding to link sentences with **transitional devices** that provide smooth passage from one idea to the next. These devices include not only *transitional words and expressions* but also *pronouns, repetition of key words and phrases,* and *parallel grammatical structure.*

1 Transitional words and expressions

Transitional words and expressions show the relationship of one term to another term, one sentence to another sentence, one idea to another idea, and even one paragraph to another paragraph. They serve as signposts that direct the reader through the passage.

The following is a list of some common transitional words and expressions and the relationships they might indicate:

ADDITION

again, also, and, besides, equally important, finally, first (second, third, and so on), furthermore, in addition, last, likewise, moreover, next, too

SIMILARITY

in a similar fashion, likewise, moreover, similarly, so

CONTRAST

although, but, even so, for all that, however, in contrast, nevertheless, nor, on the contrary, on the other hand, or, still, yet

TIME

afterward, at the same time, before, earlier, finally, in the past, later, meanwhile, next, now, previously, simultaneously, soon, subsequently

PLACE OR DIRECTION

above, beyond, here, in the distance, nearby, opposite, overhead, there, to the side, underneath

PURPOSE

for this purpose, to this end, with this object in mind

RESULT

accordingly, as a result, consequently, hence, then, therefore, thus

EXAMPLES OR INTENSIFICATION

for example, for instance, indeed, in fact, in other words, that is

SUMMARY OR CONCLUSION

finally, in brief, in conclusion, in short, in summary, on the whole, to conclude, to sum up

In the following paragraph, the transitional words and expressions are printed in **boldface:**

There were other important applications of new technology that looked ahead to the future, **too.** Thaddeus Lowe was by no means the first to fly in lighter-than-air-balloons, **but** he was the first to use these craft for doing reconnaissance work on enemy positions. **Likewise,** the telegraph had been around for some years, **but** the Civil War was the first war in which it played a crucial role. **So, too,** railroads were already enjoying a robust adolescence, **but** it was during the Civil War that they found themselves making a major contribution. Barbed wire entanglements were **also** used for the first time in the Civil War, **as** were land and water mines.

Arthur M. Schlesinger, Jr.
The Almanac of American History

2 Pronouns

Pronouns link sentences by referring the reader to their antecedents (see Section 14a). In the following excerpt, notice how the pronouns in the second and third sentences link these clauses and sentences to the first sentence:

There is always a teahouse wherever you go in the Orient. **Some** are big with red pillars and gleaming orange-yellow roofs; **many** have tables in a garden among scented flowers and lotus ponds; a **few** are huge houseboats carved to look like dragons floating on the water. But **most** of **them** are just plain, unornamented, regular restaurants.

Maj Leung
The Chinese People's Cookbook

3 Repetition and parallel structure

Repetition of key words and phrases and the use of **parallel grammatical structure** (see Section 21c) provide emphasis and clear transition from one thought to another. In the following paragraph, notice how the repetition of the word *know* drives home the author's point. Notice also that the last three sentences are in parallel form: each is made up of a clause beginning with *if* followed by a clause beginning with *you will*. This structure, along with the transitional words *then* and *Next* at the beginning of the second and third sentences, makes it easy for the reader to follow the progression of ideas from one sentence to the next.

But I am wandering from what I was intending to do; that is, make plainer than perhaps appears in the previous chapters some of the peculiar requirements of the science of piloting. First of all, there is one faculty which a pilot must incessantly cultivate until he has brought it to absolute perfection. Nothing short of perfection will do. That faculty is **memory.** He cannot stop with merely thinking a thing is so and so; he must *know* it; for this is eminently one of the "exact" sciences. With what scorn a pilot was looked upon in the old days, if he ever ventured to deal in that feeble phrase "I think," instead of the vigorous one "**I know!**" One cannot easily realize what a tremendous thing it is to **know** every trivial detail of twelve hundred miles of river and **know** it with absolute exactness. **If** you will take the longest street in New York, and travel up and down it, **conning** its features patiently until you **know** every house and window and lamp-post and big and little sign **by heart,** and **know** them so accurately that you can instantly name the one you are abreast of when you are set down at random in that street in the middle of an inky black night, **you will** then have a tolerable notion of the amount and the exactness of a pilot's **knowledge** who carries the Mississippi River in his head. And **then if** you will go on until you **know** every street crossing, the character, size, and position of the crossing-stones, and the varying depth of mud in each of these numberless places, **you will** have some idea of what the pilot must **know** in order to keep a Mississippi steamer out of trouble. **Next, if** you will take half of the signs in that long street, and *change their places* once a month, and still manage to **know** their new positions accurately on dark nights, and keep up with these repeated changes without making any mistakes, **you will** understand what is required of a pilot's peerless **memory** by the fickle Mississippi.

Mark Twain
Old Times on the Mississippi

EXERCISE 4-4

In the following excerpt, circle all the transitional devices.

Propaganda. How do we feel about it? If an opinion poll were taken tomorrow, nearly everyone would be against it. For one thing it *sounds* so bad. "Oh, that's just propaganda" means, to most people, "That's a pack of lies." But propaganda doesn't have to be untrue—nor does it have to be the devil's tool. It can be used for good causes as well as for bad—to persuade people to give to charity, for example, or to love their neighbors, or to stop polluting the environment, or to treat the English language with more respect. The real problem with propaganda is not the end it's used for, but the means it uses to achieve the end. Propaganda works by tricking us, by momentarily distracting the eye while the rabbit pops out from beneath the cloth. This is why propaganda always works best with an uncritical audience, one that will not stop to challenge or question. Most of us are bamboozled, at one time or another, because we simply don't recognize propaganda when we see it.

Donna Woolfolk Cross
"Politics: The Art of Bamboozling"

EXERCISE 4-5

In each of the paragraphs in Exercise 4-1, identify the words that give the paragraph *unity* (u); then identify the words that serve the function of *transition* (t).

4e Transitional Paragraphs

A **transitional paragraph** consists of one or two sentences whose purpose is to carry the reader from one main idea to another. Usually, a transitional paragraph sums up or emphasizes the thoughts in the preceding paragraph and announces the idea to be developed in the next paragraph. Notice how this kind of movement is accomplished in the third (transitional) paragraph in the following excerpt:

I always find myself annoyed when "intellectual" men dismiss violence against women with a yawn, as if it were beneath their dignity to notice. I wonder if the reaction would be the same if the violence were directed against someone other than women. How many people would yawn and say, "Oh, kids will be kids," if a rock group did a nifty little number called "Lynchin," in which stringing up and stomping on black people were set to music? Who would chuckle and say, "Oh, just a little adolescent rebellion" if a group of rockers went on MTV dressed as Nazis, desecrating synagogues and beating up Jews to the beat of twanging guitars?

I'll tell you what would happen. Prestigious dailies would thunder on editorial pages; senators would fall over each other to get denunciations into the Congressional Record. The president would appoint a commission to clean up the music business.

But violence against women is greeted by silence. It shouldn't be.

But this does not mean censorship, or book (or record) burning. In a society that protects free expression, we understand a lot of stuff will float up out of the sewer. Usually, we recognize the ugly stuff that advocates violence against any group as the garbage it is, and we consider its purveyors as moral lepers. We hold our nose and tolerate it, but we speak out against the values it proffers.

Caryl Rivers
"Rock Lyrics and Violence Against Women"

4f   Paragraphs of Introduction

In most essays, the **introduction** is usually restricted to the first paragraph, although longer papers might require several introductory paragraphs. The introduction is important because it shapes the reader's first impression and often serves as a deciding factor in whether the reader goes beyond it. The introduction sets the tone, establishes the writer's relation to the reader, and indicates the direction the essay will take. Avoid attempting to perfect the introduction in your first draft. You cannot expect to do your best writing the first time. Refine your introduction and thesis as you work through multiple drafts.

1   Announce the topic

The introduction can take many forms to achieve a variety of effects. It can simply identify the topic to be addressed, as in the case of the following introduction for an article on surgeons:

> Today in the United States there is one profession in which conflict of interest is not merely ignored but loudly defended as a necessary concomitant of the free-enterprise system. That is in medicine, particularly in surgery.

> George Crile, Jr.
> "The Surgeon's Dilemma"

Normally, you will take several sentences to introduce your controlling idea. You can give background information or begin with some fairly broad remarks about your subject, then narrow the focus down to the specific idea covered by your thesis. This is the approach used in the following introductory paragraph:

> I love my country as many who have been here for generations cannot. Perhaps that's because I'm the child of immigrants, raised with a conscious respect for America that many people take for granted. My parents chose this country because it offered them a new life, freedom, and possibilities. But I learned at a young age that the country we loved so much did not feel the same way about us.

> Magdoline Asfahani
> "Time to Look and Listen"

2   Catch the reader's interest

You also want to encourage your readers to keep reading. You need to engage them at the onset, especially when you cannot assume that they are interested in the subject. Here are several kinds of openings that are designed to grab the readers' attention. Depending on your topic and purpose, one of these strategies might work for you.

Surprising statement

I am sleeping hard, when the telephone rings. It's my brother, and he's calling to say that he is now my sister.

Judy Ruiz
"Oranges and Sweet Sister Boy"

Description of a scene or event

The room is dusty and ill-lighted, claustrophobic, the sort of room illegal operations are performed in. Brenda is lying on the makeshift operating table, nervously fingering her shirt and the table edges. She is young, probably no more than nineteen, with rust-colored hair and freckles, and with small, tight breasts that rise gently from her chest. A needle is punched in just below the right nipple. Her arms flinch, she winces, but she says nothing. It's a long needle, three inches.

Al Reinert
"Illegal Silicon Breast Injections"

Questions

Do non-human animals have rights? Should we humans feel morally bound to exercise consideration for the lives and well-being of individual members of other animal species? If so, how much consideration, and by what logic? Is it permissible to torture and kill? Is it permissible to kill cleanly without prolonged pain? To abuse or exploit without killing?

David Quammen
"Animal Rights and Beyond"

Quotation or dialogue

An acquaintance was telling me about the joys of rediscovering her ethnic and religious heritage. "I know exactly what my ancestors were doing 2,000 years ago," she said, eyes gleaming with enthusiasm, "and I can do the same things now." Then she leaned forward and inquired politely, "And what is your ethnic background, if I may ask?"

Barbara Ehrenreich
"Cultural Baggage"

Examples

It happens in an instant, but the scars and psychological damage can last a lifetime. An inquisitive child pulls at the handle of a pot on the stove and is scalded by a cascade of boiling water. A smoker falls asleep with a lighted cigarette and is badly burned when the bedding catches fire. An eruption of caustic chemicals engulfs a worker, eating away skin and flesh. A blast of superheated air burns a fire fighter's face and damages his lungs. Some 1.25 million Americans suffer burns every year.

Leon Jaroff
"To Hell and Back"

Facts and figures

Every two-and-a-half minutes someone in the United States is robbed at gunpoint, and every forty minutes someone else is murdered with a gun. Each year the police seize about 250,000 handguns and long guns (rifles and shotguns) from the people they arrest. Given the number of guns that the manufacturers produce each year (2.5 million long guns and 4 million handguns), the supply-and-demand equation works against the hope of an orderly society.

Steven Brill
"The Traffic (Legal and Illegal) in Guns"

These strategies are less important in academic essays and other writing aimed at readers who have a professional interest in the subject. The important thing is to craft an introduction that fits your audience, topic, and purpose.

Writing Introductions ON A WORD PROCESSOR

Draft sample introductions at the computer. Try out several strategies. You can save time by using the copy and paste functions to incorporate your thesis into each sample. Then print out the copies and review them. Decide which one works best, and move it to the beginning of your first draft. You can always revise it later or try another strategy. Be sure to save all the versions until you have finished the final draft.

4g   Concluding Paragraphs

The Latin word *concludere,* from which **conclusion** is derived, means "to shut up closely." An essay should not just stop; it should conclude—that is, it should end by emphasizing the point the writer has made.

The thesis should, therefore, be reflected in some way in the conclusion. In paragraph 8 of "Swim for Your Life" (see Section 3e), Kit Hoffman makes the point once again that American children and their parents would be healthier if they adopted swimming as their sport of choice. Although this conclusion is not a word-for-word repetition of the thesis, it is clearly a reaffirmation of the essay's main idea.

When writing a conclusion, then, remember to look back. The final paragraph or final sentence should not contain arguments, perceptions, expansions, or ideas that do not already exist within the essay. Such new ideas belong in the body of the paper, where they can receive explanation and support. Although a conclusion might contain a prediction or suggest a future action, the grounds for such elements should be clearly established in the body of the essay. In other words, the conclusion should refer to "what I have written" rather than to "what I can write next."

As with introductions, it is not necessary to come up with the perfect conclusion during the drafting stage. If an idea occurs to you while you are writing, jot it down and save it for later. You can rework it or even replace it with something more effective as your essay develops.

Some introductory strategies—questions, quotations, descriptions—are also useful in bringing an essay to a close. These methods should be combined with a restatement or reinforcement of your main idea. Here are some other strategies that are appropriate for conclusions.

1   Summary

If your essay is long and complex, your readers might appreciate a summary of the major ideas. You want to be careful, however, not to write an ending that sounds forced and simply repeats your introduction. It's a good idea to combine your summary with another strategy, such as a call for action, as is done in this example:

> If black youths are given real opportunities for education, if they are provided with meaningful jobs, if they have adequate income to care for their families, if they have hope for future mobility, then they will contribute their fair share to the larger community. We have the knowledge, the technology, and the resources to improve life chances for young black males. What we need is the compassion, commitment, and consensus to create a human environment for all youth in this country.
>
> Jewelle Taylor Gibbs
"Young, Black, and Male in America:
An Endangered Species"

¶ **4g** *Building Coherent Paragraphs*

2 Suggestions

If you are writing an analysis or a persuasive piece, a useful closing strategy involves offering suggestions—possible solutions for problems discussed in the paper. Here is the conclusion of the article about containing the proliferation of guns in the United States (the introduction is in Section 4f):

> All these small steps toward sanity are possible if we force the people who profit from America's free-wheeling gun traffic to be open, accountable, and fully responsible to law-enforcement needs. If we're going to continue to allow the RGs or the Smith and Wessons to make guns at all for civilian use, we ought to at least demand that they become partners in the effort to curb the carnage their weapons cause. When we think of people murdered or robbed at gunpoint, we have to start thinking of brand names.

Steven Brill
"The Traffic (Legal and Illegal) in Guns"

3 Consequences

Think about the long-term implications of what you have said in your paper. You might want to conclude by suggesting possible benefits or issuing a warning:

> Because propaganda is so effective, it is important to track it down and understand how it is used. We may eventually agree with what the propagandist says because all propaganda isn't necessarily bad; some advertising, for instance, urges us not to drive drunk, to have regular dental checkups, to contribute to the United Way. Even so, we must be aware that propaganda is being used. Otherwise, we will have consented to handing over our independence, our decision-making ability, and our brains.

Ann McClintock
"Propaganda Techniques in Today's Advertising"

Part

II

READING CRITICALLY
AND WRITING LOGICALLY

Most people who write well also read well—and vice versa. The two skills are so intertwined that they are often taught together. Reading not only gives you information and pleasure, but it also instills a sense of how sentences and paragraphs work. Most of the time, you get this sense without really paying attention; it just seeps into your mind with the rest of the material. By looking carefully at good writing, you will better understand the content as well as the techniques that good writers use.

5   Being a Critical Reader

Most of the reading you will do in college will be **critical reading.** This kind of reading will involve reacting to what you read—analyzing it, drawing inferences from it, and evaluating its content and presentation.

5a   Active Reading

Did you ever finish reading an assignment and realize that you hadn't taken in any ideas or information at all? Your eyes passed over the print, but you might as well have stared out the window. At such times, you know that you have been an extremely passive reader. By learning to read actively, you will be able to handle your reading assignments much more successfully. The key is to stay involved with the reading through interaction—bringing mental and emotional energy to the task. The following suggestions will help you to become a more engaged, more effective reader.

1 Preview the material

Study skills experts emphasize the value of previewing a reading—to get your mind ready for full comprehension. Previewing helps to establish a mental set that makes your brain receptive to the reading material. Here are some steps to take in previewing an article or a chapter in a book:

- Read the title. It usually gives you a clue about what's ahead.
- Read the opening paragraph in a chapter or essay. It often contains the thesis and a list of main points.
- Look over visual features. Page through the reading, paying attention to any parts that stand out from the ordinary print: introductory notes, headings, photos, diagrams, boxed material, lists, summaries, and questions. Your textbooks are specially designed to include many of these helpful features. Unfortunately, many students skip them, thinking that they are not as important as the rest. Actually, they are there to focus attention on what *is* important in the reading; they might also give you information that assists you in understanding the reading.
- Read the first sentences of a few paragraphs on each page, especially in material that doesn't include headings. This survey will give you a mental outline of the content before you read it. As a result, your comprehension will improve because you will know what to expect.
- Read the last paragraph. You will get a clear idea of where the reading is heading.

2 Annotate the text

Annotating is a means of recording your impressions, ideas, reactions, and questions *as you read*. You can write words, phrases, statements, exclamations, or questions in the margins. You can also circle important terms, underline or highlight key points, bracket unusual phrases, draw arrows between related details, or just put questions marks in the margin—anything that will help you to interact with the author's thoughts and language. These annotations will be very helpful when you are ready to discuss, review, or write about your reading assignments. Here are some of the things you might want to annotate:

- Questions that come to mind as you read.
- Important ideas that you might want to find again.
- Key facts, details, statistics, and dates.
- Points that you don't understand or need to reread.
- Ideas or details that you want to challenge.

3 Reflect on what you read

It's important to clarify and develop your initial reactions— expressed in your annotations—with further reflections. We have four modes of verbal communication: listening, reading, speaking, and writing. Different people learn best through different modes, but college learning often emphasizes just the first two: listening to course lectures and reading textbooks. When you add the other two modes to your study habits, you more than double your learning potential. Speaking in class and discussing the material with friends and classmates are important. Writing about what you have heard and read is equally important. Here are some productive ways to follow up a reading assignment:

- Have a conversation about your reading with a friend or classmate. Another person who has read the same selection will have different reactions and might be able to clarify points that stumped you. Even someone who has not read the selection might be a good sounding board to discuss the ideas with.
- Without looking at the reading, write a 100- to 200-word summary of the selection. While you write, you will feel which parts of the selection are blurry in your mind. These will be the parts that you find hard to express. Compare your

summary to the original, and revise it to make it as accurate as possible. This summary will be a fine study aid if you are going to be tested.

- You can make another study aid by constructing an outline of the important points. This outline can be a simple list of key thoughts in the order in which they appeared in the essay or chapter.

- In your journal, write a letter to the author of your selection. What would you say to him or her if you could? Do you have any questions? These might be brought up in class discussion if you have them on hand.

- If there are questions at the end of a chapter, write out your answers to them. They will help you to focus on meaning and writing technique. If there are no questions, pose some for yourself and answer them in writing.

5b　Making Inferences

In some reading material, the meaning is not completely spelled out; you have to make judgments and draw conclusions about what the writer means. You can train yourself to infer knowledge that lies below the surface meaning of the words. To *infer* means to arrive at an idea or a conclusion through reasoning. When you infer, you balance what the writer says with your own ideas and insights about what is left unsaid. This process might sound difficult, but making inferences is a skill that can be learned. The following suggestions will help to improve your ability to read between the lines:

- Read beyond the words. Fill in details and information to complete the writer's suggestions. Use the writer's hints to discover the meanings that often lie beneath the surface. But don't go too far: you should be able to point to words and phrases that support what you have inferred.

- Question yourself as you read and after you finish. You might use questions like these: Why did the author include these details? What does this example mean? How am I supposed to react to this sentence?
- Draw conclusions and speculate on outcomes. Ask yourself these questions: What is the author's purpose? What is the point or message of this selection? What am I being asked to think or do (if anything)?
- Make associations between the reading and your own experience. Relating the reading to your own observations and reflections can add richness to the meaning of a work. Have you any experiences or knowledge of the topic? To which points did you respond most strongly? Why? Did the reading challenge your thinking? How can you apply these ideas (or this information)?

5c Evaluating Texts

Evaluation is an important part of critical reading. Once you have a clear understanding of a selection, you are in a position to examine its strengths and weaknesses. Here are some useful questions to ask:

- Who is the intended audience for this selection? Do you fit into this intended audience? If not, why not?
- What words and terms are important in this selection? Has the author defined these key terms adequately and fairly? Or has the author assumed that you will accept these definitions? Do you?
- Does the author present facts or opinions—or a mixture of the two? Can you distinguish the facts from the opinions?
- What conclusions are you being asked to accept or agree with? What reasons and evidence does the author offer you to ensure your agreement? Are the reasons persuasive and

logical? Is the evidence relevant and sufficient? (See Section 6a for details about clear and logical arguments.)

- Does the author present a one-sided view of the issues? Has the author acknowledged and responded to other points of view?
- How much does the author appeal to your emotions? Are these appeals appropriate? (See Section 6d-4 for a discussion of emotional appeals.)
- Is the author's thinking logically sound? Does the author avoid logical fallacies? (See Sections 6c and 6d.)
- How trustworthy is the author's information? Is it complete and up to date? Do you need additional information?
- How successful is the presentation? Does the author accomplish his or her purpose?

6 Writing Arguments

Much of the writing that you do in college will be persuasive or argumentative in nature. On essay tests and in writing assignments, you will often be asked take a stand or support a conclusion. Even an informational report can be said to "argue" or "persuade" in the sense that it attempts to convince the reader that the writer's facts and explanations are true or believable. The skills that you use in being a critical reader will also come into play in writing arguments.

6a Building an Effective Argument

Your purpose in this type of writing is to encourage the readers to accept your point of view, solution, plan, or complaint as their own. Traditionally, the word *persuasion* refers to attempts to sway the readers' emotions, and the word *argument* refers to tactics that address the readers' logic. Many writers mix the two types of appeal. A personal testimony from a paraplegic accident victim pleading with readers to use their seat belts persuades through emotional identification. A list of statistics concerning injury rates before and after seat belt laws went into effect argues the point through rationality. A combination of the two tactics would probably be quite effective. In everyday language, *persuasion* means influence over the audience, whether emotional or rational.

Presenting a conventional argument involves five tasks:

1. State the **issue** you will address, and put it in a context. Why is it controversial or problematic? Why do people care about it? Why do people disagree about it?

2. State your main point or thesis. What point of view, solution, or stance do you wish the readers to adopt? This is your **claim.**

3. Provide well-developed **evidence** on your own side of the issue. You can develop your point through facts, statistics, examples, testimony of experts, and logical reasoning (cause and effect, analogy), just to name a few strategies. This is the longest part of a conventional argument, and each piece of evidence will probably take a paragraph or more to develop.

4. Respond to opposing viewpoints. This is called the **refutation** section. Especially when arguments against your own are widely known, you need to acknowledge them and deal with them, or your essay will have an obvious hole in it. You might minimize their importance, demonstrate that they are not logical or factual, or offer alternative ways of thinking about them.

5. Close by reminding your reader of your main point and the strength of your evidence. Many persuasive essays include

a call to action, encouraging the reader to do something in support of your cause.

Writers often alter this conventional plan, especially tasks 3 and 4. For example, a magazine articled called "Five Myths about Immigration" focuses on refutation, countering popular fears and misconceptions about immigration, one by one, and concluding with the claim that the United States does not have a serious immigration problem. An essay entitled "Why Prisons Don't Work" begins with refutation of the present system, followed by the evidence on the writer's side, instead of the other way around. In an essay entitled "A Crime of Compassion," the author gives the most space to the moving personal story of an expert on the topic of euthanasia. You can tailor your written argument to fit your topic, audience, and purpose and the nature of your evidence.

Claims, evidence, and refutation are the basic building blocks of argument. You must understand them to write persuasively and effectively.

1   Claims

The "engine" that propels any argument is its **claim.** Claims fall into three categories:

1. *Claims of fact* assert, state, or validate that something is indeed true. "Women currently do not receive equal pay for equal work."

2. *Claims of value* approve or disapprove of something related to a system of values. "Leaning to appreciate diversity is more important than learning calculus."

3. *Claims of policy* state that certain conditions, courses of action, or policies should prevail. "A six-month maternity leave policy ought to be federally mandated."

For any argument to be effective, it must be grounded in a claim that is significant, consistent with accepted beliefs or well-reasoned premises, and backed up by the available evidence.

EXERCISE 6-1

Compose three claims of fact, three claims of value, and three claims of policy from the following topic areas.

general education classes	college sports	health care reform
censorship of the arts	legalized drugs	the death penalty
sexual harassment	immigration laws	civil rights
energy conservation	prayer in the public schools	required testing for the AIDS virus
global warming	sex education	domestic violence
affirmative action	same-sex marriage	assisted suicide

2 Evidence

Evidence can come in many forms. Some of the most frequently used kinds of evidence are these:

- *Personal observation or experience.* "I visited prisons across the country and can personally attest to their negative impact on inmates." This is the least widely accepted form of evidence because it is derived from a narrow band of experience and might be unrepresentative. But it can be very persuasive in communicating the human significance of an issue.

- *Facts.* "Every state in the country has enacted mandatory sentencing laws in the past decade." Facts are noncontroversial pieces of information that can be verified through observation or by generally accepted sources; they are persuasive to the extent that they are relevant to the statement they support.

- *Relevant examples.* "Louisiana has one of the highest lockup rates in the country and imposes some of the most severe penalties, yet it also has the highest murder rate in the nation." Like facts, examples are most persuasive when they are objective and clearly relevant.
- *Testimony.* "Eminent sociologist Oscar Teufelmeister refers to the American penal system as 'graduate school for crooks.'" Testimony should come from sources that the readers will accept as credible; it carries its greatest weight when the meaning of the facts or data is not self-evident and some judgment or interpretation is required to reach a conclusion.
- *Data.* "Sixty-three percent of all federal prisoners are repeat offenders." This is probably the most readily accepted form of evidence because of its apparent objectivity and scope.

To be persuasive, all evidence in support of a claim must meet certain standards:

1. It must be reasonably up to date.

2. It must be of sufficient scope.

3. It must be relevant to the claim.

For example, you wouldn't use 1990 unemployment data in support of a 1998 policy decision (recentness). Nor would you rely on unemployment data from only one month to formulate a long-term unemployment policy (scope). Nor would you use employment data from Brazil to comment on the U.S. unemployment picture unless your argument involved an overall comparison of the two countries' economies (relevance).

3   Refutation

Arguments always presume that other points of view are possible; otherwise, there would be no reason to argue. You might

feel so strongly about an issue that you want to attack those who disagree with you and express contempt for their opinions, but that strategy can be counterproductive, especially if you are trying to influence readers who are undecided. Your case will be strengthened if you treat opposing views with respect and understanding.

This acknowledgment of and response to the opposing views is called **refutation.** There is no best place in an argument to refute the opposition. Sometimes you will want to bring up opposing arguments early and deal with them right away. Another approach is to anticipate objections as you develop your own case point by point. Wherever you decide to include your refutation, your goal is to point out problems with the opponents' reasoning and evidence. You can refute opposing arguments by showing that they are unsound, unfair, or flawed in their logic. Frequently, you will present contrasting evidence to reveal the weakness of your opponents' views and to reinforce your own position.

When an opposing argument is so compelling that it cannot be easily dismissed, you should concede its strength. This approach will establish that you are knowledgeable and fair-minded. You can sometimes accept the opponents' line of thought up to a certain point—but no further. Or you can show that their strong point addresses only *one* part of a complex problem.

EXERCISE 6-2

Imagine that you are defending three of the following statements in an argumentative essay. For each, write three points that your opposition might bring up—points that you might need to refute.

1. Government agencies protect us from harmful additives in our food.

2. Every family should consider abolishing Christmas gift giving.

3. The government should discourage the use of private automobiles by funding inexpensive, effective public transportation.

4. A mother has a responsibility to stay home with her children until they are of school age.

5. Colleges and universities should require a study-skills course of all incoming freshman.

6b Sample Argument

The following selection appeared in *U.S. News & World Report* on December 30, 1996. Although this article is a news report, it also contains an argument. The writer advances a claim of fact: that needle exchange programs are effective in reducing the rate of HIV infection. He also suggests a policy claim: that the federal ban on funding these programs should be lifted. The marginal notes identify key features and strategies in building an argument.

IGNORING THE SOLUTION

BY JOSHUA WOLF SHENK

Statement of the problem

AIDS was once the scourge of the gay community. Soon, it will be largely a drug addict's disease. Scientists believe that 50 percent of all new HIV infections occur among intravenous drug users, with an additional 20 percent or so occurring among junkies' sex partners. The syringe is the Typhoid Mary of the 1990s.

Yet what worked best in curtailing the spread of HIV among homosexuals—mass education campaigns promoting safe sex—has been ineffective with drug addicts lurking in society's shadows. What does seem to work is giving drug users clean needles. Since 1986,

Solution — some 100 small needle-exchange programs have sprouted up around the country, through which used syringes are traded for new, sterile ones—no questions asked. Often run by private groups with limited funds, these experiments have been the object of intense scrutiny by major universities and federal health agencies. The conclusion? The programs work. Stud-

Claim of fact — ies have shown up to a sevenfold reduction in all

Evidence (data) blood-borne diseases, a 33 percent projected drop in HIV infections and 25 percent fewer cases of dangerous behavior, such as needle sharing.

Further claim — Besides saving lives, these needle exchanges deliver a huge financial payoff. Consider the case of an HIV-positive addict who infects eight others in a one-year period (a very modest estimate). If each turns to

Evidence (example, data) — Medicaid to pay his or her lifetime medical costs (at an average $119,000 plus), that's about a $1 million burden for taxpayers—money that could have been saved if the one addict had been in a needle-exchange program.

Concession — Evidence for the effectiveness of needle exchanges is not airtight. Drug users who participate in needle exchanges may be more safety conscious and thus at less risk of contracting HIV in the first place.

Refutation — But studies also show that those who participate improve their own behavior over time. So evidence that

Restatement of claim needle exchanges have at least some positive effects is strong.

Evidence (expert testimony) — On balance, the studies are persuasive enough that physician Scott Hitt, chairman of President Clinton's Advisory Council on HIV/AIDS, rebuked his own president for banning the use of federal AIDS funds for needle exchanges. Hitt is joined in the endorse-

Implied claim of policy ment of needle exchanges—and the call for more federal involvement—by the National Academy of Sciences, the Centers for Disease Control and Prevention and the General Accounting Office.

Refutation of 1st objection — The administration worries that needle exchanges might increase drug use. It's a reasonable fear but one not borne out by research, according to the CDC. Only a handful of needle-exchange studies have tracked drug use, but their conclusions jibe with anecdotal evidence and common sense: While addicts prefer clean needles, they will eagerly opt for the abundant supply of dirty ones in the face of a monstrous drug craving.

Refutation of 2nd objection

Some worry that needle exchanges are the classic "Band-Aid"—dealing with HIV infection but not the underlying drug addiction. But needle exchanges have actually worked as a bridge into real treatment. One program in Tacoma, Wash., made nearly 1,000 referrals to drug treatment programs in two years. Others worry that needle exchanges, cheap as they are, will siphon funds from zero-tolerance treatment efforts. But the real problem is that all anti-addiction programs are woefully underfunded.

Evidence (example)

Refutation of 3rd objection

Conclusion

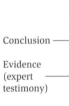

Evidence (expert testimony)

It's hard to avoid the suspicion that these concerns have less to do with science or public health than with politics; specifically, a reluctance to muddy the "just say no" message. But there's another message leaders should heed—that no one has to die needlessly. Peter Lurie, a leading University of California researcher, estimates that nearly 10,000 lives could have been saved over the past few years by an aggressive expansion of needle-exchange programs. Wasn't the war on drugs supposed to be about saving lives?

6c Using Deductive and Inductive Reasoning

The effectiveness of any argument depends on the validity of the reasoning behind it: a well-written argument must be a well-reasoned one. The concept of critical thinking was discussed in Chapter 5. As you will see here, thinking about your writing and evaluating it with a critical eye—important in all writing—is especially important when writing arguments.

The two major kinds of reasoning are inductive and deductive reasoning. **Inductive reasoning** is reasoning from the specific to the general. The word *inductive* comes from a Latin word that means "to lead into." In the inductive method, you observe a number of particular details or specific examples, and these particulars lead you to a general conclusion. Consider the following example:

> *Specific observations:* Having lived for a year in a society that practices folk medicine, you carefully observe the practices of the healers. You observe that they use a preparation made from a particular plant to treat boils. In all cases, the boil disappears within two days of the application of the plant.
>
> *General conclusions:* On the basis of your observations, you reason that this plant helps to cure boils.

To make valid use of the inductive method, you have to be sure of the following:

1. That you have enough observations.

2. That your observations are accurate and representative.

3. That your conclusion derives from these observations.

For example, suppose that the plant mentioned above did not cure three cases of boils. If your conclusion is to be valid, you must note these exceptions and explain them in terms of the conclusion. Perhaps this plant will not cure boils in people who have been treated with it previously or whose boils are especially severe. The more observations and information you accumulate, the more likely it is that your inductive conclusion will be sound.

Deductive reasoning is reasoning from the general to the specific. The word *deductive* comes from a Latin word that means "to lead from." In the deductive method, you start with a general principle and apply it to specific instances. For example, a doctor accepts the general principle that penicillin is effective against the bacteria that cause strep throat. When a patient comes in with strep throat, the doctor applies the general principle to the specific case and prescribes penicillin.

The deductive method can be expressed as a three-step process called a **syllogism.** The three steps are called the major premise, the minor premise, and the conclusion:

MAJOR PREMISE: Penicillin cures strep throat.

MINOR PREMISE: This patient has strep throat.

CONCLUSION: (Therefore) This patient will be cured by using penicillin.

The major premise is a generalization; the minor premise is a specific case; and the conclusion follows from applying the generalization to the specific instance.

To make effective use of the deductive method, you have to be sure that the general principle that you start with is true and that the situation to which you apply it is relevant. Note and account for any exceptions. For example, if the bacteria in the strep throat patient have developed an immunity to penicillin, then the principle would not be applicable to the patient's case. The more information you have about the specific situation, the more likely you will be to apply the relevant principle.

6d Avoiding Logical Fallacies

All thinking is subject to **logical fallacies,** or errors in reasoning. Test your own writing to make sure you have avoided false analogies, overgeneralizations, erroneous assumptions, appeals to emotion, faulty cause-effect analysis, either/or thinking, non sequiturs, red herrings, and circular reasoning.

1 False analogies

Analogies are comparisons. Writers use them to explain a point or to help their readers understand a difficult or unfamiliar concept. For example, a science writer might make an analogy between the way water moves in waves and the way light travels. But analogies are not proofs of a conclusion, and many times they are misleading. For an analogy to be sound, or true, the comparison must make sense: the things being compared must correspond in essential ways, and the ways in which they do not correspond must be unimportant in terms of the argument or conclusion. Consider the following **false analogy:**

> Buying a car is like buying a steak. You can't be sure how good the product is until you've bought it and used it.

This analogy is false because you can test-drive the car, but you cannot test-eat the steak. Moreover, the economic differences between the items is so great that a comparison between the purchase of one and the purchase of the other has little meaning.

EXERCISE 6-3

Explain why the following analogies are false.

1. Mr. Brown will be an excellent member for our school board because he was a colonel in the army.

2. A city council that can spend all the money it did to install electric traffic signals at the mall can afford four stop signs at the corner intersection in our neighborhood.

3. If we can put people on the moon, we should be able to find a cure for AIDS.

2   Overgeneralizations

An **overgeneralization** is a conclusion based on too little evidence or on evidence that is unrepresentative or biased. For example, imagine that you go to a major-league baseball game and observe that attendance at this game is very low. You conclude that attendance at major-league baseball games has fallen off drastically. This is an overgeneralization, since one observation—or even two or three—is not a sufficient number from which to draw a conclusion.

Here are some other examples of overgeneralization:

My nephew has used steroids to build his strength and improve his success as an athlete. This shows that these drugs are more beneficial than harmful.

The book I needed on Reyes syndrome was checked out of the library. Somebody's hoarding all the research material on this topic.

A poll of families in our neighborhood shows that a majority of them are willing to pay higher taxes to improve the public schools. I'm going to run for the school board on this platform.

Stereotyping is overgeneralization about groups of people. **Stereotypes** are the standardized mental images that result from such overgeneralization. Almost everyone believes stereotypes about one group or another, and we encounter them every day in advertising, television programs, and other media. We are all familiar with many of these stereotypes: the absentminded professor, the dumb jock, the talkative female, the dishonest car dealer, the fiery redhead, the passionate Italian lover, the miserly old person, the mean mother-in-law, the stoical male, the computer nerd.

Because stereotypes of this kind are so widely recognized as such, you can easily avoid them in your writing. A greater danger is that you will develop your own stereotypes by treating an individual as representative of a group to which the individual belongs. Try to eliminate stereotyping not only from your writing but also from your thinking.

3   Erroneous assumptions

An **assumption** is an idea that we accept as true without any proof. Sometimes, **erroneous assumptions** enter into our reasoning and confuse our thinking. Many of these assumptions are really overgeneralizations or stereotypes. They are frequently underlying ideas or beliefs that are not explicitly stated, as the following comment demonstrates:

> His autobiography must be fascinating because he is such a famous actor.

The unstated assumption here is that someone who has had a glamorous or exciting career will be able to write about it in an interesting way. There may be some truth in this conclusion, but it cannot be assumed as a general principle.

EXERCISE 6-4

Identify the overgeneralization, stereotype, or unstated assumption in each of the following statements.

1. He could not possibly be guilty of the crime, since he is a devoted family man.

2. Attaining success in politics is the goal of every student who majors in political science.

3. Unions have ruined this country's competitiveness.

4. Young women use abortion as an easy form of birth control.

5. Because they cannot reproduce, homosexuals recruit young people into their lifestyle.

4 Appeals to emotion

Writers use various techniques to arouse an emotional response that may overwhelm logic or reasoning. Among these are name calling, loaded words, and the bandwagon appeal.

Name calling, which is sometimes referred to as the **ad hominem** ("to the man") fallacy, is an attempt to discredit an idea or conclusion by attacking the person presenting it, not the idea or conclusion itself. By shifting the focus from ideas to people, writers fail to address the real issues.

> The only opposition to the new mall comes from environmentalists who care more about trees and birds than they do about the economic welfare of this community.

Loaded words are highly charged, emotional words that appeal to readers' prejudices. Readers who do not already share these prejudices are as likely to be offended as convinced by the use of loaded words.

> Because of this nation's **giveaway** policies, the **hardworking** man or woman lives in squalor while the **lazy bum** drives a Cadillac.

The *bandwagon appeal* attempts to influence people by encouraging them to put aside their powers of reasoning and simply join the crowd.

> Many of the top colleges and universities have abolished freshman composition courses. Our school should do away with them, too.

> ColaRite is the most popular soft drink in the country. Buy some and join in the fun.

EXERCISE 6-5

Each of the following statements contains a logical fallacy. For each statement, indicate whether this fallacy is a false analogy (FA), an overgeneralization (OG), an unstated erroneous assumption (UA), or an appeal to the emotions (AE).

1. Why would you want to live on a street where people have paved driveways but no garages?

2. He cannot possibly succeed in graduate school because he was a star athlete as an undergraduate.

3. All the dentists in town endorse this toothpaste, so it must be effective.

4. Only eggheads and clods belong to that fraternity. You're not planning to pledge it, are you?

5. That restaurant must serve good food because truckers stop there.

6. Purchasing a gun is no more dangerous than getting a driver's license.

7. You can't possibly understand grief unless you've had a loved one die recently.

8. Increased law enforcement and mandatory jail sentences have greatly reduced the number of drunk-driving violations. The drug problem can be solved in the same ways.

9. All patriotic citizens will object to any burning of the flag.

10. They must contribute a lot of money to the university because they always have season tickets for the football games.

5 Faulty cause-effect analysis

Often called the **post hoc** ("after this") fallacy, this logical flaw assumes a cause-effect relationship between two events, just because one precedes the other. Many superstitions are based on this error in reasoning.

It didn't rain today because, for once, I brought my umbrella.

He won the game because he was wearing his lucky T-shirt.

6   Either/or thinking

Either/or thinking is a type of oversimplification that assumes there are only two alternatives in a situation when usually there are many possibilities in between.

We have to decide whether we want clean air and water or a high standard of living.

Every woman today must choose between having a family or having a career.

7   Non sequiturs

The Latin words **non sequitur** means "it does not follow." This fallacy occurs when a speaker or writer presents a conclusion that is not the logical result of a claim or the evidence that supports the claim.

Many wild animals live longer in zoos than in the wild. Therefore all wild animals should be placed in zoos.

Jim Edgar was a popular state governor; he will make an effective president for our university.

8   Red herring

A **red herring** is an irrelevant issue that is introduced into a discussion to draw attention away from the real argument. The term refers to the practice of dragging a smelly fish across the trail to divert tracking dogs away from the real quarry.

Women may deserve equal pay, but I don't think they want the added stress and responsibility that come with those higher-paying jobs.

9 Circular reasoning

Circular reasoning occurs when a writer tries to support a claim by restating it in different words or by assuming that it has been proved.

> Public transportation is necessary because everyone needs it.

> The play is unsophisticated because it displays a naïve simplicity.

EXERCISE 6-6

Each of the following sentences contains a logical fallacy. For each statement, indicate whether the fallacy is faulty cause-effect analysis (CE), either/or thinking (EO), a non sequitur (NS), or circular reasoning (CR). Explain the error.

1. She scored very high on the test because her grandmother prayed for her success.

2. Overcrowded prisons have left us with two alternatives: let criminals loose on the street or make capital punishment a real threat.

3. Lucille does not smoke or drink; she'll be a good parent.

4. The Antarctic ozone layer decreased in October, about the same time that California had a big earthquake. If the ozone layer keeps disintegrating, we can expect more big earthquakes.

5. Juan is an impressive speaker because he always touches his listeners deeply.

6. My car wouldn't start this morning; the battery must be dead.

7. He exercises every day because thin people live longer.

8. Essays exams should be abolished because they require writing skills.

9. If you don't learn how to use a computer, you won't be able to get a good job.

10. We cannot expect that reporter to give us a fair and honest analysis of this issue, since she's a member of the liberal press.

Part

III

GRAMMAR

A complete grammar of English would explain how human beings produce and understand the thousands of utterances they say and hear daily. That is a tall order, involving study of language history, physiology, brain functions, gesture, tone, emphasis, and even silence—as well as the study of words and sentences.

But you do not need a complete and thorough theory of grammar to write well. What you need is a basic vocabulary, shared by you and your teachers and other writers, in which you can talk and think about sentences. Learning the terminology of grammar and the concepts it describes can help you to identify and correct errors in sentence form and to construct more pleasing and effective sentences.

7 Basic Sentence Grammar

The basic unit of communication in English is the **sentence.** A useful definition of a *sentence* is "a word or group of words that expresses a complete thought" and contains a subject and a verb. (Sometimes the subject is implied rather than stated.) A sentence may be as short as one word or as long as fifty words or more.

7a Sentence Patterns

English has six basic patterns for sentences. Each pattern contains a subject and a verb. Depending on the nature of the verb, the pattern may also contain *objects* or *complements* that complete the meaning of the verb. Study the parts of the sentences in the patterns that follow. The individual parts will be explained in the indicated sections.

1. Subject/intransitive verb (see Sections 7b and 7c)

   > S V
   > Her tires squealed.

2. Subject/transitive verb/direct object (see Section 7d)

   > S V   DO
   > Flying gravel hit the sidewalk.

3. Subject/transitive verb/indirect object/direct object (see Section 7d)

   > S V IO   DO
   > Her father gave Shana driving lessons.

4. Subject/transitive verb/direct object/object complement (see Section 7d)

   > S   V DO OC
   > Her driving makes him nervous.

   > S V   DO   OC
   > Shana calls her father a big worrywart.

5. Subject/linking verb/subject complement (see Section 7d)

   > S V   SC
   > Her father is a professional race car driver.

   > S   V SC
   > He usually seems calm.

6. Subject/being verb/adverb of time or place

   > S V   ADV
   > Shana is seldom here.

   > S V   ADV PHRASE
   > She is frequently in Chicago.

7b Subjects

The **subject** of the sentence is a noun or nounlike word group that answers the question "Who?" or "What?" about the predicate, or verb. The subject is the part of the sentence that performs the main action of the sentence or is described in it.

How can you identify the subject of a sentence? Form a question by putting "who" or "what" before the verb. In some sentences, the subject *performs* the action expressed by the verb.

Halfway through her performance, the **soprano** *hit* a flat note.

Captain Cook *searched* for a northwest passage to China.

Who hit a flat note? The *soprano.* Who searched for a northwest passage to China? *Captain Cook.*

In other sentences, the subject *receives* the action of the verb; that is, it is acted upon.

The **deer** *was wounded* by the hunters.

If the verb is a linking verb, such as *be* or *seem,* the subject is the person or thing identified or described.

James Boswell *was* both the friend and the biographer of Samuel Johnson.

Sometimes, one of the **expletives** *there* and *here* appears at the beginning of the sentence. These words are never the subject but simply serve to postpone the appearance of the subject, which is in the middle of the sentence. The word *it* can also be used as an expletive. The result of using initial expletives and placing the subject in midsentence is an unemphatic sentence. Placing the subject at the beginning or the end of a sentence will help you to achieve sentence *emphasis*. In both of the following sentences, the subject is printed in **boldface:**

There are **six books in this series.**

Here are **four ways to increase productivity at this plant.**

Sometimes the sentence is a command. In a command, the subject *you* is implied rather than stated.

[You] Help me with this word processing program.

Please read this chapter before the next class.

Because a prepositional phrase ends with a noun or noun substitute, people sometimes look to it for the subject of the sentence (see Chapter 8). However, the simple subject is never found in a prepositional phrase. In both of the following sentences, the simple subject is printed in **boldface** and the prepositional phrase in *italics:*

Each *of the states* chooses delegates to the convention.

Neither *of the pandas* is female.

1 The simple subject

The **simple subject** is the main noun or noun substitute in the subject.

A New Jersey **farmer** won a prize in London in 1986 for a 671-pound pumpkin.

Growing **conditions** in 1987 made the pumpkins smaller.

That year a **Canadian** took first place with a 408-pound entry.

It won its grower a cash prize and a trip to San Francisco.

Growing monstrous vegetables can be a profitable hobby.

A simple subject may consist of two or more nouns or noun substitutes (pronouns) that take the same predicate.

> **Economics** and **health** are much in the news lately.

> In ancient Greece, **war** and **athletics** were believed to be influenced by Nike, the winged goddess of victory.

> **Desire, anger,** and **pain** must be annihilated in order to reach Nirvana.

2   The complete subject

The **complete subject** consists of the simple subject and all the words that modify it. In both of the following sentences, the simple subject is printed in **boldface** and the complete subject in *italics:*

> *Wide-visioned, close-fisted* **George Halas,** *originator of the Chicago Bears,* can be described as the George Washington of pro football.

> *A hot* **bath** *and a vigorous* **massage** are good remedies for aching muscles.

Note: Throughout this book, we use the term *subject* to mean the simple subject.

7c   Predicates

The **predicate** of a sentence states either the action done by the subject or the condition of the subject; it asserts what the subject does or is. The predicate consists of a verb (a word that expresses action or a state of being) and all the words that complete the meaning of the verb.

How can you identify the predicate of a sentence? Form a question by putting "Does what?" or "Is what?" after the subject.

The pianist **played a complicated piece.**

The amateur treasure hunters **found a few valuable pieces.**

The pianist did what? *Played a complicated piece.* The amateur treasure hunters did what? *Found a few valuable pieces.*

1 The simple predicate

The **simple predicate** is the verb, which may consist of more than one word.

The cups **broke.**

Early in her reign Elizabeth **had reestablished** the Church of England.

Many accidents **could have been prevented.**

A simple predicate may include two or more verbs that take the same subject.

The small group of colonists **boarded** the British ships and **threw** their cargoes of tea overboard.

2 The complete predicate

The **complete predicate** consists of the simple predicate and all the words that modify it and complete its meaning. In the following sentence, the simple predicate is printed in **boldface,** and the complete predicate is in *italics:*

A jet flying overhead **broke** *the stillness of the night.*

EXERCISE 7-1

Underline the complete predicate in each of the following sentences and label the simple subject (S) and the simple predicate (V). Follow the examples.

```
        S          V
Vandals destroyed Rome during Nero's reign.

     S       V
Rome was destroyed.

     S       V
Rome burned furiously.

     S      V
Nero was an emperor.

     S      V
Nero remained indifferent to the fate of the city.
```

1. Most of us know the writing process.

2. The car was struck by the yellow truck.

3. The popularity of the rock group soared.

4. Speak softly and carry a big stick.

5. There are no simple answers to your question.

6. My friends and I left at intermission and adjourned to our fa-vorite hangout.

7d   Complements

A **complement** completes the meaning of a verb. The four major types of complements are the *direct object,* the *indirect object,* the *object complement,* and the *subject complement.* (See the sentence patterns in Section 7a; look carefully at patterns 2 through 5.)

1   Direct objects

A **direct object** is a noun or noun substitute that specifies the person or thing directly *receiving* the action of a transitive

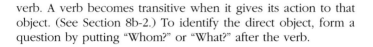
verb. A verb becomes transitive when it gives its action to that object. (See Section 8b-2.) To identify the direct object, form a question by putting "Whom?" or "What?" after the verb.

> Darwin accepted a **position** aboard H.M.S. *Beagle*.

> The congressional representative greets **everyone** warmly and then opens the **discussion.**

Darwin accepted what? A *position*. The congressional representative greets whom? *Everyone*. And opens what? The *discussion*.

2   Indirect objects

An **indirect object** is a noun or noun substitute that tells to whom or for whom or what the action of the verb is performed. A sentence can have an indirect object only if it has a direct object; the indirect object comes before the direct object. Indirect objects follow verbs that describe a giving action of some kind.

> The director gave the **plans** her approval.

> My daughter wrote **me** this poem.

Most sentences containing an indirect object can be rewritten by putting *to* or *for* before the indirect object.

> The director gave her approval **to the plan.**

> My daughter wrote this poem **for me.**

3   Object complements

An **object complement** is a noun or adjective that completes the action of a transitive verb by renaming or modifying the direct object. A sentence can have an object complement only if its verb has a direct object. The action of the verb imparts a change of some kind to that object.

The storm made the bridge **unsafe.**

The news report declared it a **hazard.**

You can often insert *to be* between the direct object and the object complement.

The storm made the bridge *to be* **unsafe.**

The news report declared it *to be* a **hazard.**

Sometimes the object complement is signaled by *as,* which we call an **expletive.** In some cases, the *as* is optional:

We elected Raoul president of the senior class.

We elected Raoul *as* president of the senior class.

And in some cases, the *as* is required:

I know her *as* a good friend.

The noun object complement always follows the direct object. Occasionally, the adjective object complement may precede the direct object:

     S   V   OBJ COMP   DIR OBJ
The judge ruled **impossible** the impartiality of a trial held in the victims' community.

4 Subject complements

A **subject complement** is a noun or adjective that completes an intransitive linking verb and renames or describes the subject. (See Section 8b-2.)

The dance recital was an exciting **event.**

Martha Graham became a principal **innovator** in modern dance.

The noun *event* renames *recital,* and the noun *innovator* renames *Martha Graham.*

In a sentence like this, the linking verb serves as an equal sign. The noun on the left-hand side of the linking verb equals the noun on the right-hand side. Because it is part of the predicate, a noun subject complement is also called a *predicate noun* or *predicate nominative.*

An adjective subject complement (also called a *predicate adjective*) follows an intransitive linking verb and describes the subject.

> Isadora Duncan's style of dancing seemed **revolutionary** to her contemporaries.

> The critic's review of the recital was especially **sarcastic.**

The adjective *revolutionary* describes *style* (a "revolutionary style"); the adjective *sarcastic* describes *review* (a "sarcastic review").

EXERCISE 7-2

In each of the following sentences, underline the complete subject once and the complete predicate twice. Circle both the simple subject and the simple predicate. Then identify any complements and classify them as direct object (DO), indirect object (IO), object complement (OC), or subject complement (SC).

1. Environmental biology is a popular program of studies in this part of the country.

2. Frank Lloyd Wright designed the house next to ours.

3. Some European nations have successfully encouraged the official use of two or even three languages.

4. The discussion group named Judy their official spokesperson.

5. We should give our children every educational opportunity.

6. The therapist made her client comfortable.

EXERCISE 7-3

Make up sentences that conform to the following patterns. The abbreviations correspond to the following elements in the sentence: S (subject), V (verb), DO (direct object), IO (indirect object), OC (object complement), SC (subject complement), ADV (adverb of time or place).

1. S V
2. S V SC
3. S V DO

4. S V IO DO
5. S V DO OC
6. S V ADV

---

8   Word Classes: The Parts of Speech

Words have traditionally been classified into eight categories, called the **parts of speech:** noun, verb, adjective, adverb, pronoun, preposition, conjunction, and interjection. Early grammarians came up with these categories to make their description of English conform to the word categories of Latin grammar. More recently, however, grammarians have looked closely at English and have identified two main categories of words: the **form classes** and the **structure classes.** These two groups divide words in English according to their form, their meaning, and their functions in the sentence.

In general, the words in the form classes provide the primary content in a sentence; the structure classes describe the grammatical or structural relationships. You can think of the form-class words as the bricks of the language and the structure-class words as the mortar that holds them together.

FORM CLASSES	STRUCTURE CLASSES	
Noun	Pronoun	Conjunction
Verb	Determiner	Expletive
Adjective	Qualifier	
Adverb	Preposition	

FORM-CLASS WORDS

The distinctive feature of form-class words is that they change form: nouns have singular and plural forms, verbs have present-tense and past-tense forms, adjectives and adverbs have comparative and superlative forms. Form-class words also perform the main functions in a sentence: subject, predicate, complement.

8a Nouns

A **noun** is a word that names. Nouns may name persons, places, objects, events, or ideas.

PERSONS:	Shakespeare	actor	women	
PLACES:	Pittsburgh	prairie	suburbs	
OBJECTS:	reindeer	Bunsen burner	cassettes	
EVENTS, IDEAS, ACTIVITIES:	meeting	freedom	frustration	fire

1 Forms of nouns

Nouns can show **number.** Most nouns can be either singular or plural. (For guidelines on forming the plural of nouns, see Section 42e.)

| **SINGULAR:** | computer | success | criterion | woman | sheep |
| **PLURAL:** | computers | successes | criteria | women | sheep |

Nouns also can change form to show **possession** (and in this form are considered to show a possessive case; see Chapter 15): the *cat's* feet (the cat has feet); a *singer's* voice (a singer has a voice).

A noun is the only part of speech that can be preceded by an **article** or **determiner**—*a, an,* or *the.* A generalized noun naming something countable can be preceded by an **indefinite article**—*a* or *an* (indicating "one"): *a* cat; *an* animal; *a* woman. A noun that names something quite specific is often preceded by the **definite article**—the word *the: the* cat; *the* animal; *the* woman. Nouns also identify something very specific when preceded by certain limiting or determining words such as *this, that, these, those* (*this* cat, *that* animal), or when preceded by indefinite determining words like *first, second, last,* and by relative pronouns like *which, that, whose.*

2   Kinds of nouns

Nouns can be classified in various ways.

Proper nouns name unique and particular persons, places, objects, or ideas. Proper nouns are capitalized: *Milton; Honda; Martin Luther King, Jr.*

Common nouns name people, places, objects, and ideas in general, not in particular. Common nouns are not capitalized: *poet-dramatist; motorcycle; preacher.*

Concrete nouns name generalized things that can be seen, touched, heard, smelled, tasted, or felt: *horizon; marble; music.*

Abstract nouns name concepts, ideas, beliefs, and qualities. Unlike concrete nouns, abstract nouns name things that cannot be perceived by the five senses: *love; justice; creativity.*

Count nouns name people or things that are considered countable in English: *eggs; rats; grains.*

Mass nouns (or **noncount nouns**) name what is not considered countable: *rice; water; air.*

Collective nouns are singular in form but plural in meaning: *faculty; tribe; family.*

Compound nouns consist of more than one word. Some compound nouns are written as one word, some are hyphenated, and some are written as two or more separate words. (When in doubt, check your dictionary.)

bedroom	tomato plant	cathode-ray tube
heartland	fire insurance	father-in-law

8b Verbs

A **verb** is the key word in the predicate of the sentence (see Section 7c); it is a word that expresses action—physical or mental—or a state of being. In the following sentences, the verbs are printed in **boldface:**

Isaac Bashevis Singer **wrote** his stories and novels in Yiddish. (*physical action*)

Puritans **valued** industry and thrift. (*mental action*)

That young man **is** a famous singer. (*state of being*)

1   Verb forms

A verb has four basic forms, called **principal parts:** the present infinitive, the past tense, the past participle, and the present participle (see Chapter 12).

PRESENT INFINITIVE	PAST TENSE	PAST PARTICIPLE	PRESENT PARTICIPLE
compute	computed	computed	computing
analyze	analyzed	analyzed	analyzing
fall	fell	fallen	falling
bring	brought	brought	bringing

The **present infinitive** is the dictionary form of the verb. For example, if you wanted to know the meaning of the first verb in the chart above, you would look up *compute,* the present infinitive form, in your dictionary. The **present participle** of all verbs is formed by adding *-ing* to the present infinitive. The **past tense** and **past participle** of most verbs, called **regular verbs,** are formed by adding *-d* or *-ed* to the present infinitive. Verbs like *fall* and *bring* are **irregular verbs;** their past tense and past participle are formed in some other way. (For more information on irregular verbs, see Section 12a.)

A **verb phrase** is made up of the present infinitive, the present participle, or the past participle preceded by one or more auxiliary verbs or modals. As discussed in Chapter 12, the **auxiliary** verb *have* is used to form the perfect tense; the auxiliary verb *be* is used to form progressive tenses and the passive voice. In the following sentences, the verb phrase is printed in *italics* and the auxiliary in **boldface:**

> Edna St. Vincent Millay's first book of poems **was** *published* in 1917. (*passive voice, past tense*)

> Jacobo Timerman **has** *called* attention to the violation of human rights in Argentina. (*present perfect tense*)

2   Kinds of verbs

Action verbs

An **action verb** may be *transitive* or *intransitive.* An action verb that takes an object is **transitive.** An **object** is a word (a noun or noun substitute) that completes the idea expressed by the verb. (See Section 7d).

> Marie and Pierre Curie successfully **isolated** *radium.*

> Professor Higgins **introduced** *Eliza Doolittle* to society.

When the subject of a transitive verb performs the action received by the object, the verb is said to be in the **active voice.** The verbs in the preceding sentences are **transitive active.**

A transitive verb is in the **passive voice** when the active-voice object has become subject of that verb; the active-voice subject may appear as the actor only in a phrase with an introductory preposition such as *by.*

Radium **was** successfully **isolated** by Marie and Pierre Curie.

Eliza Doolittle **was introduced** to society by Professor Higgins.

Only transitive verbs can be described as having voice. (For more about voice, see Section 12b-3.) An action verb that has no object is **intransitive.**

> Sometimes even good old Homer **nods.**
>
> Horace

> Consider the lilies of the field, how they **grow;** they **toil** not, neither **do** they **spin.**
>
> Matthew 6:28

State-of-being verbs

State-of-being verbs may be *linking* or *nonlinking.* They are, however, always **intransitive** because they never take objects. Instead, they take subject complements. (See Section 7c-4.)

A **linking** verb expresses a state of being or condition and connects its subject to a word that describes or identifies that subject. The most common linking verb is *be,* including its forms: *am, is, are, was, were, will be, have been,* and so on.

Radiotherapy **is** the treatment of disease with radiation.

Woody Guthrie **was** a popular folksinger.

Americans **were** aghast at the sinking of the *Lusitania.*

Other common linking verbs are *appear, become, feel, grow, look, remain, seem, smell, sound,* and *taste.*

> Houdini **became** world-famous for his daring escapes.

> The true fate of Amelia Earhart **remains** a mystery.

A linking verb connects the subject to a subject complement. A subject complement may be either a noun, which identifies the subject, or an adjective, which describes the subject. (See Section 7d-4.)

> *Napoleon* was a brilliant **general.** (*noun subject complement*)

> After his defeat at Waterloo, *Napoleon* was **disconsolate.** (*adjective subject complement*)

A **nonlinking** state-of-being verb is not followed and completed by a subject complement but may be followed by an adverb modifier of time or place.

> Yesterday we **were** upstream from their camp.

> The next performance **is** at eight o'clock.

Auxiliary or helping verbs

Forms of the verbs *be* and *have* can help show important shifts in meaning in various forms of the main verb that signal **tense** and **mood.** (See Chapter 12.) When they serve this helping function they are called **auxiliary** or **helping verbs.**

> **MAIN VERB:** She *goes.*
> **AUXILIARY VERBS:** She *is* going; she *has* gone; they *have been* going.

Modals are used to form questions, to help express a negative, to emphasize, to show future time, and to express such conditions as possibility, certainty, or obligation. The words *do, does, did; can, could; may, might, must; will, shall; would, should;* and *ought to* are modals. A verb phrase may include both auxiliaries and modals. In each of the following sentences, the verb phrase is printed in *italics* and the modal in **boldface:**

> For a democracy to work, its citizens **must** *participate.*

> The election **may** *be decided* on the basis of personality.

Sometimes an auxiliary or modal is separated from the main part of the verb.

> **Do** you *know* the full name of the Imagist poet H. D.?

> The price of gold **has** not ***been*** *falling.*

Verbs change form to display three characteristics: *tense, voice,* and *mood;* these are discussed and demonstrated in Chapter 12.

EXERCISE 8-1

Underline the simple components of the following sentences and use these abbreviated labels: subject (S), transitive verb (TV), intransitive verb (IV), linking verb (LV), passive voice verb (PV), object (O), and subject complement (SC). See the following example:

>   S   TV   O
> The marines rescued the pilot.

1. A wave of patriotism swept across the country during the Gulf War.

2. It was a stark contrast to the time of the Vietnam War.

3. Yellow ribbons were attached to doors and trees in honor of our military personnel.

4. Many people flew flags day and night.

5. Rallies in support of our troops were held in most large cities.

6. It seemed a genuine outpouring of national pride.

7. The percentage of women in the military reached its highest point in our history.

8. The popularity of a military career soared.

9. Many of the troops were honored with parades throughout America.

10. The yellow ribbons are no longer visible in most places.

8c   Verbals

A **verbal** is not a "part of speech" but a grammatical form derived from a verb that does not function as a verb in a sentence. A verbal functions as a noun, an adjective, or an adverb. There are three types of verbals: *participles, gerunds,* and *infinitives.* Infinitives and participles are explained in Section 8b-1.

1   Participles

The **present participle** and the **past participle** of most verbs can be used as adjectives. (For information on how participles are formed, see Section 8b-1.)

A **dancing** bear is an image associated with Theodore Roethke.

The peace between the two wars has been compared to a **held** breath.

He prefers **iced** tea.

2   Gerunds

A **gerund** is a verb form that is spelled in the same say as the present participle, with an *-ing* ending, but a gerund is used as a noun, not an adjective, in a sentence.

The problems of **parenting** were discussed at the symposium.

The school taught **reading** and **writing** but little else.

3   Infinitives

The present infinitive and the present perfect infinitive of a verb can be used as nouns, adjectives, or adverbs. The **present infinitive** is the *to* form of the verb (e.g., *to go*); the **present perfect infinitive** is the *to have* form (e.g., *to have gone*).

She wanted **to resign** at first but finally decided **to stay.** (*nouns*)

King Lear is considered a difficult play **to stage.** (*adjective*)

They were sorry **to have left** before you arrived. (*adverb*)

Sometimes the word *to* in the infinitive is understood rather than stated.

Therapists must help their patients cope with life's problems.

Therapists must help their patients **to** cope with life's problems.

EXERCISE 8-2

Underline the verbals in the following sentences and identify each verbal as a participle (P), a gerund (G), or an infinitive (I).

1. Do most people believe that listening, seeing, or hearing is the same thing as doing?

2. Should state governments be allowed to regulate the arts?

3. Depending on where one lives, sales of certain recordings may be prohibited unless labeled.

4. Analyzing the effects of such warnings on purchases has not yet revealed an impact on sales.

5. To be able to buy unlabeled recordings is a right that many people cherish.

8d Adjectives

An **adjective** is a word that modifies, or describes, a noun or pronoun. It limits or makes clearer the meaning of the noun or pronoun.

The **efficient** *secretary* organized the schedule. (*modifies a noun*)

He is **efficient.** (*modifies a pronoun*)

They are still **popular** though **their** *composer* died in 1937. (the first *modifies a pronoun;* the second *modifies a noun*)

By describing a quality or a condition, an adjective answers the question "What kind?"

The England of the Anglo-Saxons was not a **unified** *country,* but a land divided into **separate** *kingdoms.*

The *riddles* in **Anglo-Saxon** *poetry* were **clever** and **humorous.**

1   Forms of adjectives

Most adjectives have a comparative form to compare two things and a superlative form to compare three or more.

	COMPARATIVE	SUPERLATIVE
rich	richer	richest
beautiful	more beautiful	most beautiful
bad	worse	worst

(For more information about the comparative and superlative forms of adjectives, see Chapter 16.)

2   Placement of adjectives

Adjectives can usually be identified by their position in a sentence. For example, an adjective will fit sensibly into any of the following blanks.

The _____ person was very _____.

The _____ object was removed.

It seems _____.

8e   Adverbs

An **adverb** is a word that modifies, or limits the meaning of, a verb.

During the Harbor Festival the tall ships *sailed* **gracefully** into the bay.

My brother-in-law **always** *drives* **fast** on the highway.

1   Kinds of adverbs

An adverb modifies by answering one of the following questions: (1) "When?" (2) "Where?" (3) "How?" (4) "How often?" and (5) "To what extent?"

Adverbs of time answer the question "When?"

We *will discuss* the matter **soon.**

Environmentalists warn that we *must* **eventually** *reach* an equilibrium with nature.

Adverbs of place answer the question "Where?"

The ambassador *encountered* an Islamic revival **everywhere** in the Middle East.

Faith healers *look* **upward** and **inward** for cures for disease.

Note that nouns can function as adverbs of time and place.

The symposium *was held* **yesterday.**

Some students *go* **home** every **weekend.**

Adverbs of manner answer the question "How?" They tell in what manner or by what means an action was done.

The movie-going public **enthusiastically** *embraces* disaster films.

Adverbs of frequency answer the question "How often?"

The teacher **repeatedly** *praised* his students for their achievements.

Adverbs of degree answer the question "To what extent?"

My friends and I **thoroughly** *enjoyed* the new Stephen King novel.

2 Forms of adverbs

Many adverbs can be formed by adding the suffix *-ly* to an adjective. An additional spelling change is sometimes required.

The artist's style was **delicate.** (*adjective*)
The artist painted **delicately.** (*adverb*)

The general's actions seemed **heroic.** (*adjective*)
The general acted **heroically.** (*adverb*)

Most adverbs have comparative and superlative forms.

	COMPARATIVE	SUPERLATIVE
profoundly	more profoundly	most profoundly
fast	faster	fastest
well	better	best

(For more information about the comparative and superlative forms of adverbs, see Section 16c.)

STRUCTURE-CLASS WORDS

Unlike form-class words, **structure-class words** (also called *function words*) do not change in form. Although they convey little meaning or content, they are very important because of the structural sense they contribute to sentences. Structure-class words are among the most common words in the language.

8f Pronouns

The term **pronoun** covers a wide variety of words, many of which function in very different ways. Some pronouns change form, but most of them act as structure-class words, providing important information about the structural or grammatical relationships in a sentence.

A **pronoun** is a word that stands for or takes the place of one or more nouns. When a pronoun refers to a specific noun, that noun is called the **antecedent** of the pronoun. In the following sentences, the arrows indicate the *italicized* antecedents of the pronouns in **boldface** type:

Because *vitamins* can have toxic side effects, **they** should be administered with care.

A pronoun may also have another pronoun as an antecedent.

Most of the old records are scratched. **They** cannot be replaced.

Each of the mothers thought **her** child should receive the award.

Certain pronouns may lack a specific antecedent.

Who can understand the demands made upon a child prodigy?

Everyone knew that **something** was wrong.

There are seven categories of pronouns: *personal, demonstrative, indefinite, interrogative, relative, intensive,* and *reflexive.*

1   Personal pronouns

Personal pronouns take the place of a noun that names a person or a thing. Like nouns, personal pronouns have numbers, genders, and cases. This means that they can be singular or plural; that they can be masculine, feminine, or neuter; and that they can function in the subjective, the objective, or the possessive case. (For more information about pronoun case, see Chapter 15.) In addition, personal pronouns are divided into three "persons": **first-person pronouns** refer to the person(s) speaking or writing, **second-person pronouns** refer to the person(s) being spoken or written *to,* and **third-person pronouns** refer to the person(s) or thing(s) being spoken or written *about.* The following is a list of all the personal pronouns:

	SINGULAR	**PLURAL**
FIRST PERSON:	I, me, my, mine	we, us, our, ours
SECOND PERSON:	you, your, yours	you, your, yours
THIRD PERSON:	he, him, his	they, them, their, theirs
	she, her, hers	
	it, its	

2 Demonstrative pronouns

Demonstrative pronouns point to someone or something. The demonstrative pronouns are *this* and *that* and their plural forms *these* and *those*.

Demonstrative pronouns are usually used in place of a specific noun or noun phrase.

> The sandwiches I ate yesterday were stale, but **these** are fresh.

> James named the character Mrs. Headway, for **that** was her chief characteristic, her ability to make headway.

In addition, demonstrative pronouns are sometimes used to refer to a whole idea.

> Should we welcome the electronic age? **That** is a good question.

If you use a demonstrative pronoun in this way, be sure that the idea it refers to is clearly stated and not just vaguely suggested. (See Chapter 14.)

3 Indefinite pronouns

Indefinite pronouns do not take the place of a particular noun, although sometimes they have an implied antecedent. Indefinite pronouns carry the idea of "all," "some," "any," or "none." Some common indefinite pronouns are listed below:

everyone	somebody	anyone	no one
everything	many	anything	nobody

Some indefinite pronouns are plural, some are singular, and some can be either singular or plural.

> **Everything** *is* going according to plan. (*singular*)
>
> **Many** *were* certain that the war, which officially started on July 28, 1914, would be over before autumn. (*plural*)
>
> **Some** of the material *was* useful. (*singular*)
>
> **Some** of the legislators *were* afraid to oppose the bill publicly. (*plural*)

For more information on the number of indefinite pronouns, see Section 13e.

4   Interrogative pronouns

Interrogative pronouns are used to ask a question.

who   whom   whose   what   which

Who, whom, and *whose* refer to people. *What* and *which* refer to things.

> **What** were the effects of the Industrial Revolution on Europe during the first decade of the twentieth century?
>
> **Who** is Barbara McClintock, and for **what** is she best known?
>
> **Which** of the economic depressions have been most damaging?

5   Relative pronouns

Relative pronouns are used to form adjective clauses and noun clauses (see Section 8c on these topics).

| who | whom | that | whoever | whichever |
| whose | which | what | whomever | whatever |

Who, whom, whoever, and *whomever* refer to people. *Which, what, that, whichever,* and *whatever* refer to things. *Whose* usually refers to people but can also refer to things.

> The Black Emergency Cultural Coalition is an organization **whose** members have dedicated themselves to the elimination of racism in the arts.

> The food was given away to **whoever** wanted it.

For more information about the relative pronouns, see Sections 13e, 14a, and 15a.

6   Intensive pronouns

Intensive pronouns are used to emphasize their antecedents. They are formed by adding *-self* or *-selves* to the end of a personal pronoun.

> The detectives **themselves** did not know the solution.

> The producer wasn't sure **herself** why the show was a success.

7   Reflexive pronouns

Reflexive pronouns are used to refer to the subject of the clause or verbal phrase in which they appear. They have the same form as intensive pronouns.

> During her illness Marjorie did not seem like **herself.**

> If you have young children in the house, take precautions to prevent them from electrocuting **themselves** accidentally.

> This plant can fertilize **itself.**

EXERCISE 8-3

In each of the following sentences, underline the pronoun and label it as personal (P), demonstrative (D), indefinite (I), interrogative (?), relative (REL), intensive (INT), or reflexive (REF).

1. Although almost everyone likes sweet candy, I myself have never had a sweet tooth.

2. Those look very attractive; however, I work too hard for my money to pay the cost.

3. Many languages have important common features that enable them to be placed in language families.

4. To whom do you wish to speak and what is the nature of your visit?

5. Our English language has borrowed immensely from the vocabulary of more than 200 languages over the years.

8g   Determiners

A **determiner** is a word that introduces a noun. Unlike adjectives, determiners do not have a comparative or superlative form, and they do not describe a noun; instead, they identify or quantify it. There are four types of determiners: (1) **articles** (*a, an, the*); (2) **quantifiers** (*two, three, first, second, some, few, several, many, any, enough,* etc.); (3) **possessives** (*my, our, your, his, her, its, their, Sheila's, a friend's,* etc.); and (4) **demonstratives** (*this, that, these, those*).

Most noun phrases begin with at least one determiner:

> **your** chemistry book, **the** latest horror movie, **this** extraordinary photograph, **an** important event, **several** new students, **all my** children, **every six** weeks, **the first few** times, **our neighbor's** old car

8h Qualifiers

A small group of words act as **qualifiers** to alter or intensify the meaning of an adjective or adverb:

We worked **rather** slowly.

She is **very** intelligent.

Some qualifiers are used with the positive form of adjectives and adverbs:

quite beautiful, **too** rapidly, **almost** there

Other qualifiers are used with the comparative forms of adjective and adverbs:

still better, **even** sooner, **much** nicer

Some *-ly* adverbs are used as qualifiers with certain adjectives:

dangerously close, **particularly** harmful, **especially** difficult, **absolutely** true

8i Prepositions

Prepositions are connecting words. Each of the following prepositions shows a different relationship between the noun *stump* and the actions expressed by the verbs:

The rabbit jumped **over** the stump, ran **around** the stump, sat **on** the stump, hid **behind** the stump, and crouched **near** the stump.

The group of words beginning with a preposition and ending with a noun or pronoun (called its *object*) is a *prepositional phrase.* Prepositional phrases function in a sentence as adjectives or adverbs. (See Section 9a.)

Prepositions are among the most familiar and frequently used words in the language because they orient things and actions in space and time. The following is a list of common prepositions:

COMMON PREPOSITIONS

about	concerning	past
above	despite	save (meaning
across	down	"except")
after	during	since
against	except	through
along	for	throughout
among	from	till
around	in	to
at	inside	toward(s)
before	into	under
behind	like	underneath
below	near	until
beneath	of	unto
beside	off	up
between	on	upon
beyond	onto	with
but (meaning	out	within
"except")	over	without

A **compound preposition** is made up of more than one word. The following are some commonly used compound prepositions:

ahead of	in front of	out of
as for	on top of	together with
in back of		

Prepositions appear only in and at the beginning of prepositional phrases. In the following sentence, the prepositions are printed in **boldface** and the prepositional phrases in *italics:*

The term "metaphysical poets" was coined **by** *Samuel Johnson* **in** *the eighteenth century.*

Note: The *to* in the infinitive form of a verb (such as *to describe*) is not a preposition. (For more information on prepositional phrases, see Section 9a.)

8j Conjunctions

Conjunctions are words that are used to join other words, phrases, clauses, or sentences. There are three types of conjunctions: *coordinating conjunctions, correlative conjunctions,* and *subordinating conjunctions.*

1 Coordinating conjunctions

A **coordinating conjunction** joins elements of equal grammatical rank. These elements may be single words, phrases, or independent clauses. (See Chapter 9.) The common coordinating conjunctions are:

> and   or   for   yet   but   so   nor

In the following sentences, the coordinating conjunctions are printed in **boldface,** and the elements being joined are printed in *italics:*

> The children of *Queen Victoria* **and** *Prince Albert* married into many of the other ruling houses of Europe.
>
> *Some enjoy Matthew Arnold primarily for his poetry,* **but** *others respect him more for his criticism.*
>
> The flax is then soaked *in tanks, in streams,* **or** *in pools.*

Conjunctive adverbs

Words like the following, called **conjunctive adverbs,** may make clear the connection between *independent clauses* (clauses that can stand by themselves as sentences), but they cannot—as conjunctions can—join the clauses.

accordingly	hence	otherwise
also	however	still
besides	moreover	therefore
consequently	nevertheless	thus
furthermore		

In the following sentences, the conjunctive adverbs are in **boldface** and the independent clauses in *italics*. Notice that a semicolon precedes a conjunctive adverb that appears between independent clauses.

> *She wanted to photograph the building in the early morning light;* **therefore,** *she got up at dawn on Saturday.*

> *For years the elderly have moved from the North to Florida to retire;* **however,** *today many are returning to the North to be near their children.*

2 Correlative conjunctions

Correlative conjunctions are coordinating conjunctions that are used in pairs. The most common correlative conjunctions are these:

both . . . and	not only . . . but also
either . . . or	whether . . . or
neither . . . nor	

In the following sentence, the correlative conjunctions are in **boldface:**

> **Whether** you go **or** stay makes no difference to us.

3 Subordinating conjunctions

Subordinating conjunctions join clauses that cannot stand by themselves as sentences. They join subordinate, or dependent, clauses to main, or independent, clauses. (See Chapter 9.) The following are some common subordinating conjunctions:

after	if	than
although, though	in order that	that
as	in that	unless
as if	inasmuch as	until
as long as	now that	when
as much as	once	where
because	provided that	whereas
before	since	wherever
even though	so long as	whether
how	so that	while

8k Expletives

An **expletive** is a word that has a grammatical function in a sentence but has no meaning of its own. The most common expletive in English is the word *there*. Writers and speakers use this expletive to shift the actual subject of a sentence to a more emphatic position.

Several new specialty shops are in the mall.

There are several new specialty shops in the mall.

Here and *that* can also function as expletives.

Here are your glasses on the counter where you left them.

I know **that** she loves me.

In most cases, an expletive can be dropped from the sentence.

Your glasses are on the counter where you left them.

I know she loves me.

EXERCISE 8-4

Circle the prepositions in the following sentences. Then underline each conjunction and label it a coordinating (CO), correlative (COR), conjunctive adverb (CJ), or subordinating conjunction (SUB).

1. Neither rain nor sleet nor hail nor snow is said to deter the delivery of mail in this country.

2. Some find solitude by means of going to the lakeshore; however, I prefer the quiet of a wooded area.

3. More and more people are feeling the need for relief from everyday pressures, but most people are not in a position to do anything about it.

4. Not only men but also women deliver the mail in our neighborhood for the postal service.

5. Instead of being in crowds of people all the time, we, therefore, need time for ourselves and opportunities to reflect on life.

EXERCISE 8-5

Label the class of each underlined word: pronoun (PRN), determiner (DET), qualifier (QUAL), preposition (PREP), conjunction (CONJ), or expletive (EXP).

1. I found some <u>very</u> rare stamps <u>and</u> postmarks <u>on</u> an old envelope.

2. <u>Four</u> friends of mine <u>from</u> the dorm played cards <u>while</u> they waited in line <u>for</u> tickets to the concert.

3. <u>You</u> know <u>that</u> I cannot sell <u>this</u> ticket <u>to</u> you <u>unless</u> you show some identification.

4. <u>There</u> are <u>too</u> many people in <u>the</u> elevator.

5. The shipment <u>of</u> supplies arrived <u>even</u> sooner than <u>we</u> expected.

9 Phrases, Clauses, and Sentences

PHRASES

A **phrase** is a group of words that does not contain a subject and a predicate but that functions as a noun, adjective, or adverb in a sentence. There are several types of phrases. This section discusses *prepositional phrases* and *verbal phrases.*

9a Prepositional Phrases

A **prepositional phrase** consists of a preposition, the object of the preposition, and all the words modifying this object. In the following sentences, the prepositional phrases are in **boldface,** and the prepositions and their objects in ***boldface italics:***

> ***In* many *cultures*** whale meat has been an essential source ***of protein.***

> Some ***of these cultural groups*** resent efforts ***by conservationists*** to protect the whale, since these efforts would restrict the groups' ability to obtain food and would conflict ***with their traditions.***

Note: The word *to* with the infinitive (e.g., *to obtain*) is not a preposition and does not introduce a prepositional phrase.

Usually a prepositional phrase functions as an adjective or an adverb.

The *computer* **for the home** may become as common as the typewriter. (*adjective*)

The phrase "fruit *fresh* **from the farm**" has become quite *popular* **in merchandising circles.** (*adverbs*)

9b   Verbal Phrases

A **verbal phrase** consists of a verbal and all its complements and modifiers. (To review verbals, see Section 8c.) There are three types of verbal phrases: *participial phrases, gerund phrases,* and *infinitive phrases.*

1   Participial phrases

A **participial phrase** consists of a present or past participle and all its modifiers and complements. It acts as an adjective in a sentence. In the following sentences, the participial phrases are in **boldface** with the participles in ***boldface italics:***

Throughout his life, Whitman adhered to the beliefs ***summarized*** **in the preface to his book.**

A man ***curled*** **in the fetal position** with his arm ***covering*** **his head** is the subject of one of Rodin's most moving sculptures.

Absolute phrases

A participle modifying its own subject instead of a noun or noun substitute in the sentence creates an **absolute phrase.** An absolute phrase must be set off from its sentence by a comma.

Their voices *raised* in song, the settlers rode out of sight.

The wind *having disappeared,* the boat drifted idly with the current, **sails *hanging* limp, the passengers *complaining* but *refusing* to touch the oars.**

2   Gerund phrases

A **gerund phrase** consists of a gerund and all its modifiers and complements. A gerund phrase acts as a noun in a sentence. In the following sentences, the gerund phrases are in **boldface** with the gerunds in ***boldface italics:***

For Freud, ***remaining* in Vienna** became impossible once the Nazi forces invaded Austria in 1938.

***Running* five miles a day** keeps a person in good condition.

3   Infinitive phrases

An **infinitive phrase** consists of the present infinitive or the present perfect infinitive form of the verb and all its modifiers and complements. It acts as a noun, an adjective, or an adverb. In the following sentences, the infinitive phrases are in **boldface** with the infinitives in ***boldface italics:***

***To know* him** is ***to love* him.** (*nouns*)

Hard work is one way ***to gain* success in business.** (*adjective*)

She is proud ***to have dedicated* her life to music.** (*adverb*)

CLAUSES

A **clause** is a group of words with a subject and a predicate. A clause may be *independent* or *dependent*.

A clause that is structurally independent, that can stand by itself, is called an *independent clause*. A clause that is structurally dependent, that cannot stand by itself, is called a *dependent clause.* A subordinating conjunction is used at the beginning of a dependent clause to show the relation between this clause and the independent clause to which it is attached. In the following sentences, the subordinating conjunction is printed in **boldface** and the dependent clause in *italics:*

> The tepee was an improvement over the traditional tent **because** *it had a smoke hole at the top.*

> **When** *a chief died,* his heir erected a totem pole to honor him.

(For more information on clauses, see Chapter 21.)

9c   Independent Clauses

An **independent clause** is a group of words with a subject and a predicate that expresses a complete thought. In other words, an independent clause is structurally independent and can stand by itself as a simple sentence.

> The Spanish conquistadors heard the legend of El Dorado, the Man of Gold.

> Some soldiers of fortune traveled down the Amazon.

Coordination occurs when two or more independent clauses are joined together with a coordinating conjunction, such as *and, or,* or *but.*

> They heard the legend, **and** they slaughtered many thousands to fulfill it.

9d   Dependent Clauses and Subordination

A **dependent clause** is a group of words with a subject and a predicate. Because dependent clauses cannot stand by themselves as sentences, they must be attached to or be part of an independent clause. They are often called *subordinate clauses* because they are structurally subordinate to the independent clause. **Subordination** occurs when a dependent clause is attached to an independent clause with a subordinating conjunction or a relative pronoun. In this sentence, the independent clause appears in **boldface** and the subordinate clause in *italics:*

> *Because they heard the legend,* **they slaughtered many thousands.**

Usually, a dependent clause begins with a subordinating word, which may be a subordinating conjunction or a relative pronoun. There are three types of dependent clauses: *adjective, adverb,* and *noun clauses.*

1   Adjective clauses

An **adjective clause,** or **relative clause,** functions as an adjective and modifies a noun or pronoun. Usually, an adjective clause begins with a relative pronoun: *who, whose, whom, that,* or *which.*

> Jazz is a musical *form* **that originated among black Americans.**

In this sentence, the subject of the adjective clause is *that,* and the simple predicate is *originated.*

An adjective clause also can begin with a relative adverb—*when, where, why.*

> The *shop* **where I bought the bracelet** is near here.

Sometimes an adjective clause modifies the entire idea expressed in the preceding clause.

> On her birthday, John asked Susan to marry him, **which made her very happy.**

2   Adverb clauses

An **adverb clause** functions as an adverb in a sentence. It usually modifies the verb in another clause but sometimes modifies an adjective, an adverb, or an entire sentence. An adverb clause usually begins with a subordinating conjunction that shows the relation of the adverb clause to the word or words it modifies. (To review subordinating conjunctions, see Section 8j-3.)

> The grandfather clock *experienced* renewed popularity **after Henry Clay Works published his song "My Grandfather's Clock."** (*modifies the verb* experienced)

(For information on using commas with adverb clauses, see Sections 28c-3, 28d-2, and 28e.)

3   Noun clauses

A **noun clause** acts as a noun in a sentence. In other words, it can function as a subject, an object, or a predicate nominative. Usually, a noun clause begins with one of the following subordinating words: *that, how, what, whatever, whenever, wherever, whichever, who, whoever, whose, why.*

> **That she would run for President** seemed a certainty. (*subject*)

EXERCISE 9-1

Circle all the prepositional phrases in the following sentences. Bracket each dependent clause in the sentences and label the subject (S) and verb (V) in each. Then identify each dependent clause as an adjective clause (AJ), an adverb clause (AV), or a noun clause (NC).

1.   Whenever one thinks of American classical music, the name of Leonard Bernstein comes to mind.

2. Because of his experience in conducting, composing, playing the piano, and teaching, Bernstein, who lived in New York, was considered a very significant musical celebrity.

3. Having attended the Boston Latin School, Bernstein graduated from Harvard, becoming, in 1943, assistant conductor of the New York Philharmonic Orchestra.

4. When Bernstein assumed the conductorship of the orchestra in 1958, he was the first native-born American to be named its music director, establishing another first in his career.

5. While Bernstein enjoyed success as a pianist and composer, he also achieved acclaim when he narrated television programs featuring classical music.

SENTENCES

Sentences can be classified according to the number and kinds of clauses they contain. The four basic types are *simple, compound, complex,* and *compound–complex sentences.*

9e Types of Sentences

1 Simple sentences

A **simple sentence** contains only one independent clause and no dependent clause.

Hokusai and Kunisada are two important Japanese artists.

Sacajawea, a Shoshone Indian, worked as a guide and an interpreter on the Lewis and Clark expedition.

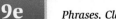
2   Compound sentences

A **compound sentence** contains two or more independent clauses and no dependent clause.

> The goddess Eos granted Tithonus his request for immortality, but he forgot to ask for eternal youth.

> First dice the celery; then peel and chop the onion; next brown the meat in a frying pan.

3   Complex sentences

A **complex sentence** contains one independent clause and one or more dependent clauses.

> After the museum bought one of his paintings, Cortez was interviewed on a local cable program.

> Because it is noted for its ability to weave intricate webs, the spider is a fitting symbol for the storyteller, or spinner of tales.

4   Compound–complex sentences

A **compound–complex sentence** contains two or more independent clauses and one or more dependent clauses.

> A group of painters called "neorealists" is turning back to representational styles, and the mass public, which never quite embraced abstract art, is responding enthusiastically to these artists' work.

> In the last twenty years, medicine has made major advances; doctors, for example, now perform bone-marrow transplants, procedures that, though risky, offer new hope to patients whose diseases were once considered terminal.

EXERCISE 9-2

Identify each of the following sentences as simple (SI), compound (CD), complex (CX), or compound–complex (CC). Underline the simple subject (S) and the simple predicate (P) of each clause.

1. Faced with both a shrinking student population and rising costs, many colleges and universities across the country are simultaneously attempting to raise more money and cut budgets.

2. Because colleges need to concentrate their funds, some deans are cutting budgets by eliminating entire academic departments.

3. Some colleges have hired strategic planners; others have contracted out their food service operations to cut back costs.

4. Because investments have stopped their rapid rise, schools no longer expect huge monetary returns on their endowments; however, some continue to expand their enrollments, although the majority do not.

5. The combination of deep budget cuts and five-figure tuition costs at some private colleges may force students to the less expensive public sector.

Part

IV

SENTENCE FORM

To write a good sentence, it is not enough to have a good idea. You have to express your idea in a form that your readers will understand. The form of a sentence has to follow certain conventions, traditional guidelines that are generally understood and accepted. The conventions of written English are much like rules of etiquette; they are essential for helping people to communicate clearly and effectively with one another. In fact, you know most of these conventions so well that you follow them without even thinking about them. Some, however, you might need to review.

10   Fragments

Use sentence fragments judiciously. For formal writing avoid using them except in special situations.

A **sentence fragment** is an incomplete sentence punctuated as if it were a complete sentence. A sentence fragment lacks a subject, a predicate, or both or is a subordinate clause presented as if it were a sentence.

10a   Fragments Lacking a Subject

Avoid punctuating as a sentence a group of words that lacks a subject.

To eliminate a sentence fragment lacking a subject, simply add a subject to this group of words or connect it to another sentence containing its subject.

NOT:	Jean Rhys was born in the West Indies. And evoked the magic of these islands in *Wide Sargasso Sea*.
BUT:	Jean Rhys was born in the West Indies and evoked the magic of these islands in *Wide Sargasso Sea*.

NOT:	Most Americans had considered World War II a just war. Were willing to give their lives for their country. But many came to think Vietnam was an unjust war. And were repelled by the slaughter of their sons.
BUT:	Most Americans had considered World War II a just war and were willing to give their lives for their country. But many came to think Vietnam was an unjust war and were repelled by the slaughter of their sons.

10b Fragments Lacking a Predicate

Avoid punctuating as a sentence a group of words that lacks a predicate.

A predicate must be a finite, or complete, verb. Some verb forms require an auxiliary verb or a modal in order to be finite. (To review auxiliary words and modals, see Section 8b-2.)

To eliminate a sentence fragment that lacks a predicate, add a finite verb or an auxiliary verb or modal to make the verb finite, or connect the fragment to another sentence that contains its verb.

NOT:	People of many different nationalities together on the same block.
BUT:	People of many different nationalities live together on the same block.

NOT:	The sun rising over the rooftops.
BUT:	The sun was rising over the rooftops.

NOT:	The alumni already given millions of dollars for the new library.
BUT:	The alumni have already given millions of dollars for the new library.

NOT:	In the back of the theater were standing-room-only ticket holders. And latecomers impatient for their seats.
BUT:	In the back of the theater were standing-room-only ticket holders and latecomers impatient for their seats.

10c Phrase Fragments

Avoid punctuating a phrase as a sentence.

To eliminate a phrase fragment, simply make it part of an independent clause.

NOT:	We swerved when we saw the deer. Running across the highway.
BUT:	We swerved when we saw the deer running across the highway.

NOT:	The professor rode with two officers in their squad car for six weeks. To learn about police work firsthand.
BUT:	To learn about police work firsthand, the professor rode with two officers in their squad car for six weeks.

NOT:	The highlight of the show was appearances by several guest stars. Cho Liu, for example, one of the country's finest ballerinas.
BUT:	The highlight of the show was appearances by several guest stars—Cho Liu, for example, one of the country's finest ballerinas.

NOT:	Because of public opposition. The city refused to grant permission. For a skyscraper to be built on the site of the church.

BUT: Because of public opposition, the city refused to grant permission for a skyscraper to be built on the site of the church.

10d Dependent Clause Fragments

Avoid punctuating a dependent clause as a sentence.

A dependent clause usually begins with a subordinating word, which may be a subordinating conjunction or a relative pronoun. (To review dependent clauses, see Section 9d.)

One way to eliminate a dependent clause fragment is to remove the subordinating word. Another way is to connect the dependent clause to an independent clause.

NOT: Because Charlene was fluent in French.

BUT: Charlene was fluent in French.

NOT: Before Harrison wrote his term paper. He prepared an outline.

BUT: Before Harrison wrote his term paper, he prepared an outline.

NOT: Harold Macmillan felt it imperative for Britain to develop a firm relationship with de Gaulle. Even though the United States opposed official recognition of him.

BUT: Harold Macmillan felt it imperative for Britain to develop a firm relationship with de Gaulle, even though the United States opposed official recognition of him.

NOT: Although John Muir is often pictured as a genial and perhaps somewhat innocent nature guide. He was actually a shrewd, strong-willed, thoughtful man. Who was an effective political lobbyist for conservation.

BUT: Although John Muir is often pictured as a genial and perhaps somewhat innocent nature guide, he was actually a shrewd, strong-willed, thoughtful man who was an effective political lobbyist for conservation.

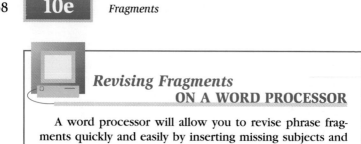

Revising Fragments
ON A WORD PROCESSOR

A word processor will allow you to revise phrase fragments quickly and easily by inserting missing subjects and verbs. You can also join phrases and dependent clauses to related sentences by deleting punctuation and altering capitalization. You might even want to use the cut and paste functions to experiment with the placement of these word groups before you attach them to the independent clauses.

EXERCISE 10-1

Revise the following items to eliminate any sentence fragments. One of the items contains no fragments.

1. In the not-too-distant past, television sets were very costly to repair.

2. Placing the painting behind the couch. The room appeared larger

3. Where is the book I gave you? Over there?

4. I am not going on that trip. Unless you also agree to go.

5. Through the seemingly endless night. The train continued over the mountain.

10e Intentional Fragments

We use fragments often, especially in speech. We see them in advertising and in newspapers and magazines. In formal writing, they can be used appropriately, but only occasionally, to ask and answer questions, to emphasize a point, to record exclamations in dialogue, and to provide transition between ideas. Note the use of fragments in the following passages by professional writers. (The fragments are printed in *italics*.)

> There has been a flood of new studies of the Wild Child: historical, literary, psychological. The story is still evocative, "good to think with." But there is something new. There is a new focus for a forbidden experiment. *A new mind that is not yet a mind. A new object, betwixt and between, equally shrouded in superstition as well as science.* This is the computer.
>
> **Sherry Turkle**

> Hating to ask questions and never trusting the answers has defined the type of reporting I do. What I do is hang around. *Become part of the furniture. An end table in someone's life.* It is the art of the scavenger: set a scene, establish a mood, get the speech patterns right.
>
> **John Gregory Dunne**

As you can see from these passages, fragments can be used effectively in formal writing. However, unless you have a well-thought-out reason for using fragments, avoid them in formal writing and consult your instructor before using them.

11 Comma Splices and Fused Sentences

Separate sentences correctly from one another.

A **run-on sentence** occurs when two or more complete sentences are written as though they were one sentence. Two types of errors result in a run-on sentence: *comma splices* and *fused sentences*.

11a Comma Splices

Avoid separating two independent clauses with only a comma, unless the clauses are very short and closely related.

A comma is sometimes used between clauses of two or three words, especially if the clauses are in parallel grammatical form.

> One sings, the other dances.

> The grass withers, the flowers fade.

In general, however, using only a comma between two independent clauses is considered a serious grammatical error called a **comma splice.**

NOT: Researchers are attempting to program robots to see, this procedure is much more complicated than you might expect.

BUT: Researchers are attempting to program robots to see. This procedure is much more complicated than you might expect.

OR: Researchers are attempting to program robots to see, but this procedure is much more complicated than you might expect.

NOT: Some monasteries during the Middle Ages had fine libraries, in these libraries monks copied and illuminated manuscripts.

BUT: Some monasteries during the Middle Ages had fine libraries; in these libraries monks copied and illuminated manuscripts.

OR: Some monasteries during the Middle Ages had fine libraries, in which monks copied and illuminated manuscripts.

A comma splice also occurs when a comma (instead of a semicolon) is used between two independent clauses joined by a transitional phrase or conjunctive adverb (in **boldface**).

NOT: The exhibit at the museum was well reviewed and well pro-
moted, **consequently,** there were long lines for tickets.

BUT: The exhibit at the museum was well reviewed and well pro-
moted; **consequently,** there were long lines for tickets.

NOT: When the smoke alarm sounded in the middle of the night,
Melissa jumped out of bed and rushed to get her family out
of the house, **in the meantime,** her neighbor called the fire
department.

BUT: When the smoke alarm sounded in the middle of the night,
Melissa jumped out of bed and rushed to get her family out
of the house; **in the meantime,** her neighbor called the fire
department.

11b Fused Sentences

Avoid writing two independent clauses without any punctuation between them.

This error is called a **fused sentence.**

NOT: The school was closed because of the snowstorm not knowing this, some students showed up for classes.

BUT: The school was closed because of the snowstorm. Not
knowing this, some students showed up for classes.

OR: Not knowing that the school was closed because of the
snowstorm, some students showed up for classes.

NOT: First boil the squash until it is tender then cut it open and
scoop out its insides.

BUT: First boil the squash until it is tender; then cut it open and
scoop out its insides.

OR: First boil the squash until it is tender, and then cut it open
and scoop out its insides.

Although there are many ways of correcting fused sentences,
these are the four most common:

1. Make two sentences by adding a period at the end of the first clause and capitalizing the first word of the second clause.

   NOT: Doctors are again using leeches these creatures can prevent the problem of clotting that occurs after reattachment surgery.

   BUT: Doctors are again using leeches. These creatures can prevent the problem of clotting that occurs after reattachment surgery.

2. Add a coordinating conjunction between the two clauses. Place a comma before the coordinating conjunction unless the two clauses are very short.

   NOT: Maria washed the car Carlos mowed the lawn.

   BUT: Maria washed the car **and** Carlos mowed the lawn.

3. Rewrite one of the independent clauses as a dependent clause.

   NOT: The cat wanted her breakfast she mewed loudly at the foot of the bed.

   BUT: **When** the cat wanted her breakfast, she mewed loudly at the foot of the bed.

Revising Comma Splices and Fused Sentences
ON A WORD PROCESSOR

Your word processor will allow you to revise comma splices and fused sentences without having to retype whole sentences. You can divide fused and spliced sentences by inserting periods and capital letters. You can also insert semicolons or coordinating conjunctions to join independent clauses. If you insert subordinating conjunctions to turn an independent clause into a dependent one, use the cut and paste functions to find the best place to attach the dependent clauses.

4. If the two clauses are closely related, place a semicolon between them.

> **NOT:** Cindy found the movie disappointing Lee thought it was wonderful.
>
> **BUT:** Cindy found the movie disappointing; Lee thought it was wonderful.

EXERCISE 11-1

Eliminate the run-on sentence in each of the following items. Identify the error as a comma splice (CS) or a fused sentence (FS).

1. Some cities recently banned cigarette vending machines, it makes it harder for children to purchase cigarettes.

2. Several coats were left behind by the audience a few looked expensive.

3. We had difficulty lighting the fire, the smoke billowed into the room from the fireplace.

4. Place the cups on the table the napkins go on the left side.

5. It makes no sense to me, go if you want to.

EXERCISE 11-2

Eliminate the fragments and run-on sentences in each of the following items.

1. *Harassment* means "to trouble, worry, or torment someone" it comes from a French word that means "to set a dog on."

2. Harassment can be physical and verbal. Also sexual.

3. The results of physical harassment are easily seen the results of verbal harassment are harder to detect.

4. Because the verbal harassment can be sexual. Women are most often the victims.

5. Confronting the harasser is a way to stop it people differ on the prevention strategies.

12   Verb Forms

12a   Principal Parts for Regular and Irregular Verbs

Use the appropriate form of the verb.

English verbs have four principal parts, or forms: present infinitive, past tense, past participle, and present participle. (See Section 8b-1.) The **present infinitive** is the base form of the verb, the form that appears in the dictionary. Regular verbs add *-ed* or *-d* to their present infinitive to form the **past tense** and **past participle.**

paint	painted	cook	cooked
dance	danced	slice	sliced

Irregular verbs form the past tense and past participle in a variety of other ways.

PRESENT INFINITIVE	PAST TENSE	PAST PARTICIPLE
begin	began	begun
catch	caught	caught
draw	drew	drawn
put	put	put
sing	sang	sung

You can use a dictionary to find the principal parts of a verb. In most dictionaries, after the abbreviation "*v.*" or at the end of the definitions for the verb, the entry gives the principal parts and the third-person singular present tense form of the verb. When the past tense and past participle are the same, the entry lists only three forms of the verb. When the past tense and past participle are different, the entry lists four forms.

The fourth form is called the **present participle,** always formed by adding *-ing* to the infinitive. (See Section 8b-1.)

dance: danced, dancing, dances

begin: began, begun, beginning, begins

draw: drew, drawn, drawing, draws

Most people have few problems using the proper forms of regular verbs. Many, however, do have problems with the past tense and past participle of irregular verbs. A list of common irregular verbs follows.

IRREGULAR VERBS

PRESENT INFINITIVE	PAST TENSE	PAST PARTICIPLE
arise	arose	arisen
awake	awoke	awaked
be	was, were	been
bear	bore	born (borne)

PRESENT INFINITIVE	PAST TENSE	PAST PARTICIPLE
become	became	become
begin	began	begun
bind	bound	bound
bite	bit	bitten
blow	blew	blown
break	broke	broken
bring	brought	brought
build	built	built
burst	burst	burst
catch	caught	caught
choose	chose	chosen
cling	clung	clung
come	came	come
creep	crept	crept
deal	dealt	dealt
dig	dug	dug
dive	dived, dove	dived
do (does)	did	done
draw	drew	drawn
drink	drank	drunk
drive	drove	driven
eat	ate	eaten
fall	fell	fallen
feel	felt	felt
flee	fled	fled
fling	flung	flung
fly	flew	flown
forbid	forbade, forbad	forbidden
forget	forgot	forgotten, forgot
forgive	forgave	forgiven
freeze	froze	frozen
get	got	got, gotten
give	gave	given
go	went	gone
grow	grew	grown

PRESENT INFINITIVE	PAST TENSE	PAST PARTICIPLE
hang (objects)	hung	hung
hang (people)	hanged	hanged
have (has)	had	had
hit	hit	hit
know	knew	known
lay	laid	laid
lead	led	led
lend	lent	lent
lie	lay	lain
lose	lost	lost
mean	meant	meant
pay	paid	paid
prove	proved	proved, proven
ride	rode	ridden
ring	rang	rung
rise	rose	risen
run	ran	run
say	said	said
see	saw	seen
seek	sought	sought
send	sent	sent
set	set	set
shake	shook	shaken
shine (give light)	shone	shone
shine (polish)	shined	shined
shrink	shrank	shrunk
sing	sang	sung
sink	sank, sunk	sunk, sunken
sit	sat	sat
slay	slew	slain
speak	spoke	spoken
spin	spun	spun
spit	spit, spat	spit, spat
spring	sprang, sprung	sprung
steal	stole	stolen

PRESENT INFINITIVE	PAST TENSE	PAST PARTICIPLE
sting	stung	stung
stink	stank	stunk
swear	swore	sworn
swim	swam	swum
swing	swung	swung
take	took	taken
teach	taught	taught
tear	tore	torn
think	thought	thought
thrive	throve, thrived	thriven, thrived
throw	threw	thrown
wear	wore	worn
weep	wept	wept
win	won	won

Over the years, some irregular forms have been eliminated from the language, and others are in the process of changing. As you can see from the preceding list, the preferred past tense form of *dive* is now *dived,* not *dove.* The preferred past participle form of *prove* is *proved,* not *proven.*

12b Verb Forms for Tense, Voice, and Mood

1 Tense

Tense is the time expressed by the form of the verb. The six tenses are the *simple present, present perfect, simple past, past perfect, simple future,* and *future perfect.* Each of these tenses has a progressive form that indicates continuing action.

	BASIC FORM	**PROGRESSIVE FORM**
SIMPLE PRESENT:	compose(s)	is (are) composing
PRESENT PERFECT:	has (have) composed	has (have) been composing
SIMPLE PAST:	composed	was (were) composing
PAST PERFECT:	had composed	had been composing
SIMPLE FUTURE:	will (shall) compose	will (shall) be composing
FUTURE PERFECT:	will (shall) have composed	will (shall) have been composing

Usually, the simple present, the simple past, and the simple future are referred to as the present, the past, and the future tense, respectively.

The time of an action does not always correspond exactly with the name of the tense that is used to write about the action. For example, in special situations, the present tense can be used to write about events that occurred in the past or will occur in the future as well as events that are occurring in the present.

Present tense

In general, the **present tense** is used to write about events or conditions that are happening or existing now.

She **lives** in Austin, Texas.

An accountant **is preparing** our tax returns.

They **are** dissatisfied with their grades.

The present tense is also used to write about natural or scientific laws or timeless truths, events in literature, and habitual action.

Some bacteria **are** beneficial, but others **cause** disease.

No one **lives** forever.

> Sherlock Holmes and his archenemy, Dr. Moriarity, apparently **perish** together.

> She **goes** to work every day at eight.

The past tense can also be used to write about events in literature. Whichever tense you choose, be consistent.

The present tense can be used with an adverbial word or phrase to indicate future time. In the following sentences, the adverbs that indicate time are *italicized:*

> This flight **arrives** in Chicago *at 7:30 P.M.*

> *Next week* the class **meets** in the conference room.

The verb *do* is used with the present infinitive to create an emphatic form of the present tense.

> You **do know** your facts, but your presentation of them is not always clear.

> He certainly **does cover** his topic thoroughly.

Present perfect tense

The **present perfect tense** is used to write about events that occurred at some unspecified time in the past and about events and conditions that began in the past and might still be continuing in the present.

> The novelist **has incorporated** theories of psycholinguistics into his mysteries.

> Their new line of greeting cards **has been selling** well.

> The two performers **have donated** the profits from their concert to charity.

Past tense

The **past tense** is used to write about events that occurred and conditions that existed at a definite time in the past and do not extend into the present.

The study **explored** the dolphin's ability to communicate.

The researchers **were studying** the effects of fluoridation on tooth decay.

The word *did* (the past tense of *do*) is used with the present infinitive to create an emphatic form of the past tense.

In the end he **did vote** against the bill.

Despite opposition, she **did make** her opinions heard.

Past perfect tense

The **past perfect tense** is used to write about a past event or condition that ended before another past event or condition began.

She voted for passage of the bill because she **had seen** the effects of poverty on the young.

The researchers **had tried** several drugs on the microorganism before they found the right one.

He **had been painting** for ten years before he sold his first canvas.

Future tense

The **future tense** is used to write about events or conditions that have not yet begun. (See the Glossary of Usage for *shall, will.*)

Her next book **will continue** the saga of the Anderson family.

The voters **will be deciding** the role of religion in the schools.

We **shall stay** in London for two weeks.

Future perfect tense

The **future perfect tense** is used to write about a future event or condition that will end before another future event or condition begins or before a specified time in the future.

Before I see him again, the editor **will have read** my short story.

By October, she **will have been singing** with the City Opera five years.

For more information on the use of tenses, see Sections 17e–17h.

2 Some guidelines for use of tense forms

The following rules will help you to select the appropriate verb form.

Use the past tense form to indicate simple past time.

NOT:	We **seen** him in the library yesterday.
BUT:	We **saw** him in the library yesterday.

NOT:	His clothing **stunk** from the skunk's spray.
BUT:	His clothing **stank** from the skunk's spray.

Use the past participle form with auxiliary verbs *have* and *be*.

NOT:	**Have** you **chose** a major?
BUT:	**Have** you **chosen** a major?

NOT:	If you don't lock up your bike, it **will be took.**
BUT:	If you don't lock up your bike, it **will be taken.**

Use the past participle form with a contraction containing an auxiliary verb.

NOT: **He's drove** all the way from Miami.

BUT: **He's driven** all the way from Miami.

NOT: **She'd** never **flew** in an airplane before.

BUT: **She'd** never **flown** in an airplane before.

3 Voice

Voice indicates whether the subject of the clause or sentence performs or receives the action of the transitive verb.

Active and passive voice

The verb and the clause are in the **active voice** when the subject performs the action of the verb. (See also Section 8b-2.)

The President **announced** his decision.

The journal **offers** insights into contemporary poetry.

When the subject no longer performs the action but is removed or expressed in a phrase, then the verb and the clause are in the **passive voice.** The passive voice of a verb consists of a form of *be* followed by the past participle of the verb.

The decision **was announced** by the President.

Insights into contemporary poetry **are offered** by the journal.

Many sentences written in the passive voice, like the two preceding examples, contain a phrase beginning with the word *by*. This phrase usually tells who or what actually performed the action, if the phrase has not been omitted.

4 Mood

Mood refers to the form a verb uses to express a statement, a command, a wish, an assumption, a recommendation, or a condition contrary to fact. In English there are three moods: the *indicative,* the *imperative,* and the *subjunctive.*

Indicative mood

The **indicative mood** is used to make a factual statement or to ask a question.

> William Carlos Williams **lived** in Paterson, New Jersey.
> **Did** William Carlos Williams live in Paterson, New Jersey?

> Kublai Khan **was** the grandson of Genghis Khan.
> **Was** Kublai Khan the grandson of Genghis Khan?

Imperative mood

The **imperative mood** is used to express a command or a request. In a command, the subject *you* is often not stated, but understood.

> **Bring** me the newspaper.

> **Don't** ever **come** here!

> Please **close** that door.

Subjunctive mood

The **subjunctive mood** is used to indicate a wish, an assumption, a recommendation, or a condition contrary to fact.

> He wished he **were** rich. (*wish*)

> If this **be** true, the validity of the collection is in doubt. (*assumption*)

It is mandatory that he **dress** appropriately. (*recommendation*)

If I **were** mayor, I would solve the problems of this city. (*condition contrary to fact*)

The form of a verb in the subjunctive is often different from the indicative in the third-person singular in the present tense. There, the subjunctive does not have the final *s* of the indicative form.

INDICATIVE	SUBJUNCTIVE
he speaks	he speak
she manages	she manage
it works	it work

The subjunctive of the verb *to be* differs from the indicative in both the present and past tenses.

PRESENT TENSE

INDICATIVE		SUBJUNCTIVE	
I am	we are	(if) I be	(if) we be
you are	you are	(if) you be	(if) you be
he/she/it is	they are	(if) he/she/it be	(if) they be

PAST TENSE

INDICATIVE		SUBJUNCTIVE	
I was	we were	(if) I were	(if) we were
you were	you were	(if) you were	(if) you were
he/she/it was	they were	(if) he/she/it were	(if) they were

The subjunctive appears to be falling into disuse. However, it is still preferred in writing for expressing a condition contrary to fact, and it is required in *that* clauses of recommendation, wish, or command and in a few idiomatic phrases.

If she **were** in command, we would not be having this problem.

In Kipling's tale, Danny wished that he **were** king.

He resolved that if need **be,** he would study night and day.

12c Appropriate Forms for Troublesome Verbs

Master troublesome pairs of verb forms.

Because of similarity in form and related meanings, *the transitive and intransitive senses* of certain pairs of verbs are frequently confused. (See Section 8b-2.) The following pairs of verbs often give people trouble: *lie* and *lay; sit* and *set; rise* and *raise; sneak* and *sneaked.*

1 *Lie* and *lay*

The verb *lie* means "recline." The verb *lay* means "put" or "place." Do not confuse the principal parts of these verbs.

PRESENT INFINITIVE	PAST TENSE	PAST PARTICIPLE	PRESENT PARTICIPLE
lie	lay	lain	lying
lay	laid	laid	laying

The problem most people have with these verbs is using a form of *lay* when they mean *lie. Lie* is intransitive; it does not take an object. *Lay* is transitive; it does take an object.

Lie on the floor. (*no object*)

Lay the *book* on the table. (*object*)

NOT: Why is Millie **laying** on the couch in the nurse's office?
BUT: Why is Millie **lying** on the couch in the nurse's office?

NOT: Peter **laid** in the sun too long yesterday.
BUT: Peter **lay** in the sun too long yesterday.

NOT: She had just **laid** down when the telephone rang.

BUT: She had just **lain** down when the telephone rang.

2 *Sit* and *set*

The verb *sit* means "be seated." The verb *set* usually means "place" or "put in a certain position." Do not confuse the principal parts of these verbs.

PRESENT INFINITIVE	PAST TENSE	PAST PARTICIPLE	PRESENT PARTICIPLE
sit	sat	sat	sitting
set	set	set	setting

The problem most people have with these verbs is using a form of *set* when they mean *sit*. *Sit* is intransitive; it does not take an object. *Set* is usually transitive; it does take an object.

Sit in the chair by the fireplace. (*no object*)

Please **set** the *table* for me. (*object*)

Note: Set is sometimes intransitive: *The sun sets.*

NOT: Some people **set** in front of the television far too much.

BUT: Some people **sit** in front of the television far too much.

NOT: He **set** up until two in the morning, waiting for his daughter to come home from her date.

BUT: He **sat** up until two in the morning, waiting for his daughter to come home from her date.

3 *Rise* and *raise*

The verb *rise* means "go up" or "get into a standing position." The verb *raise* means "lift." Do not confuse the principal parts of these verbs.

PRESENT INFINITIVE	PAST TENSE	PAST PARTICIPLE	PRESENT PARTICIPLE
rise	rose	risen	rising
raise	raised	raised	raising

Rise is intransitive; it does not take an object. *Raise* is transitive; it does take an object.

Without yeast, the bread will not **rise.** (*no object*)

After they won the game, they **raised** the school *banner*. (*object*)

NOT: They **rose** the curtain before the cast was fully assembled on stage.

BUT: They **raised** the curtain before the cast was fully assembled on stage.

NOT: Every morning they **rise** the blinds before leaving for work.

BUT: Every morning they **raise** the blinds before leaving for work.

NOT: He **rose** his voice in order to be heard.

BUT: He **raised** his voice in order to be heard.

4   *Sneak* and *sneaked*

The verb *sneak* means "to move quietly and in a way to avoid detection." It is a regular verb and forms its past tense and past participle by adding *-ed* to the base form: *sneaked*. A tendency exists in the spoken language to treat *sneak* as if it were an irregular verb with a past tense and past participle of "snuck." This is considered inappropriate in writing.

NOT: I **snuck** around the house in my bare feet.

BUT: I **sneaked** around the house in my bare feet.

EXERCISE 12-1

Identify the inappropriate verb form (or forms) in each of the following sentences. Replace it with the appropriate form.

1. Yesterday I see the book.

2. The cat stinked up the kitchen when the dog begin to growl.

3. The play begin at 8:00 P.M. tonight.

4. Sit this pillow beside you when you lay on the couch.

5. She weared the rain coat although the sun shined.

6. I creeped into my brother's room and turn the stereo down.

7. The cup fall on the brick floor and crack.

8. I shone the silver vase and polish it.

9. Sit the flowers on the table so they don't fell.

10. The car past so close to us that we almost fall down.

11. You would of went to the movies if you was careful of your timing.

12. My notebook was stole and it show up in a trash can.

13. Greg laid in bed all morning and exercise in the afternoon.

14. Have you chose your dress for the dance?

15. The painter had rose the ladder before his helper said "raised it."

Revising Verb Forms
ON A WORD PROCESSOR

Use the search function to check for verbs that you know you have trouble with, especially *lie/lay, sit/set,* and *rise/raise.* If you cannot tell which form of a verb you need (such as *lie* or *lay*), choose another word; the thesaurus feature will give you some suggestions to try.

13   Subject–Verb Agreement

Make a verb agree with its subject in number and person.

The agreement of singular or plural subjects with singular or plural verbs requires only one form change in standard dialect verbs. This change occurs in the present tense and with a third-person singular subject. The change is the addition of *-s* or *-es* to the basic present tense form.

The cushion **feels** soft.	The tomato **tastes** ripe.
The goose **flies** south.	He **brushes** his hair.

No change in verb form occurs with other singular subjects or with plural subjects.

	SINGULAR	**PLURAL**
FIRST PERSON:	I **feel**	We **feel**
SECOND PERSON:	You **fly**	You **fly**
THIRD PERSON:	It **tastes**	They **taste**

Except for the verb *do*, the modal auxiliaries (*may, can, will,* and so on) do not add *-s* or *-es* in third-person singular present tense. The auxiliary *have* changes form to *has*.

The verb *be* changes to indicate number in both the present tense and the past tense and in both the first person and the third person.

PRESENT TENSE		**PAST TENSE**	
I am	we are	I was	we were
you are	you are	you were	you were
he/she/it is	they are	he/she/it was	they were

To agree with a singular or plural verb form, the noun or pronoun in the subject must also show a matching singular or plural form. (See Sections 7f and 42e for singular and plural formation.) Some kinds of subjects present special problems with subject–verb agreement. The following rules will help you to choose the appropriate verb forms.

13a Compound Subjects

1 Compound subject with *and*

In general, use a plural verb form with a compound subject joined by the word *and*.

A **compound subject** consists of two or more nouns that take the same predicate.

> *Shatonda and Sal* **make** films for a living.
>
> *History and biology* **were** his best subjects.
>
> *Ted and his friends* **are supporting** Lopez for mayor.

Use a singular verb form with a compound subject joined by *and* if the compound is considered a single unit.

> *Pork and beans* **is** a popular dish.
>
> The *bow and arrow* **is** still regarded as a useful weapon.

Use a singular verb form with a compound subject joined by *and* if the parts of the compound refer to the same person or thing.

> My *friend and guest* **is** the artist Katya Hyeska.
>
> His *pride and joy* **was** his 1962 convertible.

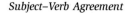
2 Compound subject with *or* or *nor*

With a compound subject joined by *or* or *nor* or by *either . . . or* or *neither . . . nor,* make the verb agree with the subject closer to it.

> The *cat or her kittens* **have pushed** the vase off the table.
>
> *Either the employees or their supervisor* **is** responsible.
>
> *Neither the camera nor the lenses* **were broken.**

13b Intervening Phrases or Clauses

Make the verb agree with its subject, not with a word in an intervening phrase or clause.

1 Intervening phrases

> Several *people* in my club **subscribe** to that magazine.
>
> The *books* by that writer **are** very popular.
>
> The *picture* hanging between the windows at the top of the stairs **is** a portrait of the artist's mother.

Phrases introduced by *together with, as well as, in addition to, accompanied by,* and similar expressions do not affect the number of the verb.

> The emerald *bracelet,* as well as her other jewels, **is** in the safe.
>
> The *novel,* together with the plays that she wrote when she was much younger, **establishes** her reputation.
>
> His *wit,* accompanied by his excellent grasp of the facts, **makes** him a sharp interviewer.

2 Intervening clauses

> The *books* that are in my briefcase **are** about Russian history.

The *people* who came to the concert that was canceled **are receiving** rain checks.

The *doctor* who is attending these patients **is** Ellen Okida.

13c Collective Nouns

A collective noun may take either a singular or a plural verb form.

Usually, a collective noun refers to a group of people or things as a single unit. When this is the case, the collective noun is singular and the verb form should be singular.

The *army* **needs** the support of the civilian population.

The *flock* **is heading** toward the west end of the lake.

The *group* **is selling** tickets to raise money for charity.

Sometimes a collective noun refers to a group of things or people as individuals. When this is the case, the collective noun is plural and the verb form should be plural.

The *jury* **are arguing** among themselves; six believe the defendant is guilty, two think he is innocent, and four are undecided.

The *congregation* **disagree** about whether to keep the church open during the week.

Some people think that using a plural verb form with a collective noun sounds awkward. You can avoid this problem by inserting "the members of" or a similar expression before the collective noun.

The *members* of the jury **are arguing** among themselves; six believe the defendant is guilty, two think he is innocent, and four are undecided.

The *members* of the congregation **disagree** about whether to keep the church open during the week.

13d Nouns Plural in Form but Singular in Meaning

Use a singular verb form with nouns plural in form but singular in meaning.

The following are some common words that are plural in form but singular in meaning:

checkers	ethics	molasses	pediatrics
civics	mathematics	mumps	physics
economics	measles	news	statistics

Checkers **is called** draughts in Great Britain.

Measles **is** a contagious childhood disease.

The *news* **is broadcast** around the clock on some radio stations.

The words *pants, trousers,* and *scissors* are considered plural and take a plural verb form. However, if they are preceded by the words *pair of,* the verb form is singular, since *pair* is the subject.

The *scissors* **need** to be sharpened.

The *pair* of scissors **needs** to be sharpened.

The *pants* **match** the jacket.

The *pair* of pants **matches** the jacket.

13e Indefinite and Relative Pronoun Subjects

1 Indefinite pronoun subjects

The following indefinite pronouns are considered singular. Use a singular verb form with them.

anybody	either	neither	one
anyone	everybody	nobody	somebody
each	everyone	no one	someone

Neither **is** willing to go with me.

Everybody **is going to vote** on Tuesday.

Do not be confused by prepositional phrases that follow the indefinite pronoun. The verb must agree with its subject, not with the object of a preposition.

Each of the apartments in the north wing of the building **has** a fireplace.

Either of those methods **is** feasible.

The following indefinite pronouns are considered plural. Use a plural verb form with them.

both   few   many   several

Few **are** certain enough of their beliefs to take a stand.

Several **are** riding their bicycles to school.

Both of the paintings **were** sold at the auction.

The following indefinite pronouns may be singular or plural. If the noun to which the pronoun refers is singular, use a singular verb form. If the noun is plural, use a plural verb form.

all   any   enough   more   most   some

All of the *money* **was** recovered. (*singular*)

All **was** recovered. (*singular*)

All of these *records* **are** scratched. (*plural*)

All **are** scratched. (*plural*)

Most of the *cake* **was** eaten. (*singular*)

Most **was** eaten. (*singular*)

Most of the *guests* **were** hungry. (*plural*)

Most **were** hungry. (*plural*)

The indefinite pronoun *none* is considered singular because it means "no one." It takes a singular verb.

None of the books **was** missing.

2   Relative pronoun subjects

A verb whose subject is a relative pronoun should agree with the antecedent of the pronoun.

The man *who* **narrates** the film has a raspy voice. (*singular antecedent*)

The radios *that* **were made** in Japan are selling well. (*plural antecedent*)

The newspaper, *which* **was founded** in 1893, is closing. (*singular antecedent*)

The phrase *one of* is worth mentioning. Usually, the relative pronoun that follows this phrase is plural because its antecedent is a plural noun or pronoun. Therefore the relative pronoun takes a plural verb form.

The man is one of the hostages *who* **are** in most danger.

Ralph is one of those *who* never **gain** weight.

However, when the words *the only* come before this phrase, the relative pronoun is singular because its antecedent is *one*. Therefore it takes a singular verb form.

This is the only one of Mark's songs *that* **has been published.**

Mitch is the only one of those men *who* **is** athletic.

13f Titles

Use a singular verb form with a title, even if the title contains plural words.

> *Guys and Dolls* **was** a popular Broadway musical.
>
> *60 Minutes* **is** on television tonight.
>
> *Wuthering Heights* **tells** the story of a doomed love.

13g Units of Measurement, Time, and Money

Use a singular verb form with a plural noun phrase that names a unit of measurement, a period of time, or an amount of money.

> *Five miles* **is** too far to walk to school.
>
> *One hundred years* **is** the usual life span for the crocodile.
>
> *Twenty-five thousand dollars* **is** a good salary for this job.

13h Inverted Sentence Order

Use a verb that agrees with its subject, even when the subject follows the verb.

> Outside the building **were** *crowds of* spectators.
>
> From the chimneys **rises** thick black *smoke*.
>
> On the wall **are** *portraits* of her ancestors.

Do not be confused by sentences beginning with the expletives *there* and *here*. These words are never the subject.

There **is** a *chicken* roasting in the oven.

Here **are** the *groceries* you asked me to pick up.

13i Agreement with Subject, Not Subject Complement

Use a verb that agrees with the subject, not with the subject complement.

A firm *moral sense* and a *belief* in the goodness of human beings **were** his inheritance.

His *inheritance* **was** a firm moral sense and a belief in the goodness of human beings.

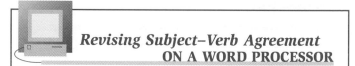

Revising Subject–Verb Agreement
ON A WORD PROCESSOR

You can use the search function to locate *and, or,* and other relevant conjunctions to check for compound subjects. The search function will also help you to locate expletive constructions—*there is, there are, there was, there were, here is, here are*—to make sure the verb agrees with the inverted subject, not with the word *there* or *here.*

Grammar checkers are not completely successful in dealing with subject-verb agreement. They fail to notice some problems and will sometimes flag sentences that are correct. When in doubt, use your handbook and your own good sense to revise subject-verb agreement errors.

EXERCISE 13-1

Revise any of the following sentences in which a verb does not agree with its subject. Some of the sentences are correct as written.

1. Your pair of trousers are on the table.

2. Either the foreman or the supervisor made the error.

3. There is a caterpillar and two blue birds in the porch.

4. The choir stand beside each other, with the tallest singers in the back row.

5. Neither of us really like popcorn.

6. The entrance to the movie and the arcade are on the same corner.

7. Watching basketball and football games on television constitute his favorite pastime.

8. Whoever took my ticket realize its value.

9. Does the manager or the umpire control the length of time involved?

10. Rising early in the morning, cooking my own breakfast, and waiting in a long line is not my idea of fun.

11. None from that committee are here.

12. How many of you participating in this contest has seen a video-tape of last year's results?

13. She is the only one of our family who have graduated from college.

14. Your gym shoes, along with gym shorts and a shirt, seem appropriate to bring.

15. My brother and sister, as well as a cousin, are going with us today.

16. *The Canterbury Tales* are considered Chaucer's best poetry.

17. The supervisor will welcome each of the prospective employees who complete the application form.

18. Are you certain that $16 are a reasonable price?

19. Each of the coats and hats in the pile were correctly identified.

20. The arrangement of the flowers on both sides of the stage presents an impressive sight.

14 Pronouns: Agreement, Reference, and Usage

By themselves, most **pronouns,** or noun substitutes, have little meaning. For a pronoun's meaning to be clear, it usually must have a clear antecedent (the word or words to which the pronoun refers), and it must agree with its antecedent in number and gender.

After the *pilot* checked **her** instruments, **she** prepared for takeoff.

After the *pilots* checked **their** instruments, **they** prepared for take-off.

14a   Pronoun–Antecedent Agreement

1   Indefinite pronouns as antecedents

Use a pronoun that agrees in gender and number with an indefinite pronoun antecedent.

Use a masculine pronoun with an indefinite pronoun that refers to a masculine noun and a feminine pronoun with an indefinite pronoun that refers to a feminine noun. Use a neuter, or indeterminate, pronoun with an indefinite pronoun that refers to a neuter noun.

> Twenty men are in the training program. *Each* is a unique individual with **his** own goals and ideals.

> Twenty women are in the training program. *Each* is a unique individual with **her** own goals and ideals.

> Fifty businesses contributed to the charity. *Each* is unique, with **its** own goals and aspirations.

Many times, however, a singular indefinite pronoun refers to a group consisting of both men and women, which implies plurality, as in the following sentence:

> Everyone should cast _____ vote in the next election.

What should the pronoun in the blank be? Traditionally, a masculine pronoun (*his*) was used in such constructions to refer to an antecedent that included both men and women. Today, most people consider this usage sexist and prefer to use *his or her.* However, a paragraph or a paper can become tedious and calls attention to itself if it is filled with too many pairs of *his or her, he or she, him or her,* and so on. Here are three suggestions for rewriting sentences like this to avoid the problem of pronoun choice.

1. Make the pronouns plural.

   All should cast **their** votes in the next election.

2. Use an article (*a, an,* or *the*) in place of the possessive pronoun.

   Everyone should cast **a** vote in the next election.

3. Rewrite the sentence more extensively.

   Everyone should vote in the next election.

(See also Chapter 25.)

2 Relative pronouns

Use the appropriate relative pronoun.

The pronouns *who, whom,* and *whose* refer to people. They may also refer to animals that are thought of in human terms and called by name. The pronoun *that* usually refers to animals and things, but it is sometimes used to refer to people. The pronoun *which* refers to animals and things.

The *ballplayer* **who** broke Babe Ruth's career home run record is Hank Aaron.

The *movie* **that** Mikiko saw last night was *Terms of Endearment.*

Orwell's *1984,* **which** was published in 1949, is still in print.

Someone **whom** voters can trust will win the election.

Do not use *what* as a relative pronoun.

NOT: The stereo **what** I want costs $300.
BUT: The stereo **that** I want costs $300.

To avoid an awkward sentence, use the possessive pronoun *whose* to mean "of which."

NOT: The car the windshield wipers **of which** are not working failed to pass inspection.

BUT: The car **whose** windshield wipers are not working failed to pass inspection.

A relative pronoun takes its number from its antecedent. The number of the relative pronoun determines the number of any other pronouns used with it.

Students **who** show **their** identification cards will get a discount.

A *man* **who** cannot make up **his** mind is of no use to this company.

3   Compound antecedent

Use a plural pronoun to refer to a compound antecedent joined by *and.*

Evita and Juan have finished **their** assignments.

The judge and the district attorney have completed **their** terms of office.

When the antecedent is a compound joined by *or* or *nor* or by *either . . . or, neither . . . nor,* or *not only . . . but also,* make the pronoun agree with the part of the compound that is closer to it.

Neither the district attorney nor the defense *lawyers* stated **their** cases clearly.

Not only the jurors but also the *judge* found **his** attention wandering.

4   Collective nouns as antecedents

Use a singular pronoun with a collective noun antecedent if the members of the group are thought of as one unit. Use a plural pronoun if the members are thought of as individuals.

> After winning the race, the *crew* placed **its** trophy on the mantelpiece.

> The leader asked the *group* to lower **their** voices.

EXERCISE 14-1

Underline the pronoun in each of the following sentences. If the pronoun does not agree with its antecedent, rephrase the sentence. One of the sentences is correct as written.

1.   Somebody put their book on the radiator.

2.   Each of those in the group proudly displayed their prize.

3.   Not only the band but also the director saw their chances of winning the contest fade.

4.   Is it true that anything is better than nothing?

5.   The person which gave you those directions was mistaken.

14b   Pronoun Reference

1   Vague reference

Provide a clear antecedent for each pronoun that needs one.

In general, do not use a pronoun to refer to the entire idea in a previous sentence or clause or to an antecedent that has not been clearly stated.

VAGUE: Ahmed usually taps his feet, rolls his eyes, and fidgets when he is nervous, **which** annoys his girlfriend.

The pronoun *which* refers vaguely to the entire idea of Ahmed's behavior when he is nervous.

CLEAR: Ahmed's habit of tapping his feet, rolling his eyes, and fidgeting when he is nervous annoys his girlfriend.

VAGUE: Lou is an excellent mechanic, and she uses **this** to earn money for college.

The pronoun *this* refers vaguely to the idea of Lou's skill as a mechanic.

CLEAR: Lou is an excellent mechanic, and she uses her skill to earn money for college.

VAGUE: The tourists stared in awe as the great Christmas tree in Rockefeller Center was lit. They listened in rapt attention to the speeches and sang along with the carolers. **It** was something they would tell their friends about back home.

CLEAR: The tourists stared in awe as the great Christmas tree in Rockefeller Center was lit. They listened in rapt attention to the speeches and sang along with the carolers. The spectacle was something they would tell their friends about back home.

VAGUE: Now that her children were away at school, she felt free to pursue her own interests for the first time in years. Perhaps she would get a job. Perhaps she would go back to school. Suddenly she felt alive again. Until this moment, she hadn't realized how badly she had needed **this.**

CLEAR: Now that her children were away at school, she felt free to pursue her own interests for the first time in years. Perhaps she would get a job. Perhaps she would go back to school. Suddenly she felt alive again. Until this moment, she hadn't realized how badly she had needed a change in her life.

2 Ambiguous reference

Do not use a pronoun that could refer to either of two or more antecedents.

AMBIGUOUS: Malcolm told Henry that **he** had won a trip to France.

The pronoun *he* could refer to either Malcolm or Henry. If it refers to Malcolm, rewrite the sentence to make this reference clear.

CLEAR: Malcolm told Henry, "I have won a trip to France."
OR: Malcolm, who had won a trip to France, told Henry the news.

If the pronoun refers to Henry, rewrite the sentence a different way.

CLEAR: Malcolm told Henry, "You have won a trip to France."
OR: Malcolm knew that Henry had won a trip to France and told him so.

AMBIGUOUS: Marika met Dr. McCluskey when **she** visited the lab last week.

The pronoun *she* could refer to either Marika or Dr. McCluskey.

CLEAR: When Marika visited the lab last week, she met Dr. McCluskey.
CLEAR: When Dr. McCluskey visited the lab last week, Marika met her.

AMBIGUOUS: In the saga, Luke Skywalker and Han Solo are at first rivals. Both want to win the affection of the princess. As the saga progresses, however, the two young men gain respect for each other, until finally the rivalry ends when **he** discovers he is Leia's brother.

The pronoun *he* could refer to either Luke or Han.

CLEAR:	In the saga, Luke Skywalker and Han Solo are at first rivals. Both want to win the affection of the princess. As the saga progresses, however, the two young men gain respect for each other, until finally the rivalry ends when **Luke** discovers he is Leia's brother.
AMBIGUOUS:	Fourteenth-century Europe was scarred by war and plague. It is hard to tell which was worse. The figures given by the chroniclers differ, but according to some accounts, **it** reduced the population by a third.
CLEAR:	Fourteenth-century Europe was scarred by war and plague. It is hard to tell which was worse. The figures given by the chroniclers differ, but according to some accounts, **plague alone** reduced the population by a third.

14c Pronoun Usage

Do not use a personal pronoun immediately after its antecedent.

Pronouns are often used this way in conversation to emphasize the antecedent, but this construction is inappropriate in writing.

NOT:	The dictator **he** would not give up any of his power.
BUT:	The dictator would not give up any of his power.
NOT:	Cuckoos **they** lay their eggs in other birds' nests.
BUT:	Cuckoos lay their eggs in other birds' nests.

Use a pronoun ending in *-self* or *-selves* only when an antecedent for this pronoun appears in the sentence. (See reflexive pronouns, Section 8f-7.)

I bought the tickets for Doris and **myself.**

pr/agr

NOT: Give the tickets to Doris and **myself.**
BUT: Give the tickets to Doris and **me.**

NOT: The invitation was addressed to his wife and **himself.**
BUT: The invitation was addressed to his wife and **him.**

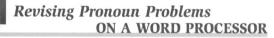

Revising Pronoun Problems
ON A WORD PROCESSOR

You can use the search function to locate specific pronouns to verify clear reference and agreement with antecedents. Check relative pronouns (*who, whom, which*) for vagueness and incorrect form; look at masculine pronouns (*he, him, his*) to make sure you have avoided sexist usage; find reflexive pronouns (*myself, himself,* etc.) to see whether you have used them correctly. The delete and insert functions will allow you to change pronouns and reword sentences without having to retype a whole page.

EXERCISE 14-2

Rephrase any of the following sentences that contain pronoun agreement, reference, or usage problems.

1. Some of the players, they had had a wonderful time.

2. The professor and the dean completed his plans this morning.

3. Alice and Tasha were no longer roommates after she got a bid to join the sorority.

4. Why didn't you tell Juan and myself about the picnic?

5. The shirt, although very highly priced, it was my least favorite gift.

6. The people crowded around the car after the accident; it was a mess.

7. Please accept this token of our esteem on behalf of our committee and myself.

8. After the drivers checked the tires, they were ready to go.

9. Each of those present lit their candle on signal.

10. The students in the park, which traveled with us, were noisy.

15 Pronoun Case

15a Subjective, Possessive, and Objective

Personal pronouns take the form of the *subjective,* the *possessive,* or the *objective case,* depending on their use in the sentence. The pronouns *who* and *whoever* also have different forms to indicate case.

SUBJECTIVE:	I, you, he, she, it, we, they, who, whoever
POSSESSIVE:	my, mine, your, yours, his, her, hers, its, our, ours, their, theirs, whose
OBJECTIVE:	me, you, him, her, it, us, them, whom, whomever

He wrote *The Way to Rainy Mountain.* (*subjective*)

Scott Momaday has increased **our** awareness of the daily struggle of Native Americans. (*possessive*)

Many awards have been given to **him.** (*objective*)

The author is **he.** (*subjective*)

Most people have little trouble choosing the appropriate case when a personal pronoun is used by itself. Many do have trouble, though, when the pronoun is part of a compound structure. Almost everyone has trouble at times with *who* and *whom* and with *whoever* and *whomever*.

1 In compound subjects and objects

Place a pronoun that is part of a compound subject in the subjective case.

> **NOT:** Fanny and **me** have tickets for the football game.
> **BUT:** Fanny and **I** have tickets for the football game.

> **NOT:** Neither Wally nor **him** is on the wrestling team.
> **BUT:** Neither Wally nor **he** is on the wrestling team.

Place a pronoun that is part of a compound direct object or a compound indirect object in the objective case.

> **NOT:** The fly ball bounced off the fence and then hit Christine and **I.**
> **BUT:** The fly ball bounced off the fence and then hit Christine and **me.** (hit . . . me)

> **NOT:** Give Mel and **she** the blueprints so that they can check the measurements.
> **BUT:** Give Mel and **her** the blueprints so that they can check the measurements. (Give . . . her)

Place a pronoun that is part of a compound object of a preposition in the objective case.

> **NOT:** Although there are thirty people competing, everyone knows the race is really between you and **I.**

> **BUT:** Although there are thirty people competing, everyone knows the race is really between you and **me.**

> **NOT:** The symposium is being conducted by Dr. Fell and **she.**

> **BUT:** The symposium is being conducted by Dr. Fell and **her.** (by . . . her)

> **NOT:** Several of **we** amateurs were allowed to play in the pro tournament.

> **BUT:** Several of **us** amateurs were allowed to play in the pro tournament. (of us, *not* of we)

2   In subject complements

Place a pronoun that is part of a subject complement in the subjective case. (See linking verbs, Section 8b-2.)

> **NOT:** The people to see for tickets are Juan and **him.**
> **BUT:** The people to see for tickets are Juan and **he.**

> **NOT:** The winners are Dara and **her.**
> **BUT:** The winners are Dara and **she.**

In speech, many people accept the informal use of the objective case of the pronoun following the verb *be*. In formal writing, however, the subjective case is still required in this construction.

> **INFORMAL:** It is **me.**
> **FORMAL:** It is **I.**

> **INFORMAL:** Was it **him** who asked you to the dance?
> **FORMAL:** Was it **he** who asked you to the dance?

3   After *than* or *as*

In an elliptical, or incomplete, clause, place the pronoun in the case it would be in if the clause were complete.

NOT:	Demetrius is stronger than **him.**
BUT:	Demetrius is stronger than **he.** (than he is)
NOT:	No one could have worked more skillfully than **her.**
BUT:	No one could have worked more skillfully than **she.** (than she did)

4 In appositives

Place a pronoun that is part of a compound appositive in the same case as the noun to which the appositive refers.

An **appositive** is a noun or noun substitute that renames or identifies the noun or noun substitute preceding it.

NOT:	The partners—Willie, Travis, and **me**—plan to open a bicycle repair shop in July.
BUT:	The partners—Willie, Travis, and **I**—plan to open a bicycle repair shop in July.
NOT:	Only two people, the manager and **him,** knew the combination of the safe.
BUT:	Only two people, the manager and **he,** knew the combination of the safe.

5 Before verbals or verbal phrases

Place a pronoun that precedes a gerund or gerund phrase in the possessive case. A noun follows this rule also.

NOT:	The audience applauded **them** dancing.
BUT:	The audience applauded **their** dancing. (the performers')
NOT:	I resented **him** criticizing me in front of my friends.
BUT:	I resented **his** criticizing me in front of my friends. (my dad's)

Place a pronoun that precedes a participle or participial phrase in the objective case.

NOT: I heard **his** starting the car.

BUT: I heard **him** starting the car.

NOT: Phil had seen **their** racing to class.

BUT: Phil had seen **them** racing to class.

To decide which case of the pronoun to use, you have to decide whether the verbal following it is a gerund or a participle. Look at the next two sentences:

I can hear your singing.

I can hear you singing.

Both of these sentences are grammatically correct, but they have slightly different meanings. In the first sentence, *singing* is a gerund modified by the possessive pronoun *your;* in the second sentence, *singing* is a participle that modifies the objective pronoun *you.* The first sentence emphasizes an action, *singing,* while the second sentence emphasizes the performer of the action, *you.* Thus in writing sentences like these, you can often convey different shades of meaning by using the possessive or the objective case of the pronoun.

6   *Who* and *whom; whoever* and *whomever*

In conversation, many people no longer use *whom* or *whomever* except directly after a preposition. In writing, however, you should always be careful to distinguish between *who* and *whom* and between *whoever* and *whomever.*

Use *who* and *whoever* as the subject of a sentence or clause.

Who founded the American Red Cross? (*subject of sentence*)

The book is about Clara Barton, **who** founded the American Red Cross. (*subject of clause*)

Whoever lost the book will have to pay for it. (*subject of clause*)

Use *whom* and *whomever* as the direct object or the object of a preposition.

> **Whom** shall I call? (*direct object*)
>
> **Whomever** the *Union Leader* endorsed enjoyed a substantial advantage. (*direct object*)
>
> The person to **whom** I gave the packages was Pete. (*object of preposition*)

How can you tell whether the pronoun should be *who* or *whom*? For sentences, mentally rephrase the question as a declarative statement. Then substitute *who* for *he, she,* or *they,* or *whom* for *him, her,* or *them.*

> (*Who/Whom*) founded the American Red Cross?
> **She** founded the American Red Cross.
> **Who** founded the American Red Cross?
> (*Who/Whom*) shall I call?
> I shall call **him.**
> **Whom** shall I call?

For clauses, follow the same process. Rephrase the clause as a statement, and substitute *who* for *he, she,* or *they,* or *whom* for *him, her,* or *them.*

> The person (*who/whom*) founded the American Red Cross was Clara Barton.
> **She** founded the American Red Cross.
> The person **who** founded the American Red Cross was Clara Barton.
>
> The writer (*who/whom*) she enjoyed most was Dickens.
> She enjoyed **him** most.
> The writer **whom** she enjoyed most was Dickens.
>
> (*Whoever/Whomever*) the *Union Leader* endorsed enjoyed a substantial advantage.

The *Union Leader* endorsed **him.**

Whomever the *Union Leader* endorsed enjoyed a substantial advantage.

If words intervene between the pronoun and the main verb of the sentence or clause, mentally delete them as you rephrase.

(*Who/Whom*) <u>did he think</u> he had offended?

He had offended **them.**

Whom did he think he had offended?

One person (*who/whom*) <u>the newspaper said</u> was killed was actually unhurt.

She was killed.

One person **who** the newspaper said was killed was actually unhurt.

The stores gave away the food to (*whoever/whomever*) <u>they knew</u> could use it.

They could use it.

The stores gave away the food to **whoever** they knew could use it.

Revising Pronoun Case
ON A WORD PROCESSOR

You can use the search function to locate *who, whom, whoever,* and *whomever* and then analyze the sentence to be sure that you have the correct case.

Grammar checkers can flag some incorrect pronouns and explain the rules for using *I* or *me, he* or *him, she* or *her, we* or *us, they* or *them, who* or *whom.* But don't assume that a computer program will catch all incorrect pronouns.

EXERCISE 15-1

Select the appropriate form of the pronoun in each of the following sentences.

1. Her family and (we/us) attended the special concert honoring Bach and Handel.

2. All the arrangements were made by Susan and (I/me).

3. Two of us—Kathleen and (I/me)—went to the recital early to get the tickets.

4. In the year 1882, both Bach and (he/him) died.

5. Perhaps Bach is a more prolific composer than (he/him), but Handel is more popular.

6. The two of them—Handel and (he/him)—were from Germany.

7. Some music lovers think that Handel is easier to listen to than (he/him).

8. Some organists object to (his/him) writing organ concertos because of his training.

9. Yet, (he/him) wrote great orchestral accompaniments for his oratorios.

10. (Who/Whom) are we to believe in these matters when others say that Bach is indeed more popular than (he/him)?

EXERCISE 15-2

Select the appropriate form of the pronoun in each of the following sentences.

1. If you scan the crowd carefully, you will locate the young woman (who/whom) you are looking for.

2. The woman in charge, (who/whom) you must first see, has gone to lunch.

3. Mary's brother, (who/whom) she admits is envious, will manage her mayoral campaign.

4. (Who/Whom) do you plan to see?

5. (Who/Whom) do you suspect has the higher grades?

6. (Whoever/Whomever) submits the least expensive bid will probably get the job.

7. The inspiration of the coach, (who/whom) never gives up, impressed the visitors.

8. The manager will employ (whoever/whomever) he can find (who/whom) is willing to work long hours.

9. (Whoever/Whomever) do you think that will be?

10. The musician, (who/whom) taught for many years, retired at the age of sixty.

16   Adjectives and Adverbs

An **adjective** is a word that modifies a noun or a pronoun.
An **adverb** is a word that modifies a verb.

Avoid confusing these two parts of speech.

ADJECTIVE	ADVERB
happy	happily
graceful	gracefully
most	almost

Although most adjectives and adverbs have different forms, a
few words can function as both. Among them are the following:

deep	hard	late	loud	slow	very
far	high	little	low	straight	well
fast	kindly	long	parallel	tight	wild

16a   Misused Adjective Forms

Avoid using an adjective to modify a verb, an adjective, or an
adverb. Use an adverb or qualifier instead.

NOT: The lawyer answered very **quick.**

BUT: The lawyer *answered* very **quickly.**

NOT: The director thought Marie's reading was **near** perfect.

BUT: The director thought Marie's reading was **nearly** *perfect.*

NOT: The group performing at the club plays **real** well.

BUT: The group performing at the club plays **really** *well.*

Do not be confused by words separating the adverb from the word it modifies. For example:

The lawyer *answered* each of her client's questions very **quickly.**

Avoid using an adjective ending in *-ly* in place of an adverb or an adverb phrase.

Although the suffix *-ly* usually signals an adverb, a few adjectives end in *-ly* too. For example:

earthly	ghostly	holy	lovely
friendly	heavenly	homely	manly

Do not mistake these adjectives for adverbs or try to use them as adverbs. Either use another word or express your idea as a phrase.

NOT: A figure was moving **ghostly** through the darkened room.

BUT: A figure was moving **like a ghost** through the darkened room.

OR: A figure was moving **ghostlike** through the darkened room.

NOT: They do not generally answer the questions of American tourists **very friendly.**

BUT: They do not generally answer the questions of American tourists **in a very friendly way.**

OR: They do not generally answer the questions of American tourists **very pleasantly.**

16b Misused Adverb Forms

Avoid using an adverb to modify a direct object. Use an adjective as an object complement instead. (See Section 7d-3.)

Think about the difference in meaning between the following two sentences:

The instructor considered the student's paper intelligent.

The instructor considered the student's paper intelligently.

In the first sentence, the adjective *intelligent* modifies the direct object *paper*. It tells what opinion the instructor held of the paper. In the second sentence, the adverb *intelligently* modifies the verb *considered*. It tells in what manner the instructor considered the paper.

NOT: He keeps his workstation **tidily.**

BUT: He keeps his *workstation* **tidy.**

NOT: She considers her grades **excellently.**

BUT: She considers her *grades* **excellent.**

NOT: The jury found the defendant **guiltily.**

BUT: The jury found the *defendant* **guilty.**

Avoid using an adverb after a linking verb. Use the corresponding adjective instead as a predicate adjective. (See Sections 7d-4 and 8e-2.)

NOT: After the operation, the patient felt **badly.**

BUT: After the operation, the *patient* felt **bad.**

NOT: This proposal sounds **sensibly** enough.

BUT: This *proposal* sounds **sensible** enough.

NOT: After he took that cooking course, his meals tasted **differently.**

BUT: After he took that cooking course, his *meals* tasted **different.**

Two words that are especially confusing are *good* and *well*. *Good* is always used as an adjective. *Well* is usually used as an adverb, but it can also be used as an adjective that means "healthy" or "satisfactory."

> The preliminary *findings* look **good.** (*adjective*)
>
> Janet *dances* **well.** (*adverb*)
>
> The town crier shouted, "*All* is **well!**" (*adjective*)

Notice the difference between the following two sentences:

> He feels good.
> He feels well.

The adjective *good* describes the person's mood. The adjective *well* describes his health.

Some verbs can be used as both action verbs and linking verbs. (See Section 8e-2.) These verbs include the following:

die	go	look	taste
feel	grow	smell	turn

ACTION: The customs officer *looked* **carefully** through our luggage. (*adverb*)

LINKING: This *book* looks **interesting.** (*adjective*)

ACTION: The cute little puppy *grew* **quickly** into a 150-pound dog. (*adverb*)

LINKING: After drinking the potion, the old *man* grew **young** before our very eyes. (*adjective*)

ACTION: He *died* **peacefully** in his sleep. (*adverb*)

LINKING: The *poet* died **young.** (*adjective*)

16c Comparative and Superlative Forms of Adjectives and Adverbs

Form the comparative of most one-syllable adjectives and adverbs by adding the suffix *-er* (or *-r*) to the base, or positive, form of the word. Form the superlative of most one-syllable adjectives and adverbs by adding the suffix *-est* (or *-st*) to the base form.

POSITIVE	COMPARATIVE	SUPERLATIVE
slow	slower	slowest
late	later	latest
deep	deeper	deepest

Form the comparative of most longer adjectives and adverbs by placing the word *more* before the base word. Form the superlative of most longer adjectives and adverbs by placing the word *most* before the base word.

POSITIVE	COMPARATIVE	SUPERLATIVE
graceful	more graceful	most graceful
gracefully	more gracefully	most gracefully
sensible	more sensible	most sensible
sensibly	more sensibly	most sensibly

Some adjectives and adverbs have irregular comparative and superlative forms.

POSITIVE	COMPARATIVE	SUPERLATIVE
good well	better	best
bad ill badly	worse	worst
many much	more	most
little (quantity)	less	least

A dictionary usually lists the *-er* and *-est* comparative and superlative forms for adjectives and adverbs that have these forms.

Use the comparative form to compare two things. Use the superlative form to compare three or more things.

> This dish is **spicier** than that one.
> This dish is the **spiciest** one on the menu.
>
> Harry is a **more skillful** carpenter than his partner.
> Harry is the **most skillful** carpenter in town.
>
> Lois works **harder** than Carol.
> Lois works the **hardest** of the three students.
>
> Sharon speaks **more distinctly** than her sister.
> Sharon speaks the **most distinctly** of anyone in her family.

Avoid using the superlative form when only two things are being compared.

> **NOT:** Of the two sexes, women live **the longest.**
>
> **BUT:** Of the two sexes, women live **longer.**
>
> **NOT:** Both of the proposals were reasonable, but Johnson's was **the most complex.**
>
> **BUT:** Both of the proposals were reasonable, but Johnson's was **more complex.**
>
> **NOT:** Henry James and Edith Wharton both wrote of a certain type of society—the society of the very rich and the very secure—and of the effects of this society on the idealistic woman. It is hard to say whose vision was the **clearest.**
>
> **BUT:** Henry James and Edith Wharton both wrote of a certain type of society—the society of the very rich and the very secure—and of the effects of this society on the idealistic woman. It is hard to say whose vision was **clearer.**

Avoid making double comparisons (comparisons using both *-er* or *-est* and *more* or *most*).

> **NOT:** He was **more wealthier** than John D. Rockefeller.
> **BUT:** He was **wealthier** than John D. Rockefeller.
>
> **NOT:** It is the **most sleekest** craft on the lake.
> **BUT:** It is the **sleekest** craft on the lake.

Avoid comparing words such as *complete, dead, perfect, round, square,* and *unique.*

These words, called *absolutes,* name conditions that cannot be compared. For example, people are either dead or not dead; one person cannot be *more dead* than another person. If something is perfect, something else cannot be *more perfect.* Except for *dead,* however, you can compare the steps in reaching these conditions. For example, something may be *more nearly perfect* than something else, or one thing may be *the most nearly complete* of three.

> **NOT:** His solution was **more perfect** than John's.
> **BUT:** His solution was **more nearly perfect** than John's.

Revising Adjective and Adverb Use ON A WORD PROCESSOR

You can use the search function to locate words such as *real* and *really, bad* and *badly,* and *good* and *well.* Then you can check to see whether you used the proper form.

You can also search for *more, most, less,* and *least* to see whether you have chosen the appropriate comparative or superlative. Some word-processing programs enable you to search for specific sets of letters, not just separate words. If you think you have problems with comparatives and superlatives, you can use this feature to search for *-er* and *-est* words.

16d Double Negatives

Use only one negative word to express a negative meaning.

A **double negative** occurs when two negative words are used to make a negative statement. Although this device was often used in earlier centuries to emphasize the idea of negation, it is not acceptable in standard modern English.

NOT:	Felicity **didn't** bring **nothing** to the party.
BUT:	Felicity **didn't** bring **anything** to the party.
OR:	Felicity brought **nothing** to the party.
NOT:	I **don't** know **no one** by that name.
BUT:	I **don't** know **anyone** by that name.
OR:	I know **no one** by that name.
NOT:	She **can't hardly** see in this light.
BUT:	She **can hardly** see in this light.

EXERCISE 16-1

Identify the incorrect adjective and adverb forms in each of the following sentences and explain why the usage is incorrect.

1. Visiting the showroom to view new cars makes many people feel happily.

2. When one narrows one's choices to two cars, it's always difficult to decide which one is the attractiver.

3. The colorfully instrument gauges look nicest in the day than at night.

4. The salesperson I met yesterday was not at work today because he felt badly and was sent home.

5. When I was asked to make a price offer, I didn't have nothing appropriate planned.

6. We couldn't hardly wait to go for a test drive.

7. After turning a corner, a truck came dangerous close to hitting us.

8. It happened so quick there wasn't hardly nothing to do but hit the brakes.

9. The salesperson with us sighed weary and shook his head.

10. When we got back, the salesperson anxious took the key from me and didn't speak to no one.

---

17   Shifts and Mixed Constructions

Although variety is desirable in writing, some kinds of variety are not desirable. Shifting for no good reason from the active to the passive voice or from the past to the present tense is confusing and irritating to the reader. Be consistent in your use of number, person, tense, voice, and mood. You will also want to maintain a logical sequence of tenses to indicate when events happen in relation to one another.

SHIFTS

17a In Number

Avoid shifting pronouns awkwardly and inconsistently between the singular and the plural.

Many shifts of this kind are actually problems with pronoun–antecedent agreement. (See Section 14a.)

INCONSISTENT:	Just before **a person** speaks in public, **they** should do several relaxation exercises.
CONSISTENT:	Just before **a person** speaks in public, **he or she** should do several relaxation exercises.
OR:	Just before speaking in public, a person should do several relaxation exercises.
INCONSISTENT:	**A warthog** may appear ungainly, but **these animals** can run at a speed of 30 miles an hour.
CONSISTENT:	**A warthog** may appear ungainly, but **this animal** can run at a speed of 30 miles an hour.
OR:	**Warthogs** may appear ungainly, but **these animals** can run at a speed of 30 miles an hour.
INCONSISTENT:	**Anyone** who travels to Greece will see many sites about which **they** have read.
CONSISTENT:	**People** who travel to Greece will see many sites about which **they** have read.
OR:	**Travelers** to Greece will see many sites about which **they** have read.

17b In Person

Avoid shifting pronouns awkwardly between the second person and the third person.

All nouns and all indefinite pronouns are in the third person. However, personal pronouns may be in the first person, the second person, or the third person.

	SINGULAR	PLURAL
FIRST PERSON:	I, me, my, mine	we, us, our, ours
SECOND PERSON:	you, your, yours	you, your, yours
THIRD PERSON:	he, him, his she, her, hers it, its	they, them, their, theirs they, them, their, theirs

INCONSISTENT:	It has been said that unless **you** have a knowledge of history, **a person** is condemned to repeat its mistakes.
CONSISTENT:	It has been said that unless **you** have a knowledge of history, **you** are condemned to repeat its mistakes.
OR:	It has been said that without a knowledge of history, a person is condemned to repeat its mistakes.
INCONSISTENT:	When **a person** reads Jefferson's *Notes on Virginia,* **you** are amazed by his wide range of interests.
CONSISTENT:	When **people** read Jefferson's *Notes on Virginia,* **they** are amazed by his wide range of interests.
OR:	People who read Jefferson's *Notes on Virginia* are amazed by his wide range of interests.
INCONSISTENT:	As **we** read about the slaughtering of the rhinoceros for its horn and the elephant for its tusks, **one** becomes appalled by the selfishness of humankind.
CONSISTENT:	As **we** read about the slaughtering of the rhinoceros for its horn and the elephant for its tusks, **we** become appalled by the selfishness of humankind.
OR:	Reading about the slaughtering of the rhinoceros for its horn and the elephant for its tusks, one becomes appalled by the selfishness of humankind.

17c In Voice

Avoid shifting verbs awkwardly between the active voice and the passive voice.

INCONSISTENT:	André-Jacques Garnerin **made** the first parachute jump, and the first aerial photographs **were taken** by Samuel Archer King and William Black.
CONSISTENT:	André-Jacques Garnerin **made** the first parachute jump, and Samual Archer King and William Black **took** the first aerial photographs.
INCONSISTENT:	A group of ants **is called** a colony, but you **refer** to a group of bees as a swarm.

CONSISTENT: A group of ants **is called** a colony, but a group of bees **is referred** to as a swarm.

17d In Mood

Avoid shifting verbs awkwardly between the indicative, imperative, and subjunctive moods.

INCONSISTENT: First **brown** the onions in butter. Then you **should add** them to the beef stock.

CONSISTENT: First **brown** the onions in butter. Then **add** them to the beef stock.

INCONSISTENT: If I **were** president of this club and he **was** my second in command, things would be very different.

CONSISTENT: If I **were** president of this club and he **were** my second in command, things would be very different.

(See also mood, Section 12b-4.)

EXERCISE 17-1

Rephrase each of the following items to eliminate awkward shifts in number, person, voice, and mood.

1. A person must bring a check, not cash, when you purchase license plates.

2. Before you begin to criticize someone, one should consider what that person might have been through.

3. Because interest rates are so low now, an investor should take their decisions seriously.

4. Anyone who tries to cook this recipe will not understand what she or he have read.

5. A person cannot help but be impressed when you see the football team run onto the field.

17e In Verb Tense

Maintain a logical sequence of tenses to indicate when events happen in relation to one another.

The English tense system might seem complicated, but most of the time, native speakers of the language have few problems using it correctly. One problem is shifting unnecessarily from one tense to another. Some writers have the opposite problem: They do not change tenses when they should to show that one event happened before or after another. The following sections cover some of the most common problems with sequence of tenses.

Avoid shifting awkwardly between the present tense and the past tense.

When writing about literature or history, you can often use either the present tense or the past tense. However, if you start writing in the present tense, continue writing in that tense. If you start writing in the past tense, continue writing in that tense.

INCONSISTENT:	At the end of the war, Ezra Pound **is accused** of treason. He **was confined** at St. Elizabeth's Hospital, where he **spends** the next twelve years.
CONSISTENT:	At the end of the war, Ezra Pound **is accused** of treason. He **is confined** at St. Elizabeth's Hospital, where he **spends** the next twelve years.

INCONSISTENT:	Lincoln **came** to national attention as a result of a series of debates with Stephen A. Douglas. Although he **loses** the senatorial election to Douglas, two years later he **gains** the Republican nomination for president.
CONSISTENT:	Lincoln **came** to national attention as a result of a series of debates with Stephen A. Douglas. Although he **lost** the senatorial election to Douglas, two years later he **gained** the Republican nomination for president.

17f Tense with Clauses

If you begin a sentence in the present tense, shift to the past tense or the present perfect tense when you begin to write about past action.

NOT:	To a large extent, we **remember** Alice B. Toklas because she **is** Gertrude Stein's friend.
BUT:	To a large extent, we **remember** Alice B. Toklas because she **was** Gertrude Stein's friend.
NOT:	Today he **supports** moving the embassy, but just three weeks ago he **opposes** this action.
BUT:	Today he **supports** moving the embassy, but just three weeks ago he **opposed** this action.

Use the past perfect tense to indicate that one past action occurred before another past action.

NOT:	Hitler **purged** the Nazi Party before he **gained** complete control of the state.
BUT:	Hitler **had purged** the Nazi Party before he **gained** complete control of the state.
NOT:	They **double-checked** the results of their experiment because they **made** an error.

BUT: They **double-checked** the results of their experiment because they **had made** an error.

Use the future perfect tense to indicate that an action in the future will occur before another future action.

NOT: By next Tuesday we **will cover** half the course.

BUT: By next Tuesday we **will have covered** half the course.

NOT: When they **pay** off the loan, they **paid** twice the cost of the car.

BUT: When they **pay** off the loan, they **will have paid** twice the cost of the car.

17g Tense with Infinitives

Use the present infinitive to express action that occurs at the same time as or later than the action of the main verb. Use the present perfect infinitive to express action that occurs before the action of the main verb.

NOT: They **need to purchase** their tickets by now.

BUT: They **need to have purchased** their tickets by now. (*The need is in the present; the purchase, if it happened, was in the past.*)

NOT: The designer **had hoped to have gotten** the job.

BUT: The designer **had hoped to get** the job.

Compare the following three sentences:

He **would like to review** the book favorably. (would like *in the present* to review *in the present*)

He **would have liked to review** the book favorably. (would have liked *in the past* to review *in the past*)

He **would like to have reviewed** the book favorably. (would like *in the present* to have reviewed *in the past*)

17h Tense with Participles

Use the present participle to express action that occurs at the same time as the action of the main verb. Use the present perfect participle or the past participle to express action that occurs before the action of the main verb.

The present perfect participle of a verb consists of the word *having* followed by the past participle of the verb: *having done, having been, having seen,* and so forth.

NOT: **Winning** the battle, the general planned the next day's campaign.

BUT: **Having won** the battle, the general *planned* the next day's campaign. (*action of participle occurred before action of main verb*)

NOT: **Being encouraged** by her friends, she eagerly filled out the form for entrance in the marathon.

BUT: **Having been encouraged by her friends,** she eagerly *filled out* the form for entrance in the marathon. (*action of participle occurred before action of main verb*)

OR: **Encouraged** by her friends, she eagerly *filled out* the form for entrance in the marathon.

EXERCISE 17-2

Correct any error in the sequence of tenses in the following sentences. Identify any correct sentences.

1. We were wishing for a dry spring season even though winter had come late.

2. He was late for class, parking his car so far away.

3. By the end of this week, we will cover half of this course's syllabus.

4. We all regretted to have missed your presentation.

5. He had been relieved to visit you, having waited for the directions for over a week.

MIXED CONSTRUCTIONS

17i Mixed Sentence Structure

Maintain a consistent sentence structure. Do not start a sentence with one type of structure and end it with another type.

INCONSISTENT: First rub olive oil over the outside of the chicken; then salt the chicken lightly, but no pepper.

The writer of the preceding sentence begins with an independent clause, continues with another independent clause, and then concludes beginning with the conjunction *but,* indicating that another independent clause will follow. However, the writer then ends the sentence with a phrase rather than a clause. The problem can be eliminated by turning the phrase into a clause.

CONSISTENT: First rub olive oil over the outside of the chicken; then salt the chicken lightly, but do not pepper it.

Another kind of mixed sentence structure is created by clauses that are not clearly related to one another.

INCONSISTENT: When your parents were poorly educated and you
yourself have attended substandard schools, what
kind of odds for success are those?

In this sentence, the writer begins with an adverb clause that should
modify a word in an independent clause. However, the independent
clause that follows does not contain any word for the adverb clause
to modify. To correct the problem, simply provide such a word.

CONSISTENT: What kind of odds for success do you have when
your parents were poorly educated and you yourself have attended substandard schools?

INCONSISTENT: Those black pilots who fought so valiantly during
World War II, many people do not even know of
their existence.

Here the writer begins with a noun modified by an adjective
clause but does not provide a predicate for the noun. Instead,
the sentence ends with an independent clause that is not grammatically related to what precedes it.

CONSISTENT: Many people do not even know of the existence of
those black pilots who fought so valiantly during
World War II.

The following sentence is from a television program about training business executives to answer (or evade) reporters' questions:

INCONSISTENT: How you could be a newsperson and work with
people you might one day have to interview, I
could not do it.

CONSISTENT: As a newsperson, I could not work with people I
might one day have to interview.

OR: I do not understand how you could be a newsperson and work with people you might one day have
to interview.

18 Dangling and Misplaced Modifiers

Sentence introductory phrases must clearly and logically modify the nouns or pronouns that follow them, or the result becomes nonsense. Modifying words or phrases must be placed close to the words they modify, or ambiguity in meaning results.

18a Dangling Modifiers

An introductory phrase must clearly and sensibly modify the noun or pronoun that follows it.

A phrase that does not do this is called a **dangling modifier,** because it is not clearly attached to the rest of the sentence.

UNCLEAR: **Frightened by the huge, gnarled tree outside his window,** his head dived under the covers.

In the sentence above, the introductory participial phrase seems to modify *his head,* but it was obviously not the boy's head, but the boy himself, who was frightened. A simple way to revise this sentence is to rewrite the independent clause so that it begins with the noun that the introductory phrase actually refers to.

CLEAR: **Frightened by the huge, gnarled tree outside his window,** the boy hid his head under the covers.

UNCLEAR: **Unable to make a living in Detroit,** relocating to Houston seemed a good idea.

The introductory phrase does not sensibly modify *relocating,* the gerund that follows it. This sentence can also be revised by rewriting the independent clause so it begins with the noun or pronoun that the introductory phrase actually refers to.

| CLEAR: | **Unable to make a living in Detroit,** she thought relocating to Houston was a good idea. |
| OR: | **Unable to make a living in Detroit,** she thought she might move to Houston. |

Another way to revise the sentence is to turn the phrase into a clause.

| CLEAR: | **Because she was unable to make a living in Detroit,** relocating to Houston seemed a good idea. |

Here are some more examples of dangling modifiers:

UNCLEAR:	**While trying to control my temper,** the sergeant forced me to do a hundred push-ups.
CLEAR:	**While trying to control my temper,** I was forced by the sergeant to do a hundred push-ups.
OR:	**As I tried to control my temper,** the sergeant forced me to do a hundred push-ups.

| UNCLEAR: | **As a young girl,** my grandfather told me stories of his life in Korea. |
| CLEAR: | **When I was a young girl,** my grandfather told me stories of his life in Korea. |

A few introductory phrases are idiomatic. They modify the entire sentence, not a particular word.

To tell the truth, no one knows where he is.

Relatively speaking, my grades are not that bad.

As a matter of fact, the sea is not wine-red but blue.

18b Misplaced Modifiers

Place a modifying word or phrase as close as possible to the word it modifies. Carefully avoid placing it so that it seems to refer to a word other than the one you intended.

The placement of a modifier in a sentence is very important. Notice the difference in meaning between the following two sentences:

He **almost** spent two hundred dollars.
He spent **almost** two hundred dollars.

In the first sentence, *almost* modifies the verb *spent*. It tells us that he did not complete his action. In the second sentence, *almost* modifies *two hundred*. It tells us that the amount he spent came close to, but did not total, two hundred dollars.

Misplaced modifiers make a sentence confusing or even ridiculous, as shown in the following examples:

UNCLEAR:	He almost spoke for two hours.
CLEAR:	He spoke for **almost** two hours.
UNCLEAR:	She only quoted from three sources.
CLEAR:	She quoted from **only** three sources.
UNCLEAR:	He sang a ditty about filling a bottomless hole with his sister.
CLEAR:	**With his sister,** he sang a ditty about filling a bottomless hole.
OR:	He sang a ditty **with his sister** about filling a bottomless hole.
UNCLEAR:	He described his years spent alone on the island after the rescue.
CLEAR:	**After the rescue,** he described his years spent alone on the island.

Avoid misplacing a modifier that will create a **split infinitive.**

Writers occasionally **split infinitives** by inserting words or phrases between the word *to* and the verb. In the following phrases, the infinitive is in **boldface,** and the word that splits the infinitive is in *italics:*

To *exactly* **know**
To *truly* **have known**

Revise such awkward constructions to eliminate the split. Although recommendations on the use of split infinitives vary, it is best to avoid using them in formal writing.

Revising Modifier Placement
ON A WORD PROCESSOR

To improve the clarity and effectiveness of modifiers, you can use the cut and paste functions to move words, phrases, and clauses. Remember that you might also need to alter punctuation, capital letters, and even wording when you make these changes; you can use the delete and insert functions to perform such revisions.

Grammar checkers can flag split infinitives, but they do not alert you to other misplaced and dangling modifiers. You have to rely on your own editing skills or those of a peer editor for remedying such problems.

18c Squinting Modifiers

Avoid placing a modifier in such a way that it could refer to either the preceding or the following element in the sentence.

Such a modifier is called a **squinting modifier.**

UNCLEAR: The mayor announced **in March** he would run for re-election.

Was it the announcement or the election that was in March?

CLEAR:	The mayor announced he would run for reelection in March.
CLEAR:	In March, the mayor announced he would run for reelection.
UNCLEAR:	Carlson said **today** he is leaving for California.
CLEAR:	Carlson said he is leaving for California today.
CLEAR:	Today Carlson said he is leaving for California.
UNCLEAR:	Professor Quinn asked us **before we left** to turn in our papers.
CLEAR:	Before we left, Professor Quinn asked us to turn in our papers.
CLEAR:	Professor Quinn asked us to turn in our papers before we left.

EXERCISE 18-1

Revise each of the following sentences to eliminate the problem in sentence structure.

1. The actor nearly ate all of his supper and then only rested an hour before the performance.

2. The soldiers ran quickly turning their weapons toward the target.

3. Shipped directly from Peru every day, shoppers are able to purchase fresh corn in March.

4. Searching for the apples she dropped on the sidewalk, the bus departed without her.

5. Walking down the street, the house looked pleasant and bright.

19   Sentence Completeness

Sentence predication must be accurate both grammatically and logically. A writer who is making a comparison has to keep a number of points in mind in addition to using the appropriate comparative or superlative form of an adjective or adverb. Be certain that your comparisons are sensible, complete, and unambiguous; do not omit anything necessary to make your meaning clear.

19a   Faulty Predication

Make the subject and predicate of a sentence fit together both grammatically and logically.

A sentence with a poorly matched subject and predicate is said to have **faulty predication.**

> **NOT:**   More versatile and more manageable account for the popularity of the latest breed of home computers.

In the preceding sentence, the writer used two adjectives as the subject of the predicate *account for . . . computers.* A subject, however, must always be a noun or a noun equivalent.

> **BUT:**   Their greater **versatility** and increased **manageability** account for the popularity of the latest breed of home computers.

Other sentences with faulty predication are grammatically acceptable but make no sense or do not say what the writer intended.

> **NOT:**   Flattery and snobbery are people who will not be effective as political advisers.

The nouns *flattery* and *snobbery* do not sensibly fit the predicate *are people*.

> **BUT:** The flatterer and the snob will not be effective as political advisers.
>
> **NOT:** My opinion of his latest movie is poorly directed and ineptly filmed.

According to the preceding sentence, it is the writer's opinion that is poorly directed and ineptly filmed. Obviously, the writer meant to say this of the movie, not of the opinion.

> **BUT:** In my opinion, his latest movie is poorly directed and ineptly filmed.
>
> **OR:** My opinion of his latest movie is that it is poorly directed and ineptly filmed.
>
> **NOT:** Our criminal justice system, which allows the victims of crime to suffer more than the perpetrators of crime, should be punished more severely.

The subject *our criminal justice system* does not fit the predicate *should be punished more severely*.

> **BUT:** Our criminal justice system, which allows the victims of crime to suffer more than the perpetrators of crime, should be changed.
>
> **OR:** Our criminal justice system should be changed so that perpetrators of crime suffer more than their victims.

Avoid using an adverb clause as a subject or as a subject complement.

> **NOT:** Because the British were occupying Philadelphia is the reason the Liberty Bell was moved to Allentown during the Revolutionary War.

The word *because* introduces what must be an adverb clause.

> **BUT:** Because the British were occupying Philadelphia, the Liberty Bell was moved to Allentown during the Revolutionary War.

> **NOT:** The reason the Liberty Bell was moved to Allentown during the Revolutionary War is because the British were occupying Philadelphia.

Change this *because* adverb clause to a noun clause, or omit it.

> **BUT:** The reason the Liberty Bell was moved to Allentown during the Revolutionary War is **that** the British were occupying Philadelphia.

> **NOT:** The year 1778 is when the Liberty Bell was returned to Independence Hall.

> **BUT:** The Liberty Bell was returned to Independence Hall in 1778.

> **NOT:** Ironically, England is where the Liberty Bell was cast.

> **BUT:** Ironically, the Liberty Bell was cast in England.

19b False Comparisons

Be careful that your comparative statements compare what you intended to compare. Do not compare things that are essentially unlike.

> **FALSE:** Mark's smile was broader than Dora.

In the preceding sentence, the writer is trying to compare Mark's smile with Dora's smile. But the sentence as written compares Mark's smile with Dora herself.

> **VALID:** Mark's smile was broader than **Dora's.**

> **FALSE:** Her style of dressing is like the 1980s.

The preceding sentence compares a style of dressing with a period of time. Obviously, it should compare this style of dressing with the style of dressing popular in that period.

> **VALID:** Her style of dressing is like **that of** the 1980s.

> **FALSE:** Tuition at private colleges has become much more expensive than state colleges.

> **VALID:** Tuition has become much more expensive at private colleges than **at** state colleges.

19c Incomplete Comparisons

Avoid introducing the idea of a comparison without specifying one of the things being compared.

> **INCOMPLETE:** This cake tastes better.

Tastes better than what?

> **COMPLETE:** This cake tastes better than any of the others.

> **INCOMPLETE:** Growing up in a small town is different.

Different from what?

> **COMPLETE:** Growing up in a small town is different from growing up in a large city or a suburb.

19d Ambiguous Comparisons

Avoid making a comparative statement that has two possible meanings.

> **AMBIGUOUS:** I know Eliot better than Pound.

The preceding sentence is unclear. You can interpret it in two ways.

CLEAR:	I know Eliot better than I know Pound.
CLEAR:	I know Eliot better than Pound knows him.
AMBIGUOUS:	I can recall the family vacation we took when I was five better than my sister.
CLEAR:	I can recall the family vacation we took when I was five better than my sister can recall it.
CLEAR:	I can recall the family vacation we took when I was five better than I can recall my sister.

19e Omitted Comparative Words

Avoid omitting the words *as* or *than* when they are necessary in a comparative construction.

NOT:	The candidate was better prepared although not as well spoken as her opponent.
BUT:	The candidate was better prepared **than,** although not as well spoken as, her opponent.
NOT:	His grades were as good, if not better than, his brother's.
BUT:	His grades were as good **as,** if not better than, his brother's.
NOT:	All of their friends were as poor or even poorer than they.
BUT:	All of their friends were as poor **as** they or even poorer. (*than they* is understood)

Use the word *other* or *else* when you compare one thing with other members of the group to which it belongs.

NOT:	The flutist plays more beautifully than any member of the orchestra.
BUT:	The flutist plays more beautifully than any **other** member of the orchestra.
NOT:	Hal can throw farther than anyone on his team.
BUT:	Hal can throw farther than anyone **else** on his team.

| NOT: | The clipper cut through the water more gracefully than any of the ships. |
| BUT: | The clipper cut through the water more gracefully than any of the **other** ships. |

EXERCISE 19-1

Rephrase the following sentences to eliminate any false, ambiguous, or incomplete comparisons. Where necessary, supply any comparative words that have been omitted.

1. He paid more for his car than his father.

2. She likes ice cream better than Rudolpho.

3. This soda goes flat quicker.

4. Some believe the tuba is harder to play than almost any instrument.

5. The color of her eyes is the same as the car.

20 English as a Second Language

This chapter serves as a reference guide for multilingual students of composition for whom English is not a native language. It reviews the main features of English that are distinctive to the language and likely to prove troublesome to learners because of interference with features of other languages. The section's organization groups topics into nouns and associated words, modifiers (adjectives, adverbs, qualifiers), and verbs and associated structures.

20a Nouns, Articles, and Other Determiners

Nouns can be classified in many ways (see Section 8a), including as countable or noncountable (mass nouns). **Count nouns** name things that are counted separately in English, such as *pens, computers,* and *bottles.* **Noncount nouns** name things that are not counted separately in English, such as *gold, water,* and *happiness.* This section explains these nouns and the determiners that are used with them. A **determiner** is a word or group of words that introduces a noun. Some determiners signal that a noun is to follow; others indicate quantity or identify the noun in some other way. (See Section 8g.) There are three types of determiners to consider: articles, quantifiers, and demonstratives.

1 Noncount and count nouns

Almost all noncount nouns belong to one of several categories. Reviewing these lists will help you to recognize such nouns.

ABSTRACTIONS, EMOTIONS, IDEAS:	intelligence, health, love, timidity, ignorance, luck, patience, advice
FOODS:	beef, butter, ice cream, celery, sugar, rice, coffee, oil
LIQUIDS:	cream, water, soup, tea, milk, coffee, gasoline, perfume
AREAS OF STUDY:	architecture, chemistry, art, sociology
ANIMATE COLLECTIONS:	humanity, personnel, youth, mankind
INANIMATE COLLECTIONS:	equipment, furniture, hardware, luggage, jewelry, money
FORCES OF NATURE:	wind, water, thunder, sunlight, hail, heat, gravity, lightning
ACTIVITIES:	reading, hiking, shopping, swimming, golf, football, soccer, tennis, homework

Noncount nouns name generalized things that do not have plural forms, such as *laughter, peace, yogurt,* and *dirt,* and are never preceded by the articles *a* or *an.*

Count nouns name things that can be counted and can be made plural, such as *pen, computer, bottle, apple,* and *hour.* Count nouns are preceded by the indefinite articles *a* or *an,* by the definite article *the,* and by other determiners. (See Section 20a-4.)

2 Indefinite articles

A noun may refer to a single indefinite, unspecified person, place, or thing. Such count nouns are indicated as singular in English by the use of one of the **indefinite articles** *a* or *an* (meaning any unspecified *one*): *a glass, an owl.* These nondefinite singular count nouns require an indefinite article or some other determiner in front of them. Use *a* before words beginning with a pronounced consonant and *an* before words beginning with a vowel sound: *a* house, *an* hour.

Nondefinite count nouns that are plural can be used without any determiner: *Glasses* break easily; *owls* live in barns. (See Section 20a-5.)

3 Definite articles

A noun may refer to a definite person, place, or thing. Such nouns—count or noncount—are signaled by the use of the **definite article** *the.* The definite article can be used with either singular or plural nouns. Use the definite article in the following instances:

- After the first time a noun is mentioned in the same context.

FIRST MENTION:	We saw two cars in the driveway.
	Put rice in a bowl.
SUBSEQUENT MENTION:	*The* cars belong to Juanita.
	Stir *the* rice with a spoon.

- Before a noun that refers to something the reader knows or whose meaning is obvious from the context.

  Park *the* car.

- Before a noun referring to something unique.

  the Missouri River; *the* Vietnam War

- Before the superlative forms of adjectives.

  the wisest person; *the* best manners

- Before a noun described by restrictive phrases or clauses. Such phrases and clauses answer the question "Which one?" or "Which ones?" about the nouns they modify. (See also Section 28d-1.)

  The driver *in the car* is ill.

  The student *who arrived late* missed the bus.

If your native language lacks articles (e.g., Japanese or Russian), you might need help to distinguish between definite and indefinite articles.

4 Other determiners

Nouns may be signaled or marked by **determiners** other than articles. **Quantifiers** are used to signal how much or how many of something.

  some tablets (indefinite number)

  ten tablets (definite number)

  his tablet (possession)

  some grass (indefinite amount)

Some *quantifier* words precede only count nouns. Other quantifiers precede only noncount nouns to indicate an amount. A few quantifiers can precede both kinds of nouns: *a lot of, lots of,* etc. Both kinds of nouns may be preceded by possessive-case nouns or pronouns to indicate possession.

USED WITH COUNT NOUNS

AN INDEFINITE ITEM (SINGULAR)	A DEFINITE ITEM (SINGULAR)
a banana	*the* banana
any banana	*his, her* banana
either banana	*each* banana
neither banana	*another* banana

AN INDEFINITE NUMBER (PLURAL)	A DEFINITE NUMBER (PLURAL)
few bananas	*no* bananas
a few bananas	*all* bananas
several bananas	*both* bananas
some bananas	*one, two,* etc. bananas
lots of bananas	*their* bananas
many bananas	
any bananas	
more bananas	
most bananas	

USED WITH NONCOUNT NOUNS

AN INDEFINITE AMOUNT	A DEFINITE AMOUNT
little rice	*no* rice
	none of the rice
a little rice (a little of the rice)	*all* rice
	all of the rice
some rice (some of the rice)	*some of* the rice
much rice (much of the rice)	*much of* the rice
more rice (more of the rice)	*lots of* the rice
most rice (most of the rice)	*more of* the rice
	most of the rice

The **demonstratives**—*this, that, these, those*—point to a noun and indicate its distance, in either space or time, from the speaker or writer. *This* and *these* indicate that a noun is close to you in space or time. Use *this* with noncount nouns and singular count nouns; use *these* with plural count nouns.

NOT: *These* information from the library is very useful.
BUT: *This* information from the library is very useful.

NOT: *These* computer works just fine.
BUT: *This* computer works just fine.

That and *those* indicate that a noun is distant either in time or space. Use *that* with noncount nouns and singular count nouns; use *those* with plural count nouns.

NOT: *Those* soup that you made yesterday tasted spicy.
BUT: *That* soup that you made yesterday tasted spicy.

NOT: In *that* days, women were not sent to colleges and universities.
BUT: In *those* days, women were not sent to colleges and universities.

5   No determiner

Some nouns can be used without determiners of any kind. These include proper nouns (*John, Chicago*), noncountable nouns (*salt, water*), abstract nouns (*justice, grief*), and sometimes plural count nouns (*apples, students*). Here are some sentences containing nouns that have no determiner preceding them:

You should include raw *vegetables* in your diet.

Animals need *oxygen* to survive.

Children sometimes require a lot of attention.

Irina listens to *music* to relax.

Yusef likes to give *advice,* but he does not like to receive it.

Everyone wants *peace* and *prosperity* to prevail.

EXERCISE 20-1

Identify the nouns in the following phrases as S/C (singular count), P/C (plural count), NC (noncount), D (definite), I (indefinite), or O (no determiner).

1. Wild game roams the prairie.

2. Demetrius played in a wild soccer game.

3. Crackers taste best when fresh.

4. Is the candy sweet?

5. Do you have enough money to purchase furniture and jewelry?

EXERCISE 20-2

Identify the noun quantifiers and demonstratives in the following sentences by circling them. Then rewrite the sentences, changing the determiners.

1. Most of the people ate several hotdogs.

2. Some sand is in those shoes.

3. Either these people here know where to go or those people over there do.

4. Any student can recite both poems today.

5. Much rain fell before several students found their umbrellas.

20b Adjectives, Adverbs, and Qualifiers

An **adjective** is a word that modifies a noun or pronoun, as in "*big* dog." An **adverb** modifies a verb, as in "ran *quickly*." And **qualifiers** modify adjectives and adverbs, as in "*very* big dog." Most adjectives and adverbs have different forms, but some words can function as both. Use correct order when placing adjectives, adverbs, and qualifiers in a sentence.

1 Placement of single-word adjectives

Place the modifier for a noun as close to the noun as possible. Single-word adjectives are usually placed before the noun or after a linking verb. Note that adjectives do not show any change in form in modifying either a singular or a plural noun.

The *happy* dog ran into the house.   The dogs are *happy*.
The *tired* boy rested on the couch.   The boys were *tired*.

Native speakers of such languages as Spanish, Italian, Vietnamese, or others that place the adjective after the noun may tend to do the same in English. If so, you might also need to be careful not to inflect the adjective in number to agree with the noun, as in *cars blues;* revise this to *blue cars*.

2 Placement of noun modifiers

When two nouns appear together, the first noun is considered the modifier and the second noun is considered the word modified. The order of the words becomes important because a reversal of the order will result in a different meaning.

chicken broiler = a broiler to cook a chicken in
broiler chicken = a chicken to be cooked in a broiler

3 Placement of cumulative adjectives

Cumulative adjectives are groups of adjectives that are accumulated to form a whole group of words modifying the noun that follows them.

> He gave her *an old green crystal perfume* bottle.

When adjectives are accumulated in this way, they tend to fall into typical sequences in a normal English sentence. The listing below shows the typical order of sequence:

First Possessives precede numbers: my *first* date; Larleen's *sixteenth* birthday

Second Cardinal numbers precede ordinal numbers: my *first six* attempts

Third Following possessives and numbers come size, shape, age, and color in that order: *small, square, new, red* tiles

Fourth After these come, in order: nationality, religion: *German Lutheran; Iranian Moslem*

Fifth Following these are material modifiers (sometimes nouns used as adjectives): *wooden kitchen* furniture; *copper cooking* pans

EXAMPLE: *His last big old Japanese Zen steel* gong

Cumulative adjectives are not separated by commas. The use of three or more adjectives to modify a noun is fairly unusual.

4 Present and past participles as adjectives

Present participles and **past participles** are verbals used as adjectives. (See Section 8c.) Note how their meanings differ:

PRESENT PARTICIPLE	PAST PARTICIPLE
The teacher is *boring*.	The teacher is *bored*.
(The teacher causes other people to be bored.)	(The teacher experiences boredom.)

5 Placement of adverbs

Adverbs enjoy relative freedom of placement within a sentence. But **adverbs of frequency,** such as *always, never, often,* and *usually,* are placed after the verb *be* or before the main verb.

NOT: Moonlit nights are considered *usually* romantic.
BUT: Moonlit nights are *usually* considered romantic.

NOT: Our football team plays *usually* well.
BUT: Our football team *usually* plays well.

Note: These adverbs are placed differently with auxiliary verbs and are often found after the first in a group of auxiliaries.

Our games have *usually* been played at night.

Adverbs other than those of frequency can be placed relatively freely in the sentence.

Quickly he arose.
He *quickly* arose.
He arose *quickly*.

But you should avoid placing an adverb between the verb and its direct object.

NOT: The audience left *hurriedly* the concert hall.
BUT: The audience *hurriedly* left the concert hall.

6 Placement of qualifiers

A qualifier is usually placed before the word it modifies.

Sleepy children can be *very* cranky.

The bus will arrive *very* soon.

Limiting qualifiers, such as *almost, even, just, nearly, only,* and *simply,* must be placed immediately before the word they modify.

Only I ate cake and ice cream. (Denotes *who* ate)

I ate *only* cake and ice cream. (Denotes *what* was eaten)

EXERCISE 20-3

Determine the misplaced or incorrect modifiers in the following sentences and correct them.

1. The Chinese ancient temple was red and small.

2. The drive to the city usually is surprising.

3. Tom wore the shirt dress to the dance.

4. The trip to the prison was depressed.

5. Later we arrived, sad and discouraging, at the brick red schoolhouse.

20c Verb Forms

1 Auxiliary verbs and modals

Auxiliary verbs, or helping verbs (such as *be, have, do*), are used to form questions, express negations, show emphasis, and denote future time. (See Section 8b-2.) In addition, **modal auxiliary** verbs express conditions such as possibility, certainty, or obligation. The modal verbs include *can, could, may, might, must,* *will, shall, would, should,* and *ought.* A verb phrase may include both auxiliary and modal verbs.

Note also that many expressions of future time include *shall* or *will* when expressing future time as part of a future tense.

> They *will* meet at the bus station next week.
> *Shall* I see you tomorrow?

Only one modal is used with each main verb in standard English.

NOT:　She *might can* do it.
BUT:　She *might* do it.

NOT:　I *would can* guess where it went.
BUT:　I *can* guess where it went.

Use the base form of the main verb after all modals.

NOT:　She can *plays* soccer well.
BUT:　She can *play* soccer well.

NOT:　He might *attends* today.
BUT:　He might *attend* today.

Use *could, might,* and *would* with the base form of the main verb to express past time.

NOT:　He *can* play the guitar well last week.
BUT:　He *could* play the guitar well last week.

NOT:　He *will* sing it last year every evening.
BUT:　He *would* sing it last year every evening.

Use the base form of *have* or *be* when the modal is followed by a verb in the perfect or progressive form.

NOT: He *could* not *has* done it earlier.
BUT: He *could* not *have* done it earlier.

NOT: He *could* *is* doing it today.
BUT: He *could* *be* doing it today.

2 Using auxiliaries with perfect and progressive tenses

The **perfect tense** of a verb consists of *to have* plus the past participle (*-ed*) form of the verb. The form of *have* used determines the tense. (See Section 12b-1.)

has walked	present perfect tense
had walked	past perfect tense
will have walked	future perfect tense

(Review tense in Section 12b-1.) Remember to use the past *participle* of the verb instead of the past *tense* to express the perfect tenses. Be certain that the present tense form of *have* agrees with its subject in the present perfect tense.

NOT: He *have* written good papers.
BUT: He *has* written good papers.

The **progressive tense** of a verb consists of a form of the verb *be* (*am, are, is, was, were, be, has been, is being*) plus the present participle (*-ing*) form of the verb. Be certain that the present and past tense forms of *be* agree with their subjects.

is singing	present progressive tense
was singing	past progressive tense
will be singing	future progressive tense

Use the auxiliary verb *have* to form the perfect progressive tenses.

have/has been singing   have/had been singing

3   Verbs that do not form progressive tenses

Some verbs, as a general rule, are not used in the progressive tenses. Following are some of the types of verbs that do not form progressive tenses:

- Verbs of sense perceptions: *hear, see, smell, taste*

  EXCEPTION: *Feel* often appears as progressive: She is *feeling* good today.

- Linking verbs and verbs that indicate qualities or states of being: *appear, be, have, seem*

  EXCEPTIONS: When some of these express an active meaning, they may form progressives: He's *appearing* on stage tonight. She is *having* [i.e., giving birth to] a baby.

- Verbs of attitudes, emotions, and intellectual states: *imagine, intend, want, wish, hate, dislike, like, pity, behave, disagree, prefer, realize, suppose, understand*

  EXCEPTIONS: *think* and *wonder:* He is *thinking* about home. She is *wondering* about the test.

4   Forming the passive voice

The **passive voice** of a verb consists of a form of *be* followed by the past participle (*-ed*) form of the verb. (See Section 12b.)

> She *was appointed* to the committee.
> Anxiety *can be caused* by tension.
> The lamp *was removed* from the room.

Be certain to select the past participle verb form, not the base form or past tense form, to write the passive voice. Use special care in selecting irregular verbs: *is torn, was begun, is frozen.* Also be sure the auxiliary form of *be* agrees with the subject.

> A cloth *is* placed on the tables each evening.
> The cloths *are* placed there daily.

Note that **intransitive verbs** cannot be made passive. Only **transitive verbs,** which can have a direct object, can be made either active or passive. (See Section 12b-3.)

transitive verb   direct object
     ↓   ↓

The dog *ate* the candy. The candy *was eaten* quickly.

Consult either Section 12c or your dictionary for a discussion of common troublesome transitive and intransitive verbs.

5   Two-word verbs

Some verbs are regularly followed by a particle (an adverb or preposition) that changes or modifies the meaning of the verb; such verbs are called **two-word verbs.** Some commonly used two-word verbs follow (ellipsis indicates that the particle can be separated from the main verb by a direct object):

ask . . . out	hand on	run out of
break down	hand . . . out	shut . . . off
burn up	help . . . out	speak to
call . . . off	hooked on	speak up
call on	leave . . . out	stay up
call . . . up	look into	take . . . off
clean . . . up	look . . . over	take . . . out
come across	look . . . up	take . . . over
count on	make . . . up	talk . . . over
drop . . . off	pick . . . up	think . . . over
fill . . . up	point . . . out	throw . . . out
get along	put . . . away	try . . . on
get rid of	put . . . off	try . . . out
give . . . away	put . . . on	turn . . . on
give in	put . . . out	wake up
give . . . up	put . . . together	wear . . . out
go over	put up with	wear upon
grow up	quiet . . . down	
hand . . . in	run across	

Two-word verbs may be transitive or intransitive.

TRANSITIVE: ask for, call on, fill out
INTRANSITIVE: help out, catch on, give in

Transitive two-word verbs may be separable or inseparable. **Inseparable** two-word verbs are never separated by a direct object.

NOT: The teacher will probably not *call* Mary *on* today.
BUT: The teacher will probably not *call on* Mary today.

With **separable** two-word verbs, the direct object *can* separate the verb and the particle.

My cousin *gave* her old typewriter *away.*

In general, follow these rules:

1. Do not separate the verb and the particle of inseparable two-word verbs. Place the noun or pronoun object *after* the particle.

   I did not *hear about* the **accident.**

   We will *listen for* your **signal.**

2. A noun object of a separable two-word verb may be placed *between* the verb and the particle or *after* the particle.

   She *brought back* the **bicycle.**

   She *brought* the **bicycle** *back.*

3. A pronoun object of a separable two-word verb must be placed between the verb and the particle.

   NOT: We *gave away* **it.**
   BUT: We *gave* **it** *away.*

EXERCISE 20-4

Underline the incorrect verb forms in the following sentences and replace them with the correct verb forms.

1. I has sent the book to my sister.

2. She will disregards the message.

3. They was singing before the game started.

4. The cat could not has done it alone.

5. The meat is smelling spoiled.

6. I have trouble getting colds over.

7. There's a fire: put out it.

6   Gerunds and infinitives following verbs

Some verbs can be followed by **gerunds,** other by **infinitives,** and still others by either gerunds or infinitives. No rules exist to govern this usage; familiarization with verbs and memorization are the only keys. (Review gerunds and infinitives in Sections 8c-2 and 8c-3.)

VERB + GERUND	VERB + INFINITIVE
I *practice* **swimming.**	I *refuse* **to swim.**
mind	*admit*
appreciate	*mean*
miss	*agree*
avoid	*arrange*
postpone	*need*
come	*offer*
practice	*beg*
consider	*plan*

VERB + GERUND	VERB + INFINITIVE
prevent	*claim*
delay	*pretend*
deny	*decide*
recommend	*promise*
discuss	*deserve*
regret	*expect*
remember	*seem*
enjoy	*have*
resist	*hope*
fall	*wait*
risk	*intend*
finish	*want*
stop	*wish*
go	*manage*
suggest	
tolerate	
imagine	
keep	

VERB + GERUND OR INFINITIVE

I *like* **swimming.**
I *like* **to swim.**

begin	*like*
cannot bear	*love*
cannot stand	*prefer*
continue	*start*
hate	

Two-word verbs always take a gerund object rather than an infinitive object.

> **NOT:** I *cut down on* **to jog.**
> **BUT:** I *cut down on* **jogging.**

EXERCISE 20-5

Select the entry in each pairing that correctly (C) uses a gerund or an infinitive after the verb.

1a. I regret signing the letter.
 b. I regret to sign the letter.

2a. She plans attending the meeting.
 b. She plans to attend the meeting.

3a. He claims to feel ill.
 b. He claims feeling ill.

4a. I do not tolerate teasing very well.
 b. I do not tolerate to tease very well.

5a. It seems being true.
 b. It seems to be true.

7 Writing conditional sentences

Conditional sentences use main clauses and subordinate clauses introduced by *if, when/whenever,* or *unless.* They report two kinds of events: (1) *real* conditions that actually exist or existed or that might be possible in the future and (2) *unreal* conditions in the present, the past, or the future.

1. Verb tenses for real conditions in the present, past, or future

For reporting real conditions in the present and past, use the same tense in both clauses.

If I *walk* home, I *get* tired.
Whenever I *walked,* I *got* tired.

Use the present tense of the verb to state a condition that might be possible in the future. In the same sentence, use the future tense to state the result of that condition.

If I **get** a letter from her, I *shall go* to Boston.
When I **get** a letter from her, I *shall go* to Boston.

2. Verb tenses for unreal conditions

Use the past tense of the verb to state a condition that might not necessarily exist in the future. In the same sentence, use the past tense form of an auxiliary (*could, should, would, might*) to state an improbable result of the condition.

If she **received** the book, she *would* probably *read* it by tonight.
She **might read** the book by tonight if she *received* it.

Use the *were* form of the verb to state a wish in the present that might occur in the future. The object of the wish is expressed in a *that* clause, although the coordinating word *that* may be omitted. The auxiliary verbs *could* and *should* can be used to express the object of the wish.

I wish [that] I **were** somewhere else.
I wish [that] I **could be** somewhere else.

She wishes [that] she **were** on vacation now.
She wishes [that] she **could be** on vacation now.

Use the past perfect tense in the *that* clause to express a wish made in the present or the past for something that might have occurred in the past.

I wish [that] it **had been** you who sent me the book.
I wished [that] it **had begun** before we got there.

Use the base form of the verb in the *that* clause to state a recommendation, suggestion, or special request.

She **recommends** [that] you *stay* at home.

> She **suggests** [that] he *arrive* on time.
> She **requests** [that] you *be* prompt.

EXERCISE 20-6

Underline the incorrect verb forms in each of the following sentences and correct them.

1. I wish that I was on vacation this week.

2. When the ticket arrive in the mail, Jose will goes to the concert.

3. If she receives the money yesterday, she would have spent it all today.

4. The mayor requests that she votes for him.

5. The woman wish that it has been my brother who sends me the package yesterday.

20d Verbs in Sentences

1 Expletives

An **expletive** is a word such as *there, here,* or *it* that occupies the subject position in a sentence, often as the first word in a sentence. However, the expletive does not function as the sentence's subject; it refers to the subject, which is usually shifted to the middle of the sentence. The subject is printed in **boldface** in the following sentences, which begin with expletives:

> There is **one cookie** remaining.
> There are **many people** present.
> Here is the **best recipe** in the book.
> It is a **tale** told by an idiot.
> It may be a hard **way** to get started.

Although an expletive serves as an introductory word and does not serve as the subject of the sentence, it cannot be omitted from the sentence (as in many languages). Be certain, however, that the verb agrees with the *subject* rather than the expletive.

> **NOT:** There **is** four cups.
> **BUT:** There **are** four cups.

2 Word order in questions

Interrogative sentences ask a question: *Where is my book? Did you go there? You saw him?* When *who* or *what* functions as the subject of an interrogative sentence, the auxiliary verb *do* is not used and normal word order is followed.

> **Who** are you? **What** is the matter?
> **Who** went there? **What** went ahead of us?

When *who* or *what* functions as the object in an interrogative sentence, a form of the auxiliary verb *do* is used and the word order is inverted, with the object placed at the beginning of the sentence.

> **What did** the person choose? **What did** you ask?
> **Whom did** the person choose? **Whom did** you ask?

3 Verb tense in reported speech

When reporting someone else's words, writers may use either **direct quotation** or **reported speech** (indirect discourse). In direct quotation, the speaker's exact words are enclosed in quotation marks. In reported speech, the writer changes the speaker's verb tense.

> **DIRECT QUOTATION:** The professor said, "Let us read Shakespeare today."
> **REPORTED SPEECH:** The professor said that we would read Shakespeare today.

For "yes/no" questions, use *if* or *whether* in reported speech; for "or" questions, use *whether*.

DIRECT QUOTATION: **"yes/no" question**

I asked the professor, "Will we read Shakespeare?"

"or" question

I asked the professor, "Will we read Shakespeare or Ibsen?"

REPORTED SPEECH: **"yes/no" question**

I asked the professor *if* we would read Shakespeare.

"or" question

I asked the professor *whether* we would read Shakespeare or Ibsen.

Use the infinitive (*to* + base form) of the verb to report commands in reported speech.

DIRECT QUOTATION: The professor replied, "**Review** the other dramas first."

REPORTED SPEECH: The professor told us **to review** the other dramas first.

The present tense in a direct quotation changes to the past tense in reported speech. The auxiliary verbs *do* and *does,* if part of the quotation, also change to the past tense.

DIRECT QUOTATION: The assistant to the president said, "I **advise** Americans to maintain free trade in the Pacific area."

REPORTED SPEECH: The assistant to the president said that he **advised** Americans to maintain free trade in the Pacific area.

DIRECT QUOTATION: "I **do** not foresee a solution to the problem," said the assistant.

REPORTED SPEECH: The assistant told us [that] he **did** not foresee a solution to the problem.

(*That* may be omitted at the beginning of a clause containing reported speech.)

Change the present progressive tense of direct quotations to the past progressive tense in reported speech.

DIRECT QUOTATION: "I **am learning** to read critically," said Lola.
REPORTED SPEECH: Lola said she **was learning** to read critically.

Change the present tense of the modals *can, will,* and *may* in direct quotations to their past tense forms of *could, would,* and *might* in reported speech. Do not change other modals.

DIRECT QUOTATION: Our captain said, "We **can** do it."
  Our captain said, "We **will** do it."
  Our captain said, "We **may** do it."
  Our captain said, "We **shall** do it."

REPORTED SPEECH: Our captain said [that] we **could** do it.
  Our captain said [that] we **would** do it.
  Our captain said [that] we **might** do it.
  Our captain said [that] we **shall** do it.

Change the present perfect tense or past tense of direct quotations to past perfect tense in reported speech.

DIRECT QUOTATION: The server volunteered, "I **have carried** twenty full trays during the last hour."
  The server volunteered, "I **carried** twenty full trays during the last hour."

REPORTED SPEECH: The server volunteered that she **had carried** twenty full trays during the last hour.

EXERCISE 20-7

Cross out the incorrect verb forms or the unnecessary words in each of the following examples of reported speech and replace them with the correct forms or words. One set is correct.

1.a. Direct quotation: "Can I go now?" asked the student.

  b. Reported speech: The student asked can I go now.

2.a. Direct quotation: "We may have to ride the bus today," said Mara.

  b. Reported speech: Mara said that we might have to ride the bus today.

3.a. Direct quotation: "Wait for the whistle," said the coach.

  b. Reported speech: The coach said wait for the whistle.

4.a. Direct quotation: Juan said, "I have waited for you for three hours."

  b. Reported speech: Juan said that he waited for me for three hours.

5.a. Direct quotation: Shatonda replied, "I sing every day."

  b. Reported speech: Shatonda replied that she sings every day.

Part

V

CLEAR SENTENCES

21 Coordination, Subordination, and Parallelism

The structure, emphasis, and logic of any group of sentences greatly depend on how the group's independent statements and clauses are related to each other. The relationship established through **coordination** in **compound sentences** (see Section 9e-2) is one of balance between statements of equal weight and emphasis. **Complex sentences** (see Section 9e-3) are developed through **subordination** to set up closely linked logical relationships between statements—links in which one clause is dependent on another to complete its meaning. Many kinds of sentences are also written to establish an expressed or implied comparison between related statements or elements. To make sense, these need to be written in a carefully matched structure of **parallelism.**

21a Coordination

Use **coordination** in a balanced structure to link two independent clauses together with a coordinating conjunction to form a compound sentence.

Independent clauses that are joined in coordination are considered to be of approximately equal weight or importance. (See Sections 9c and 9e-2.) In effect, in such a sentence, two or more equally important statements are linked as if by a "plus" sign. The following example shows two independent clauses stated separately and then paired in coordination, joined by punctuation and a coordinating conjunction (shown in **boldface**):

SEPARATE: The football game ended at dusk. For three hours afterward all the local restaurants were crowded.

COORDINATED:	The football game ended at dusk, **and** for three hours afterward all the local restaurants were crowded.

1   Coordination with coordinating conjunctions

Words and phrases, as well as clauses, can be linked by using the basic **coordinating conjunctions** preceded by a comma to show specific balanced relationships between elements: *and* shows a simple addition (I jumped, *and* I gasped.); *or/nor* is used to show choice (You go *or* I go.); *but/yet* is used to show contrast (I am close, *yet* I'm not ready.). (See Section 8j-1.)

Two other coordinating conjunctions—*so* and *for* preceded by a comma—can link independent clauses. A causal relationship between the first clause and the second is shown with *for* (I must lie down, *for* I am sick at heart.); a resultant relationship between the first and second clauses is shown by *so* (I was sick at heart, *so* I lay down.).

2   Coordination with conjunctive adverbs

When preceded by semicolons to join independent clauses, **conjunctive adverbs** (see Section 8j-1) can establish significant balanced relationships between the clauses:

RELATIONSHIP	CONJUNCTIVE ADVERB	COORDINATED CLAUSES
ADDITION:	*also, besides, furthermore, moreover*	A used car can be reliable; furthermore, it's cheap.
CONTRAST:	*however, nevertheless, still, nonetheless*	You can check it carefully; still, it may be a lemon.
CAUSE/EFFECT:	*accordingly, consequently, thus, therefore, hence*	I asked my service garage to check that car; hence, my chances of avoiding problems should be good.

| **CHOICE:** | *otherwise* | It has to be clean; otherwise, I won't buy. |
| **TIME SEQUENCE:** | *then, subsequently, afterward* | I'll get an okay from my garage; then I'll buy the car. |

3 Overuse or misuse of coordination

While coordination can be used to create a number of interesting balanced relationships between independent clauses, some writers may get carried away with a repetitive accumulation of clauses glued together with the conjunctions *and* or *but* in a thoughtless manner. As you rewrite a paragraph, think about the kinds of relationships and links you want.

> **MISUSED:** We finally located a big car lot and we looked around for quite a while, but I didn't see much of interest, and it seemed I didn't know a good-looking car from a lemon. My friend and I kicked about forty tires and we opened lots of doors, and then a salesperson started talking fast about convertibles, but we didn't trust anything we saw, so we left.
>
> **REVISED:** We finally located a big car lot; afterward we looked around for quite a while. I didn't see much of interest; furthermore, I didn't seem to know a good-looking car from a lemon. My friend and I kicked about forty tires, and we opened lots of doors. A salesperson started talking fast about convertibles; consequently, we really didn't trust anything we saw. We left.

21b Subordination

Use **subordination** to form sentences with two or more closely linked statements involving a dependent clause.

Subordination occurs when a dependent clause (one that cannot stand alone) is intimately linked with an independent clause using a subordinating conjunction or a relative pronoun. (See Section 9-d.) In the following sentence, the dependent clause appears in *italics* and the subordinating conjunction in **boldface.**

SUBORDINATED: **Because** *the football game ended at dusk,* all the local restaurants were crowded for three hours.

1 Subordination with adjective clauses

An **adjective clause** is a group of words with a subject and a predicate that modifies a noun or a pronoun. Usually, an adjective clause begins with a relative pronoun. Notice how the choppy sentences in the following examples can be combined through the use of adjective clauses:

SEPARATE: The birthplace of Jean Rhys is Dominica. Dominica is one of the Windward Islands.

COMBINED: The birthplace of Jean Rhys is Dominica, which is one of the Windward Islands.

SEPARATE: William W. Warner described blue crabs as "beautiful swimmers." He wrote a study of the Chesapeake Bay. The book won a Pulitzer Prize.

COMBINED: William W. Warner, whose study of the Chesapeake Bay won a Pulitzer Prize, described blue crabs as "beautiful swimmers."

SEPARATE: Holmes had been seated for some hours in silence with his long, thin back curved over a chemical vessel. In this vessel he was brewing a particularly malodorous product.

COMBINED: Holmes had been seated for some hours in silence with his long, thin back curved over a chemical vessel in which he was brewing a particularly malodorous product.

Sir Arthur Conan Doyle
"The Adventure of the Dancing Men"

2 Subordination with adverb clauses

An **adverb clause** is a group of words with a subject and a predicate that functions as an adverb in a sentence. Usually, an adverb clause begins with a subordinating conjunction (such as *because, after,* or *so that*) that shows the relation of the adverb clause to the word or words it modifies. Notice how the choppy sentences in the following examples can be combined through the use of adverb clauses:

SEPARATE: He was never in a battle. Nevertheless, he wrote movingly about war.

COMBINED: Although he was never in a battle, he wrote movingly about war.

SEPARATE: My wife and I both work at home. Quintana therefore has never had any confusion about how we make our living.

COMBINED: Because my wife and I both work at home, Quintana has never had any confusion about how we make our living.

John Gregory Dunne
"Quintana"

3 Subordination with noun clauses

Use a **noun clause** as a noun in a sentence, functioning as a subject, an object, or a subject complement.

Usually, a noun clause begins with one of the following subordinating words: *that, how, what, whatever, whenever, wherever, whichever, who, whoever, whose, why.*

SEPARATE: What he said is what he knows. It would fit in a thimble!

COMBINED: **What he knows** would fit in a thimble! (*noun clause as subject*)

SEPARATE: There is a reason why the United States refused to join the League of Nations. This book explains the reason.

COMBINED: The book explains **why the United States refused to join the League of Nations.** (*direct object*)

Revising for Sentence Style
ON A WORD PROCESSOR

You can use the search function to find coordinating conjunctions, especially *and,* to see whether you have overused or misused coordination. You can use various features of your word-processing program to delete coordinating conjunctions, add subordinating words, move clauses, change punctuation, and experiment with various ways to improve the flow and variety of your sentences. These alterations are much easier and faster to manage on a word processor than on a typewriter.

EXERCISE 21-1

Use adjective clauses, adverb clauses, and noun clauses to form one sentence from each of the following groups of sentences.

1. All addictions can be considered neurotic. Addictions are departures from usual, healthy impulses. Healthy impulses can also be exaggerated.

2. A walk in the woods can reveal many ecosystems of great complexity. Most of these ecosystems have been heavily affected by human population.

3. Your feelings are not facts. Your feelings really count. Your feelings can count as a mirror of the way you are thinking.

4. I went to visit their new house. It was nice. It is built on a hill.

5. She must make three important decisions by the end of the month. The three are how to pay the bills, where to find a new job, and where to seek medical attention.

21c Parallelism

Use the same grammatical form for elements that are part of a series or a compound construction.

Sentence elements that have the same grammatical structure are said to be *parallel*.

The speech was **concise, witty,** and **effective.**
Today's "supermom" is both **a mother** and **an executive.**
He tried to be honest **with himself** as well as **with others.**

When elements that are part of a series or a compound construction do not have the same form, a sentence is said to have **faulty parallelism.**

Repeat articles, prepositions, and the word *to* before the infinitive to make the meaning of a sentence clear.

The audience applauded the composer and lyricist.

The preceding sentence is clear if the composer and the lyricist are the same person. It is misleading if they are not the same person. Repeat the article *the* to indicate two people.

The audience applauded **the** composer and **the** lyricist.

UNCLEAR: She was a prominent critic and patron of young poets.
CLEAR: She was **a** prominent critic and **a** patron of young poets.

UNCLEAR:	She quickly learned to supervise the maid and cook.
CLEAR:	She quickly learned to supervise **the** maid and **the** cook.
CLEAR:	She quickly learned **to** supervise the maid and **to** cook.
UNCLEAR:	His father had taught him to shoot and ride a horse.
CLEAR:	His father had taught him **to** shoot and **to** ride a horse.

Place elements joined by a coordinating conjunction in the same grammatical form. Balance a noun with a noun, an adjective with an adjective, a prepositional phrase with a prepositional phrase, and so on.

NOT PARALLEL: The scientific community in general regarded him

      adjective   adjective   noun
        ↓   ↓   ↓

as **outspoken, eccentric,** and a **rebel.**

PARALLEL: The scientific community in general regarded him

      adjective   adjective   adjective
        ↓   ↓   ↓

as **outspoken, eccentric,** and **rebellious.**

NOT PARALLEL: In *Searching for Caleb,* the protagonist is a

    noun   noun   clause
     ↓   ↓   ↓

wife, a **mother,** and **she tells fortunes.**

PARALLEL: In *Searching for Caleb,* the protagonist is a

    noun   noun   noun
     ↓   ↓   ↓

wife, a **mother,** and a **fortune-teller.**

                             adjective
                              ↓

NOT PARALLEL: Reviewers praised the play for its **realistic**

    noun
     ↓

portrayal of a sensitive young woman and

noun clause
↓

because it gave a penetrating depiction of a family.

adjective
↓

PARALLEL: Reviewers praised the play for its **realistic**

noun
↓

portrayal of a sensitive young woman and

adjective   noun
↓   ↓

its **penetrating depiction** of family life.

prepositional phrase
↓

NOT PARALLEL: A hobbit is a creature **with a hearty appetite** and

adjective clause
↓

who loves home.

verb
↓

PARALLEL: A hobbit is a creature who **has** a hearty appetite

verb
↓

and **loves** home.

Place elements joined by correlative conjunctions in parallel form.

NOT PARALLEL: He was not only **her husband** but also **she considered him her friend.**

PARALLEL: He was not only **her husband** but also **her friend.**

NOT PARALLEL: Knute Rockne would be either **a science teacher** or **someone who coached football.**

PARALLEL:	Knute Rockne would be either **a science teacher** or **a football coach.**
NOT PARALLEL:	After his vision, Scrooge becomes not only **a generous man** but also **happy.**
PARALLEL:	After his vision, Scrooge becomes not only **a generous man** but also **a happy one.**

Revising for Parallelism
ON A WORD PROCESSOR

You can use your word processor to identify and revise problems with parallelism. With the search function, locate coordinating and correlative conjunctions, and check the parallelism in sentences that contain these words. If you discover problems, you can delete the nonparallel parts and replace them with parallel ones. You can also move words and phrases to correct misplacements with correlative conjunctions.

Take care with the placement of correlative conjunctions.

| NOT PARALLEL: | Solar energy is **both** used to heat houses **and** to run small appliances. |

In the preceding sentence, the first part of the correlative conjunction (*both*) is followed by a verb, but the second part (*and*) is followed by an infinitive. The problem can be corrected by moving *both* to a later position in the sentence so that it, too, is followed by an infinitive.

| PARALLEL: | Solar energy is used **both** to heat houses **and** to run small appliances. |

NOT PARALLEL:	She would **either** run as the presidential candidate **or** the vice presidential candidate.
PARALLEL:	She would run as **either** the presidential candidate **or** the vice presidential candidate.
NOT PARALLEL:	He **not only** wanted money **but also** fame.
PARALLEL:	He wanted **not only** money **but also** fame.

EXERCISE 21-2

Revise each of the following sentences to eliminate the faulty parallelism.

1. For hobbies she enjoys collecting stamps and to go to the movies.

2. Not only did we have to pay the admission fee but also stand in line.

3. He was interested only in sports: basketball, football, and running in races.

4. We agreed neither to go to lunch nor to the movies.

5. He really is a person with concern for others and who loves people.

---

22   Conciseness

Choose words that express your thoughts precisely and concisely and avoid padding your writing with extra words.

22a Wordiness and Repetition

1 Avoiding superfluous words

One way to achieve conciseness is to eliminate wordy expressions. Notice how each of the following phrases can be changed to a single-word equivalent.

WORDY	CONCISE
at all times when	whenever
at that point in time	then
at this point in time	now
because of the fact that	because
be of the opinion that	think
bring to a conclusion	conclude
by means of	by
due to the fact that	because
during the time that	while
have a conference	confer
in the event that	if
in spite of the fact that	although
make reference	refer
on a great many occasions	often
prior to this time	before
until such time as	until

You can also make your writing more concise by deleting superfluous words, using exact words, and reducing larger elements to smaller elements. Notice how the following sentence is improved when the author uses these revision strategies:

WORDY: In the month of December in the year 1991, those who were flying in space on board the spaceship that was named *Endeavor* made an attempt to catch hold of and perform a repair job on a satellite that had been disabled.

CONCISE: In December 1991, astronauts aboard the spaceship *Endeavor* attempted to grab and repair a disabled satellite.

The words *the month of* and *in the year* add nothing to the meaning of the sentence; they simply fill up space and can be deleted. The noun phrase *those who were flying in space* can be replaced by one exact noun—*astronauts*. The words *that was named* are also deadwood. The phrase *made an attempt* can be reduced to the more direct *attempted, catch hold of* to *grab,* and *perform a repair job on* to *repair*. The clause *that had been disabled* can be reduced to the single word *disabled*.

> **WORDY:** A man named Allan Dwan, who was a pioneer in the field of filmmaking, began his career as a director in the year 1910.
>
> **CONCISE:** Allan Dwan, a pioneer filmmaker, began directing in 1910.
>
> **WORDY:** The film that is called *The Birth of a Nation* and that was made by D. W. Griffith has caused a lot of controversy among people.
>
> **CONCISE:** D. W. Griffith's film *The Birth of a Nation* is highly controversial.

Avoid the wordiness that comes from overuse of prepositional phrases, the weak verb *be,* and relative pronouns.

> **WORDY:** The book examines the twentieth century **in terms of** its wars, depressions, and social changes.
>
> **CONCISE:** The book examines the twentieth century, its wars, depressions, and social changes.
>
> **WORDY:** The car **that** was parked on the street, **close to** the curb is the **kind of** car **that** I have always wanted to own.
>
> **CONCISE:** I have always wanted a car like the one parked at the curb.

2   Avoiding expletives

Try to avoid the constructions *it is, it was, there is,* and *there was*. Like the passive voice, these constructions are sometimes useful and appropriate, but often they are an unnecessarily wordy way of introducing an idea. Notice how the following sentences are improved by eliminating the unnecessary constructions:

WORDY: It is known that there is a need for security in children.
CONCISE: Children need security.

WORDY: It is a fact that the painting is a forgery.
CONCISE: The painting is a forgery.

WORDY: There is a need among modern people to gain an understanding of the risks of modern technology.
CONCISE: We need to understand the risks of modern technology.

3 Avoiding redundancy

Another cause of wordiness is redundant elements, words or phrases that unnecessarily repeat the idea expressed by the word to which they are attached. For example, the phrase *to the ear* is redundant in the expression *audible to the ear* because *audible* itself means "able to be perceived by the ear." Here is a list of some other common expressions that contain redundant elements:

REDUNDANT	CONCISE
and etc.	etc.
bibliography of books	bibliography
mandatory requirements	requirements
refer back	refer
tall in height	tall
collaborate together	collaborate
visible to the eye	visible
repeat again	repeat
advance forward	advance
negative complaints	complaints
humorous comedy	comedy
close proximity	proximity
expensive in price	expensive
past history	history
continue to remain	remain
component parts	components
free gift	gift

NOT: The plot of Le Carré's **fictional novel** *The Little Drummer Girl* involves the **emotionally passionate** claims of the Israelis and the Palestinians.

BUT: The plot of Le Carré's **novel** *The Little Drummer Girl* involves the **passionate** claims of the Israelis and the Palestinians.

NOT: Copies of the **biography of his life** quickly **disappeared from sight** on the shelves, although the book was **large in size** and **heavy in weight.**

BUT: Copies of the **biography** quickly **disappeared** from the shelves, although the book was **large** and **heavy.**

Repetition has an important place in writing. It can be used effectively to emphasize a point or to complete a parallel structure. However, needless or excessive repetition weakens your writing. You can eliminate it by deleting the repeated words or by substituting synonyms or pronouns for them.

NOT: Lady **Macbeth** urges **Macbeth** to murder the **king** so that **Macbeth** can become **king.**

BUT: Lady **Macbeth** urges **her husband** to murder the **king** so that **he** can gain **the crown.**

NOT: After deciding to film the movie in a **shopping mall,** they examined thirty **shopping malls** until they found the right **shopping mall.**

BUT: After deciding to film the movie in a **shopping mall,** they examined thirty **malls** until they found the right **one.**

22b Flowery Language

Wherever possible, use simple and direct words and phrases instead of showy and pretentious ones.

FLOWERY: Travelers on the road of life cannot help looking back and considering the possibility of whether any companion on this lonely journey will remember them after they have passed from this vale of tears.

DIRECT: People cannot help wondering whether anyone will remember them after they die.

FLOWERY: Even a person who passes his daily hours by contemplating the strange little tricks played on unsuspecting victims by cruel and relentless fate receives a jolt that shakes him to the depths of his being when, at the Huntington Library, he sets his eyes upon the pass that Lincoln inscribed in his own hand to allow his trusted bodyguard to be absent from his side on that fateful night of April 14, 1865.

DIRECT: Even people who appreciate the ironies of life receive a jolt when, at the Huntington Library, they see the pass that Lincoln wrote for his bodyguard to have the night off on April 14, 1865.

FLOWERY: The streets of this fair city were graced on this day of May 19, 1984, by the arrival of Hank Morris, an artist of more than well-deserved distinction.

DIRECT: The distinguished artist Hank Morris arrived in town on May 19, 1984.

22c   Directness of Assertion

In general, try to construct your sentences so that your ideas are expressed as forcefully and directly as possible. You can achieve force and directness by using action verbs and by writing in the active voice.

1   Action verbs

Action verbs give power and precision to your writing, whereas the overuse of the verb *be* weakens your writing. Note how the sentences in the following examples are strengthened when the verb *be* is replaced with an action verb:

| WEAK: | Her face **was** a wall of brown fire. |
| STRONG: | Her face **flashed** a wall of brown fire. |

James Alan McPherson
"The Story of a Scar"

| WEAK: | Everywhere, in the bathroom too, there were prints of Roman ruins that **were** brown with age. |
| STRONG: | Everywhere, in the bathroom too, there were prints of Roman ruins **freckled** brown with age. |

Truman Capote
Breakfast at Tiffany's

| WEAK: | Their feet **were** no longer on firm sand but **were** on slippery slime and painful barnacled rock. |
| STRONG: | Their feet **lost** the firm sand and **slipped** on slime, **trod** painfully on barnacled rock. |

Michael Innes
The Man from the Sea

2 The active voice

The **active voice** is often more direct and forceful than the passive voice. In the passive, which always involves some form of the verb *to be* plus a past participle, the subject is acted upon instead of doing the acting. (See Section 8b.) Notice the difference between the active and passive voices:

ACTIVE:	Zeus **overthrew** Kronos, his father.
PASSIVE:	Kronos **was overthrown** by Zeus, his son.
ACTIVE:	At the Rubicon, Caesar **made** a decision.
PASSIVE:	At the Rubicon, a decision **was made** by Caesar.

As you can see, it takes more words to express an idea with a passive verb—unless you leave out the performer of the action. Thus a passive sentence like this one,

A decision on the matter **has been made** by the court,

takes longer to read and process than the active version,

The court **has decided** the matter.

Sometimes, however, the passive voice can be the best way to convey information, especially when you want to stress the action or the receiver of the action.

The President **was elected** by a comfortable majority

The schools **were consolidated** in 1953.

EXERCISE 22-1

Review each of the following sentences to eliminate wordiness, needless repetition, or flowery language.

1. In this modern world of ours in which we find ourselves, no living and breathing human being can avoid the ravages of technological advances.

2. Studies that have been made by environmentalists decry the results of cutting the Amazon forests.

3. We will have our meetings on as many occasions as required.

4. We were beyond the announced starting time due to the fact that it snowed this evening.

5. The music was audible to the ear although the stage was barely visible to the eye.

> ### *Revising for Directness*
> ### ON A WORD PROCESSOR
>
> You can use the search function to locate forms of the *to be* verb (*am, is, are, was, were, been*) and then determine whether you can replace them with stronger verbs or whether you want to recast passive sentences into active voice. Since many word-processing programs allow multi-word searches, you can also search for expletive constructions (*it is, it was, there is, there were*) to see how many you have used and to decide whether they are useful and appropriate.
>
> Grammar checkers will flag some common redundancies, such as *true fact,* and some wordy expressions, such as *in order that.* They will also alert you to passive constructions. But their usefulness is limited in helping you to make your writing more active and direct.

23   Variety and Emphasis

A **sentence** is a group of words that contains a subject and predicate and functions as an independent clause. Writing correctly is a mechanical act of applying rules of grammar, but writing *effectively* involves more. It involves the choices you make in forming sentences by combining the various types of clauses and phrases with directness of assertion and devices of emphasis. To make a strong impression on the reader, you need to use your ear as much as your eye; that is, you need to listen to your sentences as well as to write them. Writing **effective sentences** helps you to achieve a distinctive writing **style.**

23a Variety of Sentence Structure

As a writer, you have a responsibility to hold your reader's interest. Besides, if you don't get and hold interest, you have little chance of achieving your writing goal. One way to hold interest is to vary your sentence structure. Just as the speaker who talks in a monotone will quickly lose the listener's attention, the writer who uses only one sentence structure will soon lose the reader's attention.

The following passage has been rewritten in a monotonous style. Notice that most of the sentences are short and choppy and that all begin with the word *you:*

> You see things vacationing on a motorcycle in a way that is completely different from any other. You are always in a compartment in a car. You are used to it. You don't realize that through that car window everything you see is just more TV. You are a passive observer. You are bored by everything moving by you in a frame.
>
> You lose the frame on a cycle. You are completely in contact with it all. You are *in* the scene. You are not just watching it anymore. You are overwhelmed by the sense of presence. You know that the concrete whizzing by five inches below your foot is the real thing. You know it is the same stuff you walk on. You see it is right there. You can't focus on it because it is so blurred. You can, however, put your foot down and touch it anytime. You are always immediately conscious of the whole thing. You are conscious of the whole experience.

Consider how the passage is improved by varying the sentence structure.

You see things vacationing on a motorcycle in a way that is completely different from any other. In a car you're always in a compartment, and because you're used to it you don't realize that everything you see is just more TV. You're a passive observer and it is all moving by you boringly in a frame.

On a cycle the frame is gone. You're completely in contact with it all. You're *in* the scene, not just watching it anymore, and the sense of presence is overwhelming. That concrete whizzing by five inches below your foot is the real thing, the same stuff you walk on; it's right there, so blurred you can't focus on it, yet you can put your foot down and touch it anytime, and the whole thing, the whole experience, is never removed from immediate consciousness.

Robert M. Pirsig
Zen and the Art of Motorcycle Maintenance

1   Variety in sentence length

Do not be afraid to make your sentences long enough and complex enough to express complex ideas. Using several short sentences to state what amounts to one complete thought causes a choppy and disjointed effect. Such writing gives the reader no idea what you consider important and what you consider relevant but less important. For example, read the following paragraph:

Francis opened the trunk lid. An odor filled the attic air. It was the odor of lost time. The odor was a cloying reek of imprisoned flowers. It unsettled the dust. It fluttered the window shades.

Now read how the novelist William Kennedy combined the ideas in these short, choppy sentences into a single sentence:

When Francis opened the trunk lid the odor of lost time filled the attic air, a cloying reek of imprisoned flowers that unsettled the dust and fluttered the window shades.

William Kennedy
Ironweed

Notice that the ideas in the second and third sentences of the paragraph form the main clause of Kennedy's sentence (*the odor of lost time filled the attic air*), whereas the ideas in the other sentences are expressed as subordinate clauses and appositives. Thus the idea of the odor's filling the air is given the most importance, and the other ideas are given less emphasis.

Many professional writers use short, clipped sentences to create a sense of urgency or suspense in narrative writing. In most of the writing you will do for school or other purposes, however, you will often need to use a mixture of both shorter and longer, more complex sentences to express your ideas. As you write and as you revise your earlier drafts, consider whether two or more short sentences might be more effective if they were combined into one. Some of the more common ways to combine sentences are by the use of appositives; adjective and adverb clauses; and prepositional, verbal, and absolute phrases.

2 Appositives for variety

An **appositive** is a word or group of words that defines or renames the noun that precedes it. Notice how the choppy sentences in the following examples can be combined through the use of appositives:

SEPARATE:	The ailanthus was brought to America by a distinguished Philadelphia importer. His name was William Hamilton.
COMBINED:	The ailanthus was brought to America by a distinguished Philadelphia importer, William Hamilton.
SEPARATE:	The ailanthus grows in the most meager of environments. Its name means "the tree of heaven."
COMBINED:	The ailanthus, "the tree of heaven," grows in the most meager of environments.
SEPARATE:	Beside the river was a grove of tall, naked cottonwoods so large that they seemed to belong to a bygone age. These cottonwoods were trees of great antiquity and enormous size.

COMBINED:	Beside the river was a grove of tall, naked cotton-woods—trees of great antiquity and enormous size—so large that they seemed to belong to a bygone age.

Willa Cather
Death Comes for the Archbishop

3   Adjective clauses for variety and emphasis

An **adjective clause** modifying a noun or a pronoun usually begins with a relative pronoun such as *who, whose, whom, that,* or *which*. Sentences can be smoothly combined through the use of adjective clauses. In the following examples, **boldface** clauses made from short statements are linked to key concepts in combined complex sentences.

SEPARATE:	Charlie Parker was known as Bird. He played for a while with the Billy Eckstine band.
COMBINED:	*Charlie Parker,* **who was known as Bird,** played for a while with the Billy Eckstine band.
SEPARATE:	Jazz critics have extolled John Coltrane. His penetrating, raspy sound has been imitated by many other players.
COMBINED:	Jazz critics have extolled *John Coltrane,* **whose penetrating, raspy sound has been imitated by many other players.**
SEPARATE:	Jazz began as an American art form. It is being internationalized by players such as the Argentinian Gato Barbieri.
COMBINED:	Jazz, **which began as an American art form,** is being internationalized by players such as the Argentinian Gato Barbieri.

4   Adverb clauses to subordinate ideas

An **adverb clause,** a clause that functions as an adverb in a sentence, usually begins with a subordinating conjunction (such as *because, after,* or *so that*). Short statements or sentences can be combined through the use of adverb clauses. In the following examples, **boldface** clauses made from short statements are linked to key words in new complex sentences:

SEPARATE:	Is the Golden Gate Bridge a long one? The Verrazano Bridge is quite long.
COMBINED:	Is the Golden Gate Bridge as *long* **as the Verrazano Bridge is?** (*modifies the adjective* long)
SEPARATE:	She speaks very persuasively. She does better than I.
COMBINED:	She speaks *more persuasively* **than I do.** (*modifies the comparative adverb* more persuasively)

Sometimes an adverb clause is elliptical, or incomplete, with the verb omitted but understood.

Is the Golden Gate Bridge as long **as the Verrazano Bridge** (is)?
She speaks more persuasively **than I** (speak).

5 Prepositional phrases for modification

A **prepositional phrase** consists of a preposition, a noun or pronoun called the object of the preposition, and all the words modifying this object. Notice how the choppy sentences in the following examples can be combined through the use of prepositional phrases:

SEPARATE:	Jack London died at the age of forty. He had become an extremely popular writer.
COMBINED:	Before his death at the age of forty, Jack London had become an extremely popular writer.
SEPARATE:	She had a genius for painting. She also had a talent for writing.
COMBINED:	In addition to her genius for painting, she had a talent for writing.

SEPARATE: His Royal Highness Prince Philippe gave me an audience. He was prince of Araucania and Patagonia. The audience was on a drizzling November afternoon. It was at his public relations firm. The firm was on the Faubourg Poissonière.

COMBINED: On a drizzling November afternoon, His Royal Highness Prince Philippe of Araucania and Patagonia gave me an audience at his public relations firm on the Faubourg Poissonière.

Bruce Chatwin
In Patagonia

6 Participial phrases for combining ideas

A **participial phrase** consists of a participle and all its modifiers and complements. Notice how the choppy sentences in the following examples can be combined through the use of participial phrases:

SEPARATE: Washington resigned as general. He then returned to his plantation.

COMBINED: Having resigned as general, Washington returned to his plantation.

SEPARATE: The producers planned a two-part miniseries. This miniseries would tell the story of the Native American experience from the Native American point of view.

COMBINED: The producers planned a two-part miniseries telling the story of the Native American experience from the Native American point of view.

OR: The two-part miniseries planned by the producers would tell the story of the Native American experience from the Native American point of view.

SEPARATE: We are given a thimbleful of facts. We rush to make generalizations as large as a tub.

COMBINED: Given a thimbleful of facts, we rush to make generalizations as large as a tub.

Gordon W. Allport

> # *Revising for Sentence Variety*
> ## ON A WORD PROCESSOR
>
> You can use the cut and paste functions to shift phrases and clauses and to combine sentences. Look for a series of short sentences to combine through coordination or subordination. You can then use various word-processing functions to delete repeated words, insert subordinating conjunctions, rewrite phrases, and adjust punctuation right on screen—without having to retype the entire paper. Be sure to save your revisions frequently.

7 Absolute phrases for combining ideas

An **absolute phrase** is a group of words with a subject and a nonfinite verb (a verb form that cannot function as a sentence verb). When the verb is a form of *be,* it is sometimes omitted but understood. Notice how the choppy sentences in the following examples can be combined through the use of absolute phrases:

SEPARATE:	The war was over. The nation turned its attention to reconstruction of the Union.
COMBINED:	The war being over, the nation turned its attention to reconstruction of the Union.
OR:	The war over, the nation turned its attention to reconstruction of the Union.
SEPARATE:	The plane finally came to a stop. The passengers were breathing sighs of relief.
COMBINED:	The plane finally came to a stop, the passengers breathing sighs of relief.
SEPARATE:	Breakfast had been eaten. The slim camp outfit had been lashed to the sled. The men turned their backs on the cheery fire and launched out into the darkness.

COMBINED: Breakfast eaten and the slim camp outfit lashed to the sled, the men turned their backs on the cheery fire and launched out into the darkness.

Jack London
White Fang

EXERCISE 23-1

Use prepositional phrases, participial phrases, or absolute phrases to form one sentence from each of the following groups of sentences.

1. The lawyer rose to her feet. Her face was smiling. Her eyes sparkled. She shook hands with the nervous client.

2. The candidates for the mayor's office appeared on television. Both are male. Both are wealthy. Both are young. Both failed to impress most of the viewers.

3. We walked through the field. It was waist-high with wheat. It felt like we were wading in water.

4. The historical building is located north of town. It is beside the highway. A creek flows on one side of it. Pine trees grow on the other side.

5. Lots of people study nursing these days. A shortage of nurses no longer exists. There are both male and female nurses.

EXERCISE 23-2

Use appositives, adjective clauses, or adverb clauses to form one sentence from each of the following groups of sentences.

1. The student senate will consider three issues this afternoon. The three are recycling paper, the alcohol policy on campus, and election campaigns.

2. The British medieval poet's name is Chaucer. He wrote *The Canterbury Tales*. It is a collection of stories and some poems.

3. Your feelings are not facts. Your feelings really count. Your feelings can count as a mirror of the way you are thinking.

4. Some drugs are used to treat hypertension. Hypertension means high blood pressure. The drugs lower amine chemical levels in the brain. These drugs cause side effects for some people.

5. All addictions can be considered neurotic. Addictions are departures from usual, healthy impulses. Healthy impulses can also be exaggerated.

6. Perfectionists are very hard to live with. Perfectionists cannot accept flaws. Most things they see are flawed. Everything, then, is unacceptable, even personal relationships.

7. Thick blue smoke from a car's exhaust pipe means the engine is burning oil. The engine probably needs an overhaul. An overhaul is expensive.

23b Emphasizing Important Elements

Construct your sentences to emphasize the important elements. You can achieve emphasis through careful choice of words, proper subordination, or any one of the following methods.

1. Achieve emphasis by placing important elements at the beginning or at the end of a sentence, particularly at the end.

   UNEMPHATIC: It is not known why more boys than girls are autistic.

   EMPHATIC: Why more boys than girls are autistic is unknown.

   UNEMPHATIC: The trip was not as bad as, but worse than, I feared it would be.

   EMPHATIC: The trip was not as bad as I feared it would be—it was worse.

2. Achieve emphasis by changing loose sentences into periodic sentences. In a loose sentence, the main clause comes first; modifying phrases, dependent clauses, and other amplification follow the main clause.

   Jane Eyre would not declare her love for Mr. Rochester, although the fortune-teller pressed her for the information when they were alone together on that dark and mysterious night.

   In a periodic sentence, the main clause comes last.

   Although the fortune-teller pressed her for the information when they were alone together on that dark and mysterious night, Jane Eyre would not declare her love for Mr. Rochester.

   Periodic sentences are less commonly used than loose sentences and therefore are more emphatic. They give emphasis to the idea in the main clause by saving this idea for last.

LOOSE: The fortune-teller was really Mr. Rochester, although she claimed to be a gypsy from a nearby camp who had come simply to tell the ladies' futures.

PERIODIC: Although she claimed to be a gypsy from a nearby camp who had come simply to tell the ladies' futures, the fortune-teller was really Mr. Rochester.

LOOSE: It's easy to choose between love and duty if you are willing to forget that there is an element of duty in love and of love in duty.

PERIODIC: If you are willing to forget that there is an element of duty in love and of love in duty, then it's easy to choose between the two.

Jean Giraudoux

LOOSE: Emancipation will be a proclamation but not a fact until justice is blind to color, until education is unaware of race, until opportunity is unconcerned with the color of men's skins.

PERIODIC: Until justice is blind to color, until education is unaware of race, until opportunity is unconcerned with the color of men's skins, emancipation will be a proclamation but not a fact.

Lyndon B. Johnson

3. Achieve emphasis by writing balanced sentences. A balanced sentence presents ideas of equal weight in the same grammatical form, thus emphasizing similarity or disparity between the ideas. (See parallelism, Section 21c.)

UNBALANCED: Generally the theories we believe we call facts, and the facts that we disbelieve are known as theories.

BALANCED: Generally, the theories we believe we call facts, and the facts we disbelieve we call theories.

Felix Cohen

UNBALANCED: Money—in its absence we are coarse; when it is present we tend to be vulgar.

BALANCED: Money—in its absence we are coarse; in its presence we are vulgar.

Mignon McLaughlin

4. Achieve emphasis by inverting normal word order. In most English sentences, the usual word order is subject-verb-complement. Changing this order makes a sentence stand out.

UNEMPHATIC: He gave his property to the poor.

EMPHATIC: His property he gave to the poor.

UNEMPHATIC: Indiana Jones walked into the Temple of Doom.

EMPHATIC: Into the Temple of Doom walked Indiana Jones.

UNEMPHATIC: Long hours of hard work lie behind every successful endeavor.

EMPHATIC: Behind every successful endeavor lie long hours of hard work.

UNEMPHATIC: The lens, which helps to focus the image, is in the front of the eye.

EMPHATIC: In the front of the eye is the lens, which helps to focus the image.

Revising for Emphasis
ON A WORD PROCESSOR

You can use the cut and paste functions to move sentence parts and rearrange clauses and phrases. The word processor lets you experiment with sentence order. Begin by saving the original; then try several of the methods for achieving emphasis described in this chapter. With the delete and insert capabilities, you can easily make needed changes in punctuation and capitalization. If you don't like the revisions, you can always return to the saved copy.

EXERCISE 23-3

Revise each of the following sentences to make it more forceful or to emphasize important elements. Where appropriate, change the verb *be* to an action verb, change the passive voice to the active voice, place important words at the beginning or at the end of the sentence, turn a loose sentence into a periodic sentence, turn an unbalanced sentence into a balanced sentence, and invert word order.

1. Many politicians say that transporting garbage from the eastern states to the midwestern states is caused by greed and not a lack of space for landfills.

2. There are many reasons for opposing capital punishment.

3. A proposal to abolish grading in all freshman courses was made in the student senate just before the preannounced time for adjournment.

4. A New York court recently ruled that a gay lover had the right to remain in his deceased partner's rent-control apartment having qualified as a member of the deceased's family.

5. Slanting can be interpreted as presenting something with a special interest but propaganda is simply called disseminating one's beliefs.

6. All great cultures of the past were dependent on creativity and creativity depended on intelligent people.

7. As expected, the soprano was a vision of beauty and stepped up to the footlights.

8. The little boy's wagon was struck by the ice cream vendor's truck.

9. Some people believe that there is nothing positive about being in isolation and that it is merely a remote place or a frame of mind that results in loneliness and depression.

10. Being in a state of solitude and daydreaming are not the same things because there exists a fine line between the two.

Part

VI

DICTION AND STYLE

Diction is the choice and use of words in writing. Good diction helps you reach your audience, achieve your purpose, maintain an appropriate tone, and write with style.

24   Appropriate Word Choice

Whenever you write, the most basic decision you have to make about diction is whether to use formal or informal English. **Formal English,** as its name suggests, adheres strictly to the conventions of standard English. Most of the writing you do in college or in a profession—term papers, formal essays, theses, reports—should be in formal English. **Informal English** takes a more relaxed attitude to the conventions of standard English and may include contractions, colloquialisms, jargon, and sometimes even slang. It is appropriate for informal writing situations—journal and diary entries, informal essays, and creative writing in which you try to capture the sound of everyday speech.

INFORMAL: The delegates **were savvy about the fact** that the document they were signing **wasn't** perfect.

FORMAL: The delegates **understood** that the document they were signing **was not** perfect.

INFORMAL: The candidate **slammed** her opponent for often **changing his tune** on the issues.

FORMAL: The candidate **criticized** her opponent for often **changing his views** on the issues.

INFORMAL: Stickley furniture may not be **real smooth,** but **it's pricey** and **fresh.**

FORMAL: Stickley furniture may not be **very comfortable,** but **it is expensive** and **fashionable.**

A good dictionary will not only help you to determine whether a word or expression is formal or informal but also provide other useful information. Following is a list of three good desk dictionaries and a sample listing from the first one:

1. *The American Heritage Dictionary.* 3rd coll. ed. Boston: Houghton Mifflin, 1994.

2. *Webster's New World Dictionary of the American Language.* 3rd coll. ed. New York: Simon & Schuster, 1995.

3. *Random House Webster's College Dictionary,* 2nd ed. New York: Random House, 1997.

Pronun-ciation | **doubt** (dout) *v.* doubt-ed, doubt-ing, doubts.— *tr.* **1.** To be undecided or skeptical about. **2.** To tend to disbelieve; distrust: *doubts the promises of all politicians.* **3.** *Archaic.* To suspect; fear.—*intr.* To be undecided. | Forms and usage as a verb

Definition as a noun | —*n.* **1.** A lack of conviction or certainty. **2.** A lack of trust. **3.** A point about which one is uncertain or skeptical. **4.** An uncertain state of affairs: *an outcome still in doubt.*—*idioms.* beyond (or without) doubt. Without question; certainly; definitely, no doubt. **1.** Certainly. **2.** Probably. [ME *douten* < OFr. *douter* < Lat. *dubitare,* to waver.] —doubt´er *n.* | Etymology

Explan-ation of usage | **Usage:** *Doubt* and *doubtful* are often followed by clauses introduced by *that, whether,* or *if.* A choice among the three is guided by the intended meaning of the sentence, but considerable leeway exists. Generally, *that* is used when the intention is to express more or less complete rejection of a statement: *I doubt that he will even try* (meaning, "I don't think he will even try"); or, in the negative, to express more or less complete acceptance: *I don't doubt that you are right.* On the other

Explanation of usage

hand, when the intention is to express real uncertainty, the choice is usually *whether: We doubt whether they can succeed. It is doubtful whether he will come.* According to a majority of the Usage Panel, *whether* is the only acceptable choice in such examples; a minority would also accept *if* (which is more informal in tone) or *that.* In sum, *that* is especially appropriate to the denial of uncertainty or to implied disbelief but is sometimes used also when the intention is to express real uncertainty. *Doubt* is frequently used in informal speech, both as verb and as noun, together with *but: I don't doubt but* (or *but what*) *he will come. There is no doubt but it will be difficult.* These usages should be avoided in writing; substitute *that* or *whether* as the case requires.

Syllabication

doubt•ful (dout´fəl) *adj.* 1. Subject to or tending to cause doubt; uncertain: *It's doubtful if*

Beginning of list of related words

24a Slang

Slang is extremely informal language. It consists of colorful words, phrases, and expressions added to the language, usually by youthful or high-spirited people, to give it an exciting or ebullient flavor. Carl Sandburg described slang as "language that rolls up its sleeves, spits on its hands, and goes to work."

Slang is usually figurative and highly exaggerated. Each generation has its own slang; for example, in the 1960s, someone who was approved of was *cool;* in the 1970s, such a person was *with it;* in the 1980s, *awesome;* and in the 1990s, *phat* (fat) or *dope.* Although slang often begins as street language, some of it becomes so popular that with time it is accepted as part of formal language. Until a slang term becomes accepted, however, it is usually inappropriate in college writing.

SLANG: Some parents **came apart** when they were **clued in to** how some children's programs on the **idiot tube** were really just extended commercials.

FORMAL: Some parents **became upset** when they were **made aware of** how some children's **television** programs were really just extended commercials.

SLANG: Elizabeth Blackwell was **spaced out** by the nineteenth century's view of the ideal woman, but she managed to find a doctor who was **wired with** her goal of studying medicine.

FORMAL: Elizabeth Blackwell was **disheartened** by the nineteenth century's view of the ideal woman, but she managed to find a doctor who was **sympathetic to** her goal of studying medicine.

Slang can be used judiciously for effect in formal writing. When you use slang this way, do not enclose it in quotation marks or underline it.

The educated were turning in their diplomas for guitars, the rich were trading in their furs for jeans and love beads, and the middle-aged were pretending they were fifteen, not fifty; in fact, during this topsy-turvy time, everyone seemed to be **going nuts.**

She was thoughtful, politically aware, well spoken, and well educated, but the movie directors of the 1950s preferred **airheads.**

As he grew older, he realized that his **old man** had been smarter than he thought.

24b Colloquialisms

Colloquial language is the conversational and everyday language of educated people. **Colloquialisms** are the words and expressions that characterize this language. Though not as informal as slang, colloquial language is generally still too casual to be considered appropriate for formal writing.

COLLOQUIAL:	The meeting will begin at 7:00 P.M. **on the dot.**
FORMAL:	The meeting will begin **promptly** at 7:00 P.M.
COLLOQUIAL:	In *Bodily Harm,* Rennie realizes she is **in a jam** when she opens the box and finds illegal guns.
FORMAL:	In *Bodily Harm,* Rennie realizes she is **in trouble** when she opens the box and finds illegal guns.
COLLOQUIAL:	When Colonel Pickering expresses doubt as to Higgins's ability to make a lady of Eliza, Higgins **tells him to put up or shut up.**
FORMAL:	When Colonel Pickering expresses doubt as to Higgins's ability to make a lady of Eliza, Higgins **invites him to make a bet.**

Notice how the following sentences are improved when the colloquial qualifiers are replaced by more formal adverbs:

COLLOQUIAL:	Harriet Tubman was a **terribly** brave woman, for she made several trips back into slave territory to lead fugitives into freedom.
FORMAL:	Harriet Tubman was a **truly** brave woman, for she made several trips back into slave territory to lead fugitives into freedom.
COLLOQUIAL:	General Harrison considered Tecumseh's plan to force the United States to relinquish its claims to Indian lands **awfully** clever, but not workable.
FORMAL:	General Harrison considered Tecumseh's plan to force the United States to relinquish its claims to Indian lands **extremely** clever, but not workable.
COLLOQUIAL:	Television viewers were **pretty** moved by the program about nuclear war.
FORMAL:	Television viewers were **greatly** moved by the program about nuclear war.

24c Jargon

Jargon is the special language used by people in a particular field or group to communicate with others in the same field or group. The problem with jargon, or "shop talk," is that people outside the group have trouble understanding it. Language aimed at people with specific technical or professional knowledge may be appropriate for some classes, but it is not appropriate for most general college writing. If you must use a technical term in general college writing, make sure you define it.

Consider the following excerpt, which captures the strangeness of some computer jargon:

> A system for visual data interpretation should address format conversion, data storage and retrieval, the user interface, visualization methods, and capture of results on film or videotape. Frequently, data *format conversion* is required to convert floating-point numbers generated at irregular mesh points to integers in a rectilinear array. To ensure interactive speeds, it is important to consider *data storage and retrieval.*

> **E. J. Farrell et al.**
> *Visual Interpretation of Multidimensional*
> *Computations and Transistor Design*

Someone who is familiar with computer programming will easily understand this paragraph. However, the general audience at which you aim most of your college writing will not; this audience will need to know the meaning of the terms *format conversion, data storage and retrieval, user interface, visualization methods, floating-point numbers, irregular mesh points,* and *rectilinear array.*

24d Gobbledygook

Gobbledygook, or inflated diction, is stuffy, pretentious, inflated language that often contains an abundance of jargon. It is found in much government, legal, and academic writing, as well as in many other places, and it is sometimes called *governmentese* or *legalese.* Avoid gobbledygook, because it obscures meaning and lends both a timid and a pompous quality to your writing.

appr

24d *Appropriate Word Choice*

Revising Inappropriate Language
ON A WORD PROCESSOR

Eliminating slang, colloquialisms, jargon, and gobbledy-gook is especially easy to do on a word processor. Simply delete the inappropriate words, and insert a carefully chosen alternative. Grammar checkers can be useful in identifying jargon; they usually advise against using words like *effectuate* or *facilitate.* Many grammar programs also flag slang and some colloquialisms.

A major advocate of eliminating gobbledygook, especially from government writing, is Rudolf Flesch. In his book *How to Write Plain English,* he shows how Oregon's income tax instructions were rewritten to eliminate gobbledygook.

ORIGINAL

Deceased persons. A return must be made by the executor or administrator of the decedent's estate or by the surviving spouse or other person charged with the care of the property of the deceased. If the surviving spouse or next of kin desires to claim the refund, an affidavit should be submitted with the return. This affidavit (Form 243) is available at all Oregon Department of Revenue district offices, or it can be obtained by writing the Oregon Department of Revenue, State Office Building, Salem, Oregon 97310.

REVISED

My husband died last year. Can I file for him? Yes. The husband or wife of someone who dies, or the legal representative, must file the return. Use the form the person would have used if living. If you claim a refund, attach Form 243 to show you have the right to the deceased person's refund. Write for Form 243 to: Oregon Department of Revenue, Salem, Oregon 97310, or pick it up at any of our district offices.

EXERCISE 24-1

Rephrase each of the following sentences in formal English.

1. Grasp the circular receptacle by its protuberance and slowly rotate it until the minute particles deposited therein explode into almost weightless edibles.

2. Don't give me any jazz on the reasons why you miss the beat every time we're supposed to meet my parents.

3. He was caught red-handed with his hand in the cookie jar by the security guard.

4. Her shoes are rad but she still looks like a granola.

5. After an awesome scoring drive, the fullback hot-dogged in the end zone and high-fived the other players.

6. I can't deal with all these problems anymore.

7. She kind of got mad when she got stood up for the dance.

8. His set of wheels cost a bundle.

9. I haven't a clue as to why people call her a "tie-dye."

10. His new specs have colored panes and he still visits a shrink.

25   Sexist and Biased Language

In your writing, it is important to avoid language that could offend or alienate your audience and leave you open to charges of unfairness and prejudice.

25a Sexist Language

Sexist language is the use of words that inappropriately call attention to gender. Such language tends to stereotype individuals, usually women. It reflects outmoded usage, unfairly and incorrectly excludes an entire sex, and is often demeaning. Using the word *mankind,* for instance, when you are referring to all people, discriminates against women by excluding them. Substituting a gender-neutral term such as *all people, humanity,* or *humankind* eliminates the sexist language; it is fair to both sexes.

As a writer, you must be as accurate as you can be. Avoiding sexist language will enable you to fulfill this goal. But sexist language, or any biased language, poses a bigger threat than simply affecting your accuracy. Words have incredible power; the images they create last a lifetime. Special care should be taken to choose the appropriate words that will enable you to communicate effectively and to show consideration for another's point of view. The following guidelines will help you recognize sexist language and eliminate it from your writing:

Avoid using the word *man* or nouns ending in *-man* when discussing both sexes.

Replace any masculine-marked words in your writing with gender-free alternatives such as these:

MASCULINE-MARKED WORDS	ALTERNATIVES
fellow man	other people, humans
forefathers	ancestors
kinsman	relative
layman	ordinary person, nonspecialist
man	person, individual
(to) man	to care for, to work in, to staff
spokesman	speaker, representative
statesman	leader
workmanship	skilled work, quality job

Converting the suffix *-man* to *-person* often works, as in *chairperson* or *salesperson*. However, this practice can be awkward, as in *cave person* or *committee person*. Using sex-free solutions such as *cave dweller* or *committee member* is more effective. Similarly, avoid using feminine-marked terms such as *schoolgirl* or *mother tongue* when *student* or *native language* would work just as effectively.

Rewrite to avoid stereotyping jobs and social roles by gender.

Replace the words *salesman, chairman, mailman,* and *businessman* with the gender-free terms *sales representative, chair, mail carrier,* and *business executive*. Similarly, use such terms as *housekeeper* instead of *cleaning woman, homemaker* instead of *housewife,* and *flight attendant* instead of *stewardess* or *steward*. Recognize that the use of gender-specific terms for occupations is quickly disappearing as various groups and organizations substitute neutral job titles for those traditionally identified as male or female.

Watch for the use of language that expresses traditional and outdated assumptions about male and female occupations and roles.

Consider these sentences:

> **NOT:** A doctor uses his skill and physical strength in the operating room while a nurse uses her compassion at the bedside.
>
> **BUT:** Doctors and nurses use their skill, physical strength, and compassion in the operating room and at the bedside.
>
> **NOT:** When cleaning their homes, women should be thorough.
>
> **BUT:** It's important to be thorough when cleaning house.

Be consistent when naming individuals and identifying their occupations. Failing to do so implies a real or imagined value judgment about the person, the occupation, or both.

> **NOT:** The corporate president, John Martinez, and his lovely wife Linda, a lawyer and mother of two, attended the gala.
>
> **BUT:** The corporate president, John Martinez, and his wife, the lawyer Linda Ostacco, attended the gala.

Also, it is appropriate to identify a married woman by her own name instead of her husband's name. When writing the names of male or female authors, artists, composers, and so on, write the full name the first time it appears. Subsequent references should be made by last name only, without a title: **not** Mr. Hemingway **but** Hemingway; **not** Miss Dickinson **but** Dickinson.

Check for demeaning language or for language that presents a stereotypical view of the way the sexes behave.

In your writing, avoid referring to women as *girls, ladies,* or *young ladies.* Sexist terms such as *lady lawyer, coed,* and *gal Friday* should be avoided. Instead use the words *lawyer, student,* and *assistant.* Replace terms such as *male dancer* and *male nurse* with *dancer* and *nurse.* Similarly, watch for phrases such as *cute girls* and *rowdy boys* that reinforce stereotypes about the way men and women act.

Rewrite your sentences to avoid using the generic pronoun *he* when referring to all human beings.

In the past, generic *he* was acceptable when referring to men and women:

Nobody wants a failing grade to be on *his* record.

Everyone can be successful if *he* is given a chance.

In fact, for many years, students were taught to use the male pronouns *he, him,* or *his* as antecedents or references for indefinite pronouns. In the first sentence, *his* refers to *nobody,* indirectly suggesting that only males are in danger of failing. In the second, *he* refers to *everyone,* indirectly suggesting that only males are capable of success. Indefinite pronouns such as *nobody* and *everyone* are gender neutral. Combining them with masculine pronouns like *he* and *his* results in sexist language. The following strategies might help you to eliminate this inadvertent sexism.

1. Recast your sentences to make the pronouns plural.

   No *individuals* want failing grades on *their* records.

   People can be successes if *they* are given a chance.

2. Try eliminating the pronoun by using an article (*a, an,* or *the*) in its place.

   Nobody wants *a* failing grade recorded.

   Everyone can be successful if given *a* chance.

3. Rewrite the sentence using *he or she* (or *she or he*) whenever you refer to a singular indefinite pronoun such as *everyone* or *nobody.*

   Nobody wants a failing grade on *his or her* record.

   Everyone can be successful if *she or he* is given a chance.

   Be aware that with repeated use this type of construction leads to stilted writing. Strings of *his or her* constructions quickly bore most readers. Note too that the use of *s/he* or *he/she* has not gained widespread acceptance.

Any of the methods shown here for revising sex-specific pronouns (see also Section 8f on pronouns) are correct, although you will probably find it easier to make words plural whenever appropriate. Plural is neither masculine nor feminine; it refers to both collectively.

25b Biased Language

Biased language, whether sexist language or derogatory language directed at a group, race, religion, or nationality, should be avoided in writing. Also take care to avoid assigning stereotypical physical or behavioral characteristics to members of a particular group. Pay special attention to the language you choose. Keep these guidelines in mind:

1. Mention race and cultural heritage only if you make an important point by doing so. When you do, use specific and accurate language.
   - Combine descriptive terms with *American* for people whose forebears come from another country: *Japanese American, Cuban American,* and the like.
   - The term *Asian* is too broad to be useful, and *Oriental* is no longer used; specific designations such as *Chinese, Korean,* and *Indonesian* are more precise and effective.
   - *Hispanic* is also very broad; use specific terms such as *Mexican, Spanish,* and *Puerto Rican* when you can.

2. Use terminology preferred by the people you're writing about.
   - The term *African American* is favored by many whose ancestors came from Africa, but *black* is still widely used, and some publications use *Black*.

Choosing Appropriate Words
ON A WORD PROCESSOR

The general functions of word-processing programs will help you to delete inappropriate words and substitute acceptable ones with ease. You can use the search function to look for masculine pronouns or the words *man* and *men;* then check to be sure your usage is fair and nonsexist.

Grammar checkers are effective at flagging sexist words, but they might also flag words such as *girl* and *man* when they aren't being used in a sexist way. You don't need to avoid words like *man* or *girl* entirely, but you do have to use common sense when selecting language that is accurate and inoffensive.

- Both *Native American* and *American Indian* are acceptable for indigenous peoples. For natives of the Arctic regions, *Inuit* is preferred over *Eskimo*.
- *Gay* and *lesbian* are the terms preferred by those whose sexual orientation is toward their own sex, although *homosexual* is also acceptable.
- Many people over age sixty-five don't want to be called *elderly, old,* or even *senior citizens*. The best thing to do is to use specific numbers: *late sixties, early seventies*.
- Don't call college students and young working adults *boys, girls,* or *kids*. They deserve to be called *men* and *women*.

3. Mention a person's disability or illness only when it's relevant, and avoid words such as *crippled* or *victim*. People do not *suffer* from these disorders; they live with them the way other people live with other imperfections.
   - Terms such as *visually impaired* or *paraplegic* are simply descriptive and acceptable.

■ A useful strategy is to mention the person first and then his or her illness or disability: "my cousin Joan, who is diabetic" or "Kerri's father, who has multiple sclerosis."

4. Eliminate language that suggests negative class connotations, such as *redneck, white trash, welfare mother, fraternity boy, wealthy snob, hick,* and *city slicker.*

EXERCISE 25-1

Identify the biased language in the following sentences and supply an acceptable substitute. One sentence is acceptable as is.

1. The hard hats frequent that bar, but the chicks prefer the one downtown.

2. Our school has basketball teams for both men and girls.

3. Everyone was requested to move to her or his seat.

4. Mankind's inhumanity spreads throughout history.

5. Ask the kid at the desk what time the postman arrives.

6. Those guys play football like a bunch of old ladies.

7. The waitress tripped over the busboy's foot.

8. In that coed dormitory, boys and girls live on alternate floors.

9. John is considered the black sheep of the family.

10. Firemen, policemen, scrubwomen, and hairdressers all joined in the singing.

26 Exact Word Choice

Choose words that express your thoughts precisely. Avoid settling for a near-synonym or an almost-right word, but pay attention to shades of meaning, nuances, and context.

26a Specific and General Words

Specific words are precise, focused, and restricted in scope. General words are not focused; they refer to a large group or a wide range of things. For example, compare the following general and specific words:

GENERAL:	painter	make	hungry	some
SPECIFIC:	Mary Cassatt	coerce	voracious	thirty-five

The word *painter* refers to a whole group of people. *Mary Cassatt* refers to just one. The word *make* refers to a wide range of actions; *coerce* limits this range, meaning "to make someone do something or to make something happen through the use of force or pressure." The word *hungry* indicates a desire for food or for something else, but *voracious* indicates that this desire is overwhelming and insatiable. The word *some* indicates a number larger than a few, but *thirty-five* indicates a specific number.

Consider how the following sentences are improved through the use of a specific word:

GENERAL:	The **official** was accused of **working** for a **foreign government.**
SPECIFIC:	**Alger Hiss** was accused of **spying** for the **Soviet Union.**

GENERAL: This **woman,** who is best known for **longer things,** also wrote **several good** ghost stories, which are collected in a **book.**

SPECIFIC: **Edith Wharton,** who is best known for her **novels,** also wrote **eleven riveting** ghost stories, which are collected in *The Ghost Stories of Edith Wharton.*

GENERAL: **Some writers** are **liked** for their **sense of humor.**

SPECIFIC: **Dorothy Parker and Robert Benchley** are **appreciated** for their **wry, and sometimes biting, wit.**

Of course, general words do have a place in your writing. They introduce topics that you can later elaborate on or narrow. When you use a general word, however, consider narrowing the scope of this word later in your writing, if not immediately. Always search for an alternative before using adjectives and adverbs such as *good, nice, bad, very, great, fine, awfully, well done,* or *interesting.* Words like these are so general, that is, have so many meanings, that, paradoxically, they convey almost no meaning at all.

26b Concrete and Abstract Words

Concrete words create vivid impressions. They name things that can be seen, touched, heard, smelled, or tasted—in other words, things that can be perceived by the senses. The words *skyscraper, microfilm, buzzer, gourmet, pizza,* and *porcupine* are concrete words. **Abstract words** name concepts, ideas, beliefs, and qualities—in other words, things that cannot be perceived by the senses. For example, the words *democracy, honesty, childhood,* and *infinity* are abstract words. Use abstract words with care, because, in general, they create less intense impressions and so are often ineffective.

ABSTRACT: He argued that this nation could no longer accept poverty.

CONCRETE: Hungry children crying themselves to sleep, families evicted from their homes and sleeping in the streets, old people in cold-water flats surviving by eating cat food—these are conditions, he argued, that we as Americans can no longer tolerate.

ABSTRACT: Immigrants came to America in search of a better life.

CONCRETE: Immigrants came to America to farm their own land, to earn a living wage, to put a roof over their heads and food in their stomachs, and to speak and believe as they wished without fear of being thrown in jail.

ABSTRACT: One reason supermarkets began to replace ma-and-pa grocery stores is that they offered more variety.

CONCRETE: One reason supermarkets began to replace ma-and-pa grocery stores is that they offered not one brand of peas, but seven brands; not one kind of coffee, but six kinds; not one type of paper towel, but ten in five different colors—all under one roof.

Abstract words do have a place in your writing. However, too many of them can create an impression of vagueness. When you use abstract words, try to provide concrete examples to make their meaning vivid. Compare the following pairs of sentences. The second sentence in each pair contains a concrete example that clarifies the meaning of the abstract word or words in the first sentence.

Hating people is self-destructive.
Hating people is like burning down your own house to get rid of a rat.

Harry Emerson Fosdick

Circumstance makes heroes of people.
A light supper, a good night's sleep, and a fine morning often made a hero of the same man who by indigestion, a restless night, and a rainy morning would have proved a coward.

Earl of Chesterfield

Americans are absorbed in the present but are unaware of the past. We Americans are the best informed people on earth as to the events of the last twenty-four hours; we are not the best informed as to the events of the last sixty centuries.

Will and Ariel Durant

EXERCISE 26-1

Each of the following sentences is vague or unclear. Rewrite each sentence, replacing general and abstract words with specific or concrete ones.

1. Contemporary architects are designing new shapes for interior spaces.

2. People avoid unpleasantries.

3. Keeping a houseplant is not as time consuming as keeping a pet.

4. Some men's clothing was on sale sometime last week.

5. The media objected to the mayor's decision.

26c Denotation and Connotation

Besides their **denotation,** or basic dictionary definition, many words also have **connotations**—associations that the word brings to mind and emotions that it arouses. Words that have the same dictionary meaning may have quite different connotations. For example, consider the following two sentences:

The clothes at this boutique are quite **cheap.**
The clothes at this boutique are quite **inexpensive.**

Improving Word Choice
ON A WORD PROCESSOR

If you think that you need to use a more precise word or one with different connotations, the thesaurus feature of your word-processing program will give you suggestions to consider. For example, for the word *childish,* you might be given these choices: *immature, infantile, puerile, adolescent,* and *babyish.* If one of those seems more fitting for the tone and purpose of your writing, then you can automatically substitute it into your text. A thesaurus does not define words; it just lists synonyms. You will have to consult a collegiate dictionary to make sure your choice conveys the exact meaning you want.

Both *cheap* and *inexpensive* have the dictionary meaning of "not expensive." However, *cheap* carries a negative connotation of low value, but *inexpensive* carries a positive connotation of fair value.

When you write, you must choose words with the appropriate connotations.

INAPPROPRIATE:	The quality of **childish** innocence shines through her poetry.
APPROPRIATE:	The quality of **childlike** innocence shines through her poetry.
INAPPROPRIATE:	The editorial praised the candidate for being **egocentric.**
APPROPRIATE:	The editorial praised the candidate for being an **individualist.**
INAPPROPRIATE:	In 1873, the Supreme Court prevented Myra Bradwell from becoming a lawyer, because it did not consider the law an **effeminate** profession.

APPROPRIATE: In 1873, the Supreme Court prevented Myra Brad-
well from becoming a lawyer, because it did not
consider the law a **ladylike** profession.

Some words have such strong connotations that they are said to
be *loaded*. When used, they go off with a deafening emotional
bang. For example, the words *slumlord, witch-hunt,* and *imperi-
alism* are all loaded. Their connotative effect drowns out their
denotative meaning. Be careful of loaded words, because they
can make your writing appear biased.

EXERCISE 26-2

In each of the following pairs, the words have the same or almost
the same denotative meaning but different connotations. Write a sentence for each word that shows that you understand its connotative
value. You may use your dictionary to help you.

1. common/vulgar   6. corrupt/dishonest

2. donation/giveaway   7. mutter/mumble

3. hardy/bold   8. requests/demands

4. wrinkled/messy   9. ignorant/moronic

5. effete/sterile   10. customers/patrons

EXERCISE 26-3

Use figurative language to complete each of the following items in
a vivid and consistent manner.

1. The pack of dogs (the lion's den/the crashing car) sounded

   like _____.

2. From the speeding car the houses (people/cornfields) looked
   like _____.

3. As the day for the final examination approached, she felt ____

   _____.

4. The darkness was like _____.

5. The dancing couple _____.

6. The addition of _____ was like _____.

7. The mattresses in the store were _____.

8. The child's face during the birthday part was as _____ as

   _____.

9. Touching the chalkboard felt like _____.

10. Elephants and mice are as different as _____.

EXERCISE 26-4

Rewrite each of the following sentences to eliminate clichés and
euphemisms.

1. Does anyone really believe that life is just a bowl of cherries?

2. In summation, the nonessential personnel in this division will be

   vacationed by next week.

3. To add insult to injury he then asked another girl to the party.

4. He looked as strong as an ox and acted as sober as a judge.

5. The remains will be taken to the cemetery.

6. Reaching the top of the ladder of success must be a moving experience.

7. After he was brought back to reality, he was cool, calm, and collected.

8. I was told that he did away with himself.

9. A sadder but wiser person, Mary appeared tired but happy.

10. He'll have to face the music despite his diabolical skill.

Part

VII

PUNCTUATION, MECHANICS, AND SPELLING

Punctuation marks are symbols designed to help people understand what they are reading. They tell readers when to pause, when to stop, and when to read something with emphasis or emotion.

Mechanics concerns the technical aspects of writing, such as when to underline for italics, how to form contractions, when to use abbreviations, and when to use numbers. Mechanics also includes manuscript form, which concerns the conventions followed when preparing your paper, whether on a computer, with a typewriter, or by hand.

27 End Punctuation

End punctuation separates sentences and marks the end of other elements, such as abbreviations. The three end punctuation marks are the *period,* the *question mark,* and the *exclamation point.*

27a The Period

1 Periods to end sentences

Use a period to end a sentence that makes a statement.

> In 1979, the United States ceded control of the Panama Canal Zone to the Panamanian government.
> The Japanese painter Hokusai changed his style many times.

Use a period to end a sentence that makes a request, expresses a mild command, or gives directions.

Please help the needy.
Open your books to page 178.
Turn left at the next corner.

If you want the command or request to be given a great deal of emphasis or force, use an exclamation point instead of a period (see Section 27c).

Sign up now!

Use a period at the end of a sentence that asks an indirect question.

The editorial questions whether NATO is effective.
The reporter asked how the fire had started.
The doctor wondered why the patient's temperature had risen.

Use a period at the end of a request politely expressed as a question.

Will you please type this letter for me.
Will you kindly keep your voices down.

(See Section 32a for the use of the period with parentheses. See Section 34e for the use of the period with quotation marks.)

2 Conventional uses of periods

Use a period after most abbreviations and initials.

If a sentence ends with an abbreviation requiring a period, use only one period.

The first admiral in the U.S. Navy was David G. Farragut.
The Marine Corps traces its beginnings to Nov. 10, 1775.

Thomas Jefferson's home, Monticello, is near Charlottesville, Va.

The current trend in abbreviations is away from the use of periods. The following two rules are now considered standard. However, if you are in doubt about whether to use a period after an abbreviation, consult your dictionary.

Avoid using a period when abbreviating a unit of measure.

86 **m**	275 **kg**	2.4 **cm**	20 **ft**
10.5 **yd**	20 **lb**	20 **cc**	

Exceptions: For *mile* use *m.* or *mi.* to prevent confusion with *m* for *meter.* For *inch* use *in* only when there is no possibility of confusion with the word *in;* the abbreviation *in.* avoids all confusion.

Avoid using a period with acronyms or other abbreviations of businesses, organizations, and government and international agencies.

The **NAACP** has not endorsed a presidential candidate.

My mother served in the **WACs** for eight years.

The impartiality of **UNESCO** is being questioned.

27b The Question Mark

Use a question mark at the end of a sentence that asks a direct question.

Who invented the safety pin?

Have you registered to vote?

Use a question mark at the end of an interrogative element that is part of another sentence.

How can I keep my job? was the question on every worker's mind.

"Will he actively support women's rights?" she wondered.

The telegram said that Malcolm is alive—can it be true?—and will be returned to the United States on Friday.

In general, when a question follows an introductory element, use a capital letter to begin the question and a question mark to end it.

The question to be decided is, How can we improve our public transportation system?

Before buying on credit, ask yourself, Do I really need this?

A good detective inquires, What was the motive for the crime?

Usage varies somewhat on capitalization of questions following introductory elements. The more formal the question, the greater the tendency to use a capital letter. The less formal, the greater the tendency to use a lowercase letter.

FORMAL: The book raises the question, What role should the United States play in the Middle East?

INFORMAL: I wondered, should I bring my umbrella?

Use a question mark, usually in parentheses, to express doubt or uncertainty about a date, a name, or a word.

The *Vedas* (written around 1000 B.C.?) are the sacred books of Hinduism.

A dialect of Germanic, called Angleish (?), is the basis of modern-day English.

Sir Thomas Malory (?–1471) wrote *Morte d'Arthur,* an account of the exploits of King Arthur and his knights.

27c The Exclamation Point

Use an exclamation point at the end of a sentence, word, or phrase that you wish to be read with emphasis, surprise, or strong emotion.

Don't give up**!**
We shall resist this onslaught**!**
Impossible**!**
What a terrible time**!**

Avoid using the exclamation point to express sarcasm, and try not to overuse the exclamation point. Too many exclamation points are distracting and ineffective. The more you use, the less effective each one will be.

Revising End Punctuation
ON A WORD PROCESSOR

You can use the search function to find question marks and check to be sure you have used them with *direct* questions. If you find a question mark following an *indirect* question, revise the sentence or change the question mark to a period (see Section 27a-1). You can also search for exclamation points to be sure that you have used them sparingly and for good reason.

Some grammar checkers will flag sentences that begin with interrogative words (such as *Are* or *What*) and suggest that a question mark is needed. But on the whole, grammar programs are of little help with end punctuation.

EXERCISE 27-1

Identify the end punctuation that is missing from the following sentences.

1. Have you ever been to a sculpture exhibition

2. Such an exhibition is opening here on Nov. 1

3. Suspense has been growing as people catch glimpses of unusual objects being installed in the gallery

4. One sculpture consists of a large wooden scaffold dripping with heavy chains

5. A lot of people would ask, Is this a form of insanity

6. You might wonder

7. One sculptor is exhibiting a ceramic sink and toilet that look like they came from the land of Oz

8. Is it ironic that the night before the exhibit opens is Halloween

9. All Saints' Eve, or All Hallows' Eve, or Halloween, is on October 31

10. Will you please check the hours for the exhibit

28 The Comma

The **comma** groups elements within the sentence in four ways: a comma *separates coordinate elements;* it *sets off introductory elements;* it *sets off certain terminal elements;* and a pair of commas *sets off interrupting elements.*

28a Between Coordinate Elements

1 Independent clauses

Use a comma between two independent clauses (sentences) joined by a coordinating conjunction—*and, but, for, nor, or, so, yet.*

Many Caribbean people emigrated to other countries, and 700,000 of these emigrants settled in the United States within a ten-year period.

Halloween has its origins in the Celtic religious festival of the dead, but today Halloween is largely a children's holiday of tricks and treats.

Travel to the countryside to buy fresh apples, for there at roadside stands you can find many varieties not available in supermarkets.

The comma may be omitted between two short independent clauses.

She handed him the note and *he read it immediately.*
Take notes in class and *study them.*

If in doubt, use the comma.

2   Items in a series

Use commas to separate three or more items—words, phrases, or clauses—in a series.

WORDS IN A SERIES

A zoo veterinarian is called on to treat such diverse animals as elephants, gorillas, and antelopes.

Murillo, Velázquez, and El Greco were three major seventeenth-century Spanish painters.

The sporting goods store carries equipment for skiing, track, hockey, and weight lifting.

PHRASES IN A SERIES

The subway carried children going to school, adults going to work, and derelicts going nowhere at all.

The children playing hide-and-seek hid behind boulders, under bushes, or in trees.

Running in the halls, smoking in the bathrooms, and shouting in the classrooms are not allowed.

CLAUSES IN A SERIES

Edward Steichen photographed the Brooklyn Bridge, Georgia O'Keeffe painted it, and Hart Crane wrote about it.

Foster stole the ball, he passed it to Kennedy, and Kennedy made a basket.

The supermarket tabloid proclaimed boldly that the man's character was hateful, that he was guilty, and that he should be punished severely.

Note: The comma before the conjunction with items in a series is often omitted in newspapers and magazines. Follow your instructor's preference. Most handbooks recommend using the comma because it prevents misreading, as in the following cases.

Harry, Anita, and Jayne have left already.

Without a comma before the conjunction, it is possible to read such sentences as directly addressing the first person named.

Harry, Anita and Jayne have left already. (*Someone is addressing Harry and giving him information about Anita and Jayne.*)

The menu listed the following sandwiches: bologna, chicken salad, pastrami, ham, and cheese. (*five sandwiches*)

The menu listed the following sandwiches: bologna, chicken salad, pastrami, ham and cheese. (*four sandwiches*)

3 Coordinate adjectives

Use commas between coordinate adjectives that are not joined by *and.*

Coordinate adjectives each modify the noun independently.

The comic was censored for his *audacious, vulgar* routine.

The traveler paused before walking into the *deep, dark, mysterious* woods.

The advertisement requested a *cheerful, sensitive, intelligent* woman to serve as governess.

Avoid using a comma between cumulative adjectives.

Cumulative adjectives each modify the whole group of words that follow them.

He gave her a *crystal perfume* bottle.

On top of the stove was a set of *large shiny copper* pots.

She carried an *expensive black leather* briefcase.

How can you distinguish coordinate adjectives from cumulative adjectives? In general, coordinate adjectives would sound natural with the word *and* between them, since each modifies the noun independently.

The comic was censored for his audacious and vulgar routine.

The traveler paused before walking into the deep and dark and mysterious woods.

The advertisement requested a cheerful and sensitive and intelligent woman to serve as governess.

In addition, coordinate adjectives would sound natural with their order changed or reversed.

The comic was censored for his vulgar, audacious routine.

The traveler paused before walking into the mysterious, dark, deep woods.

The advertisement requested an intelligent, sensitive, cheerful woman to serve as governess.

The order of cumulative adjectives cannot be changed. For example, the following sentences make no sense:

> He gave her a perfume crystal bottle.
>
> On top of the stove was a set of copper shiny large pots.
>
> She carried an expensive leather black briefcase.

EXERCISE 28-1

Place commas where they are needed in the following sentences. One sentence is correct.

1. A smaller maple chair matched the larger one.

2. Solomon played the guitar Latitia played bass and Louella played piano.

3. The strong fortress-like building was not very inviting.

4. Over there you will find the elevators and the escalators.

5. Writers work with pen and paper and artists work with paints and canvas.

28b After Introductory Words, Phrases, and Clauses

Use a comma after an introductory word or expression that does not modify the subject of the sentence.

> Why, we didn't realize the telegram was merely a hoax.
>
> Yes, Washington did sleep here.
>
> Well, that restaurant is certainly expensive.

On the other hand, its prices are justified.

By the way, what were you doing last night?

Use a comma after an introductory verbal or verbal phrase.

Smiling, she greeted us at the door.

While sleeping, Coleridge conceived the idea for "Kubla Khan."

To sketch a tree accurately, you must first study it closely.

Hoping to find happiness at last, Poe married his cousin.

Use a comma after an introductory series of prepositional phrases.

Under cover of night, the secret agent slipped across the border.

In this album of music from the 1960s, you will find several traditional songs.

In Jack London's famous story of a fight for survival in the Arctic, the man fails to light a fire.

Use a comma after an introductory phrase if there is a possibility that the sentence will be misread without it.

The day before, he had written her a letter.

After the tournament, winners received trophies and certificates.

Without hunting, the deer would soon become too numerous for the available food supply.

Use a comma after an introductory adverb clause.

Because John F. Kennedy was assassinated on the same day Aldous Huxley died, Huxley's death was given little attention by the press.

Although the alligator once faced extinction, its numbers are now increasing dramatically.

If the earth were to undergo another ice age, certain animals would flourish.

The comma after a very short introductory adverb clause is considered optional, unless its placement prevents misreading.

28c   Before Certain Terminal Elements

1   Contrasted elements

Use a comma to set off an element that is being contrasted with what precedes it.

> Robert Graves claims he writes novels for profit, not for pleasure.

> Birds are warm-blooded animals, unlike reptiles.

2   Interrogative elements

Use a comma before a short interrogative element at the end of a sentence.

> I don't know anyone who hasn't seen at least one of Hitchcock's films, do you?

> Tom Stoppard's new play is wonderful, isn't it?

> The Vietnam War was never officially a war, or was it?

3   Terminal adverb clauses

In general, do not use a comma before an adverb clause that follows the main clause.

> Many people wept *when they saw the monument honoring the veterans of the war in Vietnam.*

> A national holiday has been established *so that Americans can honor Martin Luther King, Jr.*

> Who ruled England *before the Normans invaded it?*

However, there are several exceptions to the preceding rule:

Use a comma before a terminal adverb clause that begins with *although* or *even though.*

> Columbus found a rich world for the Spanish, although it was not the world he set out to reach.

Use a comma before a terminal adverb clause that begins with *since* or *while* when these words express cause or condition. Do not use a comma when these words express time.

CAUSE:	He advocated prison reform, *since he knew firsthand the dehumanizing effects of prison life.*
TIME:	Mighty empires have come and gone *since the world began.*
CONDITION:	Many critics praised her new play, *while others felt it was the worst she had ever written.*
TIME:	She wrote her first play *while she was vacationing in Venice.*

Use a comma before a terminal adverb clause beginning with *because* if the clause does not modify the verb nearest it.

Notice the difference in meaning between the two sentences below:

> I knew he *was absent* from work *because his supervisor was looking for him.*

> I *knew* he was absent from work, *because his supervisor was looking for him.*

In the first sentence, the adverb clause modifies *was* (*absent*). It tells why he was absent—because his supervisor was looking for him. In the second sentence, the comma tells us that the adverb clause does not modify the verb closest to it. Instead, it modifies the verb *knew*. It tells how I knew he was absent—because his supervisor was looking for him.

Use a comma before a terminal adverb clause that begins with *so that* when *so that* indicates result. Do not use a comma when *so that* indicates purpose.

> **RESULT:** *Huckleberry Finn* combines strong plot and characterization with a profound insight into the human condition, *so that it can be read by children and adults alike.*

> **PURPOSE:** Oliver Twist set out for London *so that he could escape punishment by the beadle.*

EXERCISE 28-2

Place commas where they are needed in the following sentences. One sentence is correct.

1. The rabbit nevertheless does shed fur.

2. If you hurry we will arrive there on time.

3. It will be your first visit won't it?

4. Wishing to surprise their friend they planned a birthday party.

5. She presented her paper even though she had a headache.

28d Around Interrupting Elements

1 With nonessential appositives and adjective clauses

Use commas to set off a nonessential appositive. Do not use commas to set off an essential appositive.

A nonessential, or nonrestrictive, appositive gives additional information about the noun it refers to but is not essential for the identification of the noun it renames. In the following sentences, the nonessential appositives appear in *italics:*

Duke Ellington, *a famous composer and bandleader,* helped gain acceptance for jazz as a serious musical form.

St. Augustine, *the oldest city in the United States,* was founded by the Spanish.

An essential, or restrictive, appositive identifies the noun it refers to. As its name suggests, it is essential to the meaning of the sentence. In the following sentences, the essential appositives appear in *italics:*

My friend *George* works in a bookstore.

The word *nice* has undergone many changes in meaning.

Truman Capote's book *In Cold Blood* established a new literary form.

Use commas to set off a nonessential adjective clause. Do not use commas to set off an essential adjective clause.

A nonessential, or nonrestrictive, adjective clause provides extra information about the noun it modifies but is not essential to identify the noun it modifies. In the following sentences, the nonessential adjective clauses appear in *italics:*

Dinah Washington, *whom many consider the queen of the blues,* sang with Lionel Hampton's band.

Modern dance, *which was originated by Martha Graham,* has had a profound influence on the dance world.

An essential, or restrictive, adjective clause limits or identifies the noun it refers to. It is essential to the meaning of the sentence. In the following sentences, the essential adjective clauses appear in *italics:*

The person *who buys the first ticket* will win a trip to Mexico.

The scientist *whose research is judged the most important* will be given a grant.

The performance *that they gave last night* was not up to their usual standard.

Note: The pronoun *that* is used only with essential clauses. The pronoun *which* may be used with either essential or nonessential clauses.

Whether or not an adjective clause is set off with commas can make a major difference to the meaning of a sentence. For example, compare the following two sentences:

ESSENTIAL:	The first president who was born in Virginia was George Washington.
NONESSENTIAL:	The first president, who was born in Virginia, was George Washington.

The first sentence tells you that George Washington was the first Virginia-born president. The second sentence tells you that George Washington was the first president. As additional information, it mentions that he was born in Virginia.

Now compare the next two sentences:

ESSENTIAL:	The first president who was born in New York was Martin Van Buren.
NONESSENTIAL:	The first president, who was born in New York, was Martin Van Buren.

The first sentence tells you that Martin Van Buren was the first New York-born president. This statement is true. However, the second sentence says that Martin Van Buren was the first president. This statement is obviously not true.

Finally, compare these two sentences:

ESSENTIAL:	The tenants who did not pay their rent were evicted.
NONESSENTIAL:	The tenants, who did not pay their rent, were evicted.

The first sentence tells you that only the tenants who did not pay their rent were evicted. The second sentence tells you that all the tenants were evicted. As additional information, it tells the reason they were evicted: they did not pay their rent.

2 With adverb clauses and interrupting or parenthetical adverbs

In general, use commas to set off an internal adverb clause that is parenthetical or that separates the subject of the main clause from its predicate.

> Harry Truman, although a newspaper headline prematurely declared otherwise, won the 1948 election over Thomas E. Dewey.

> Columbus, as we have seen, died without his true accomplishments recognized or honored.

Use commas to set off adverbs (*however, accordingly, moreover, nevertheless,* and so on) and transitional phrases (*in addition, to sum up, on the other hand, for example*) used parenthetically.

> Many acclaimed writers, however, have written mysteries.

> A popular mystery set in a fourteenth-century monastery, moreover, was written by a professor of semiotics.

> Edmund Wilson, on the other hand, considered mysteries simply a waste of time.

3 With parenthetical expressions

Use commas to set off a parenthetical expression within a sentence.

Expressions that comment on or give additional information about the main part of the sentence are considered parenthetical.

> Jazz, many critics believe, is America's greatest contribution to the arts.

You, like most people, probably do not know that the person responsible for the completion of the Brooklyn Bridge was a woman.

George Washington, according to the old-style calendar used by the colonists, was born on February 11.

Use commas to set off words that identify the source of a quotation within a sentence.

"The advance for the book," said Calvin Trillin, "should be at least as much as the cost of the lunch at which it was discussed."

"You can be a little ungrammatical," Robert Frost claimed, "if you come from the right part of the country."

"Just get it down on paper," advised Maxwell Perkins, "and we'll see what to do with it."

Use commas after or around words in direct address.

Here, my fellow citizens, is an issue we can agree on.

Ladies and gentlemen, may I present our speaker.

Sam, you've won the prize!

4 With dates and addresses

With dates, use commas to separate the day of the week from the month, the day of the month from the year, and the year from the rest of the sentence.

Please reply by Tuesday, January 7.

The *Titanic* hit an iceberg and sank on April 15, 1912.

The Allies landed at Normandy on Tuesday, June 6, 1944, and began the offensive that would lead to the downfall of the Third Reich.

Note: Do not use a comma when only the month and the day (e.g., April 15) or only the month and the year (e.g., April 1912) are given or when the following form is used: 15 April 1912.

With addresses, use a comma to separate the name from the street address, the street address from the city, and the city from the state. Use a comma after the zip code (or after the state if no zip code is given) to separate the entire address from the rest of the sentence. Do not use a comma between the state and the zip code.

> The book is available from the Macmillan Publishing Company, 866 Third Avenue, New York, New York 10022.

> He lived at 579 Montenegro Avenue, Frisco, Colorado, until 1982.

Checking Comma Use
ON A WORD PROCESSOR

If you have problems with comma use, you can use the search function in your word-processing program to find the commas in your writing. As you review them, make sure you know a rule to justify each one. Pay special attention to pairs of commas that set off interrupting elements; if you have left one of them out, you can insert it and the computer will automatically reformat your sentence.

Grammar checkers give little advice about commas, although some can tell you that a comma is usually used before *which* but not before *that* (see Section 28d-1).

EXERCISE 28-3

Place commas where they are needed in the following sentences. One sentence is correct as written.

1. I did not know where you went!

2. In spite of what the driver said the police officer still wrote a traffic citation.

3. "If everyone will contribute" reminded the chairperson "we can raise the money quickly."

4. She moved to 892 Durham Way Granger Indiana on August 13 of this year.

5. Lyndon Johnson formerly a grade-school teacher in Texas became president after John Kennedy was assassinated.

28e Unnecessary Commas

Avoid using a comma to separate a subject from its predicate.

NOT: The album that he recorded last year, sold over a million copies.

BUT: The album that he recorded last year sold over a million copies.

OR: The album, which he recorded last year, sold over a million copies.

NOT: The painting hanging on the wall, was of the last duchess.

BUT: The painting hanging on the wall was of the last duchess.

NOT: How a bill becomes a law, was the subject discussed in class today.

BUT: How a bill becomes a law was the subject discussed in class today.

Avoid using a comma to separate a verb from its complement.

NOT: Did you know, that chimpanzees can communicate through sign language?

BUT: Did you know that chimpanzees can communicate through sign language?

NOT: After discussing the issue for several hours, we realized that our decision must be, to place safety concerns before cost considerations.

BUT: After discussing the issue for several hours, we realized that our decision must be to place safety concerns before cost considerations.

NOT: The speaker declared that the government must let us know, why we are involved in this conflict.

BUT: The speaker declared that the government must let us know why we are involved in this conflict.

Avoid using a comma between cumulative adjectives.

NOT: She declared him to be a handsome, young man.
BUT: She declared him to be a handsome young man.

NOT: He was sentenced to a nine-year, prison term.
BUT: He was sentenced to a nine-year prison term.

NOT: She wore a knee-length, red, suede shirt.
BUT: She wore a knee-length red suede shirt.

Avoid using a comma to separate the two parts of a compound subject, a compound verb, or a compound complement.

NOT: High ceilings, and cathedral windows are two features I look for in a house.

BUT: High ceilings and cathedral windows are two features I look for in a house.

NOT: The skier cleaned his boots, and then sprayed them with a water repellent.

BUT: The skier cleaned his boots and then sprayed them with a water repellent.

NOT: For breakfast she ordered a ham omelet, and a side dish of home fries.

BUT: For breakfast she ordered a ham omelet and a side dish of home fries.

Eliminating Unnecessary Commas ON A WORD PROCESSOR

If you tend to use too many commas, use the search function to locate the commas in your writing. Then check their use, making sure that you have a rule to justify each one. When you delete unnecessary commas, your word-processing program will automatically reformat the sentences for you.

Avoid using a comma to separate two dependent clauses joined by *and*.

NOT: They promised that they would obey the laws of their new country, and that they would uphold its principles.

BUT: They promised that they would obey the laws of their new country and that they would uphold its principles.

NOT: Anyone who attends this school, and who lives off-campus must sign this list.

BUT: Anyone who attends this school and lives off-campus must sign this list.

NOT: He wrote that he would stop loving her when dogs could fly, and when fish could sing.

BUT: He wrote that he would stop loving her when dogs could fly and fish could sing.

Avoid using a comma to separate the parts of a comparison.

NOT: During the five months she spent alone in the woods, she was more productive, than she had ever been before.

BUT: During the five months she spent alone in the woods, she was more productive than she had ever been before.

NOT: The situation is not as bad, as we had expected.

BUT: The situation is not as bad as we had expected.

NOT: It is difficult to imagine another museum containing such a magnificent collection of medieval art, as the Cloisters in New York City.

BUT: It is difficult to imagine another museum containing such a magnificent collection of medieval art as the Cloisters in New York City.

Avoid using a comma before an opening parenthesis. You may, however, use a comma after a closing parenthesis.

NOT: David McCullough, who wrote *The Path Between the Seas*, (winner of the National Book Award) visited the Panama Canal.

BUT: David McCullough, who wrote *The Path Between the Seas* (winner of a National Book Award), visited the Panama Canal.

EXERCISE 28-4

Circle any unnecessary commas that appear in the following sentences. One sentence is correct as written.

1. Things were not as bleak, on June 23, 1991, as they appeared to be later in the year.

2. Do you, by chance, know where to register for the marathon race to be held in Akron, Ohio?

3. They claimed that they did not see the intruder, and that they could not, therefore, identify him or her.

4. William Faulkner, an industrious and prolific writer, (who won a Nobel Prize for Literature), lived in Oxford, Mississippi.

5. They decided to meet in Paris, France, on, July 25, 1995.

EXERCISE 28-5

Place commas where they are needed in the following sentences, and circle any unnecessary commas that appear.

1. Computers are used in many writing classes although at one time (about fifteen years ago) the practice would have been considered odd.

2. Computers were first used as drill and practice machines to help students overcome problems with spelling punctuation grammar and even in some cases pronunciation.

3. Gradually, computers became accepted, in college writing classes, as students arrived with increasing computer literacy.

4. In many cases although teachers did not like to admit it their students knew more about using the machines than they did.

5. But software (computer programs) that operated on one manufacturer's machines, most often, did not operate on other machines.

6. The result, was a proliferation of software that, was very mixed in quality.

7. Nevertheless the computer market settled to a few major manufacturers and software improved, in both quality and quantity.

8. The next advance, in software for writing, around 1975–1980, occurred when programs devoted to prewriting appeared.

9. Students found these programs both helpful, and interesting because they could generate, more writing more quickly.

10. Some of these were based on freewriting and others on brainstorming clustering and the pentad.

11. At the same time many teachers (the enlightened ones!) recommended that students use the computer's word processing capabilities to write the final drafts of essays.

12. "A new age of anxiety " as one professor stated "began when students submitted essays with right-justified margins page numbers in the wrong places and paragraphs lacking indentation."

13. Furthermore the students experienced anxiety because so many of them despite precautions "lost" their essays in the computer.

14. After overcoming this, particular problem students found that the advantages of editing essays, on the computer outweighed the disadvantages.

15. The finished product produced, on a laser printer looks so professional that it is worth the initial anxiety.

---

29   The Semicolon

The **semicolon** links independent clauses or separates items in a series. The semicolon indicates a pause longer than that taken for a comma but not as long as that taken for a period.

29a Between Independent Clauses

Use a semicolon between two closely related independent clauses that are not joined by a coordinating conjunction.

> Years ago caviar was an inexpensive food often given away free at taverns; today it is one of the most expensive foods in the world.

> Truffles are the food of the rich; turnips are the food of the poor.

> Truffles are the food of the rich; turnips, the poor.

The comma in the preceding sentence indicates that a part of the second clause has been left out.

Use a semicolon between two independent clauses joined by a conjunctive adverb or by a transitional phrase.

> Columbus sent cacao beans back to Spain; however, the Spanish were not particularly impressed.

> Cortez brought back more cacao beans; moreover, he brought back the knowledge of how to prepare them.

> In some cultures insects are considered delicacies; for example, the ancient Romans thought the cicada a delightful morsel.

Use a semicolon between two independent clauses joined with a coordinating conjunction if one or both of these clauses contain internal commas or if the clauses are particularly complex.

With fairly short clauses, either a comma or a semicolon is acceptable.

> Persephone was the daughter of Demeter, the goddess of agriculture, and she was represented by the pomegranate, the symbol of fertility.

Persephone was the daughter of Demeter, the goddess of agriculture; and she was represented by the pomegranate, the symbol of fertility.

With longer and more complex clauses, the semicolon is preferred.

In Greek mythology Persephone was the daughter of Demeter, the goddess of agriculture; and she was represented by the pomegranate, the symbol of fertility, of which she ate the seeds after Hades carried her down into the underworld.

In Italy during the Renaissance, the inside of the opened pomegranate, which is divided into compartments containing colorful seeds, was used as the basis for a popular fabric design; and in the Middle East during ancient times, this beautiful fruit figured prominently in the decorative arts.

Because of its abundance of seeds, some Westerners find the pomegranate, which originated in the Middle East, unpalatable as a food, although pleasing as a decoration; but supporters of the pomegranate, of whom there are many, find the seeds no drawback, since they like to chew these crunchy tidbits.

29b Between Items in a Series

Use semicolons to separate items in a series if the individual items are long or contain commas.

In the language of flowers, each flower represents a particular attribute: belladonna, which is a deadly poison, silence; citron, which produces a sour, inedible fruit, ill-natured beauty; blue periwinkle, which is small and delicate, early friendship.

The guide grouped wildflowers into many families, four of which were the cattail family, Typhaceae; the arrowhead family, Alismataceae; the yellow-eyed grass family, Xyridaceae; and the lizard-tail family, Saururaceae.

;

Checking Semicolons
ON A WORD PROCESSOR

You probably use semicolons infrequently, so you should check each use. The search function will locate places where you have used semicolons. Be sure that they separate independent clauses or items in a series that contain commas.

Grammar checkers will alert you to some misused semicolons. They will also flag some run-on sentences, some of which can be corrected by inserting a semicolon (see Section 11b).

29c Misused Semicolons

Avoid using a semicolon between noncoordinate elements.

NOT: In Shakespeare's *Hamlet,* after Ophelia is rebuffed**;** she communicates her despair through the language of flowers.

BUT: In Shakespeare's *Hamlet,* after Ophelia is rebuffed**,** she communicates her despair through the language of flowers.

NOT: She became famous for her photographs of wildflowers**;** especially for those of mountain laurel.

BUT: She became famous for her photographs of wildflowers**,** especially for those of mountain laurel.

EXERCISE 29-1

Circle sections where a punctuation mark should be replaced by a semicolon or where a semicolon should be placed in each of the following sentences. Insert a comma where needed after a conjunctive adverb. Two of the sentences are correct as written.

1. Several of the most beautiful bulbous flowers belong to the tulip family, others belong to the narcissus family.

2. Most tulips bloom in the early spring, others in late spring.

3. The colors of tulips range over the entire spectrum, however red appears to be the most favored color.

4. Wealthy people in eighteenth-century Europe, enchanted with tulips from the Middle East, paid vast sums of money for one bulb, in many cases, the cost exceeded thousands of dollars.

5. Today, tulip bulbs are sold for very reasonable prices nevertheless some varieties, especially hybrids, are very expensive.

6. The most popular varieties of tulips include the Darwin, which can be as large as a tennis ball and grows sixteen inches high, the lily-flowered, which has pointed petals resembling the daylily and also grows tall and the parrot whose petals resemble feathers and which grows about seven inches high.

7. Tulips are planted in the fall, they bloom in the spring.

8. Tulips prefer a well-drained sandy soil; however, some varieties adapt to other soils easily.

9. Cutting some varieties of tulips for display in a vase can be risky; the cut flowers require a lot of water and, if the supply is not replenished often, the flowers quickly droop.

10. Most people associate the tulip with the country of Holland, nevertheless a major tulip festival occurs every spring in the city of Holland, Michigan.

---

30 The Colon

The **colon** introduces elements that explain, illustrate, or expand the preceding part of the sentence. It calls attention to the word, phrase, clause, or quotation that follows it.

30a Before Elements Introduced Formally

Use a colon when formally introducing a statement or a quotation.

Capitalize the first word of a formal statement or a quotation.

> One of the guiding principles of our government may be stated as follows: All people are created equal.

> Though Murphy's identity is not known, Murphy's Law seems to be a truth: "If anything can go wrong, it will."

Use a colon when formally introducing a series of items.

> The picture gallery at the Vatican contains magnificent treasures: Raphael's *Madonna of Foligno,* Titian's *Madonna of San Niccolô dei Frari,* Leonardo's *St. Jerome,* Caravaggio's *Deposition,* Rouault's *Autumn,* and Utrillo's *The Church of St. Auxonne.*

From 1933 through 1981, unsuccessful assassination attempts were made on the lives of the following presidents: Franklin Roosevelt, Harry Truman, Gerald Ford, and Ronald Reagan.

Nine planets circle the sun: Mercury, Venus, Earth, Mars, Jupiter, Saturn, Uranus, Neptune, and Pluto.

30b Before Formal Appositives

Use a colon before a formal appositive, including one beginning with a phrase such as *namely, that is, specifically,* or *in other words.*

In many cases, a dash would also be appropriate in this situation.

The scholar wrote mysteries for one reason and one reason only: to make money.

Domenikos Theotocopoulos, whom many consider one of the greatest painters of all times, is better known by his pseudonym: El Greco.

In 1961, Kennedy made one of the toughest decisions of his presidency: *namely,* to back the invasion at the Bay of Pigs.

Notice that the colon in the third example appears *before* the word *namely.*

30c Between Two Independent Clauses

Use a colon between two independent clauses when the second clause explains or expands the first.

Cubism was more than a new movement: it was a revolution.

After reading the letter, he did something that surprised me: he laughed.

The clause following the colon may begin with a capital or a lowercase letter. However, a lowercase letter is preferred.

30d In Salutations and Bibliographical Entries

Use a colon after a salutation in a formal letter or speech.

> Dear Dr. Jacoby:
>
> Ladies and Gentlemen:
>
> Members of the Board:

Use a colon between the city and the publisher in a bibliographical entry.

> Boston: Allyn & Bacon
>
> London: John Murray
>
> Chicago: The University of Chicago Press

Use a colon between a title and its subtitle.

> *Tutankhamen: The Untold Story*
>
> *Nooks and Crannies: An Unusual Walking Tour Guide to New York City*
>
> *The Seeing Hand: A Treasury of Great Master Drawings*

30e Misused Colons

Avoid using a colon after a form of the verb *be,* after a preposition, or between a verb and its object.

> **NOT:** Three devices the ancient Romans used to tell time were: sundials, water clocks, and sand-filled glasses.

BUT: Three devices the ancient Romans used to tell time were sundials, water clocks, and sand-filled glasses.

OR: The Romans used three devices to tell time**:** sundials, water clocks, and sand-filled glasses.

NOT: In 1966, France effectively withdrew from NATO, which thereafter consisted of**:** Belgium, Canada, Denmark, Great Britain, Greece, Iceland, Italy, Luxembourg, the Netherlands, Norway, Portugal, Turkey, the United States, and West Germany.

BUT: In 1966, France effectively withdrew from NATO, which thereafter consisted of Belgium, Canada, Denmark, Great Britain, Greece, Iceland, Italy, Luxembourg, the Netherlands, Norway, Portugal, Turkey, the United States, and West Germany.

NOT: The store manager ordered**:** six microwave ovens, four dishwashers, seven coffee makers, and eleven toasters.

BUT: The store manager ordered six microwave ovens, four dishwashers, seven coffee makers, and eleven toasters.

Checking Colons
ON A WORD PROCESSOR

Because you probably seldom use colons, you should check each use. With the search function, find the colons in your writing, and check to make sure that you have used each one correctly. Make sure that you have not placed a colon between a verb and its complement, after a preposition, or after a form of the verb *be* (see Section 30e).

Grammar checkers do not catch missing or misused colons.

EXERCISE 30-1

Place a colon where it is necessary in each of the following sentences.

1. The teacher responded by quoting Michaelangelo "Trifles make perfection but perfection is no trifle."

2. The players could not understand the coach's logic in other words, his reasoning processes appeared to be faulty.

3. No one realized how tired she was until the evidence became indisputable specifically, she collapsed.

4. He purchased supplies needed for the weekend picnic hot dogs, buns, potato chips, and soda.

---

31 The Dash

The **dash** is less formal than the colon. It is used to give *emphasis* or clarity to extra information in a sentence. Dashes should be used sparingly in college writing. When typing, produce a dash by two hyphens without a space before, after, or between them (--).

31a With an Introductory Series

Use a dash to separate an introductory series from its summarizing clause.

His own party, the opposition, and the public—all were astounded by his resignation.

Chaucer, Shakespeare, Malory—these were her favorite writers.

31b With Parenthetical Elements

Use dashes to set off a parenthetical element that you wish to emphasize.

> The castle was surrounded by a moat and contained—I found this astounding—an actual dungeon.

> On his first day as a volunteer, he fought a fire in—of all places—the firehouse.

Use dashes to clarify a parenthetical element that contains *commas.*

> Of our first five presidents, four—George Washington, Thomas Jefferson, James Madison, and James Monroe—came from Virginia.

> The first recorded Olympic Games—which, you will be surprised to know, this reporter did not see—were held in 776 B.C.

31c With Terminal Elements

Use a dash to introduce informally a terminal element that explains or illustrates the information in the main part of the sentence.

> They pledged to prevent what seemed inevitable—war.

> He battled his worst enemy—himself.

> Willie little appreciated her greatest attribute—her sense of humor.

Use a dash to introduce informally a terminal element that is a break in thought or a shift in tone.

> Raquel confessed that she was desperately in love—with me.

> No one loves a gossip—except another gossip.

"But she said she had——I can't believe it," Patrick exclaimed.

EXERCISE 31-1

Indicate where dashes may be placed in each of the following sentences.

1. Bach, Beethoven, Brahms, Bruckner all these composers were represented on one program.

2. Three of Beethoven's compositions the "Eroica Symphony," the "Leonore Overture," and the "Choral Fantasy" were performed before the intermission.

3. It was a long concert to put it mildly!

4. The Bach selection no one will believe this was an unknown, rarely played sinfonia.

5. When the concert ended, guess who the conductor asked to take a bow the cellist.

---

32 Parentheses

Parentheses enclose information or comments that break the continuity of the sentence or paragraph. Unlike the dash, which tends to emphasize, parentheses *minimize* the importance of the material they enclose and therefore should be used sparingly. The information within parentheses should be of such a nature that it may be omitted without changing the essential meaning of the sentence.

32a With Incidental Comments and Additional Information

Use parentheses to enclose comments or additional information that you do not wish to emphasize.

On August 11, 1960, Chad (see map) became independent.

Charles Darwin (1809–1882) was a contemporary of Abraham Lincoln.

Ibsen's *A Doll's House* (which was quite revolutionary for its time) ends with Nora's walking out on her husband.

Do not use a capital letter or a period for a parenthetical sentence within another sentence. Use a capital letter and a period for a parenthetical sentence that stands by itself.

SENTENCE WITHIN ANOTHER SENTENCE

After the Civil War, carpetbaggers (their name came from their habit of carrying their belongings in a bag made of carpet material) took advantage of Southern blacks who had just been given the vote.

Demosthenes warned the Athenians against King Philip of Macedon (he felt King Philip was a threat to their liberty).

The Democratic Party (this is the party founded by that lover of liberty, Thomas Jefferson) was divided on the question of slavery.

Notice that in the second example, the period ending the main sentence goes *outside* the closing parenthesis.

SENTENCE STANDING BY ITSELF

In the fifteenth century, Christian I founded the Oldenburg dynasty. (In modern Denmark, the ruling family traces its roots to him.) Christian II, however, was removed from the throne in 1523.

Elizabeth Barrett Browning is remembered in part for her beautiful love poems. (She died in 1861.)

In the original *King Kong,* the huge creature climbed what was then the tallest building in the world, the Empire State Building. (In the second version of the movie, he climbed the World Trade Center.) There he was attacked by airplanes.

Notice that the period ending the parenthetical sentence goes *inside* the closing parenthesis.

32b With Items in a Series

Use parentheses to enclose numbers and letters designating items in a series.

When accepting a credit card from a customer, you should (a) check the customer's signature against the card, (b) call the credit-card company for approval, and (c) write the approval code on the credit slip.

In the nineteenth century, the United States was involved in four wars: (1) the War of 1812, (2) the Mexican War, (3) the Civil War, and (4) the Spanish–American War.

32c With Other Punctuation Marks

Place a comma, semicolon, or colon *outside* a closing parenthesis.

Although most Americans have heard of the Battle of Lexington and Concord (which occurred on April 19, 1775), many do not know that it is commemorated as Patriots' Day in Massachusetts.

Maine has successfully preserved its northern moose population (the moose is Maine's official state animal); however, the state's deer population is now endangered by the growing moose herd.

The candidate carried only six states (plus the District of Columbia): Georgia, Hawaii, Maryland, Minnesota, Rhode Island, and West Virginia.

Place a question mark or exclamation point *inside* a closing parenthesis if the parenthetical expression itself is a question or an exclamation.

> Sean was astonished when he opened the door to his room and found a letter (who could have put it there**?**) lying on the floor.

> The Founding Fathers considered many different animals (Benjamin Franklin suggested the turkey**!**) before they decided to make the bald eagle the national symbol of the United States.

Place a question mark or exclamation point *outside* a closing parenthesis if the sentence is a question or exclamation but the parenthetical expression is not.

> Did you know that Lewis Carroll wrote *Alice in Wonderland* for a real girl named Alice (Alice Liddell)**?**

> Never was I more surprised than when I found wild berries growing in a New York City park (there were both raspberries and blackberries)**!**

33   Brackets

Brackets enclose information inserted into quotations, and they take the place of parentheses within parentheses. Brackets are used mainly in formal writing.

33a With Inserted Information

Use brackets to enclose information inserted into direct quotations for clarification.

"The fellow [Rubens] mixes blood with his colors," claimed Guido Reni.

The comedian quipped, "From the moment I picked your [S. J. Perelman's] book up until I laid it down, I was convulsed with laughter. Someday I intend reading it."

"Government [in a democracy] cannot be stronger or more tough-minded than its people," said Adlai Stevenson.

Use brackets to enclose editorial comments inserted into quoted material.

According to Clarence Darrow, "The first half of our lives is ruined by our parents [how many people under twenty agree with this!] and the second half by our children."

Notice that the exclamation point is placed inside the closing bracket because it is part of the editorial comment.

The word *sic* or *thus* enclosed in brackets is used to indicate that an incorrect or seemingly incorrect or inappropriate word is not a mistake on the part of the present writer but appears in the original quotation.

Jane Austen parodied the popular melodramatic fiction of her day in "Love and Freindship [*sic*]," which she completed at the age of fourteen.

Notice that the comma is placed *outside* the closing bracket and that *sic* is italicized.

33b With Parentheses

Use brackets to replace parentheses within parentheses.

Some humpback whales reach a length of over fifty feet. (See p. 89 [chart] for a comparison of the sizes of whales.)

> Several books are available on the life and times of "Boss" Tweed. (For a revisionist picture of Tweed, we suggest Leo Hershkowitz's *Tweed's New York* [Garden City: Anchor Press/Doubleday, 1977].)

Notice that the period is placed *inside* the closing parenthesis because the entire sentence is enclosed by parentheses.

> The reading list contains several books dealing with the issue of freedom of the press (for example, Fred W. Friendly's *Minnesota Rag: The Dramatic Story of the Landmark Supreme Court Case that Gave New Meaning to Freedom of the Press* [New York: Random House, 1981]).

Notice that the period is placed *outside* the closing parenthesis because only part of the sentence is enclosed by parentheses.

Special Punctuation Marks
AND YOUR WORD PROCESSOR

You can use the search function to locate any dashes, parentheses, or brackets in your writing. Check these marks to be sure that they conform to accepted usage. Because you can modify your writing on a word processor without completely retyping, you can try out alternative forms of punctuation to create emphasis and vary style.

EXERCISE 33-1

Add parentheses and/or brackets where necessary to enclose information in each of the following sentences.

1. According to the famous British jurist, "The road to judgement

   sic is not a strait jacket."

2. During the Middle Ages, carols were also dances. They were not limited to the Christmas season either see examples 9 and 10 in the text.

3. In the past thirty years, the map of Africa see plate in text has changed drastically.

4. After agreeing on a budget compromise, the chair of the Senate budget committee Democrat–Indiana changed her mind.

5. We all helped to give him John a surprise birthday party.

34 Quotation Marks

Quotation marks enclose quoted material and certain kinds of titles. They are always used in pairs.

34a For Direct Quotations

Use quotation marks to enclose a direct quotation—the exact words of a speaker or writer.

> When one character says to Mae West, "My goodness, those diamonds are beautiful," West replies, "Goodness had nothing whatever to do with it."

> In *The Code of the Woosters,* Bertie vividly describes the aunt he fears: "Aunt Agatha, who eats broken bottles and wears barbed wire next to the skin."

The opening lines set the tone of the poem: "I will be the gladdest thing / Under the sun!" (*The slash indicates the end of a line in a poem.*)

When writing dialogue, begin a new paragraph each time the speaker changes.

"This coat costs $25.00," said the seller at the flea market.

"That's too much," said the customer.

"Did I say $25.00?" responded the seller. "I meant $15.00."

34b Block Quotations

When quoting a **prose** passage of considerable length, you omit quotation marks when you use the block quotation form. The Modern Language Association's (MLA) guidelines advise **block quotation** form for four or more lines of prose; the American Psychological Association (APA) specifies its use for passages of forty or more words. Type the material double-spaced. If you are using MLA form, indent ten spaces or one inch from the left-hand margin. Further indent three spaces or a quarter inch for a paragraph, but only where a paragraph appears in the original. APA guidelines suggest that you indent only five spaces from the left-hand margin, indenting five additional spaces for a paragraph. Note that the right margin does not change and that double-spacing separates the quote from the text. These instructions apply principally to material that is being prepared for publication. Your instructor may adjust these rules for class assignments and may suggest single-spacing in block form.

Here is an example following MLA rules:

In a speech he made in New York in 1911, Woodrow Wilson underscored the importance of business:

> Business underlies everything in our national life,
> including our spiritual life. Witness the fact that in
> the Lord's Prayer the first petition is for daily bread.
> No one can worship God or love his neighbor on an
> empty stomach.

Following is an example of APA rules:

In Psychological Types, Jung stated the following:

> The dynamic principle of fantasy is play, which belongs also
> to the child, and as such it appears to be inconsistent with
> the principle of serious work. But without this playing with
> fantasy no creative work has ever yet come to birth. The
> debt we owe to the play of imagination is incalculable.

When quoting four or more lines of *poetry,* double-space lines and indent, according to MLA guidelines, one inch or ten spaces, or five fewer if the poetic lines are long (APA style recommends spaces as with prose quotations). Type the poem line for line, following the spatial arrangement of the original. Do not use quotation marks.

Thoreau, as he explains in Walden, or Life in the Woods, lived
less than two miles from the village of Concord and yet felt that
he was living on a distant star, like the shepherd in the
anonymous poem he quotes:

> There was a shepherd that did live,
>   And held his thoughts as high
> As were the mounts whereon his flocks
>   Did hourly feed him by.

34c For Quotations within Quotations

Use single quotation marks to enclose quoted material contained within a quotation.

> In "Silence," Marianne Moore wrote: "My father used to say, 'Superior people never make long visits.' "

> The British humorist Robert Morley once joked, "Beware of the conversationalist who adds 'in other words.' He is merely starting afresh."

> Jensen looked up from his research and declared, "I've found the answer. It was Henry Clay who said, 'I would rather be right than President.' "

34d For Titles of Short Works

Use quotation marks to enclose the quoted titles of short stories, short poems, one-act plays, essays, articles, subdivisions of books, episodes of a television series, songs, short musical compositions, and dissertations.

> In his poem "Son of Frankenstein," Edward Field reveals the loneliness of the Frankenstein monster.

> In the second half of *Brideshead Revisited,* entitled "A Twitch upon the Thread," Charles returns from South America, and Lord Marchmain returns to Brideshead to die.

> Joan Didion details the pattern of shopping malls in "On the Mall."

Use underlining for the titles of longer works (see Section 36a).

34e With Other Punctuation Marks

Place a period or a comma *inside* a closing quotation mark.

In "Perseid**,**" John Barth writes, "Stories last longer than men, stones than stories, stars than stones**.**"

"I don't want to talk grammar**,**" Eliza Doolittle says in *Pygmalion*. "I want to talk like a lady**.**"

"After all**,**" says Scarlett, "tomorrow is another day**.**"

Place a semicolon or a colon *outside* a closing quotation mark.

The critic wrote that the play demonstrated the playwright's "dissatisfaction with satisfaction"**;** this comment, I felt, was more preposterous than the play itself.

In the American detective story, few women are private eyes. One of the best known of these women appears in Stuart Palmer's "The Riddle of the Twelve Amethysts"**:** Hildegarde Withers.

Place a question mark or an exclamation point *inside* a closing quotation mark if the quotation itself is a question or exclamation.

The song I was trying to recall is "Will You Love Me in December**?**"

Upon reaching the summit of Mount Everest, Sherpa Tensing declared, "We've done the bugger**!**"

Place a question mark or an exclamation point *outside* the closing quotation mark if the sentence is a question or exclamation but the quotation itself is not.

Who first said, "Big Brother is watching you"**?**

What a scene she caused by saying, "I don't want to"**!**

If both the sentence and the quotation are questions or exclamations, use only one question mark or exclamation point, and place it *inside* the closing quotation mark.

Why did she cause a scene by asking, "Who is that woman**?**"

Of course, the rules for using other punctuation marks with quotation marks apply to single quotation marks as well.

> Harold asked, "Do you know who coined the term 'the brain trust**'?"** (*Question mark ends Harold's quotation.*)

> Gordon said, "I can hear the crowd shouting, 'Long live the king**!' "** (*Exclamation point ends quotation within quotation.*)

Checking Quotation Marks
ON A WORD PROCESSOR

Use the search function to locate quotation marks, and check to be sure that you have placed commas and periods *inside* the quotation marks (i.e., *before* the closing mark). Also be sure that every opening quotation mark is balanced with a closing quotation mark.

34f Misused Quotation Marks

Do not use quotation marks to enclose indirect quotations.

> **NOT:** The seer declared that **"**they would win the war against the Macedonians.**"**
>
> **BUT:** The seer declared that they would win the war against the Macedonians.
>
> **NOT:** The editorial proclaimed that **"**the president would win the next election.**"**
>
> **BUT:** The editorial proclaimed that the president would win the next election.

Note: The word *that* is usually used to introduce an indirect quotation, *not* a direct quotation.

Do not use quotation marks to enclose a title used as the heading of a paper, theme, or essay.

> Suicide and the Modern Poet
>
> Science Fiction in the 1930s
>
> Communication among Chimpanzees

EXERCISE 34-1

Identify where quotation marks are needed in the following sentences. Three of the sentences do not need quotation marks.

1. Horace is credited with the now proverbial saying, Taste is not a matter to be disputed.

2. Although you all mean well, said the music director, nothing can substitute for practice.

3. The professor admonished, Remember to get a good night's rest before the examination day.

4. The chairperson advised that we all needed to try our very best in this endeavor.

5. A native of Indiana, James Whitcomb Riley has come to be known as the Hoosier poet.

6. Yet to come, said the announcer, is the winner.

7. The editor claimed that he could not reveal the name of the reporter who wrote the article.

8. The anxious student asked, Did anyone here see my brown book bag?

9. John Keats ended his poem, To Autumn, with the line, And gathering swallows twitter in the skies.

10. If you view Picasso's painting, <u>The Tragedy</u>, after reading Márquez's short story, Tuesday Siesta, the impact is astounding.

---

35   Ellipsis Points and the Slash

35a   Ellipsis Points

    Ellipsis points are equally spaced dots, or periods. They indicate that part of a quotation has been omitted.

Use three ellipsis points within a quotation to indicate that part of the quotation has been left out, or omitted. To distinguish between your ellipsis points and the spaced periods that sometimes appear in written works, put square brackets around the ellipsis dots that you add.

Partial quotations do not need ellipsis points at beginning and end.

> **NOT:**   The politician declared that Indians have " • • • a reverence for the life-giving earth • • • •"
>
> **BUT:**   The politician declared that Indians have "a reverence for the life-giving earth."

When typing, leave a space before the first bracket, a space between each of the points, and a space after the last bracket.

In *The Other America: Poverty in the United States,* Michael Harrington writes: "They [the poor] are not simply neglected **[• • •]** they are not seen."

In *The Quiet Crisis,* Stewart Udall writes: "The most common trait **[• • •]** is a reverence for the life-giving earth, and the native American shared this elemental ethic: the land was alive to his touch, and he, its son, was brother to all creatures."

The Atlantic Charter states: "Eighth, they believe that all of the nations of the world **[• • •]** must come to the abandonment of the use of force."

Use a period and three ellipsis points to indicate that the end of a sentence has been left out of a quotation.

Huck said, "It most froze me to hear such talk **[• • •]** . Thinks I, this is what comes of my not thinking."

The review said, "The book promises a cornucopia of unusual characters **[• • •]** . That promise is fully realized."

35b The Slash

Use a slash to indicate that a pair of options exist.

She wants to go to the movies but he wants us to go bowling; either/or will suit me fine.

He prefers diet soda/low calorie yogurt.

Use a slash to indicate the end of a line of poetry when you are citing three lines or fewer and when you are not using the block form of citation. Note that a space precedes and follows the slash.

Wordsworth's poem begins: "My heart leaps up when I behold / A rainbow in the sky."

Avoid using a slash to form the construction *s/he*, a nonstandard usage for *she and he;* instead, write the phrase as *she or he* or as *he or she*.

36 Italics or Underlining

Underlining in a typed or handwritten paper serves the same purpose as *italics* in a published or computer-generated work. It highlights or sets apart certain titles, words, or phrases.

36a For Titles

Underline or, on the computer, use an italic font for the titles of books, full-length musical compositions, paintings, television series, plays, and long poems and the names of newspapers, magazines, ships, boats, and aircraft.

The Light in the Forest (*book*)

Madame Butterfly (*opera*)

The Rape of the Lock (*long poem*)

the Mayflower (*ship*)

Be careful to underline only the exact title or name. Do not underline words added to complete the meaning of the title.

the Atlantic magazine (*The word* magazine *is not part of the name.*)

the London Times or the Times of London (London *is not part of the name.*)

Be careful to underline all the words that make up the title.

> <u>The Decline and Fall of the Roman Empire</u> (The *is part of the title.*)
>
> <u>A Childhood</u> (A *is part of the title.*)
>
> <u>Standard & Poor's New Issue Investor</u> (Standard & Poor's *is a part of the title.*)

(Do not underline the heading of your own papers.)

36b For Words

Underline foreign words or phrases that are not commonly used in English, or use an italic font on the computer.

In general, a word or phrase need not be underlined if it is listed in a standard English dictionary. For example, the Spanish word *siesta,* the French phrase *coup de grace,* and the Latin phrase *ad infinitum* are now considered part of English and are not underlined.

> German women were traditionally expected to confine themselves to <u>Kinder,</u> <u>Kirche,</u> <u>Küche.</u>
>
> <u>Chacun à son goût</u> proved a difficult principle to apply in this case.
>
> The great English public schools attempted to follow the ideal of <u>mens sana in corpore sano.</u>

Underline letters, words, or phrases being named or use an italic font on the computer.

> How many <u>i</u>'s are in <u>Mississippi</u>?
>
> His life demonstrates the meaning of the word <u>waste.</u>
>
> What is the derivation of the phrase <u>on the ball</u>?

In most cases, it is also appropriate to use quotation marks instead of underlining for this purpose.

Underline words and phrases for emphasis, or use an italic font on the computer.

> I did <u>not</u> say I would do that.
>
> You <u>must</u> stop overeating!
>
> You plan to do <u>what</u>?

Do not overuse this device. Too much underlining or italics weakens the effect. Emphasize only what deserves emphasis.

Underlining, Italics, AND WORD PROCESSORS

Most word-processing programs and computer printers allow you to use italic type, but sometimes this type is not very distinctive. Before you choose an italic font, look at a sample printout; if the italics are difficult to read, use underlining instead. You should also check your teacher's preferences; some instructors prefer underlining even if their students can produce italics.

EXERCISE 36-1

Specifically identify which items require underlining in each of the following sentences, and explain why.

1. The novel Buffalo Girls was written after Larry McMurtry was awarded the Pulitzer Prize for his novel Lonesome Dove.

2. The word fallacy derives from a Latin word, fallacia, which means deceit.

3. Two popular magazines in the men's dormitory are Gentlemen's Quarterly and Popular Mechanics.

4. Beowulf was the first long epic poem in the English language.

5. His biography reveals that his grandparents sailed to this country on the Queen Elizabeth II.

37   **The Apostrophe**

37a **In Possessive Forms**

The possessive case forms of all nouns and of many pronouns are spelled with an apostrophe. The following rules explain when to use an apostrophe for possessive forms and where to place the apostrophe.

Note: Do not be misled by the term *possessive*. Rather than trying to see "ownership," consider the possessive case form as an indication that one noun modifies another in some of the ways adjectives do. (See Section 8d.) Consider these examples:

a **week's** vacation	the **flower's** fragrance
Egypt's history	a **car's** mileage
the **river's** source	your **money's** worth

1   Singular nouns

To form the possessive of a singular noun, add an apostrophe and *s*.

Kirsoff's review emphasized the **dramatist's** outstanding contribution to the arts.

A **woman's** effort to free herself from the past is the concern of Alice **Walker's** novel, *Meridian*.

The Greeks tried to appease **Zeus's** anger, just as the Romans tried to avoid **Jupiter's** wrath.

Usage varies for singular nouns ending in *s*. Many writers follow the regular rule for singular nouns and add an apostrophe and *s*.

The **boss's** salary is three times that of her assistant.

We discussed **Keats's** sonnets in class today.

But it is also acceptable to form the possessive of such singular nouns by adding only an apostrophe.

The **witness'** testimony seemed vague and unconvincing.

Macmillan published **Yeats'** first collection of poetry in 1939.

2   Plural nouns

To form the possessive of a plural noun that does not end in *s*, add an apostrophe and *s*.

The **women's** proposal called for a day-care center to be set up at their place of employment.

Dr. Seuss is a well-known name in the field of **children's** literature.

The store has introduced a new line of **men's** fragrances.

To form the possessive of a plural noun that ends in *s*, add an apostrophe alone.

The **doctors'** commitment to their patients was questioned at the forum.

The course highlights two **composers'** works—Haydn and Mozart.

3 Compound nouns

To form the possessive of a compound noun, make the last word possessive.

> Do most people welcome a **mother-in-law's** advice?
>
> As a result of the **Vice President's** remarks, the student council members asked for his removal from the ticket.
>
> The editorial defended the **police officers'** conduct in the case.

4 Noun pairs or nouns in a series

To show joint possession, add an apostrophe and *s* to the last noun in a pair or a series.

> Sociologists were concerned that the **royal couple's** announcement would set off a new baby boom in Britain.
>
> **Lennon and McCartney's** music had a dramatic effect on their contemporaries.

To show individual possession, add an apostrophe and *s* to each noun in a pair or series.

> **Anne Tyler's** and **Sam Shepard's** styles have many similarities.
>
> The **President's** and the **Vice President's** duties are clearly defined.

5 Nouns naming periods of time and sums of money

To form the possessive of a noun naming a period of time or a sum of money, add an apostrophe and *s* or an apostrophe if the noun is plural.

> The value of **today's** dollar is less than the value of last **year's** dollar.
>
> Taxes can easily swallow several **days'** pay.

6   Indefinite pronouns

To form the possessive of some indefinite pronouns, add an apostrophe and *s*. (Note that *each, both, all,* and some others can have no possessive form.)

> We can learn from **each other's** mistakes.
>
> How we can improve our care of the elderly is a subject on almost **everyone's** mind.

7   Personal pronouns

Do not use an apostrophe with the possessive forms of personal pronouns.

> Her analysis of the problem was more complete than **yours.**
>
> The druids' methods of telling time were quite different from **ours.**
>
> Our troops are better prepared than **theirs.**

37b In Plural Forms

Add an apostrophe and *s* to form the plural of words being named, letters of the alphabet, abbreviations, numerals, and symbols. The apostrophe may be omitted with capitals without periods: TVs, UFOs, PhDs.

> One drawback of this typeface is that the capital *i*'s and the lower-case *l*'s look exactly alike.
>
> Avoid weakening your argument by including too many *but*'s and *however*'s.

37c For Omissions

Use an apostrophe to indicate that part of a word or number has been omitted.

> In **'64** the Beatles invaded the United States with a new style of rock **'n'** roll.

> The manager told the singer to "go out and knock **'em** dead."

37d In Contractions

A **contraction** is a shortened form of a word or words. Contractions are widely used in speech and in informal writing.

Use an apostrophe to indicate a missing letter or letters in a contraction.

> Winning at cards **wasn't** Tony's only claim to success.

> Enrique claimed that enough attention **isn't** being paid to the threat of environmental pollution.

Note: It's is a contraction meaning "it is" or "it has." *Its* is a possessive pronoun meaning "belonging to it" and does not require an apostrophe.

> **It's** your turn to drive today.

> The dog covered **its** right eye with **its** paw.

Do not confuse the two.

In general, avoid contractions in formal writing.

> **INFORMAL:**   During his lifetime, Mark Twain **didn't** receive the serious critical attention he deserved.
>
> **FORMAL:**   During his lifetime, Mark Twain **did not** receive the serious critical attention he deserved.

Apostrophes
AND WORD PROCESSORS

Grammar checkers usually catch missing apostrophes in common contractions, such as *isn't,* and they will flag some errors with possessives. But they cannot analyze the problem. You have to decide whether to add an apostrophe and, if so, whether to put it before or after the *s.*

EXERCISE 37-1

In each of the following groups, circle the items that show the incorrect use of an apostrophe or that omit a necessary apostrophe.

1. everyone's person, no ones car, anyones' boss

2. our chairs, it's fun, her' bracelet

3. it's house, our home, its' there

4. one of your's, brother-in-law's pencil, two of ours

5. a seasons toil, a day's wages, an hour's labor

6. Mary' and Bill's book, Juan's and Alfredo's stereo, Jim's and Ed's computer disk (*individual ownership*)

7. John's and Mary's apartment, Stephanie and Ophra's car, Luis'
   and Maria's sonnets (*joint ownership*)

8. mens' coats, women's scarves, sheeps' wool

9. didn't try, can't stop, do'nt do it

10. Elvis song, TV's schedule, the silent '50s

---

38 The Hyphen

38a In Compound Nouns

Use a dictionary to determine whether to spell a compound
noun with a hyphen.

Relatively few compound nouns are hyphenated; most are written either solid (as one word) or open (as two or more separate
words). The only kinds of compound nouns that are usually hyphenated are those made up of two equally important nouns and
those made up of three or more words.

>   philosopher-king   city-state   man-hour
>   mother-in-law   free-for-all   jack-of-all-trades

38b In Compound Adjectives

Hyphenate two or more words that serve as a single adjective
preceding a noun.

> **well-known** painter **law-school** degree
> **soft-spoken** man **sure-to-win** candidate
> **too-good-to-be-true** behavior

Do you know the difference between **mass-market** paperbacks and trade paperbacks?

Cheever's stories provide insight into **middle-class** suburban life.

The company is investigating both the **short-term** and the **long-term** benefits of scattered work hours.

In general, do not hyphenate such words when they follow a noun.

> painter who is **well known** degree from a **law school**
> man who is **soft spoken** candidate who is **sure to win**
> behavior that is **too good to be true**

Do you know the difference between novels that are considered **mass market** and novels that are considered trade?

Cheever's stories provide insight into the lives of suburban people who are **middle class.**

The benefits of scattered work hours are both **short term** and **long term.**

Do not hyphenate two or more words that precede a noun when the first of these words is an adverb ending in *-ly.*

> Critics attacked the President's **rapidly expanding** budget.

> When the famous rock group first came to this city, the police were called in to restrain the crowd of **wildly screaming** teenagers.

> The government's **widely criticized** policies are the subject of the debate on television today.

Use a hanging hyphen after the first part of a hyphenated compound adjective used in a series, where the second part of the compound adjective is implied but omitted.

both **paid-** and complimentary-ticket holders

both **short-** and long-term disability

all **first-, second-,** and third-year students

38c In Compound Numbers and Fractions

Hyphenate spelled-out numbers from *twenty-one* through *ninety-nine* and spelled-out fractions used as adjectives.

In spelled-out numbers larger than *ninety-nine,* do not use a hyphen before or after *hundred, thousand,* and so forth.

> **Two hundred fifty-seven** people were killed in the fire.

> The installation of computers has effected a **one-third** increase in productivity and an expected **three-quarter** growth in profits.

> The novel had **thirty-two** chapters in its first version, but the revised version has **forty-one.**

Do not hyphenate spelled-out fractions used as nouns.

> About **one half** of Yugoslavia is covered with mountains.

> Only **three eighths** of the adults in this community voted in the last election.

38d With Prefixes and Suffixes

In general, do not use a hyphen between a prefix and its root or a suffix and its root. However, there are a few exceptions:

Use a hyphen between a prefix and its root to avoid ambiguity.

the **re-creation** of the world	*but*	tennis as **recreation**
to **re-count** money	*but*	to **recount** an event
a **co-op** apartment	*but*	a chicken **coop**

Use a hyphen between a prefix and its root when the last letter of the prefix and the first letter of the root are the same vowel or when the first letter of the root is capitalized.

sem**i-i**ndustrial   ant**i-i**ntellectual
supr**a-a**uditory   r**e-e**cho
un-**A**merican   pro-**W**estern

Exceptions: Frequent usage may allow the elimination of the hyphen. (Consult the dictionary.)

cooperation   preempt   reexamine

Use a hyphen between the prefixes *all, ex* ("former"), and *self* and their roots and between the suffix *elect* and its root.

all-star   all-time
ex-senator   ex-husband
self-control   self-sufficient
mayor-elect   president-elect

38e For Word Division at the End of a Line

In general, writers no longer divide words at the ends of lines. If a word will not fit on a line, just leave the line short and begin the word on the next line. The word-wrap feature of word-processing programs will take care of this procedure automatically. If you choose to divide a word, consult a dictionary about where the break should occur.

EXERCISE 38-1

Circle the correct form of each word in parentheses in the following sentences:

1. (Twenty one/Twenty-one) lawyers worked on the case for the corporation and produced (well-researched/well researched) opinions that proved to be (thought-provoking/thought provoking).

2. The (all state/all-state) team included several (all-star/all star) players that became (all time/all-time) greats in football.

3. He said that (one fifth/one-fifth) of those people present were fooled by (mass-media/mass media) efforts to sway opinion.

4. The (well-known/well known) speaker attended a university that is (world-famous/world famous).

5. The (city-county/city county) building is located near the (short-term/short term) parking lot.

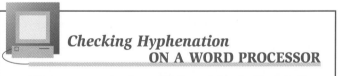

Checking Hyphenation
ON A WORD PROCESSOR

Most grammar checkers will flag missing hyphens in fractions (*two-thirds*) and compound numbers (*fifty-four*). The spelling program can also tell you how to spell some compound words, but you should consult a dictionary when you are in doubt.

EXERCISE 38-2

Circle any correctly hyphenated words in each of the following groups.

1. self-discipline, semi-independent, un-intelligent

2. semi-dilapidated, mid-winter, all-ready

3. bishop-designate, chairperson-elect, old-senator

4. excitedly-screaming, true-to-life, a hundred-thirty-one

39 Abbreviations

In general, avoid abbreviations in formal writing. However, abbreviations are acceptable in certain situations.

39a For Titles or Designations

Use an abbreviation for the following designations preceding names:

Mr.	Messrs.	St. (Saint)
Mrs.	Mmes.	Mt. (Mount)
Ms.	Dr.	Rev. (unless preceded by *the*)

Is **Mrs.** Dalloway a fully realized character?

For what musicals are **Messrs.** Rogers and Hart responsible?

Rev. James Spenser read the service.

Note: Spell out *Reverend* when it is preceded by *the*.

The **Reverend** James Spenser read the service.

Avoid using an abbreviation for any other designation preceding a name.

NOT: No one was surprised when **Pres.** Reagan said that he would run again.

BUT: No one was surprised when **President** Reagan said that he would run again.

NOT: Are you campaigning for **Sen.** Jones?

BUT: Are you campaigning for **Senator** Jones?

NOT: In his new book, **Prof.** Rosenthal discusses the use of imagery in the poetry of Ted Hughes.

BUT: In his new book, **Professor** Rosenthal discusses the use of imagery in the poetry of Ted Hughes.

Use an abbreviation preceded by a comma for a designation or an academic degree following a name.

Jr.	Ph.D. or PhD (Doctor of Philosophy)
Sr.	Ed.D. or EdD (Doctor of Education)
B.A. or BA (Bachelor of Arts)	
M.A. or MA (Master of Arts)	M.B.A. or MBA (Master of Business Administration)
M.S. or MS (Master of Science)	
D.D.S. or DDS (Doctor of Dental Science)	J.D. or JD (Doctor of Jurisprudence)
D.D. or DD (Doctor of Divinity)	D.V.M. or DVM (Doctor of Veterinary Medicine)
M.D. or MD (Doctor of Medicine)	

The speaker will be Thomas Dean, **Jr.**

The academy announced the appointment of Marion Unger, **Ph.D.,** as chair. (*or* **PhD** *without periods*)

Avoid using the abbreviation *Dr.* before a name that is followed by an abbreviation denoting a doctoral degree. Using both is redundant.

39b For Acronyms and Organizational Abbreviations

Use abbreviations without periods for many well-known agencies, organizations, and businesses and for other familiar abbreviations using capital letters.

> The newspaper accused the **CIA** of covert activities in that country.
>
> The **YMCA** is presenting a revival of Arthur Miller's *All My Sons.*
>
> The candidate sought the support of the **AFL-CIO.**

An **acronym** is a pronounceable word made from initials or parts of words. Consult your dictionary about its capitalization and be sure to explain, in parentheses, an acronym that might be unfamiliar to your readers.

> The next meeting of **OPEC** will be an important one.
>
> Bring your **scuba** (**s**elf-**c**ontained **u**nderwater **b**reathing **a**pparatus) equipment with you.
>
> America's **Zip** Code (**z**one **i**mprovement **p**lan) has improved the postal service.
>
> The lecture explained **quasars** (quasi-stellar objects).

39c In Dates and Numbers

With numerals, use the abbreviations *B.C.* or *BC* (before Christ) and *A.D.* or *AD* (*anno Domini,* "in the year of the Lord") for dates. Use the abbreviations *A.M.* or *AM* or *a.m.* (before noon) and *P.M.* or *PM* or *p.m.* (after noon) for time.

> Confucius, China's most important teacher and philosopher, was born in 551 **B.C.**
>
> In **AD** 37, Caligula was made emperor of Rome.
>
> The child was born at 6:37 **a.m.**

The abbreviation *B.C.* or *BC* should be put after the date, and the abbreviation *A.D.* or *AD* is usually put before the date. However, the practice of putting *AD* after the date is now also considered acceptable. *BC* and *AD* are sometimes replaced with the abbreviations *B.C.E.* (Before the Common Era) and *C.E.* (Common Era), respectively.

A.M. or *AM* and *P.M.* or *PM* may be written with either capital or lowercase letters, but be consistent within a single piece of writing. Lowercase letters require periods—*a.m.* or *p.m.*

Use the following abbreviations for common Latin words and expressions when appropriate:

c. or *ca.* (about)	*etc.* (and others)
cf. (compare)	*i.e.* (that is)
e.g. (for example)	*viz.* (namely)

Moses (*c.* 1350–1250 BC) led his people out of slavery.

Taoism is based on the teachings of Lao-zu (**cf.** Confucianism).

Monotheistic religions (**e.g.,** Christianity and Islam) worship only one god.

Do not overuse these Latin abbreviations. Where possible, try substituting the English equivalent.

Spell out the names of days and months.

NOT: The first game of the World Series will be played on **Oct.** 11.

BUT: The first game of the World Series will be played on **October** 11.

NOT: It snowed heavily on the first **Sat.** in **Dec.**

BUT: It snowed heavily on the first **Saturday** in **December.**

Spell out the names of cities, states, and countries, except in addresses.

NOT: He came to **N.Y.C.** to study music.

BUT: He came to **New York City** to study music.

NOT: Emily Dickinson was born in Amherst, **Mass.**

BUT: Emily Dickinson was born in Amherst, **Massachusetts.**

Checking Abbreviations ON A WORD PROCESSOR

You can use the spell checker in your word-processing program to check for irregular abbreviations. Because these programs include only the most generally accepted abbreviations, you should reconsider your use of any abbreviations that the spell checker brings to your attention.

39d Avoiding Unconventional Abbreviations

Spell out first names.

NOT: The editor of the collection is **Thom.** Webster.

BUT: The editor of the collection is **Thomas** Webster.

In names of businesses, spell out the words *Brothers, Corporation,* and *Company,* except in addresses or in bibliographic information in research papers.

NOT: She was employed by the firm of Magnum **Bros.**

BUT: She was employed by the firm of Magnum **Brothers.**

NOT: The employees at Thomas Smythe and **Co.** are on strike.

BUT: The employees at Thomas Smythe and **Company** are on strike.

In formal, nontechnical writing, spell out units of measure.

NOT: The pamphlet claims that anyone who is more than ten **lbs.** overweight is a candidate for a heart attack.

BUT:	The pamphlet claims that anyone who is more than ten **pounds** overweight is a candidate for a heart attack.
NOT:	How many **qts.** of milk did you sell?
BUT:	How many **quarts** of milk did you sell?

In technical writing, abbreviations are acceptable and often preferred.

40 Numbers

A **number** is a symbol that represents a specified quantity or location. In formal, nontechnical writing, we use numbers only in specific instances.

40a Numbers versus Words in Sentences

Use numbers for quantities that cannot be written as one or two words.

> During its first year, the book sold only **678** copies.
>
> Last Saturday this shop sold **1,059** doughnuts.

However, avoid beginning a sentence with a number.

> **Nine hundred seventy-six** people bought tickets for the concert, but only 341 attended.
>
> **Three hundred sixteen** photographs of San Francisco are on exhibit.

Spell out all numbers that can be written as one or two words and that modify a noun.

She sang a medley of **sixteen** Sondheim songs.

The gestation period for a rabbit is about **thirty-one** days.

We need **one hundred** squares to make this quilt.

Use numbers for decimals or fractions.

We had **2½** inches of rainfall last month.

What do they mean when they claim that the average family has **2.3** children?

When one number immediately follows another, spell out the first number and use a numeral for the second number.

He ran in **two 50**-meter races.

We have **three 6**-foot ladders in the garage.

40b For Conventional Identifications

Use numbers for addresses.

702 West **74**th Street   **1616** South Street

However, it is acceptable to spell out the name of a numbered street in an address.

417 **Eleventh** Avenue   210 East **Seventh** Street

Use numbers to identify pages, percentages, degrees, and amounts of money with the symbol $ or ¢.

Turn to **page 82** for an analysis of the works of Van Gogh.

The survey found that **70.2 percent** of registered voters favor Brosnan.

An acute angle is an angle under **90°.**

The computer costs **$1,667.99.**

Use numbers for dates and for hours expressed with *a.m.* (AM) or *p.m.* (PM).

At **6:07 AM** the snow began to fall.

The First International Peace Conference, held at The Hague, began on May **18, 1899**.

Use numbers with units of measurement.

The course is **127** kilometers.

The room is **11'7" × 13'4".**

The tree is **6'5"** from the garage door.

However, simple numbers may be spelled out: ***six*** *feet*.

Use numbers with quantities in a series.

A grizzly bear can run at a speed of **30** miles per hour; an elephant, **25;** a chicken, **9;** but a tortoise, only **0.17.**

The commercial traveler logged his sales for his first five days on the job: **7, 18, 23, 4, 19.**

Use numbers recorded for identification purposes.

His Social Security number is **142-45-1983.**

For service call the following number: **(800) 415-3333.**

Flight **465** has been canceled.

EXERCISE 40-1

Underline the errors in the use of abbreviations and numbers in the following sentences. Two of the sentences contain no errors.

1. The NEH (National Endowment for the Humanities) supports many research projects.

2. The game begins at 10:10 am.

3. The next speaker in the lecture series will be Dr. Andrew Ross, Jr.

4. The Rev. Dr. Luis Ababo, Ph.D., will attend the conference.

5. Wm. Smith has been appointed chair of the I.R.S. subcommittee on corporate taxation.

6. We shall next meet on Wed., Nov. 11.

7. The founder of the Nichol Bros. Corporation arrived in the U.S. by boat 100 years ago.

8. 209 delegates assembled here at 9:30 a.m. today to open the conference.

9. She has served on the board of directors of the Girl Scouts, the Y.M.C.A., and the YWCA.

10. From here to Pittsburgh is about four hundred and twenty-two miles.

---

41 Capitalization

41a First Words of Sentences or Verses

Capitalize the first word of a sentence, the pronoun *I,* and the interjection *O.*

Many writers have created imaginary universes.

Do **I** think that life exists on other planets?

These creatures, **O** mighty Gork, come from the other side of the universe.

Capitalize the first word of a direct quotation that is a complete sentence.

At the climax of the movie, Rhett says, "**F**rankly, my dear, I don't give a damn."

The book begins with the present Mrs. de Winter recounting a dream: "**L**ast night I dreamt I went to Manderley again."

Capitalize the first word of every line of verse unless the poet has written the line with a lowercase letter.

Keats's poem ends with the lines, "**T**hough the sedge is withered from the lake / **A**nd no birds sing."

Note: In quotations, always capitalize whichever words the writer has capitalized.

41b Titles, Names, and Words Based on Names

For titles of literary works, capitalize the first and the last word and all other important words, including prepositions of five or more letters.

Avoid capitalizing articles, short prepositions, or coordinating conjunctions that do not begin or end a title. A short preposition is one that has fewer than five letters.

*The **D**ecline and **F**all of the **R**oman **E**mpire*

"**T**he **C**ase of the **I**rate **W**itness"

*Much **A**do **A**bout **N**othing*

"**O**n the **M**orning **A**fter the **S**ixties"

Capitalize both parts of a hyphenated word in a title.

> "**H**ome-**T**houghts from **A**broad"
>
> "**G**ood-**B**ye, **M**y **F**ancy!"

Capitalize abbreviations and designations that follow a name. Do not capitalize titles used as appositives.

> Eugene Anderson, **J**r.
>
> Anne Poletti, **P**h.**D**. (PhD)
>
> Louise Tate, **A**ttorney at **L**aw

Capitalize proper nouns.

Sharon	**K**eats
Andrew **J**ackson	**L**ake **M**ichigan
Portuguese	**H**awaii
Greta **G**arbo	the **E**mpire **S**tate **B**uilding
the **M**iddle **A**ges	the **R**evolutionary **W**ar

Avoid capitalizing compass points unless they are part of a proper noun: *northwest of Chicago* but *the Pacific Northwest*.

Capitalize an official title when it precedes a name.

> The guest speaker will be **C**ongresswoman Katherine Murphy.
>
> The nation mourned the death of **P**resident Lincoln.
>
> The changes were supported by **G**overnor Celeste.

Capitalize the title of a high official when it is used in place of the person's name.

> The guest speaker will be the **C**ongresswoman.
>
> The nation mourned the death of the **P**resident.
>
> The changes were supported by the **G**overnor.

Note: Do not capitalize a title that does not name a specific individual.

> Seymour Rosen, a **c**hemistry **p**rofessor, submitted an article to the magazine.

> Willie Mae Kean, a first-year **l**aw student, won the award.

> Spike Kennedy, an **i**ntern at the hospital, was interviewed on television.

Capitalize the title of a relative when it precedes a name or is used in place of a name. Do not capitalize the title if it is used with a possessive pronoun.

> **A**unt Joan   **C**ousin Mary
> **U**ncle Carlos   **G**randfather Tseng

> Is **G**randmother coming to visit?

> You look well, **G**randpa.

> My **u**ncle Bill could not come to the performance.

Capitalize proper adjectives.

> **S**hakespearean sonnet   **M**achiavellian goals
> **P**arisian style   **G**recian urn
> **I**slamic teacher   **C**hristian faith

Avoid capitalizing most proper adjectives that are part of a compound noun.

> **f**rench fries   **d**anish pastry
> **x**erox copy   **v**enetian blind

Note: Usage in this area varies. Consult your dictionary for capitalization of compound nouns formed from proper adjectives.

Capitalize the names of specific academic courses. Do not capitalize general subject areas unless the subject area is a proper noun, such as a language.

History 121	*but*	a world **h**istory course
The **M**odern **A**merican **N**ovel	*but*	an American **l**iterature course
Advanced **B**iology	*but*	a **b**iology course

Capitalization
AND YOUR WORD PROCESSOR

Many word-processing programs automatically capitalize the first word in a sentence or a word following a standard abbreviation (such as *Mr.* and *Mrs.*). In some cases, you might need to override this automatic formatting. For example, in the phrase "such as *Mr.* and *Mrs.*" the program might automatically change *and* to *And,* which you would have to undo.

Your spelling program will also flag well-known proper nouns (such as *Spain* and *Inuit*) if you have not capitalized them. But your word processor will not give you any guidance on words that are capitalized only in certain contexts (such as titles, school subjects, and directions).

41c Conventional Capitalization

Capitalize words naming the Deity, sacred books, and other religious documents and names of religions, religious denominations, and their adherents.

Jehovah	**A**llah	the **L**ord
the **B**ible	the **K**oran	the **U**panishads
Catholicism	**M**oslem	**L**utheran
Christ	**B**uddha	**G**od

Note: Pronouns referring to the Deity are usually capitalized.

Capitalize names of months, days of the week, and holidays.

April	**D**ecember	**J**anuary
Tuesday	**S**aturday	**W**ednesday
Halloween	**N**ew **Y**ear's **E**ve	the **F**ourth of **J**uly

Note: Do not capitalize the names of the seasons.

Capitalize the abbreviations *A.D.* *(AD)* and *B.C.* *(BC)*.

A.D. 172   500 **B.C.**
AD 356   275 **BC**

EXERCISE 41-1

In each of the following items, change a lowercase letter to a capital letter wherever necessary.

1. The new gender studies program includes courses in women's literature from the middle ages and renaissance to the present time.

2. The puritans and separatists left England for holland and then came to america, abandoning forever the church of England.

3. At the camp david conference, the president, the prime minister, and the king all reached agreement.

4. Several cambodians opened a restaurant, the egg roll special, which instantly became popular.

5. Most tourists in paris visit the eiffel tower and the cathedral of notre dame.

6. The initial words of "the star spangled banner" are: "o say can you see by the dawn's early light / what so proudly we hailed at the twilight's last gleaming."

7. His short story, "Memories of the southwest," really portrays his aunt Iola and uncle Irving as a loving couple.

8. Was it F. D. Roosevelt who said, "we have nothing to fear but fear itself"?

9. In France the fourteenth of July is a national holiday.

10. The course in comparative religions includes methodism, islam, confucianism, and the coptic Christians; however, it is offered only on Tuesdays and thursdays.

---

42 Spelling

Although spelling rules are not infallible, mastery of the few described here will help you. They address some of the most common spelling problems for both native and nonnative writers of English: adding suffixes to words, forming noun plurals, and choosing between *ei* and *ie*.

42a Doubling the Final Consonant

A word that ends in a consonant sometimes doubles the final consonant when a suffix is added.

Double the final consonant when adding a suffix that begins with a vowel to a one-syllable word that ends in a consonant preceded by a single vowel. This rule applies to hundreds of words in the English language.

pen + ed = penned   slip + ing = slipping   win + er = winner

Double the final consonant when adding a suffix beginning with a vowel to a two-syllable word if a single vowel precedes the final consonant and if the final syllable is accented once the suffix is added.

begin + er = beginner   commit + ing = committing   regret + ed = regretted

Do not double the final consonant when it is preceded by two or more vowels or by another consonant.

cheap + er = cheaper   sustain + ed = sustained   chant + ing = chanting

Do not double the final consonant if the suffix begins with a consonant.

ship + ment = shipment   wet + ness = wetness

Do not double the final consonant if the word is *not* accented on the last syllable or if the accent shifts from the last to the first syllable when the suffix is added.

penal + ize = penalize   beckon + ing = beckoning   prefer + ence = preference

42b Dropping or Keeping the Silent *e*

Many words end with a silent *e* (*hate, raise, come, confine*).

In general, drop a silent *e* when adding a suffix that begins with a vowel.

care + ing = caring   move + able = movable

Keep the final *e* if the suffix begins with a consonant.

care + ful = careful   move + ment = movement

Words such as *argument, truly, judgment, courageous, change-able,* and *awful* are exceptions.

42c Changing or Keeping a Final *y*

When suffixes are added to words that end in a final *y,* use the following rules.

When the *y* is preceded by a consonant, change the *y* to *i* and add the suffix.

beauty + ful = beautiful   lazy + ness = laziness   study + ed = studied

Keep the final *y* when the suffix is *ing* (studying, spying, hurrying) or for some one-syllable words such as *dry, shy,* and *sly* (dryer, shyness, slyly).

Keep the final *y* when it is preceded by a vowel, and then add the suffix.

survey + or = surveyor   play + ful = playful   stay + ed = stayed

42d Choosing between *ei* and *ie*

Use *i* before *e* except after *c* or when pronounced like the letter *a,* as in *neighbor* or *weigh.*

i BEFORE *e*	EXCEPT AFTER *c*	PRONOUNCED LIKE *a*
believe	receive	eight
pierce	deceit	vein
view	conceive	reign
shield	ceiling	sleigh

Some exceptions are *seize, either, weird, height, foreign, leisure,* and *ancient.*

Note: The rule does not apply to words in which the *ie* or *ei* is not pronounced as a unit, such as *science, piety, hierarchy,* and *deity.*

42e   Forming Noun Plurals

There are several standard rules for making nouns plural.

For most words, simply add *s.*

pot/pots	lamp/lamps
table/tables	magazine/magazines

For nouns ending in *s, ch, sh, x,* or *z,* add *es.*

toss/tosses	church/churches	dish/dishes
box/boxes	waltz/waltzes	

For nouns ending in *y,* change the *y* to *i* and add *es* if the *y* is preceded by a consonant.

jelly/jellies	quality/qualities
theory/theories	enemy/enemies

Add only *s* to proper names ending in *y.*

Mary/Marys   Germany/Germanys   McNulty/McNultys

And add only *s* if the *y* is preceded by a vowel.

> monkey/monkeys   attorney/attorneys
> display/displays   journey/journeys

For nouns ending in *o*, add *s* when the *o* is preceded by a vowel.

> radio/radios   video/videos   zoo/zoos
> patio/patios   cameo/cameos

But add *es* when the *o* is preceded by a consonant.

> hero/heroes   potato/potatoes
> echo/echoes   mosquito/mosquitoes

Exceptions are *piano/pianos, solo/solos, burro/burros,* and *memo/memos.*

Some nouns have an irregular plural.

> woman/women   man/men   child/children
> mouse/mice   tooth/teeth

And some nouns have the same form for both singular and plural.

> deer, trout, species, fish, series, moose, sheep

42f Distinguishing among Homophones

Words that sound alike or nearly alike but have different meanings and spellings are called **homophones.** The following sets of words are so commonly confused that you should double-check their every use when you proofread:

affect: a verb meaning "to influence"
effect: a noun meaning "the result of some influence"

its: a possessive pronoun meaning "of or belonging to it"
it's: the contraction for "it is" or "it has"

lose: a verb meaning "to fail to keep something"
loose: an adjective meaning "free, not securely attached"

principle: a noun meaning "a rule or general truth"
principal: an adjective meaning "most important"; also a noun
   meaning "the head of a school"

their: a possessive pronoun meaning "belonging to them"
there: an adverb meaning "that place or position"
they're: a contraction for "they are"

to: a preposition (as in *to the store*) or sign of the infinitive form of
   a verb (as in *to be*)
too: a qualifier (as in *too much, too often*) and an adverb meaning
   "also"
two: the number

your: a possessive form of "you"
you're: a contraction for "you are"

Consult the Glossary of Usage, which begins on page 574, to check for the correct use of these and other commonly confused words.

EXERCISE 42-1

Underline any misspelled words in the following paragraph. Use a dictionary if you find it helpful. Circle the words that a computer's spell checker would not detect.

The histery of education in hour country is one charac-
terised by slow but constant change. Especialy notible today are
the changes in the compesition of the student body, which now
includes varyous multicultural representations. Some think the
changes have been to slow in comming. Others are anxous that
change ocurs to fast. One thing apears clear: the campus of
today is very diferent form that of yestreday.

Checking Spelling
ON A WORD PROCESSOR

The spell checker of your word-processing program is a
useful alternative to a dictionary. You should take some time
to see how it works and use it to help you edit your writing.
Be aware, though, that spelling programs have some limitations. They cannot help you to catch wrong choices of homophones or typographical errors such as *own* for *won*. As
long as a word appears in its dictionary, the program will
not flag it as an error. You will still need to proofread and to
consult a dictionary.

EXERCISE 42-2

Choose the word in parentheses that sensibly completes each of the
following sentences. Use your dictionary when necessary or consult
the glossary of usage.

1. In order (to/too/two) obtain (to/too/two) extra tickets for the
   game, they will need to contact (there/their/they're) parents.

2. The poem meant little to the (disinterested/uninterested) student.

3. (Who's/Whose) coat is that?

4. The handle on the door is (lose/loose).

5. The (percent/percentage) of the people who smoke cigarettes is less than it was five years (ego/ago).

6. The (cite/sight/site) of the new building for the department of (pubic/public) works has not been selected.

7. The (ways/waves) hit the shore loudly during the stormy (weather/whether).

8. A loudly barking dog is an (affective/effective) burglar alarm.

9. Place the (hole/whole) bush in the (hole/whole) you dug for it.

10. In one (weak/week) many people (waste/waist) a (forth/fourth) of (their/there/they're) food servings.

Part

VIII

THE RESEARCH PAPER

The word *research* comes from an Old French word, *rechercher,* meaning "to seek out" or "to search again." A research paper or essay is one in which you seek out information about a topic from a variety of sources. However, a research paper should not be merely a recapitulation of the findings of others. It should also reflect your own ideas, understanding, and analysis.

A research paper is both informative and objective. In it, you provide information about a topic by examining a variety of sources objectively and by reaching a conclusion about these findings. The research paper will also contain a thesis or assertion supported by objective information.

A research paper is formal. It contains little, if any, colloquial language or slang and few, if any, contractions. A typical research paper contains between 2,000 and 3,000 words and runs five to fifteen pages long. A research essay contains all the characteristics of a research paper but is shorter.

---

43   Selecting and Limiting a Topic

Whether your instructor provides you with a list of topics on a specific subject matter or you have the freedom to select your own topic, begin with the question "What really interests me?" Since you will be spending several weeks researching your topic, be certain to choose one that appeals to you. What are you interested in?

- Are you interested in finding information about any particular person—Andrew Johnson? Diane Arbus? Spike Lee? Gwendolyn Brooks? Steven Spielberg?
- Are you interested in studying any particular place—Fiji? Jupiter? Egypt? The Great Plains?

- Are you interested in exploring any particular time period—
  The turn of the century? The Renaissance? The fifth century
  B.C.? The 1930s?
- Are you interested in examining any particular event—The
  Civil War? Columbus's landing in this hemisphere? The birth
  of religions in the Middle East? The first space flight to the
  moon?
- Are you interested in studying any particular object or
  activity—Clocks? Vitamins? MTV? Cooking? Field hockey?
- Are you interested in looking into a particular idea or
  doctrine—Colonialism? Multiculturalism? Transcendentalism?
  Marxism?
- Are you interested in investigating a controversial issue—
  Abortion? Steroid use by athletes? Nuclear power? Cloning?

When faced with the task of writing a research paper, many
students go blank; they can think of nothing that interests them.
You can solve this problem by using one of the methods for finding a topic described in Section 1a of this book. Begin with a
general subject; browse the Internet; thumb through magazines,
newspapers, and general reference works; look at your class
notes; or talk with friends, classmates, and instructors. A letter in
the *New York Times Book Review* got one student, Gail Young,
interested in Mercy Otis Warren, a minor author of Colonial New
England. But what could Gail write about Warren? She needed
to limit her topic.

43a Limiting Your Topic

Because your research paper will be between five and fifteen pages long, after deciding on a topic you will need to limit
it so that you can cover it effectively within these boundaries.
What aspect of your topic do you want to cover? Notice how the
following topics are narrowed:

Spike Lee → his life → his life as an artist → his movies → *Jungle Fever* → the making of *Jungle Fever*

Egypt→ the history of Egypt → the military history of Egypt → Egypt's role in Middle East peace negotiations

the fifth century BC → the fifth century BC in China → religion in China in the fifth century BC → the teachings of Confucius → modern Chinese reaction to the teachings of Confucius

the Civil War → important generals of the Civil War → General Sherman's role in the Civil War → General Sherman's Atlanta campaign

vitamins → types of vitamins → the use of vitamin supplements → vitamin therapy → the controversy over megadose vitamin therapy

transcendentalism → New England transcendentalists → the influence of transcendentalism on the works of Henry David Thoreau → the influence of transcendentalism in *Walden*

Of course, limiting your topic is not always a simple, straightforward process. It is more of a trial-and-error procedure. Your exploration of sources will lead to the discovery of a number of options or topics you can follow in your research. As you do further research, you will find yourself revising and fine-tuning that topic or finding better options to narrow down. Search for the option that not only interests you but also presents a new insight that will interest your audience. And be comfortable with the idea that limiting your topic involves experimentation and risk. This is normal.

43b   Exploring Resources

A wide array of resources is available for you to explore: books, computerized databases, periodicals, general encyclopedias, specialized encyclopedias, consultations with reference librarians, personal interviews. You probably will not need to consult all of the resources available, but you will want to explore enough of them to help you select and limit your topic.

Gail Young first consulted a general encyclopedia in the reference area of the library. It seemed obvious to her from the brief entries therein that the life of Mercy Otis Warren would not be as interesting as that of Spike Lee. But with each of their entries, the encyclopedias included a brief bibliography, a start for Gail's research. The encyclopedias also gave Gail several clues to possible areas for investigation. For example, Gail noted with surprise that the *Britannica* declares Warren's poems and plays to be of "no permanent value." What the *Americana* calls Warren's "chief work"—*History of the Rise, Progress, and Termination of the American Revolution*—was "bitterly resented" by John Adams, notes the *Britannica*. So Gail was on her way to choosing a topic: What did Warren's contemporaries think of her poems and plays? Why is her work apparently of so little worth today? What caused Adams's resentment? Was Warren an early feminist?

In Gail's case, encyclopedias provided sufficient impetus to limit the topic. But other sources of information should be consulted to validate points, discover differing views, and help you determine the scope as well as the purpose of your research. The important principle to remember is to make your exploration of resources thorough. On the one hand, avoid settling on a source or strategy that forces you to devise a specific topic or thesis too soon. On the other hand, you will not want to prolong unduly the exploration. If this searching activity does not help you limit your topic and direct you toward a purpose, perhaps you need to explore another topic.

43c Exploring Purpose

You write research papers and essays in academic and nonacademic settings for the same purpose: to gather into one document materials from a variety of sources to provide knowledge and understanding for you and your audience. But a research paper is more than merely a collection of facts; it must also contain your reactions, analysis, and thought. To give your paper focus, explore various purposes and then settle on one that will act as your preliminary thesis or as the main point of the paper. Finding a purpose carries the process of limiting the topic one step further toward the formulation of a preliminary thesis.

TOPIC LIMITATION

Spike Lee → his life → his life as an artist → his artistic output → his movies → *Jungle Fever* → the making of *Jungle Fever*

The purpose or preliminary thesis: Spike Lee, in producing the movie *Jungle Fever,* vividly portrayed racial tensions but unfairly exploited stereotypes in doing so.

Although your exact purpose in writing the research paper might change or remain unclear until you have actually explored sufficient resource materials, it is best to begin your project with at least a temporary purpose in mind. Try to arrive at a purpose that allows you to react to the topic and to get involved in the topic's exchange of ideas as in the example on Spike Lee. In other words, apply prewriting devices to your topic to help generate more thoughts about it. (See also Section 1c, Determining a Purpose.)

43d Exploring Scope

Scope concerns the size or range of your research topic. When selecting your topic, you will want to be sure that it indeed lends itself to research. If the scope of your topic is too broad, you will have difficulty finding a focus. If the scope of your topic is very narrow or if the topic is very new or subjective, you probably will not be able to locate sufficient objective information about it when exploring sources. For example, the topic *the rise in popularity of imported French cheese in the northeastern states during the last three months* will most likely not lend itself to adequate research. It is too recent. Additionally, the topic *why I like cheese* calls for subjective personal opinion, not research. The topic might be appropriate for a personal essay, but not for a research paper. You will have to consider a topic's scope even if your instructor gives you a list of research topics to choose from.

Exploring a Research Topic
ON A WORD PROCESSOR

If you want to explore a possible topic, do some freewriting or brainstorming on the word processor. You can turn off the monitor or turn down the contrast if you want to write without seeing the screen. This procedure will help you to concentrate on getting ideas out of your head onto the page—or onto the screen, in this case. Write as fast as you can, letting your mind range over the topic. Why does it appeal to you? What do you already know about it? What do you expect to learn? What kind of readers would be interested in this topic? What point would you like to make to them? Print out what you've written, and read it over. Look for points and ideas that you can explore even further. Then try another round of freewriting or brainstorming.

---

44 Doing Research

44a Scheduling Your Research Paper

Writing a research paper is a time-consuming job. This is one paper that you simply cannot put off until the last minute. Dividing the project into units will allow you to keep the work under control. For example, if your completed paper is due in six weeks, you could put yourself on a schedule something like this:

First week:	Locate your possible sources, and record all the necessary bibliographical information about them.
	Try to narrow the topic to a workable idea to investigate.
Second week:	Read and take notes.
	Settle on a preliminary thesis.
	Try to come up with a preliminary outline.
Third week:	Continue reading and taking notes.
Fourth week:	Complete your reading and note taking.
	Revise and focus your preliminary thesis.
	Arrange your notes and organize your ideas.
	Develop a complete, detailed outline.
Fifth week:	Write the first draft and let it cool.
	Begin revising and editing.
	Get someone reliable to read your second draft and tell you whether the paragraphs are coherent, the sentences are clear, and the quotations are effectively integrated.
Sixth week:	Polish the second draft or write a third one.
	Type the final draft and let it rest at least overnight.
	Proofread and edit the final draft carefully.

This is a fairly leisurely schedule. You can, of course, do the work in a shorter time if required to. You will have to be more industrious about finding sources and taking notes. Some instructors deliberately ask students to complete the project within a month to prevent procrastination. Whatever your time limit, devise a schedule for yourself and stick to it.

You should also develop a plan for efficiently tracking down your source materials. Think about how much time you have and what kinds of sources you will probably be using. A good strategy is to begin with reference works that give a broad overview of the subject, as Gail Young did when she was exploring the life of Mercy Otis Warren as a possible topic (see Chapter 43). Then move to sources that provide more detailed information. Your library's reference room contains a number of useful reference works. The chart on pages 426–427 indicates the variety of material available.

44b Finding Information

One of the first things you need to do is get acquainted with your library. Most college libraries offer orientation courses to show students how to find materials. If the course is not required, take it anyway. An orientation course is the surest way of learning your way around the library. Libraries also have tours and guidebooks telling you where to find various materials. Taking one of these tours or studying the guidebook could save you many hours of aimless wandering.

To locate all the relevant information in the library, you might need to think of headings under which your subject might be indexed. The encyclopedia and general reference works will supply you with some clues. The *Library of Congress Subject Headings (LCSH)* can be very useful in providing terms or key words to search with as well as additional terms that you might not have considered. Most of the entries in the *LCSH* give alternative terms listed as BT (broader topic), RT (related topic), and NT (narrower topic). Gail Young checked several headings and found these for Mercy Warren: Colonial American Literature, American Historians, Dramatists, and Women, among others. If you fail to find what you need, ask for help. Librarians are usually willing to answer questions and will often lead you to the material you want and give you valuable advice.

REFERENCE WORKS

ENCYCLOPEDIAS   *Academic American Encyclopedia, Collier's Encyclopedia, Encyclopedia Americana, The New Encyclopaedia Britannica*

GENERAL REFERENCES   *Contemporary Authors, Current Biography, Facts on File, United Nations Yearbook, World Almanac and Book of Facts*

ART, MUSIC, AND ARCHITECTURE   *Contemporary Artists; Encyclopedia of Architecture; Encyclopedia of Pop, Rock, and Soul; Encyclopedia of World Art; New Harvard Dictionary of Art; New Grove Dictionary of Music and Musicians; The Pelican History of Art*

BIOLOGY AND EARTH SCIENCES   *Biology Dictionary, Cambridge Encyclopedia of Life Sciences, Encyclopedia of the Environment, The Concise Oxford Dictionary of Earth Sciences, The Concise Oxford Dictionary of Ecology, Grzimek's Encyclopedia of Ecology, McGraw-Hill Encyclopedia of Environmental Science and Engineering*

BUSINESS AND ECONOMICS   *American Business Dictionary, Concise Dictionary of Business, Encyclopedia of Banking and Finance, Encyclopedia of Management, McGraw-Hill Dictionary of Modern Economics*

EDUCATION   *Encyclopedia of Education, Encyclopedia of Educational Research, International Encyclopedia of Higher Education*

HISTORY AND POLITICAL SCIENCE   *Cambridge Ancient History, Cambridge History of Africa, Cambridge Medieval History, Dictionary of American History, Dictionary of World Politics, Encyclopedia of African-American Culture and History, Encyclopedia of the Third World, Harvard Guide to American History, New Cambridge Modern History, Times Atlas of the World, Timetables of History*

LITERATURE, FILM, AND TELEVISION   *Contemporary Literary Criticism, Encyclopedia of World Literature in the Twentieth Century, International Encyclopedia of Film, International Television Almanac, Oxford Companion to American Literature, Oxford Companion to English Literature, Oxford Companion to the Theater*

PHILOSOPHY AND RELIGION   *Dictionary of the History of Ideas, Contemporary Religions: A World Guide, Encyclopedia of Ethics, Encyclopedia of Religion, A History of Philosophy*

SCIENCE AND MATHEMATICS   *Encyclopedia of Mathematics and Its Applications, Encyclopedia of Physics, Kirk-Othmer Encyclopedia of Chemical Technology, McGraw-Hill Encyclopedia of Science and Technology*

SOCIAL SCIENCES   *Asian and Asian American Studies, Dictionary of Concepts in Cultural Anthropology, Encyclopedia of Human Behavior, Encyclopedia of Psychology, Encyclopedia of Social Work, Encyclopedia of Sociology, Handbook of Hispanic Culture in the United States, Harvard Encyclopedia of American Ethnic Groups, Multiculturalism in the United States, Women's Studies Encyclopedia*

1   The library catalog

You will probably begin your search for sources by consulting the **library catalog**. Most libraries now use computer catalogs (sometimes called *public access catalogs* or *online catalogs*) that allow you to search for books and other materials at a computer terminal. The opening screen of the terminal itself will tell you how to use it. You can search by subject, title, and author, as well as by call number, shelf position, and international standard book number (ISBN). You can search for books, titles of journals, and other items owned by your library or by other libraries in your region or state.

Gail started her research by consulting the author/title headings in the online computer catalog, where she found entries listing Mercy Otis Warren's works (see the following sample online catalog entry) and some biographies, giving the location of the materials in the library, and providing other information such as publisher and date of publication, number of pages, number of illustrations, and presence of bibliography. Gail also discovered that although few of Warren's plays are available in book form, all are contained on microfilm in a collection of Colonial drama located in a special section of the library. Gail also found that Warren's history of the Revolution is in a special area for rare books because it is a facsimile of the original volume that Warren autographed and sent to Thomas Jefferson. When Gail located the books using their call numbers, she found, shelved with the Warren material, books by and about other authors of the period— suggestions for new topics if this research proved unproductive.

Gail also consulted the subject heading listing, where she found some duplicate listings. She was also able to find other books that were not under the author/title headings by looking on the shelves near the call numbers she had already gathered. Like Gail, you will want to note each source of possible relevance to your topic on a card (see sample cards at the end of this chapter and in Chapter 45) or in your computer file. Always remember to record the source's call number.

SAMPLE ONLINE CATALOG ENTRY

Screen →   Screen 1 of 2
identifi-   NO HOLDINGS IN IND - FOR HOLDINGS ENTER dh DEPRESS DISPLAY RECD SEND
cation   OCLC: 3355943   Rec stat: c Entrd: 771020   Used: 911114
     Type: a Bib lvl: m Govt pub: Lang: eng Source: c Illus:
     Repr: Enc lvl: I Conf pub: 0 Ctry: xx   Det tp: r M/F/B: ^o   Technical
     Indx: 0 Mod rec: Festschr: 0 Cont: data for
     Desc: Int lvl: Dates: 1953,1775   librarians
       1   010   a35-2531
       2   040   Wisconsin Univ. Libr. ic OCP Id OCL 1d m.c.
       3   050   0   PS858.W8 1b A
       4   092   B12 1b WE91
       5   049   INDU
Author →   6   100   1   Warren, Mercy (Otis) 1d 1728-1814, 1w dn
Title →   7   245   14   The Group, 1779.   ←————————Date of publication
       8   260   Ann Arbor, 1b William L. Clements Library,   ← City, publisher
    University of Michigan, 1c 1953.
Intro- →   9   300   [9] p., facsims, 22 p. 1c 21 cm. ←┐
ductory   10   500   A political satire in 2 acts, in verse←─────Number of
pages   11   500   Reproduction of the William L. Clements Library   pages and size
    copy of the 1st Boston ed., with t. p. reading: The Group...
    Boston, Printed and sold by Edes and Gill, 1775.   └─Description

Screen →   Screen 2 of 2
identifi-   12   651   0   United States 1x History 1y Revolution Is Drama.
cation

2   Indexes and databases

To find useful articles in magazines, newspapers, and scholarly or technical journals, you can consult a periodical index. Some of these indexes are in print form, but many of them are now available as electronic databases that can be accessed and read at a computer terminal. You search for articles in an electronic database just as you search for books in the library's online catalog: by author, title, or subject key words. Most college libraries subscribe to at least one of the following computer services, which index general periodicals: CARL Uncover, Infotrac SearchBank, National Newspaper Index, Newsbank, Periodical Abstracts, WilsonSelect.

If your library subscribes to one or more of these services, you will find them either on the online catalog terminal or on computers in the library's reference area. You might also be able to access many of these databases from your computer at home or in your dorm room if it has the necessary software and a modem. These databases provide citations and abstracts of articles; some even have complete texts of articles, which you can print out from the computer.

Specialized indexes

If you want to locate information and articles in technical and scholarly fields, you can consult specialized indexes, many of which are now available as electronic databases. You can access some of these databases from the same terminal that carries the online catalog. For others, you might have to get authorization and a password from a librarian and use a different terminal in the library. The chart on page 431 lists indexes that are available online for a variety of specific academic disciplines.

Tim Gomez, a student, chose the topic *sleep disorders* for a research paper. The database that Tim searched was *PsycINFO,* produced by the American Psychological Association and available through the Bibliographic Retrieval Services (BRS). The first descriptor Tim entered was the original broad topic, *sleep disorders,* and the query was the number of items on that topic. The computer's response—413 documents—confirmed Tim's earlier suspicion that his topic was too broad. He next entered a narrower descriptor, *nightmares.* The number of documents, though smaller, was still discouragingly high, so Tim continued the search by combining the descriptors. He asked the computer to search for material concerning first the *sleep disorders of young adults,* then of *students,* then of *young adult students,* and, finally, *college students' nightmares.* Within only a few minutes, the computer narrowed the list of sources to a workable 24 items. After the computer had located the citations that were appropriate for Tim's topic, he asked the computer to provide him with the titles of several articles and books and their subject headings to determine whether he was on target in his search. After viewing this sample Tim could obtain bibliographic information and an abstract (brief summary) of any or all of the citations.

Gail also searched her topic in a database, *America: History and Life,* produced by ABC–Clio and available on the DIALOG

SPECIALIZED ELECTRONIC INDEXES

Note: The year in parentheses indicates when coverage begins. For earlier material, you will have to consult printed indexes and bibliographies.

ART, LITERATURE, AND HUMANITIES   *America: History and Life* (1964), *Art Index* (1984), *Arts and Humanities Search* (1980), *Historical Abstracts* (1972), *Humanities Index* (1984), *MLA International Bibliography* (1963), *Music Index* (1981)

BUSINESS AND ECONOMICS   *ABI/Inform* (1971), *Business and Industry* (1994), *Business Periodicals Index* (1982), *Consumers Index* (1986), *Econ Lit* (1969), *Journal of Consumer Marketing* (1989)

EDUCATION   *ERIC (Educational Resources Information Center)* (1966), *Journal of Educational Administration* (1989), *Library Literature* (1989)

HEALTH AND MEDICINE   *BioDigest (1982), Health Reference Center Academic* (current year plus three preceding years), *Medline* (1985), *CINAHL (nursing and health)* (1982), *MDX Health Digest* (1988)

LIFE SCIENCES   *Agricola (agriculture and nutrition)* (1985), *Basic BIOSIS (biology)* (1988), *Biological & Agricultural Index* (1983), *Environment* (past six years)

NEWS, FACTS, AND PEOPLE   *Biography Index* (1984), *DataTimes* (1996), *FactSearch* (1984), *SIRS Researcher* (1988)

POLITICAL AND SOCIAL SCIENCES   *Contemporary Women's Issues* (1995), *Ethnic News Watch* (1991), *Index to Legal Periodicals* (1981), *PAIS Decade* (international affairs) (last ten years), *PsycINFO (psychology)* (1967), *SocioAbs (sociology)* (1963), *Social Science Index* (1983)

SCIENCE AND TECHNOLOGY   *Applied Science & Technology Index* (1983), *General Science Index* (1984), *GeoBase (geology and geography)* (1980), *GeoRef (earth science)* (1933), *INSPEC (physics, engineering, electronics)* (1987), *Microcomputer Abstracts* (1989)

system. Before using it, Gail had spent hours searching only a few years of printed indexes and found listings for just four articles. With the database, however, she searched 200,000 references dating back to 1964 and retrieved eleven articles in just a few minutes. Gail requested abstracts for all eleven of the articles on her topic; one of these abstracts is shown here:

SAMPLE DATABASE ENTRY

380462 14A-00632

John Adams' Opinion of Benjamin Franklin

Evans, William B.

Pennsylvania Mag. of Hist. and Biog. 1968 92(2): 220–238.

Document Type: ARTICLE

Traces John Adams' animosity toward Benjamin Franklin in 10
1807 letters to Mercy Otis Warren questioning her favorable
treatment of Franklin in History of the Rise, Progress, and
Termination of the American Revolution. Differences between
the two revolutionary giants began in 1776 when Franklin
supported a unicameral legislature in Pennsylvania, and
continued in Paris (1776–79) until their joint presence on the
Peace commission in 1780 brought an open breach when
Adams opposed Franklin's supposedly pro-French policy. Not
only differences on policy but Adams' envy and pride may
have colored his view of Franklin. Based primarily on the
papers of John Adams; 67 notes. (R. B. Mitchell)
Descriptors: Adams, John (letters, opinion); Politics, 1774–1810;
Franklin, Benjamin; Warren, Mercy Otis

Notice that since Warren's name is not in the title, Gail might have had difficulty finding this article when she searched the printed indexes. The computer, however, could also search the abstract and find the descriptor.

Most often, you will use the computer database just as you use the computerized catalog, card catalog, and other sources such as periodical indexes. Use these resources to identify books and articles that may be useful in your research and that you can then locate in your library system. (Other libraries might be available to you through an interlibrary loan.) The abstracts that are available from computer databases, like all abstracts, are merely brief summaries of the books and articles to which they refer. After reading the abstract, you will know whether the article or book is pertinent to your topic. You will then need to find and consult the article or book. Researchers often misuse abstracts, citing them in a paper instead of consulting and citing the actual source.

3 The Internet

The Internet links computers around the world; it's a vast storehouse of information that can be accessed in a number of ways. Getting on the Internet is relatively easy. All you need are a computer, a modem, and a browser (software that helps you to find places on the Internet). If you don't have a computer at home, your college library probably has a bank of computers that are hooked up to the Internet.

On the Internet, you can find government documents and archives, newsgroups, online publications, texts of published materials, and databases provided by commercial servers such as America Online, Prodigy, and Campus Networks. You can browse the noncommercial contents of the Internet through the World Wide Web.

Electronic mail

If you have used the Internet at all, it's probably been with electronic mail (e-mail), communicating with friends and family. E-mail can be a valuable research tool as well. Many people participate in special-interest discussion groups via e-mail; these groups are called *mailing lists,* and they use a *listserver* to send mail automatically to all the people on the list. Once you join a mailing list, the listserver will send you all messages on standard e-mail.

There are thousands of mailing lists, so it will be difficult to find ones on your topic. The easiest way to find a list is to check one of the directories on the World Wide Web (see page 435). One of the most popular directories is *Liszt,* which claims to list over 70,000 e-mail discussion groups. It's available at http://www.liszt.com and gives you simple instructions for searching and for subscribing to any list you might find useful.

You will want to evaluate the reliability of an e-mail source in the same way you would judge any person you have interviewed. When referring to this source in your paper, provide background on the source and indicate why he or she is qualified to give information on your topic.

Newsgroups

A newsgroup is a kind of public bulletin board containing comments, questions, and responses on a particular topic. It's more extensive and more organized than an e-mail list. Asking a question of a mailing list or a newsgroup is a good way to get information about sources and to find people who can help you with your research. The newsgroup message board keeps track of several discussions at once and organizes the messages and replies in groups called *threads.* A thread begins with the original message, or *posting,* and includes all of the replies made by every participant in the discussion. A program called a *newsreader* is used to read newsgroups and follow the threads. If your school has a news feed (a system by which newsgroup messages are exchanged among providers), you can use a newsreader to locate one or more newsgroups to follow. If you are looking for a newsgroup mailing or list that is related to your topic, you can start at Tile.Net (http://www.tile.net), a searchable site that lists hundreds of newsgroups and mailing lists. A good source for searching archived newsgroup postings is DejaNews (http://www.dejanews.com).

You should use material gathered from a newsgroup with caution. Try to confirm from other sources the reliability of any information from a newsgroup that you want to use in a research paper. And always be sure to record or store the electronic address and references from an Internet source. You will need these details for a return access—and later for documentation in your paper.

The World Wide Web

The most popular tool for searching the Internet is the World Wide Web (also called the Web and WWW). The WWW is not the same thing as the Internet; the Web is a complex system for organizing and viewing information on the Internet. The primary attraction of this system is that its documents, called *Web pages,* are linked to other pages by a technique called *hypertext*. Usually, hypertext links are underlined and appear in blue. By pointing and clicking at these links on a Web page, you can find paths to additional material, such as cross-references and explanations, on other pages and at other Web sites on the WWW. (A *Web site* is a collection of related Web pages.)

To navigate the Web, you need a *browser* program such as Netscape, Mosaic, or Microsoft Internet Explorer. On page 436 is the *home page* (the first page that appears when you access a Web site) for the Library of Congress, viewed through Microsoft Internet Explorer. The WWW is also searchable. You can use one of several different *search engines*—such as Webcrawler, AltaVista, Yahoo, Lycos, and Infoseek—to search for key words in the Web addresses, headings, or text. See pages 437–438 for the first page of results from a key word search that was conducted using Yahoo powered by AltaVista (key word: *Kwanzaa*).

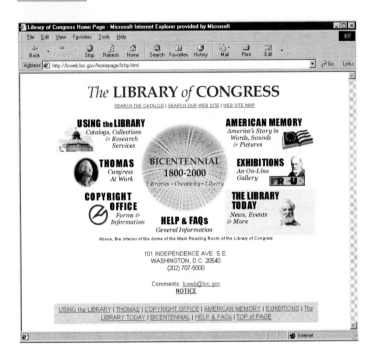

Advice about using the Web

The Internet and the Web give you access to a great deal of information that is often more current than anything available in printed sources, and the Web's hyptertext feature allows you to explore a topic quickly and thoroughly. Nonetheless, there are a couple of serious drawbacks to using the Web that you need to consider:

1. It is difficult to know how to judge the vast array of information that's available. You will find research reports, online journals, and government publications; but you will also find unsupported opinion, propaganda, inaccurate information,

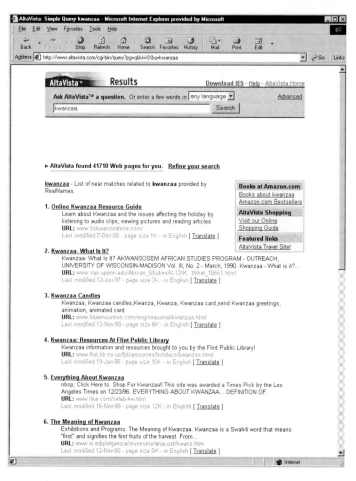

and tasteless junk. Anyone can publish on the Web; there is no editorial board to screen the material. So you must apply sound judgment in evaluating each of your electronic sources, just as you would the print sources that you find in the

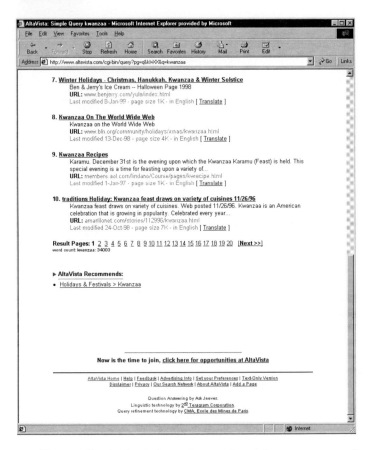

library. Check the information against other sources, and consider carefully the credentials, and the biases, of the person or organization supplying the data.

2. Searching on the Internet, especially on the WWW, can eat up a lot of valuable time. Because it's so easy to move from site to site through numerous interlinked sources, you can

spend hours browsing the Web. Your time might be better spent reading your source materials, taking notes, and writing your paper. To avoid wasting your time, always go to the Web for specific purposes, skim the sites first, and note the size and downloading time of a document before printing it out. (The slow downloading time on some equipment can consume a lot of time.)

4 Nonlibrary sources

Depending on the nature of your topic, it might be appropriate to seek information outside of your library through mailings, experiments, questionnaires, and interviews. Most corporations, municipalities, colleges, and similar organizations will respond to your inquiries for information by mailing you personal letters and/or brochures. You might opt to devise experiments modeled after the methodologies of the natural and social sciences (see Section 50a) to provide additional evidence for your research project. You might devise questionnaires that you distribute to others to obtain their opinions. Interviews are another good way to obtain information. If you decide to use an interview, you will want to prepare for it carefully in advance. Create a list of open-ended questions for the interview; avoid devising close-ended questions that can be answered with a simple "yes" or "no" because your goal is to gather information that will enhance your paper. Again, materials that are incorporated into your research from any source, whether correspondence, experiments, or interviews, require documentation to avoid plagiarism. (See Sections 46b-5 and 47b-5 on documenting nonprint sources and Section 45f on plagiarism.)

44c Primary and Secondary Sources of Information

The sources of information for a research paper can be divided into primary and secondary sources. A **primary source** gives you firsthand information about a topic. For example, for a paper on the causes of and treatment of sleep disorders of college students, a primary source would be an article by a researcher or an interview with a person who had experienced nightmares. A book describing the experiments of others is a **secondary source.** For a paper on a literary subject, primary sources would include the literature itself and the writer's letters and diaries. For Gail's literary topic on writer Mercy Otis Warren or a historical study of Warren's quarrel with John Adams or the politics of the times, primary sources would include Warren's poems and plays, Adams's letters, and records of the proceedings of the Continental Congress. Secondary sources would include critical studies of the literature, histories of the period, and biographies of Warren and Adams.

In your research, try to use as many primary sources as possible. Although for many topics you will have to use secondary sources, remember that often the closer you are to the original source, the more accurate your information will be.

Keep in mind the reliability of your sources, and ask yourself the questions in the box on the following page.

44d Compiling a Working Bibliography

A **working bibliography** is a record of sources you plan to consult for information about your topic. Since a working bibliography is open to change (you will add and delete books and articles as you do research), most instructors suggest that you record each source separately in your computer file or on 3" × 5" index cards. It is also a good idea to arrange your entries alphabetically, either by author or by category. Organizing the data that you collect makes it easier to add and delete sources and to compile your lists of **works cited,** which will appear at the end of your paper. To save time, you should also record the bibliographic information in the documentation format required by your instructor and appropriate to your discipline (see Chapters 46 and 47 on documenting research). Of course, the list of works cited will be shorter than the working bibliography because in

EVALUATING PRIMARY AND SECONDARY SOURCES

If the source is primary:
1. Is the source objective?
2. Is the author of the source an expert in the field?
3. If the source reports the results of an experiment, did the experiment follow the established procedures?
4. How recent is the information? (Obviously, this question is not important for all situations.)

If the source is secondary:
1. What is the author's reputation in the field?
2. What sources did the author use?
3. How sound are the author's conclusions?
4. How recent is the book or article? (Again, in some situations, this will not be relevant.)
5. Does the book or article examine current literature on the topic or include a survey of current research and provide documentation?
6. Was the book published by a university press or other respectable publisher, or was the article published in a reputable magazine? (An article in a scholarly journal is more likely to contain reliable information than an article in a magazine that seeks to entertain its readers.)

it, you will list only those works actually cited in your paper or essay.

For each entry that you record, be certain to include the following information:

1. The full name of the author, with the last name first (noting if the book has an editor or compiler rather than an author)

2. The complete title of the source (no abbreviations)

3. The city of publication, the publisher's name, and the date of publication

4. The library call number

5. Any other pertinent information, such as a volume or edition number

When Gail Young was preparing a working bibliography, she first consulted the general encyclopedias (*Americana, Britannica,* and *Collier's*), checking the bibliography at the end of each article about Mercy Otis Warren or John Adams. She then consulted the library catalog, a computer database, and periodical indexes. As she worked, Gail kept adding titles to her working bibliography and eliminating titles that were irrelevant to her topic. Exploring resources and compiling a working bibliography also helped Gail settle on and limit her topic. One of Gail's informal bibliography entries follows. Notice that the book she listed has two editors rather than an author:

Berky, Andrew S., and James P. Shenton, eds.
The Historians' History of the United States
New York: Putnam's, 1966.

169.12
B39
1966

45 Writing the Research Paper

Once you have selected and limited a topic and started researching, you are ready to begin taking notes and writing.

45a Taking Notes

Note taking is a way of keeping track of information that you think is important and that you might use later in your paper. Many writers compile their research notes on a computer disk; others use 4" × 6" index cards. Using this size card will prevent you from confusing your note cards with your bibliography cards. Both computer entries and note cards allow you to organize your information and then rearrange it.

It is important to be judicious when taking notes. Do not record everything you read, but only what you think will be relevant. Being selective as you take notes will help you later on because when you write the paper, you will not use all the research entries you made but will cull them, using only the information that develops your thesis. It is also important to keep track of all your sources as you take notes to ensure accurate documentation and to avoid plagiarism. (See Section 45f on plagiarism.)

What information should you put in your research notes? Each note card or computer entry should have at the top of it a subject category heading, sometimes called a *slug,* which should correspond to the headings in your working outline (see Section 45c). The slug will help you to keep your research notes organized by topic. The entry itself should consist of a summary, paraphrase, or quotation and should briefly indicate the source of the information. However, you need to include only the author and the page number, since you will already have more detailed source information in your working bibliography. If you are using more than one source by the same author, include the title or a shortened form of it.

Be sure to make a separate entry for each piece of information you record. This will help you to avoid any confusion and will make it easier for you to arrange your notes when it comes time to sit down and write the paper.

1 Summarizing

One method of taking notes is to write a summary of the information you wish to record. A **summary** presents the substance of the information in a *condensed* form. You do not use the words of the author, but you convey the thoughts of the author *in your own words*. Following is a summary Gail Young wrote:

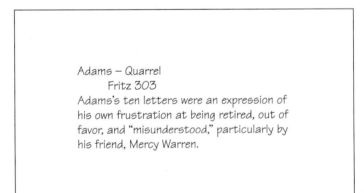

Adams – Quarrel
        Fritz 303
Adams's ten letters were an expression of
his own frustration at being retired, out of
favor, and "misunderstood," particularly by
his friend, Mercy Warren.

Compare the summary with the original source:

Actually, these letters—ten in six weeks, some running to twenty pages—were his long pent-up cry of outrage at the world in general, at his age which had reduced him to the role of a spectator, at his enemies who had defeated him, at his friends who had misunderstood him, at himself for not being sufficiently dignified (like Washington) or sufficiently genial (like Franklin) to be forgiven his foibles, and at all historians, present and future, who would not write history as he would have it written, who would not let him play his part as he knew he had played it.

Jean Fritz
Cast for a Revolution: Some
American Friends and Enemies

2   Paraphrasing

A second method of taking notes is to paraphrase the information. A **paraphrase** is a restatement of someone else's statement *in your own words*. A good paraphrase reflects your own style of writing and extracts important information but does not lose the original meaning of the statement. It is often equivalent in length to the original. Following is a paraphrase entry Gail Young wrote:

Governor Winthrop on Women
        Brown 156
If the wife of the Governor of Hartford had not
strained her weak wits by behaving like a man
and neglecting her role and duties as a female,
she would not have lost her mind.

Compare the paraphrase with the original:

> For if she had attended her household affairs, and such things as belong to women, and not gone out of her way and calling to meddle in such things as are proper for men, whose minds are stronger, &c., she had kept her wits, and might have improved them usefully and honourably in the place God had set her.

Alice Brown
Mercy Warren

Note that a paraphrase reproduces another's words without editorial comment (insertion of your own views about the text).

3 Recording quotations

A third method of recording information is to copy **quotations.** You might find that the information you wish to record has been so well expressed or contains such precise facts and details that you wish to use the exact words of the source rather than summarize or paraphrase the information. Following is a quotation Gail Young wrote:

Women and reading
    Warren, <u>The Group</u> stage directions
             n.p.
"In one corner of the room is discovered a small cabinet of books. . . . Hobb's [sic] Leviathan, Winthrop's sermons, Hutchinson's History, Fable of the Bees . . . Hoyle on Whist, Lives of the Stewarts . . . and Acts of Parliament for 1774."

When quoting, you must be extremely careful to record *the exact words of the original* if you use the quotation in your paper.

(Review Sections 34a and 34b for the use of punctuation marks with quotations.) Be sure to analyze the content of your quotations. Remember that a research paper expresses your understanding of a subject based on the information gleaned from research. Avoid overusing quotations in your paper, because too many quotations leave the reader with the impression that you did not truly master the material. If you find that you are using too many direct quotations, you can always summarize or paraphrase the quotations when you write the paper. You must also integrate direct quotations into the text of your paper. Using lead-in phrases like the following samples helps with this integration:

As Carlos Artiz has reported,

Maury Joseph counters this argument as follows:

In support of these views, Laetitia Owen points out that . . .

A fourth method of recording your information is to combine quotation and paraphrase. This method allows you to record the information *in your own words* while retaining a few particularly well-chosen words from the original. The following is a combination quotation and paraphrase Gail Young wrote:

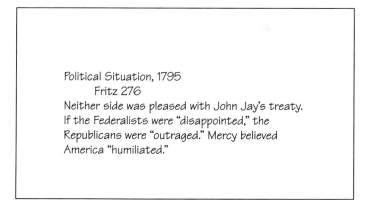

Political Situation, 1795
        Fritz 276
Neither side was pleased with John Jay's treaty.
If the Federalists were "disappointed," the
Republicans were "outraged." Mercy believed
America "humiliated."

45b Prewriting

Once you have completed your preliminary research, you will want to formulate a plan for writing. It is always a good idea to start with some **prewriting.** The prewriting will be more goal oriented than the freewriting you do when writing personal essays, but like freewriting, it will help you to generate additional ideas and decide how to organize your paper. You can begin by sorting your research notes, whether on disk or on cards, by grouping together notes with similar subject headings.

Read each category and the entries. Record your reactions, and use them as a basis for prewriting. You may brainstorm, cluster, freewrite, or use a variety of these methods. With these expanded reactions, you will be able to sketch out an initial plan of how you will proceed. Try to group the entries according to point of view: those that support your view, those that oppose it, and those that are neutral. *Temporarily* set aside entries containing information that appears irrelevant at this time. (Never throw away your research entries; they might prove useful later as your topic evolves.) Continue your research and note taking for any categories that are undeveloped, underdeveloped, or too controversial to lead, at this point, to a thesis. Do not be surprised or disappointed if you find yourself prewriting often. Prewriting is a recursive activity; you will probably have to do it more than once. (See Section 1a for more information on prewriting.)

45c Formulating a Preliminary Thesis and Constructing a Working Outline

Having completed some prewriting based on your research, you will need to plan your paper by writing a preliminary thesis and constructing a working outline.

As in an essay, your **thesis** is a sentence that expresses the idea you wish to develop in your paper. The formulation of the preliminary thesis will help you focus your research. Word this thesis carefully, but at this point, do not worry about style, because you will most likely reword your thesis many times before you are satisfied with it. Gail Young's tentative thesis stated the following: *Colonial New England author Mercy Otis Warren is best known for insulting in print her friend John Adams.* Tim Gomez's was this: *Minor anxieties and the fear of death can cause college students' nightmares, which may be relieved sometimes by simple means, or, in serious cases, only with professional help.* (For more information on the preliminary thesis, see Section 2a.)

Your **working outline** is an organizational blueprint for all the main points in your paper. It is called a working outline because you will probably change it as you do more research and begin to write. You might discover that some of the research entries that you deemed irrelevant during prewriting become pertinent. Further research could also lead you to points that you overlooked earlier, which you should add to your working outline. Your working outline need not be in perfect form, but it should be complete enough to serve as a guide as you start organizing your ideas. Take some time with your working outline. Revise it as needed because it is easier to revise an outline than a garbled first draft. Gail Young developed the following outline based on her early research. The subject headings from her research notes appear in the outline and are underlined.

Title

Preliminary Thesis: Colonial New England author Mercy Otis Warren is best known for insulting in print her best friend John Adams.

1. <u>Attitudes</u> toward women writers at that time

2. Successful <u>women writers</u> in colonial America

3. <u>John Adams's reactions</u> to her writings

4. <u>Contemporary reactions</u> to Warren's poems, plays, and her <u>History</u>

As she gathered more information about her topic, Gail added to the outline.

Revising Your Working Thesis
ON A WORD PROCESSOR

You can use your word processor to refine and improve your working thesis as you complete your research. Write several variations and compare them. Save the ones that you think are most effective and review them later. As you continue to read and take notes, return to these alternative drafts and revise them until you are ready to settle on a definite thesis. You can add and delete freely, without retyping.

Outlining
ON A WORD PROCESSOR

Preparing your outlines on a word processor has several advantages. Because it's easier to evaluate the working outline if it is typed, you can enter it into your computer, print it out, and examine it for revisions and additions. Then return to the computer and make the changes. You can also experiment with arrangement and ideas by typing two versions and printing them out to look at side by side.

You can expand the working outline to produce the formal outline that you will write from. It's easy on a word processor to indent subsections and add the Roman numerals, uppercase letters, Arabic numerals, and lowercase letters that indicate the levels of detail. You can also insert details and use the cut and paste functions to move sections and to place your thesis statement at the top of your outline. Your word-processing program might have an outline feature that will format the material automatically into an outline.

45d Constructing a Formal Outline

You will eventually want to revise your working outline and convert it into a formal outline. Many instructors require the submission of a formal outline with the paper. Your **formal outline,** in topic or sentence format, serves as a plan for your first and subsequent drafts and acts as a guide for your audience. (Review the procedures for outlining in Section 2b.) A formal outline includes a formal statement of your thesis, which has evolved from the preliminary thesis and working outline, and all of the supporting points that relate to your subject headings. Present these points in a logical sequence that you will use to develop your paper. As your paper develops, new ideas and insights on your topic may lead you to change the supporting points. Following is a portion of Gail Young's formal outline. Notice the addition of a possible title, the change in focus and point of view in her thesis, the appearance of supporting materials, and the new third point.

A New England Woman's War

Thesis: Mercy Otis Warren would probably be forgotten as an author and/or feminist but for her quarrel with John Adams.

    I. Contemporary attitudes toward women

        A. Gov. Winthrop

        B. Lord Chesterfield

    II. Women who succeeded as writers

        A. Anne Bradstreet

        B. Mercy Otis Warren

        C. Phillis Wheatley

    III. Contemporary reception of Warren's writings

        A. Poems

        B. Plays

        C. <u>History</u>

IV. John Adams's reaction
   A. To poems and plays
   B. To History
      1. Political climate
      2. Adams's personal situation
      3. Politics of Warren's family

45e Writing and Revising the Paper

The process of actually writing your research paper is much like that of writing an essay, except that you are relying to a large extent on source material outside your own mind. But you need to read these sources carefully and think about them critically to develop your own ideas about them and the topic. Using your formal outline, write a first draft, let it sit for a while, and then go back to it and begin the process of criticism and revision. (See Chapter 3 on revision.) Also, be sure to consider your paper as a piece of research. Are you relying too heavily on one or two sources? Perhaps you need to do some more research. Do you seem to be using too many quotations? Perhaps it would be more effective to summarize or paraphrase some of them. Does any section of the paper need strengthening? Perhaps you could use some of the research entries that you did not use in the previous draft. Does your paper seem like a collection of unrelated chunks of material? Perhaps you have overlooked key points in developing your topic or have failed to include logical transitions.

When Gail wrote her first draft, she gave a lot of attention to Warren's plays and poems. As she worked, Gail realized that her interest was in Warren's *History,* Adams's reaction to it, and Warren's response as part of the political controversy of the times. Gail had to revise her preliminary thesis and working outline, as her first draft revealed a slightly different emphasis. Her formal outline (on the preceding page) reflects this change in emphasis. Such changes in both the outline and the paper are easier to make if you type your first draft on a computer.

The new emphasis that Gail arrived at in her first draft was refined further when she wrote second and subsequent drafts. Experienced researchers know that one draft is rarely sufficient. The topic and the paper itself develop during the process of researching and then during the writing and revising of various drafts. In her later drafts, Gail decided to give more emphasis to Adams's personal reactions to Warren's plays because it would enable her to present Warren as an early feminist who was treated unfairly by a famous person.

The checklist on pages 454–455 for revising your research paper will help you work on your various drafts and then prepare a polished final draft.

45f Avoiding Plagiarism

In all the writing you do, it is essential that you acknowledge your sources of information and the ideas derived from those sources according to accepted guidelines. It is a matter of ethics and honesty. Although borrowing words and ideas from sources is permissible, you must indicate clearly what is borrowed both in the body of the paper and in the works cited or bibliography (explained in Chapters 46 and 47). Failure to do so is called **plagiarism,** a term derived from the Latin words *plagiarius,* "plunderer," and *plagium,* "kidnapper." Some instructors will give students a failing grade on their papers or fail them for an entire course for committing an act of plagiarism.

Plagiarism falls into two categories: using someone else's *words* or using someone else's *ideas* as if they were your own. You must be scrupulous in avoiding both categories of plagiarism in your writing. Properly cite all quotations, paraphrases, and summaries of information from other sources. The only exception to this rule is **common knowledge,** or information that is commonly known and accessible to your audience. For example, it is common knowledge that the United States participated in the Persian Gulf War and that Mark Twain wrote *Huckleberry Finn,* so you need not acknowledge sources for this information. However, information about the specific details of the air raids during the war or about Twain's use of specific dialects in the novel would not be common knowledge and would require research. You need to acknowledge your sources for such information. If you are unsure whether certain information constitutes common knowledge, document it.

REVISING YOUR RESEARCH PAPER

Ask yourself the following questions to revise and complete your paper. Also, refer to Sections 3a, 3b, and 3c on revision and to the sections noted in this checklist for more detailed information.

- **Purpose:** Is the purpose clear and is the tone consistent and appropriate for that purpose? (See Sections 1c and 43c.) Have you avoided errors in reasoning? (See Section 6c–d.)
- **Title page:** If required, have you included a title page that lists all pertinent information?
- **Title:** Is your title brief? Does it suggest the topic, tone, and purpose of the essay or does it effectively challenge interpretation?
- **Outline:** If required, have you included an outline? (See Section 2b.)
- **Thesis:** Is the thesis clear? Does it give your reader adequate direction? (See Section 2a.)
- **Opening:** Does your opening state the topic effectively? (See Section 4f.)
- **Body:** Does every part of the body relate to the thesis and increase the reader's understanding of the problem being explored? Is the body coherent? (See Sections 2c, 3a.)

- **Paragraphs:** Is the order of paragraphs logical, each relating to the thesis? (See Section 4b.) Are transitions between paragraphs clear and effective? (See Section 4d.) Is unity apparent in each paragraph as it develops its one idea? (See Section 4a.) Are supporting details specific, adequate, and logically arranged? (See Section 4a-2.)

- **Sentences:** Are sentences sufficiently varied in form to avoid monotony in style? Are your sentences constructed so that ideas are expressed forcefully and directly? Do you use action verbs and write in the active voice? Are important elements emphasized? (See Chapters 21–23.)

- **Words:** Does your choice of words express your thoughts precisely? (See Chapter 24.) Is the diction appropriate for your purpose, tone, and audience? (See Chapter 26.) Have you edited out any wordiness, repetition, and vagueness? Have you avoided sexist language? (See Chapter 25.)

- **Conclusion:** Is the conclusion effective? Does it emphasize your points without undue repetition of the thesis? (See Section 4g.)

- **Documentation:** Are all sources acknowledged according to accepted guidelines in order to avoid plagiarism? (See Chapters 46 and 47.)

- **Manuscript form:** Have you followed standard guidelines or your instructor's requirements in formatting your paper?

- **Proofing:** Have you reread and edited your final version carefully, checking punctuation and mechanics? (See Section 3d.) Have you checked for errors in usage? (See the Glossary of Usage.) Have you read your sentences backwards, from the bottom of the page up, to check spelling? (See Chapter 42.)

1 Direct quotations

All direct quotations or material taken *word for word* from another source must be documented. (See Sections 34a and 45a-3 on recording quotations.) Quotations should be enclosed in quotation marks or, if consisting of more than four lines of text, presented without quotations marks in block quotation form. (See Section 34e on punctuation with quotations, Section 34b on block quotations, and Chapters 46 and 47 on proper methods of citing sources.)

2 Paraphrases and summaries

All paraphrases and summaries need to be properly documented. As we have seen, *paraphrasing* involves *stating* the words and ideas of another person in your own words, using approximately the same number of words as the source. (See Section 45a-2.) *Summarizing* involves stating the ideas of another person in your own words in a greatly condensed form. (See Section 45a-1.) Acceptable paraphrases and summaries clearly present the author's idea, tone, and point of view. Unacceptable paraphrases and summaries distort the author's idea, tone, and point of view and often include words that are used in the original source but without quotation marks. Following are examples of unacceptable and acceptable paraphrases:

ORIGINAL TEXT OF SOURCE

Teachers have a choice. They can use word processing as a glorified typewriter, or they can use the new medium for scholarly community, creativity, and discovery. With CAI [computer-assisted instruction], software developers and teachers have the responsibility to work together to create and use software that respects the individuality of students and treats them honestly and humanely. Teachers can take good software and make it punitive, or they can soften the inflexibility of CAI programs by recommending it to certain students and, within a context, explaining its limitations.

Helen J. Schwartz
"Ethical Considerations of Educational Computer Use"

UNACCEPTABLE PARAPHRASE

As Schwartz writes, teachers can make choices. They can use word processing just like a typewriter or use it creatively. With CAI, people can work together creating and using software designed individually for students that is honest and humane. Teachers can use the software for punishment or fun, especially for bright students.

The preceding paraphrase is unacceptable for several reasons. The author's full name does not appear in the lead-in phrase. Words that are directly quoted from the source lack quotation marks, and the paraphrase reflects an inaccurate reading of the source.

ACCEPTABLE PARAPHRASE

As Helen J. Schwartz reports, teachers can use word processing in uncreative and creative ways for "scholarly community, creativity, and discovery." Teachers and software developers "work together to create" and design software that either adapts to students' individual needs or is selectively assigned to students.

This paraphrase is acceptable. It correctly identifies the author and accurately restates the source author's idea, tone, and point of view. Most unintentional plagiarism results from paraphrases that are too close to the original source. After reading a source, put it away and write your paraphrase. Then go back to the source and check your work for accuracy. Use the following checklist on avoiding plagiarism to help you evaluate your work.

3 Collusion

Collusion, a form of plagiarism, occurs when two or more people agree to devise a piece of writing that will be attributed to only one of them. Unless you are working on a collaborative assignment, all of your writing is considered to be your own work; it should not be wholly or partially written by another person. For any individual writing assignment, the idea and the organization of ideas in your paper must be your own. (Ideas of others may appear in your writing, but in each instance, the source must be properly cited.) You can incorporate into your writing ideas that have arisen from class discussion, lectures, and collaborative writing sessions, but you should not restate the ideas of the class or writing sessions simply to meet the needs of the assignment. You may revise and edit your writing with the help of others, and it is fine to discuss individual details with other people (see Section 3c on collaboration and peer critiques), but you should not have others do your writing or revising for you. Ultimately, if someone helps you significantly with your writing, you must acknowledge that help.

AVOIDING PLAGIARISM

1. Are all direct quotations accurately reproduced in my paper? Are they cited properly?

2. Do all of my paraphrases and summaries reflect the author's idea, tone, and point of view? Have I cited the author properly? Are quoted words enclosed in quotation marks?

3. Am I clear on the distinction between what information is considered common knowledge (which would *not* require documentation) and what information has been quoted, paraphrased, or summarized and needs to be documented? If in doubt, have I documented anyway?

4. Have I acknowledged each source where it occurs in my paper as well as in the works cited list or bibliography?

5. Have I avoided collusion?

46 Documenting Sources— MLA Style

To credit your sources adequately, you will need to convert your working bibliography into a formal bibliography or list of **works cited,** a list of all sources cited in your paper. It will appear on a separate page at the end of your paper and will enable your readers to verify your sources. (See Section 48a for an actual works cited listing.) Since the various disciplines have different bibliographic guidelines, before compiling your working bibliography, check with your instructor to determine which guidelines your paper should follow, whether MLA (Modern Language Association) form, APA (American Psychological Association) form, or some other form. The MLA style of documentation is used largely in the humanities and is set forth in the *MLA Handbook for Writers of Research Papers.* The *MLA Handbook* explains how to format the list of works cited and recommends the use of in-text parenthetical citations. These MLA guidelines are explained and illustrated in this chapter. For sample papers in MLA style, see Section 48a and the literary analysis paper in Chapter 49. Consult the *MLA Handbook* for situations that are not covered in this chapter's examples. See also Chapter 47 on APA and other documentation styles.

46a Preparing the List of Works Cited

According to the *MLA Handbook,* your works cited page should be formatted as follows:

1. Start the list on a new page following the text of the paper. Number each page of the list in the upper right corner, continuing the page numbers of the text. (For instance, if the text ended on page 7, the first page of the list would be page 8.)

2. Center the title "Works Cited" one inch from the top of the page. Do not underline it. (See Sections 48b and 49b for examples.)

3. Double-space between the title and the first entry, and then double-space the entire list, within entries and between entries.

4. List the sources alphabetically by author or by title for works by unknown authors. (Disregard *a, an,* and *the* in alphabetizing titles.)

5. If you follow the guidelines for your working bibliography given in Section 44d, your sources will already be listed in the proper form; simply copy the information for each source that you actually used in your paper.

6. Begin each entry at the left margin; if an entry is longer than one line, indent the subsequent lines one half inch (or five spaces if using a typewriter).

7. Remember the different formats of documentation: in-paper (parenthetical documentation; see Section 46c) and end-of-paper (works cited). Be sure to include both.

8. Look into the possibility of using a computer program to format your works cited list. This could help you save time.

Here are some guidelines for formatting works cited entries. A series of models of works cited entries follows.

1. Always include the author's full name (when given and as listed on the title page), the complete title, and the complete publication information. (See an actual list of works cited in Section 48b.)

2. Separate these three items (and any additional information) with periods followed by two spaces.

3. Give the author's last name first and separate it from the author's first name with a comma. Names of second or third authors, or the name of an editor after the author, should not be inverted. (See Section 46b.) For more than three authors, list only the first author and add "et al.," which is the Latin abbreviation for "and others." (See Section 46b.)

4. Indicate an editor or compiler by the abbreviation "ed." or "comp." or "eds./comps." if there are more than one. (See page 463.)

5. In the publication information for books, you may use the shortened form of publishers' names as listed in the *MLA Handbook* or other standard sources. Give the name of the city. Add the state or country *only* if the city alone would not be familiar or would be confusing to the reader: for example, Cambridge, MA, or Cambridge, England. Use the standard postal abbreviations for states. (See page 463 for a sample entry.)

6. In publication dates for periodicals, abbreviate the names of months except May, June, and July. Place the dates in parentheses for periodicals with continuous pagination. For online electronic information sources, try to identify a release date for the source. (See page 467.)

7. Include page numbers for a periodical article, for a work that is part of an anthology or collection, or for an introduction, preface, foreword, or afterword. Do not use *p.* or *pp.* in works cited entries. For online electronic information sources, try to identify the locator path where the source can be retrieved. (See page 467.)

8. Double-space all entries and indent the second and subsequent lines of an entry one half inch (or five spaces if using a typewriter). (See page 463.)

46b Sample MLA Works Cited Entries

1 Books

ONE AUTHOR

Boorstin, Daniel J. The Image: A Guide to Pseudo-Events in
America. New York: Atheneum, 1961.

TWO AUTHORS

Commager, Henry Steele, and Elmo Giordanetti. Was America a
Mistake? An Eighteenth-Century Commentary. New York:
Harper, 1967.

THREE AUTHORS/EDITION AFTER THE FIRST EDITION

Millet, Fred B., Arthur W. Hoffman, and David R. Clark. Reading
Poetry. 2nd ed. New York: Harper, 1968.

MORE THAN THREE AUTHORS

Adams, Russell, et al. Great Negroes Past and Present. Chicago:
Afro-American, 1964.

MORE THAN ONE BOOK BY THE SAME AUTHOR

Skinner, Cornelia Otis. Madame Sarah. Boston: Houghton, 1967.
---. Nuts in May. New York: Dodd, 1950.

Note: Use three hyphens, a period, and two spaces. (List the
works alphabetically.)

A CORPORATE AUTHOR

Group for the Advancement of Psychiatry. Symposium No. 8: Medical
Uses of Hypnosis. New York: Mental Health Material Center, 1962.

MULTIVOLUME WORK

Tolkien, J. R. R. The Lord of the Rings. 2nd ed. 3 vols. London: Allen, 1954-55.

ONE AUTHOR, PREPARED FOR PRINTING BY AN EDITOR

Franklin, Benjamin. Autobiography: An Authoritative Text. Ed. J. A. Leo. New York: Norton, 1984.

ESSAY OR SELECTION FROM AN ANTHOLOGY, COLLECTION, OR CRITICAL EDITION

Bowen, Francis. "Life of James Otis." Library of American Biography. Ed. Jared Sparks. Boston: Little, 1847.

(*Note:* You may omit the name of a publisher before 1900. The previous entry might have listed Boston, 1847.)

WITH TWO PUBLISHERS/REPRINTED/WITHOUT PUBLICATION DATE (N.D. = NOT DATED)

Boswell, James. Boswell in Search of a Wife, 1776-1779. Ed. Frank Brady and Frederick A. Pottle. 1956. New Haven: Yale UP; New York: McGraw, n.d.

WITHOUT PLACE OR PUBLISHER/REPRINTED (RPT.)

Warren, Mercy Otis. The Adulateur, a Tragedy. The Massachusetts Spy. N.p.: n.p., 1722. Rpt. in The Magazine of History 63. Tarrytown, NY, 1918.

AN INTRODUCTION, PREFACE, FOREWORD, OR AFTERWORD

Regan, M. Joanna, RSM, and Isabelle Keiss, RSM. Foreword. Tender Courage, A Reflection on the Life and Spirit of Catherine

McAuley, First Sister of Mercy. Chicago: Franciscan Herald, 1988. vii-xii.

A TRANSLATION

Aristotle. Poetics. Trans. John Warrington. New York: Dutton, 1963.

AUTHOR UNKNOWN

The Twelve Steps for Everyone. Minneapolis: Comp Care, 1990.

(*Note:* Do not use "Anonymous" or "Anon.")

AN ENCYCLOPEDIA

Academic American Encyclopedia. 21 vols. Danbury: Grolier, 1987.

A DICTIONARY

The Agriculture Dictionary. Albany: Delmar, 1991.

2   Articles in periodicals

IN A MONTHLY JOURNAL OR MAGAZINE, PAGINATION BY ISSUE

Morrison, Samuel Eliot. "Three Great Ladies Helped Establish the United States." Smithsonian Aug. 1975: 96-103.

IN A JOURNAL WITH CONTINUOUS PAGINATION

Breedan, Stanley. "The First Australians." National Geographic 173 (1991): 267-90.

IN A WEEKLY OR BIWEEKLY JOURNAL OR MAGAZINE

Seliger, S. "In the Dead of the Night." Interview with E. Hartmann. People Weekly 11 Mar. 1985: 128-30.

(*Note:* If the article is not printed on consecutive pages, write only the first number and a plus sign.)

IN A DAILY NEWSPAPER

Bohlen, Celestine. "Fragile Truce in Yugoslavia." New York Times 8
    Aug. 1991, natl. ed.: A1.

AN UNSIGNED ARTICLE

"Executive Changes." New York Times 8 Aug. 1991, natl. ed.: C3.

AN EDITORIAL

"Breakthrough for Peace." Editorial. Miami Herald 2 Aug. 1991,
    final ed.: 20A.

A BOOK REVIEW

"Do Surveys Give the Full Picture?" Rev. of What They Know About
    You, by Bernard Asbell and Karen Wynn. South Bend Tribune 4
    Aug. 1991, metro ed.: C7.

A LETTER TO AN EDITOR

Haifley, Dan. Letter. San Francisco Chronicle 30 July 1991: A16.

3   Other printed sources

A GOVERNMENT DOCUMENT

United States. Dept. of Commerce. Bureau of the Census.
    "Population Profile of the United States, 1977." Current
    Population Reports. Series P-20, no. 808. Washington: GPO,
    1979.

A BIBLICAL CITATION

The New English Bible with the Apocrypha. Oxford Study ed. New
    York: Oxford, 1970.

AN UNPUBLISHED DISSERTATION

Glenn, Jonathan A. "A New Edition of Sir Gilbert Haye's Buke of the
    Ordre of Knychthede." Diss. U of Notre Dame, 1987.

A PERSONAL LETTER

Hamel, Mohammed. Letter to the author. 12 Dec. 1992.

AN ABSTRACT

Herzberger, David K. "Narrating the Past: History and the Novel
    of Memory in Postwar Spain." Abstract. PMLA 106.1
    (1991): 190.

A CARTOON

Gross, S. Cartoon. New Yorker 31 Dec. 1990: 33.
Wright, Don. Cartoon. St. Louis Post-Dispatch 3 Aug. 1991, 3-star
    ed.: 2B.

A MAP/CHART

Wyoming. Map. Boston: Rand, 1991.
Phonetics Wheel. Chart. New York: Holt, 1988.

A PAMPHLET

Hall, Steven. The Alphabetical City. New York: Trip Builder, 1980.

4 Electronic sources

In citing electronic sources, give the same publication information as for other sources, followed by the pertinent information about the electronic source. For electronic addresses, the MLA recommends using the *uniform resource locator* (URL), enclosed in angle brackets. If a URL must be divided between two lines, break it only after a slash and don't introduce a hyphen at the break. Give the complete electronic address, including the access-mode identifier (*http, ftp, gopher, telnet, news*) and any relevant path and file names.

ARTICLES FROM AN ONLINE PERIODICAL

In general, follow the samples shown in Section 46b-2, modifying them as appropriate for the electronic source. The typical entry for a work in an online periodical consists of author's name (if given); title of the article in quotation marks; name of the periodical (underlined); volume number, issue number, or other identifying number; date of publication; the number range or total number of pages, paragraphs, or other sections (if they are numbered); date of access; and electronic address. If you cannot find some of this information, cite what is available.

"House Set to Approve Limits on Punitive-Damage Award." AP
Online 10 Mar. 1995. 18 Sept. 1998 <http://www.nytimes.com/
aponline/e/AP-Punitive-Damage.html>.

Imada, Kenneth. "A Buddhist Response to the Nature of Human
Rights." Journal of Buddhist Ethics 2 (1995): 9 pars. 21 June
1995 <http://www.cac.psu.edu/jbe/twocont.html>.

Viviano, Frank. "The New Mafia Order." Mother Jones May-June
1995: 22 pars. 17 July 1995 <http://www.mojones.com/
Mother_Jones/MJ95/viviano.html>.

MATERIAL FROM A PERIDOCALLY PUBLISHED DATABASE ON CD-ROM

The typical entry consists of the author's name, publication information for the printed source (including title and date of print publication), title of the database (underlined), publication medium (CD-ROM), name of the vendor (if relevant), and electronic publication date.

Kettel, Raymond P. "An Interview with Jerry Spinelli: Thoughts on Teaching Writing in the Classroom." English Journal 83 (1994): 61-64. ERIC. CD-ROM. SilverPlatter. Mar. 1995.

Knuuttila, Simo. "Remarks on Induction in Aristotle's Dialectic and Rhetoric." Revue Internationale de Philosophie 47 (1980): 78-88. Infotrac: Expanded Academic ASAP. CD-ROM. Information Access. Jan. 1981.

Van Wyck, Shelia M. "Harvests Yet to Reap: History, Identity, and Agriculture in a Canadian Indian Community." DAI 53 (1992): 4383. U. of Toronto, 1993. Dissertation Abstracts Ondisc. CD-ROM. Dialog. Dec. 1992.

A NONPERIODICAL PUBLICATION ON CD-ROM OR DISKETTE

Davisson, W. I. Macroeconomics. Diskette. Chicago: Emerald Distributing, 1996.

"Silly." The Oxford English Dictionary. 2nd ed. CD-ROM. Oxford: Oxford UP, 1992.

Rodes, David S. "The Language of Ambiguity and Equivocation." Macbeth. By William Shakespeare. Ed. A. R. Braunmuller. CD-ROM. New York: Voyager, 1994. 5 pp.

AN ARTICLE FROM AN ONLINE REFERENCE WORK

"The History of Western Music." Britannica Online: Macropaedia.

 Vers. 97.1.1. Mar. 1997. Encyclopedia Britannica. 29 Mar. 1997

 <http//www.eb.com:180>.

AN ONLINE POSTING

 Begin with the author's name, followed by the title of the posting in quotation marks, the words *Online posting,* and the date of the posting. Conclude with the name of the newsgroup or forum, the date of access, and the online address (in angle brackets).

Tomasson, Gunnar. "Anne Hath a Way." Online posting. 25 Feb.

 1996. The Global Electronic Shakespeare Conference. 18 Sept.

 1997 <http://www.globescope.com/ ws/will4.htm>.

WORLD WIDE WEB SITES

 Begin with the author's name (if available), followed by the title of the cited material (in quotation marks), the title of the complete work (underlined or italicized), and the publication date. Conclude with the electronic address (in angle brackets) and the date of access.

Cummings, Shelly. "Genetic Testing and the Insurance Industry."

 Electronic Genetics Newsletter. 18 Mar. 1996. 23 Dec. 1997

 <http://www.westpub.com/Educate/matchsci/insure.htm>.

AN E-MAIL COMMUNICATION

 To cite electronic mail, give the name of the writer, the title of the message (if any), a description of the message that includes the recipient (e.g., "E-mail to the author"), and the date of the message.

Morris, Richard. "Re: Mentoring Programs." E-mail to the author.

    21 Aug. 1998.

For more detailed information about citing electronic sources, consult the *MLA Style Manual,* 2nd ed. (1998) or the MLA's World Wide Web site at <http://www.mla.org>.

5 Nonprint sources

AUDIOTAPE AND VIDEOCASSETTE

Beethoven, Ludwig von. Piano Concerto no. 3 in C Minor, op. 37

    and Fantasy for Piano, Chorus and Orchestra, op. 80.

    Cond. Leonard Bernstein. New York Philharmonic Orch.

    EMI, 1983.

Alzheimer's Disease. Prod. Hospital Satellite Network. Videocassette.

    American Journal of Nursing, 1985.

FILM

It's a Wonderful Life. Dir. Frank Capra. Perf. James Stewart, Donna

    Reed, Lionel Barrymore, and Thomas Mitchell. RKO, 1946.

TELEVISION PROGRAM

Beyond Our Control. Narr. Joe Haas. Writ. and prod. Maureen

    Kline. Public service special. WNDU, South Bend, IN.

    7 Feb. 1996.

PERFORMANCE

Hamlet. By William Shakespeare. Dir. Mark Pilker. Perf. Jeremy

    Wilde. Washington Hall, Notre Dame, IN. 7 Mar. 1991.

RECORDING

Goodman, Benny. <u>Never-Before-Released Recordings</u>. Perf. Teddy
    Wilson, Zoot Sims, Ruby Braff, Roland Hanna, Urbie Green,
    Milt Hinton, and Paul Quinchette. Musical Heritage Society,
    1988.

LECTURE

Klein, Edward. "Computer-Assisted Instruction in English Grammar
    and Spelling." MLA Convention. Palmer House, Chicago.
    28 Dec. 1990.

RADIO BROADCAST

<u>Amahl and the Night Visitors</u>. By Gian Carlo Menotti. Perf. Robert
    Dure and Paula Harris. Indiana Opera North Inc. WSJV,
    Elkhart-South Bend. 9 Dec. 1990.

WORK OF ART

Seurat, Georges. <u>Sunday Afternoon at the Grand Jatte</u>. Art
    Institute, Chicago.

46c Sample In-Text Parenthetical Citations— MLA Style

The *MLA Handbook* recommends the use of in-text **parenthetical citations** to provide concise documentation directly
where a source is quoted, paraphrased, or summarized. In-text
parenthetical citations replace an outdated system of documentation requiring footnotes at the bottom of the page or at the end

of the paper. A parenthetical citation must appear in the paper each time you use material from a source. You will credit your source by citing the author's last name and identifying the location of the borrowed information with its page number, line, act, scene, or chapter, as appropriate. These parenthetical acknowledgments refer the reader to the full source information contained in the list of works cited at the end of the paper.

At times, however, you might wish to refer to the entire work within the text. In this case, give the author's name and the title of the work in the text of the paper.

> In <u>Cast for a Revolution: Some American Friends and</u>
> <u>Enemies</u>, Jean Fritz tracks the political dissention
> surrounding the war.

Or your text may give both author and location of your reference.

> Alice Brown, on page 156 of her biography, <u>Mercy Warren</u>,
> quotes Governor Winthrop's comments.

As you work through your paper, you will find yourself using parentheses for much of this information, as shown in the following examples illustrating the standard formats for MLA parenthetical citations. Consult the *MLA Handbook* for situations that are not covered here.

DIRECTLY QUOTED MATERIAL, AUTHOR'S NAME IN TEXT

> Brown says that John Adams's language was "warmer than
> that of the Courtier to Aspasia" (157).

DIRECTLY QUOTED MATERIAL, AUTHOR'S NAME IN PARENTHESES

> "Governor Winthrop . . . consigned them to the limbo they had
> earned" (Brown 156).

Note that the author's name and the page number are separated by one space without punctuation and that the punctuation closing the sentence belongs outside the end parenthesis.

At other times, your textual citations will refer to paraphrases and/or summaries.

REFERENCE TO MATERIAL, AUTHOR'S NAME IN TEXT

Fritz (259) lists the recipients of Warren's autographed copies.

REFERENCE TO MATERIAL, AUTHOR'S NAME IN PARENTHESES

Warren mailed complimentary copies to a list of distinguished friends (Fritz 259).

WORKS LISTED BY TITLE, NOT AUTHOR

In this case, you may include the title in the text or in parentheses:

The Encyclopaedia Britannica finds Warren's poems "of no value."

Judgment in our time contradicts the high praise Warren's friends gave to her poems (Encyclopaedia Britannica).

Note that you need not provide page numbers for material that is arranged alphabetically, as in an encyclopedia or a dictionary.

TWO AUTHORS WITH THE SAME SURNAME

(E. Kennedy 137)

(J. F. Kennedy 142)

TWO OR THREE AUTHORS

(Commanger and Giordaette 191-92)

(Jones, Millett, and Hoffman 21)

MORE THAN THREE AUTHORS

(Adams et al. 42)

BOOK BY A CORPORATE AUTHOR

(Group for the Advancement of Nursing 75) or a shortened
version: (Group for Nursing 75)

BOOK, PAMPHLET, OR ARTICLE WITH NO AUTHOR

(The Architect's Guide to New York 47) or a shortened
version: (Architect's Guide 47)

VOLUME AND PAGE NUMBERS OF A MULTIVOLUME WORK

(Jones 4: 9-12)

The number to the left of the colon identifies the volume; the
numbers to the right, the pages.

QUOTATION FROM AN INDIRECT SOURCE

Thomas Mann was only partly right (about the Romans, at
least) when he wrote in The Magic Mountain: "the ancients
knew how to pay homage to death" (qtd. in Crowin 139).

Always place your citation as close as possible to the material it
acknowledges, even in midsentence if it is brief.

Brown quotes Governor Winthrop (156) in his harsh
consideration of the sick wife of a fellow governor.

LITERARY PROSE WORKS

(121; ch. 4)
(231; bk. 2, ch. 3)

POEMS AND DRAMAS IN VERSE FORM

Act, scene, line(s):

>　(<u>Hamlet</u> 2.1. 10-19)

Use Arabic numerals unless your instructor specifies otherwise.
Book and line:

>　(<u>Paradise Lost</u> 4.21) or (<u>PL</u> 4.21)

Consult the *MLA Handbook* for a listing of approved abbreviations for literary titles.

QUOTATIONS OVER FOUR LINES IN LENGTH

　See Section 34b for the rules on quotations over four lines in length. Begin such quotations on a new line, indent one inch (or ten spaces if you are using a typewriter) from the left margin, and double-space the material. Do not use quotation marks. After the final punctuation mark of the quotation, skip two spaces and add the reference in parentheses. The introductory phrases for such quotations usually end with a colon.

As Norman Corwin reports, escapism dominates our television viewing:

>　On New Year's day, the parade of bowl games
>　begins early and ends late, stretching, like the old
>　British Empire, across all time zones. And as though
>　live football coverage was not enough, whole taped
>　games are played back later, throughout the season,
>　for those who may have missed them the first time
>　around.　(40)

46d Content Notes

In MLA style, you can use **content notes** to present supplemental reference information such as relevant references that do not appear in your list of works cited or additional text or commentary that might disrupt the flow of the paper. These notes appear either at the bottom of the page as footnotes or at the end of the paper as endnotes. Check with your instructor to determine which approach to use. Identify your content notes with consecutive numbers typed as raised Arabic numerals in the text of your paper. These raised numbers correspond to the numbers of the footnotes or endnotes. Set footnotes four lines from the last line of text. Indent one half inch (or five spaces if using a typewriter) to begin, and allow one space after the raised number at the bottom of the page. Note that footnotes are double-spaced.

TEXT: In her novels Maria Edgeworth makes her model women daughters, wives, and mothers rather than wage earners.[1]

NOTE: [1] When she writes about tradespeople and farmers, as in *Popular Tales,* she stresses the need for women as well as men to learn a trade in order to be morally independent.

Format endnotes as you would footnotes, but place them on a separate page at the end of the paper. Place the title "Notes" one inch from the top of the page. Indent the first line of the entry (one half inch or five spaces if using a typewriter) from the left margin and signal the endnote with a raised Arabic number. Examples of content notes can be found at the end of the sample research paper in Section 48a.

47 Documenting Sources— APA and Other Styles

Whereas MLA documentation style is used in the humanities, the guidelines of the American Psychological Association (APA) are usually required for documentation in the social sciences. In this chapter, we look at the APA style and the styles that are used in some of the other disciplines. If you use the APA style of documentation to cite sources, use the examples in this chapter as a guide in preparing your working bibliography. You will convert your working bibliography into a list of **references** (the APA equivalent of the MLA list of works cited), which will appear on a separate page at the end of your paper. (See Section 48b for an actual reference listing.) This chapter also contains examples for in-text parenthetical documentation in APA style. Consult the *Publication Manual of the American Psychological Association,* 4th edition (1994) for situations that are not covered by these examples. See Section 48b for a sample paper that uses APA style. If you have a computer program that offers APA-style formatting, using it will allow you to save time when formatting your list of references.

47a   Preparing the List of References

According to APA style, the final copy of a student's references page should be formatted as follows:

1. Start the list on a new page following the text of the paper. Number each page of the list in the upper right corner five spaces after the running head. (See Section 48b for an example.)

2. Center the title "References" two spaces beneath the page number. Do not underline the title.

3. Double-space between the title and the first entry, and then double-space the entire list within entries and between entries.

4. List the works alphabetically by author, or by title for works by unknown authors. (Disregard *a, an,* and *the* in alphabetizing titles.) Works by the same author should be listed chronologically from the earliest to the most recent publication.

5. If you follow the guidelines for your working bibliography in Section 44c, all the information you need will be found in each entry.

6. Begin each entry flush with the left margin. Subsequent lines are indented three spaces or an interval determined by your instructor. (If you are submitting a computer disk to a journal for publication, however, you should refer to the *APA Publication Manual* for formatting guidelines.)

7. Be sure to include both formats of documentation: in-paper (parenthetical documentation) and end-of-paper (references).

Here are some general APA guidelines for preparing your reference list entries. Model entries in APA style follow.

1. Include only sources that you have used in the paper.

2. Always include the names of all authors (when given and listed on the title page), the complete title, and the complete publication data for each entry in your list.

3. Separate these three items (or any additional information) with periods followed by two spaces.

4. Give the author's last name first, followed by his or her initials. Follow this format for each author of the work if there is more than one author. (See an actual list of references in Section 48b.)

5. Use capital letters for proper nouns and for the first word of titles and subtitles of books and articles. Lowercase the other parts of the title. For the titles of periodicals use customary capitalization. (See Section 48b.)

6. For more than one work by an author, repeat the author's name for each entry and arrange the works by publication date, the earliest first. (See Section 48b.)

7. List all names of multiple authors (*et al.* is not used in the list of references). See the following page for an example of a listing with multiple authors.

8. Place all publication dates in parentheses directly after the final author's name, with a period after the end parenthesis. In dates for magazine and newspaper articles, give the year first, then the month and day. Do not abbreviate the month.

9. Do not enclose the titles of articles from periodicals in quotation marks. (See Section 47b.)

10. Underline periodical titles through the volume numbers including the commas before and after these volume numbers. (See Section 47b.)

11. Precede page numbers by "p." or "pp." in referring to articles or chapters in an edited book or to articles in newspapers, but *not* in referring to journal articles. (See the following pages.)

47b Sample APA References

1 Books

ONE AUTHOR

Abernathy, C. F. (1980). <u>Civil rights: Cases and materials</u>. St. Paul: West Publishing.

TWO AUTHORS

Cook, M., & McHenry, R. (1978). <u>Sexual attraction</u>. New York: Pergamon Press.

Note: In the list of references, use the ampersand sign instead of writing the word *and*.

THREE OR MORE AUTHORS

Brusaw, C., Alfred, G., & Oliu, W. (1976). The business writer's
handbook. New York: St. Martin's Press.

GROUP OR CORPORATE AUTHOR

National Research Council. (1993). The social impact of AIDS in the
United States. York: National Academy Press.

WITH AN EDITOR

Gallegos, B. (Ed.). (1994). English: Our official language? New
York: Wilson.

ARTICLE IN A COLLECTION OR ANTHOLOGY

Emig, J. (1978). Hand, eye, brain: Some basics in the writing
process. In C. Cooper & L. Odell (Eds.), Research in composing:
Points of departure (pp. 59-72). Urbana, IL: National Council
of Teachers of English.

MULTIVOLUME WORK

Asimov, I. (1960). The intelligent man's guide to science. (Vols. 1-2).
New York: Basic Books.

LATER (SECOND OR SUBSEQUENT) EDITION

Gibaldi, J. (1998). MLA style manual and guide to scholarly
publishing (2nd ed.). New York: MLA.

2   Articles in periodicals

IN A JOURNAL WITH CONTINUOUS PAGINATION

Messner, M. (1990). When bodies are weapons: Masculinity and
violence in sport. International Review for the Sociology of
Sport, 25, 203-220.

IN A JOURNAL PAGINATED BY ISSUE

Holtug, N. (1997). Altering humans: The case for and against
human gene therapy. Cambridge Quarterly of Healthcare
Ethics, 6(2), 157-160.

IN A POPULAR MAGAZINE, MONTHLY

Neimark, J. (1991, May). Out of bounds: The truth about athletes
and rape. Mademoiselle, 196-199.

IN A POPULAR MAGAZINE, WEEKLY

Donahue, D., & Red, S. (1986, May 12). A Hyannis hitching. People,
53-56, 59.

IN A NEWSPAPER

Eskenazi, G. (1990, June 3). The male athlete and sexual assault.
The New York Times, Section 8, 1.

AN EDITORIAL

Help students—not the tax revolt [Editorial]. (1991, July 31).
Los Angeles Times, p. B6.

A BOOK REVIEW

Morris, A. (1990). The body politic: Body, language, and power
[Review of the book Sowing the body: Psychoanalysis and
ancient representations of women]. College English, 52, 570-578.

A LETTER TO AN EDITOR

Silva, J. T. (1991, August 5). The health care crisis [Letter to the
editor]. Houston-Post, p. A14.

3   Other printed sources

GOVERNMENT DOCUMENT

U.S. Department of Commerce. (1977). Population profile of the
    United States (Publication No. P-20, No. 808). Washington, DC:
    U.S. Government Printing Office.

CARTOON

Benson. (1991, August). [Cartoon]. Chicago Sun-Times, p. 8.

MAP/CHART

Wyoming. (1991). [Map]. Boston: Rand McNally.
Phonetics wheel. (1988). [Chart]. New York: Holt.

4   Electronic sources

ARTICLE FROM A FULL-TEXT DATABASE

Viviano, F. (1995, May/June). The new mafia order. Mother Jones
    [Online], 44-56. Available: Infotrac SearchBank. [1995, July 17].

ARTICLE FROM A CD-ROM

Howell, V., & Carlton, B. (1993, August 29). Growing up Tough:
    New Generation Fights for Its Life: Inner-city Youths Live by
    Rule of Vengeance. Birmingham News [CD-ROM], p. 1A
    (10 pp.). Available: 1994 SIRS/SIRS 1993 Youth/Volume 4/
    Article 56A. [1995, July 16].

ARTICLE FROM AN ONLINE ENCYCLOPEDIA

Daniel, R. T. (1995). The history of western music. In Britannica
    online: Macropaedia [Online]. Available: http//www.eb.com:
    180/cgi-bin/g:DocF=macro/5004/45/O.html [1995 June 14].

For more details about citing electronic sources, see Xia Li and Nancy Crane's *Electronic Style: A Guide to Citing Electronic Information* (Westport: Meckler, 1993), which is based on the APA style, or Janice R. Walker and Todd Taylor's *Columbia Guide to Online Style* (New York: Columbia UP, 1998).

5 Nonprint sources

PERSONAL LETTERS, TELEPHONE CONVERSATIONS, INTERVIEWS

These are cited in the text only, not in the reference list, because they consist of nonrecoverable data.

AUDIOCASSETTE

Ringer, A. B. (Speaker). (1991). Problems of codependency (Cassette Recording No. 8512). Chicago: Alcoholics Anonymous.

VIDEOTAPE

Poe, K. L. (Producer). (1991). Alzheimer's disease [Videotape]. New York: American Journal of Nursing.

FILM

Benjamin, R. D. (Producer), & Jeffries, M. K. (Director). (1990). AIDS in our schools [Film]. New York: Educational Products.

47c Sample In-Text Parenthetical Citations— APA Style

APA documentation style recommends the use of in-text parenthetical citations, as does MLA, to provide concise documentation when and where a source is used. Each source included in your parenthetical citations should appear in the list of references at the end of your paper.

The following guidelines for in-text parenthetical citations are based on the *Publication Manual of the American Psychological Association,* 4th edition, 1994.

1. Use a title in a parenthetical citation only if the author is unknown.

2. Give the year of publication in addition to the author's last name and page or line numbers for quotations.

3. Separate items in parentheses—the author's name, publication date, and page numbers—with commas. Signal page numbers with "p." or "pp." This notation is *required* for direct quotations.

4. For works with more than one and fewer than six authors, list the names of *all* the authors in the *first* textual reference. For subsequent references, if the work has two authors, cite both names; if the work has more than two authors, give only the surname of the first author, followed by "et al."

Sample APA-style parenthetical citations follow. Consult the *APA Publication Manual* for situations that are not covered here.

DIRECTLY QUOTED MATERIAL, AUTHOR'S NAME IN TEXT

According to Gringel (1991), drug habits . . .

DIRECTLY QUOTED MATERIAL, AUTHOR'S NAME IN PARENTHESES

Social behavior may be defined as the interaction of individual organisms (Judy, 1985).

SPECIFIC PART OF A SOURCE

Humans do not use these higher thought processes while speaking (Wittgenstein, 1965, p. 9).

SOURCE WITH TWO AUTHORS

Inconsistencies exist in the theories (Morris & Fox, 1978, pp. 16-17).

REFERENCE TO SEVERAL SOURCES IN THE SAME PARENTHETICAL CITATION

Some cruel experiments produce no knowledge (Oglive,

1954, p. 1195; Ryder, 1976, p. 3).

Note that multiple citations within the same parentheses are grouped alphabetically and separated by semicolons.

WORKS WITH AN UNKNOWN AUTHOR

Cite in the text the title and the year. Use double quotation marks around article or chapter titles; underline periodical and book titles.

. . . for beating the drug habit ("Saying No to Drugs," 1992).

. . . in the book Nurses as Enablers (1991).

The word "anonymous" is used with a title only if the work's author is designated as such.

PERSONAL COMMUNICATIONS (LETTERS, MEMOS, TELEPHONE CONVERSATIONS)

Give the initials as well as the surname of the source with as exact a date as possible.

R. H. Clymer (personal communication, December 8, 1992)

47d Other Documentation Styles

The MLA documentation style is generally accepted in the humanities, and the APA style is preferred in the social sciences, but other areas of study, such as mathematics and the natural sciences, prefer their own documentation styles. If you are not certain which style to use for a particular course, consult your instructor. You will find that other styles of documentation sometimes use different terminology. Other styles might, for example, refer to "bibliography" instead of "works cited" (MLA) or "references" (APA) and may prefer "footnotes" to "parenthetical citations." Regardless of the style you use, be consistent in its application. And remember when compiling your working bibliography that all documentation styles will require the same basic data: author, title, place of publication, publisher, date, and page numbers. Only the mechanics, or format, varies.

Following is a listing of some of the style manuals for other disciplines that should be available in your college library. These will give you the information you need to format citations for your courses outside of the humanities and social sciences. Also, see Sections 50b and 50c on writing in the natural and applied sciences.

Biology

Council of Biology Editors. Style Manual Committee. *CBE Style Manual: A Guide for Authors, Editors, and Publishers in the Biological Sciences.* 6th ed. Bethesda, MD: Council of Biology Editors, 1994.

Business and finance

Harrison, David. *The Spreadsheet Style Manual.* Homewood, IL: Dow Jones-Irwin, 1990.

Chemistry

Dodd, J. S., ed. *The ACS Style Guide: A Manual for Authors and Editors.* Washington: American Chemical Society, 1986.

Engineering

Michaelson, Herbert B. *How to Write and Publish Engineering Papers and Reports*. 3rd ed. Phoenix, Oryx, 1990.

Geology

Bates, Robert L., Rex Buchanan, and Martha Adkins-Heljeson, eds. *Geowriting: A Guide to Writing, Editing, and Printing in Earth Science*. 5th ed. Alexandria: Amer. Geological Inst., 1992.

Law

Columbia Law Review. *A Uniform System of Citation*. 16th ed. Cambridge: Harvard Law Rev. Assn., 1996.

Linguistics

Linguistic Society of America. "LSA Style Sheet." Published annually in December issue of *LSA Bulletin*.

Mathematics

American Mathematical Society. *The AMS Author Handbook: General Instructions for Preparing Manuscripts*. Providence: AMS, 1994.

Medicine

Iverson, Cheryl, et al. *American Medical Association Manual of Style*. 8th ed. Baltimore: Williams and Wilkins, 1989.

Music

Holoman, D. Kern, ed. *Writing about Music: A Style Sheet from the Editors of* 19th-Century Music. Berkeley: U of California P, 1988.

Physics

American Institute of Physics. *Style Manual: Instructions to Authors and Volume Editors for the Preparation of AIP Book Manuscripts*. 5th ed. New York: AIP, 1995.

Political science

American Political Science Association. *Style Manual for Political Science*. Rev. ed. Washington: Amer. Political Science Assn., 1993.

Science and technical writing

Rubens, Philip, ed. *Science and Technical Writing: A Manual of Style*. New York: Holt, 1992.

Social work

National Association of Social Workers, *Writing for NASW*. 2nd. Ed. Silver Spring: Natl. Assn. of Social Workers, 1994.

General

The Chicago Manual of Style. 14th ed. Chicago: U of Chicago P, 1993.

Turabian, Kate L. *A Manual for Writers of Term Papers, Theses, and Dissertations*. 5th ed. Chicago: U of Chicago P, 1987.

48 Sample Research Papers

Following are two model research papers. John Jansen wrote the first research paper for an English class and used the MLA documentation style, which is standard in the humanities. The paper argues the issue of equal pay for men and women for work that is judged to be of equal value. Eileen Biagi wrote the second sample research paper for a psychology class and documented it in the APA style, which is preferred in the social sciences. It reports on and analyzes career achievement motivation in women. Explanatory comments on the content and form of both papers appear on facing pages to highlight important elements. Remember that the MLA and APA styles of documentation differ on many points. Consult the appropriate sections of this handbook for specifics on each style. (See Chapter 46 for detailed guidelines on MLA documentation and Chapter 47 for APA guidelines.)

48a Sample MLA Paper

The sample paper that follows uses the documentation style recommended in the fourth edition of the *MLA Handbook for Writers of Research Papers.*

1   **Outline.** An outline, if required, precedes the first page of the paper on a separate, unnumbered page. The outline below is an informal, preliminary working outline that the author used to organize his ideas prior to and while writing the paper. The formal topic outline on the facing page could be submitted with the paper if required. Note that the formal outline uses only short phrases, omits an introduction, and uses standard outline form with Roman numerals for major categories, indented capital letters for the next series of ideas, and indented Arabic numerals for the third level. (See Section 2b on outlining.) If your outline is longer than one page, number all the pages with lowercase Roman numerals.

Working Outline: Comparable Worth

Tentative Thesis: Sexual discrimination underlies the concept of not paying equal salaries to men and women who perform jobs of equal value to an organization.

1. Introduction: Proponents and opponents of the comparable worth positions have valid viewpoints.
2. Women earn less money than men for three reasons.
3. Can comparable worth theories be used to set wage standards?
4. What is the role of job evaluation in setting wages?
5. Can compensable factors be considered without sex bias?
6. Current job evaluation procedures that appear to be objective are really subjective.
7. In reality, jobs rank differently according to various job evaluation scales.
8. Can job evaluations serve as a basis for unequal pay, which is the result of sexual discrimination?

Note: In place of an outline, an *abstract* (a summary of the essay's content and organization in two hundred words or less)

1   Outline: Comparable Worth in Salaries

Thesis: All jobs in organizations should be compared to one another using an evaluative system that is blind to gender.

  I. Unfair wages for women
      A. Women's choices
          1. Hours
          2. Job types
          3. Temporary employment
      B. Custom and tradition
 II. Comparable worth determinants
      A. Job evaluation factors
      B. Sex bias
III. Objectivity and subjectivity in evaluations
      A. The McArthur scale
      B. The Treimin scale
 IV. The solution
      A. The threat
      B. The promise

may be required. Place it on a separate page entitled "Abstract" before the essay. Double-space and center the block of type on the unnumbered page.

2   **Identification and title page format.**   A separate title page is not required by MLA guidelines; should your teacher require one, follow the specific instructions given. If you must submit an outline, place the identification on the same page as the outline.

Jansen properly omitted a separate title page. Following MLA guidelines, he placed his name and course information in a block beginning at the left margin about one inch from the top of the first page. He double-spaced and centered the title. The title includes no punctuation, underlining, or quotation marks. Jansen doubled-spaced below the title to begin the text.

3   **Paper format.**   All pages of the paper, excluding the outline and any title page, are numbered with Arabic numerals in the upper right corner, typed one half inch from the top of the page. MLA guidelines recommend typing your last name before the page number. Avoid using the abbreviation "p." before the page number.

Double-space the text of your paper with a margin of one inch at the top and bottom and on both sides of the page. Indent the first word of a paragraph five spaces from the left margin. If using a computer, set the first tab at five (or one half inch) and do not right-justify your margin without your instructor's approval.

4   **Introduction and thesis.**   Jansen's thesis statement appears in the first sentence in the form of an argumentative proposition that identifies a problem within industry. Although the thesis usually appears somewhere near the beginning of the paper, it need not be the opening sentence. By placing the thesis first, Jansen quickly informs his audience of his view on this issue. He realizes that many readers will not agree with him, so he includes opponents' views in this paragraph and offers a solution for the problem identified in the thesis. This is a good way to establish a reputation for fairness and to keep the attention of any opponents or undecided readers.

5   **In-text documentation.**   Because the names of the authors are not incorporated into the text discussion, they appear in a par-

2 John Michael Jansen
Professor M. Hall
English 102
6 November 2000

Comparable Worth in Salaries

4 Industry needs to adopt an evaluative system that is blind to gender in comparing all jobs in order to achieve comparable worth in salaries. When jobs are worth the same to an organization, those who staff the jobs should be paid the same salary. However, opponents counter that the market system properly determines wages and salaries, and that businesses and professions must base wage and salary decisions on the free market. How do we solve the dilemma, especially to provide equity to women and minorities who have suffered the most discrimination in comparable worth jobs? The solution appears to lie in adopting fair job evaluation systems that award equal pay to women and men who perform the same jobs. This would reconcile the concerns of minority workers, including women, and those of employers and taxpayers as well as labor economists, so long as all share the economic and cultural costs of such programs. As a start, this can be accomplished when all parties concerned involve themselves in implementing and funding such procedures within their own companies.

Women in the 1980s earned on the average about 30 to 35
5 percent less than men earned (Aaron and Loughy 4). It appears to be
6 common knowledge that within a corporation male janitors can

enthetical reference along with the page number on which the information is found. The abbreviation "p." for page is not used, and the parentheses are included within the sentence; a period follows them.

6   **Common knowledge.**   Jansen does not provide documentation for the views expressed about janitors and flagmen because they do not come from any particular source; they represent common knowledge that most people have about this subject matter. (See Section 45f on common knowledge.)

7   **Audience.**   Jansen gives his paper wide appeal by citing varied yet familiar occupations: janitors, secretaries, highway repair flagmen, truck drivers, teachers, female and male physicians.

8   **Use of evidence.**   Jansen cites published evidence and examples to support his thesis. In this case, he is using supporting evidence taken from a recent newspaper article. Note that the page number of the newspaper in parentheses also includes the section of the newspaper, A4.

9   **Developing the argument.**   After presenting some examples, Jansen shows how society places restrictions on the occupational choices that most women make. Note his use of the transitional phrase *on the other hand* in midparagraph to introduce two additional considerations: *custom* and *tradition.*

10   **Transition.**   Jansen accomplishes a smooth transition *between* paragraphs by using the conjunctive adverb *however* to introduce the topic sentence of the paragraph.

11   **Use of evidence.**   To exemplify and make specific his views in the previous paragraph, Jansen now cites a printed source and common knowledge.

7   earn more money than female secretaries and that highway repair
    flagmen earn more than the company's female nurse. The inequities
    extend beyond one corporation. Truck drivers, usually male, earn
    more than teachers, usually female. Problems exist even within the
    professions. Paul Recer points out that "women physicians in 1988
    earned only 62.8 percent of the pay received by male doctors [. . .] a
8   decline from 1982, when female physicians earned 63.2 percent of
    the pay of male doctors" (A4).

    Although men and women freely make career decisions in the
    same way, our culture places restrictions on women's choices. Some
    of the differences between men's and women's earnings are due to
    decisions women make about how many hours to work each week,
9   what occupations to choose, and when to enter or to leave the work
    force. On the other hand, custom and tradition also influence wages
    in different jobs and occupations, a view that acknowledges that
    women improve their relative earnings by entering jobs traditionally
    held by men. Women, who enter these same jobs and work just as
    many hours, earn, in many cases, less salary than their male
    counterparts. Recer also cites a study of the American Medical
    Women's Association that reveals that female physicians "are
    classed in the four lowest-paid specialities: general practice,
    pediatrics, psychiatry, and internal medicine" (A4).

10   However, the narrower the definition of industries and
    occupations, the greater the apparent segregation of women and
    men who hold particular jobs becomes. According to the U.S.
11   Department of Labor classifications, 37 percent of all women work in
    industries in which at least 65 percent of the employees are women

12   **Direct quotation.**   Jansen incorporates a direct quotation from Meeker, who is identified within the sentence, into his own sentence to define the concept of job evaluation. Note that a capital letter does not follow the opening quotation mark. The parenthetical reference includes only the page number because Jansen identified Meeker in the text, and a period follows the parentheses.

13   **Ellipsis within a quotation.**   The three ellipsis points, each preceded and followed by one space, indicate that Jansen did not present Meeker's full sentence. If ellipsis points appear at the end of a sentence, they are followed by a space and the appropriate end punctuation mark. The square brackets indicate that Jansen added the ellipsis points.

14   **Content note.**   The superscript number "[1]" signals the presence of an explanatory endnote placed at the end of the paper on a separate page entitled "Notes." Jansen does not place the contents of the note within the paper itself because not all readers will need an example to understand the text.

15   **Developing the argument.**   Jansen writes this expository paragraph to describe some of the complexities that are involved in devising systems of job evaluation.

16   **Quotation marks question validity.**   Jansen has placed the phrase "compensable factors" within quotation marks because of its elusive use by job evaluators; in short, he questions the validity of the concept as described in the paper.

17   **Content note.**   The superscript number "[2]" signals another explanatory endnote, which Jansen places after the text of the paper.

18   **Indirect quotation.**   Because Jansen introduces the quotation from Hutner with the conjunction "that," the quotation that follows is considered *indirect* rather than *direct;* therefore, Jansen does not enclose it in quotation marks. The indirect quotation ends at the close of the next sentence, where he places the parenthetical page citation.

19   **Developing the argument.**   Jansen closes this paragraph with a reference to *sex bias,* which he examines in the next paragraph.

(Norwood 4). Furthermore, it seems to be common knowledge that the larger the proportion of female workers in an industry, the lower the average hourly wage they receive.

Can comparable worth be used to set wage standards? To do so requires some form of job evaluation, a method of ranking jobs according to their value to the employer. Its purpose, Meeker says, is to provide a system of comparing "dissimilar work [. . .] to determine appropriate wage levels" (674). The result of the evaluation process becomes a hierarchy of job values, a model reflecting the relative worth of jobs in a governmental unit, a plant, or a firm. It seems like a good system; however, it is not always consistent.[1]

While a variety of job evaluation systems exist, they range from the simplest ranking procedures to more complicated methods based on points or scores awarded to "compensable factors," which consist of a job's skill and training requirements, its working conditions, its demands on physical and mental efforts, and the amount of responsibility for people and materials that the job requires. In the more sophisticated evaluative systems, each job receives a rank based on compensable factors followed by an attempt to relate the resulting job rankings into a wage structure. Job evaluation in this model relates to jobs, not to the worker who performs the job, even though it is the worker who is evaluated and rated.[2] Hutner writes that job content determines pay grades for each job, whereas a worker's characteristics--seniority, merit, productivity--determine the individual worker's pay within each job grade (16). At first glance this appears to be a fair system; however, it too has inconsistencies rooted in sex bias.

20   **Block quotation.**   Although it stands apart from the text as shown, a block quotation must have a logical connection with the sentence that precedes it. Jansen uses a colon, an appropriate punctuation mark to indicate that a block quotation will follow; however, other marks may be used or none, as required by the grammar of the sentence preceding the quotation. The block quotation is indented one inch or 10 spaces on each line and double-spaced. Notice that the right-hand margin of the block quotation is the *same* as that for the body of the paper. Because Jansen identifies the author and the title of the book from which he took the quotation in his text, the parenthetical reference includes only the page number. If he had not included this information in the text, the parenthetical reference would appear as follows: (Hutner 16). Note also that the period ends the block quotation and is followed by two spaces; the parenthetical reference is not part of the direct quotation.

21   **Developing the argument.**   Jansen selected the block quotation to close this paragraph because it emphasizes and summarizes the role of sex discrimination. In the next paragraph, he turns to the inequities that result from subjective judgments in establishing job evaluation models.

22   **Parenthetical citation of an author from an anthology.** Jansen identifies his paraphrase of material written by McArthur, which he discovered in an anthology (collection of essays) edited by Hartmann, and he includes the page numbers. Note that the abbreviation "pp." for pages is absent and that a hyphen mark with no spaces before or after it separates the numbers.

A critical part of the job evaluation process, from the point of view of pay equity, lies in eliminating sex bias when assessing the compensable factors. For example, when examining working conditions, most evaluators weight the rigors of traditionally male jobs, such as dirt and noise, heavier than those of traditionally female jobs, such as the stress of dealing with bosses or clients or the eye and back strain of working at sewing machines and word processors. More evaluative points may be assigned to so-called typically male jobs that involve large salaries, such as corporate sales managers, than to female jobs that involve contact with consumers, like customer service. Furthermore, in Equal Pay For Comparable Worth, Hutner reports the following:

20   If, when dollar values are assigned to the compensable factors, market values for typically female jobs are used as benchmarks for female jobs in the establishment, then discrimination in the

21   market place is carried over to the firm. (16)

Despite what appears to be the formality and objectivity of job evaluation models, the procedures appear to be judgmental throughout. In no sense do they represent an objective determination of the value of the product of each job. Subjective evaluations enter at every step of the way: in determining what attributes to include in the job evaluation, in setting the point weights for each attribute, in deciding how many points each job should get for each attribute, and in calibrating the resulting point

22   scores with pay (McArthur 53-70). An example is the range of weights attached to the degree of supervision required in an office

23 **Numbers.** Jansen properly uses Arabic numerals with percentages rather than spelling them out.

24 **Word choice.** Jansen opts to place the phrase "physical demand" in quotation marks to emphasize the elusiveness of the concept as well as the apparent use of the phrase by many people to apply only to occupations in which physical labor is more obvious. Avoid the excessive use of quotation marks for this purpose because it might confuse your audience.

25 **Developing the argument.** Jansen, having explained some examples of job evaluation systems, now discusses the problems that ensue from the lack of a uniform evaluation system, to stress the resulting inequities.

26 **The essay's conclusion.** In the last paragraph, Jansen concludes his essay by referring to the introduction and summarizing his argument. The final sentence of the essay restates the thesis to remind the reader of the point of his essay: to achieve comparable worth in salaries, companies will need to adopt evaluative systems that are blind to gender when comparing jobs.

23   job: one job evaluation scale assigns a maximum of 7 percent of total
24   points to this attribute, while another assigns 14.5 percent. "Physical
     demand" provides a maximum of 10 percent of the points for shop
     jobs but none at all for office jobs. Some job evaluation scales are
     meant to apply only to shop jobs, others only to office jobs, and still
     others to both (Treiman 66-179).

     The importance of a particular attribute in determining a job's
     rank depends not on the <u>maximum</u> proportion of total points it could
     account for, but on the <u>proportion</u> of the variation in total points of the
25   various jobs for which it actually accounts. Whatever variations occur
     depend purely on the judgment of evaluators. In other words, jobs
     rank differently according to various job evaluation scales. The
     weights assigned to job attributes actually determine the ranks of the
     jobs. In fact, different relative rankings of jobs may arise for any of a
     variety of reasons: use of different attributes or weights or variation in
     the application of a given system by evaluators. The results of simple
     correlations between the rankings of various evaluators applying the
     same job evaluation are sometimes disturbingly low (Schwab 37-52).

26   For comparable worth advocates, then, job evaluation
     constitutes both a threat and a promise. Because it typically
     rationalizes and solidifies sex discrimination in pay systems, job
     evaluation, as presently used, becomes a threat. Because it offers a
     way of measuring the relative value of jobs that are not identical, it
     becomes a promise. Moreover, job evaluation may provide the only
     evidence acceptable to the courts as proof of sex discrimination
     based on salary. Wages resulting from discriminatory pay will
     become an increasingly important issue, not only to the large
     numbers of female, ethnic, and racial members of the work force, but

27   **Content notes.** The endnotes begin on a separate numbered page entitled "Notes" with the word centered on the page one inch from the top. Notes are double-spaced and indented one half inch (or five spaces if using a typewriter) from the left margin. The note number, which is raised slightly from the line of type without punctuation, precedes by one space the content of the note. In notes that extend beyond the length of one line, as these do, subsequent lines begin at the left margin, double-spaced. Both of these notes elaborate on points that Jansen makes within the text of the paper, but he decided that the elaboration would impede the paper's flow if contained in its body. Endnotes can also contain bibliographic information that is related to the topic and of possible interest to the reader but not contained in the list of works cited. Endnotes are optional; consult your instructor.

also to their employers, to the consumers of their services, and to their male fellow workers (Hutner 18). While advocates will continue to cite cases of discrimination in salary, and opponents will argue that the labor market dictates the lower salaries, it behooves all involved (workers, employers, consumers, labor economists) to study and share the benefits and sacrifices that will follow the elimination of salary discrimination. Companies will need (or be required by federal dictate) to create and fund procedures that all businesses must follow with job evaluations determined by a panel composed of ethnically diverse members of both sexes.

27

Notes

[1] Aaron and Lougy give an example. Ranking jobs entirely on the basis of two factors, "brain" and "brawn," and assigning from 0 to 100 points for "brain" and 0 to 30 points for "brawn," brain appears to be the more important factor because it can account for 100 out of 130 maximum points. But if one assigns to most jobs similar "brain" scores (say, clustering most jobs in a 10-point range from 40 to 50 points), and if the scores are widely distributed over the 30-point range for "brawn," brawn will be more important than brains in determining the rankings. (The Comparable Worth Controversy, 28.)

[2] Aaron and Lougy state another example. Suppose one ranks jobs according to two factors, A and B, and gives scores for each factor ranging from 1 to 10. Job I gets a score of 3 for factor A and 8 for factor B. Job II receives a score of 5 for factor A and 7 for factor B. Weighting each factor equally, job II ranks ahead of job I (12 points

28   **Works cited.**   "Works Cited" lists only the works that the writer directly cites in the text.

    If your instructor requires you to list all works *consulted,* place the title "Works Consulted" on a separate page and present, in alphabetical order, all works consulted or cited. The format is the same as for works cited.

29   **Format of the list.**   The list of works cited begins on a separate, numbered page; the heading is centered one inch from the top. All lines should be double-spaced. Alphabetized entries begin with a capital letter. The first line of each entry begins flush with the left margin. Subsequent lines for an entry are indented one half inch (or five spaces if using a typewriter) from the left margin. Each entry begins with the author's surname. For works with multiple authors, invert the first author's name only. For works with more than three authors, list only the name of the first author followed by the abbreviation "et al."

30   **Page information.**   If the book as a whole is the reference, page numbers are not included.

31   **Article within an anthology or collection of essays.**   List the name of the author first, then the title of the essay in quotation marks. Note that the end punctuation goes inside the closing quotation mark. The underlined title of the anthology or collection comes next, followed by a period. "Editor" is abbreviated as "Ed." The editor's name appears in noninverted order with a period, then the place of publication and a colon, the publisher and a comma, and the year of publication and a period. The page numbers for the *entire* article appear, not merely those that identify the location of citations or paraphrases.

32   **Periodicals using continuous pagination.**   The date is identified by a volume number; the year is in parentheses. This article was accessed electronically through the InfoTrac SearchBank, a database provided by Information Access and subscribed to by the library.

33   **Government documents.**   Specific authors of government documents often are not known. If such were the case here, the entry would begin "U.S. Department of Labor" and be relocated to appear in alphabetical order. But this government report contains signed essays; the entry begins with the author's name and the title of the essay. The report was accessed through the Internet.

to 11). According factor B, for example, three times the weight of factor A, however, results in job I ranking ahead of job II (27 points to 26). (The Comparable Worth Controversy, 29.)

28   Works Cited

29   Aaron, Henry J., and Cameron M. Lougy. The Comparable Worth
30   Controversy. Washington: Brookings Institute, 1986.

     Hutner, Frances C. Equal Pay for Comparable Worth. New York:
          Praeger, 1986.

31   McArthur, Leslie Zebrowitz. "Social Judgment Biases in Comparable
          Worth Analysis." Comparable Worth: New Directions for
          Research. Ed. Heidi I. Hartmann. Washington: National
          Academy, 1985. 53-70.

32   Meeker, Suzanne E. "Equal Pay, Comparable Work, and Job
          Evaluation." Yale Law Journal 90 (1981): 674-92. InfoTrac:
          Expanded Academic ASAP. CD-ROM. Information Access. 1989.

33   Norwood, Janet L. The Female-Male Earnings Gap: A Review of
          Employment Earnings Issues. U.S. Department of Labor. Bureau
          of Labor Statistics, Report 673. Washington: GPO, Sept. 1982.
          1 Oct. 1996. <http://www.gpo.gov/lbrpt673.jnorwood.htm>.

     Recer, Paul. "Study: Health Field Still Sex-Segregated." South Bend
          Tribune 8 Sept. 1991, metro ed.: A4.

     Schwab, Donald P. "Job Evaluation Research and Research Needs."
          Comparable Worth: New Directions for Research. Ed. Heidi I.
          Hartmann. Washington: National Academy, 1985. 37-52.

     Treiman, Donald J. Job Evaluation Research: An Analytic Review.
          Washington: National Academy of Sciences, 1979.

48b   Sample APA Paper

The sample research paper that follows uses the method of documentation recommended in the fourth edition of the *Publication Manual of the American Psychological Association.*

1   **Title page format.**   APA guidelines do not explicitly prescribe a form for the title page, although the sample paper in the *APA Publication Manual* provides Biagi with a model to follow: the title, her name, and the name of the university she attends centered on the page and double-spaced. Since Biagi's paper is a class assignment, she adds the course title, the instructor's name, and the date of submission about four inches beneath her university affiliation.

2   **Page header.**   The page header is a brief encapsulation of the essay title that appears on the title page at the top right corner on the same line and five spaces to the left of the page number. Numbering and identifying pages will assist the reordering of pages in case of page misplacement and eliminate the need to include one's name alongside each page number (as is done in MLA style). On papers submitted for publication in a journal, follow *The Publication Manual of the APA,* fourth edition (especially Sections 4.06 and 4.15).

1

Career Achievement Motivation in Women

Eileen B. Biagi

University of Notre Dame

Psychology

Dr. W. Bartlett

May, 2000

3   **Abstract.**   Papers written in the APA format usually include an abstract, a brief comprehensive summary of the contents of the paper. The abstract must be exact in its content and contain no abbreviations or acronyms. The abstract may contain paraphrasing but no direct quotations. The content should be as brief as possible, yet each sentence must be informative. The content reports; it does not evaluate. An abstract for a *review* or a *theoretical paper* may not exceed 100 words and should describe the topic in one sentence; the purpose, thesis, or organizing basis and scope of the paper; the sources used (such as published literature, personal observation); and the conclusions and implications or applications. An abstract of a *report* of an empirical study may not exceed 960 characters (120 words) and includes the problem under investigation, and, as appropriate, the subjects of the study (number, age, sex, species, etc.), the experimental method (apparatus, data-gathering method, drugs or medications used), the findings (including statistical information), and the conclusions and implications or applications.

If your instructor requires a formal outline, it will take the same form as the outline that accompanies the MLA-style paper in this chapter. It begins on a separate unnumbered page, and only short phrases are used. Roman numerals indicate major categories; indented capitals and then Arabic numerals, indented further, indicate subsidiary categories.

3   Abstract

Historically, women and men have differed in their career
orientations. Farmer (1987) attempts to explain these differences
with her model of career and achievement motivation. She proposes
that interaction among personal, environmental, and background
factors determines an individual's level of achievement motivation.
Specific results of her study are presented and compared with other
research. Support exists for her assertion that gender differences in
this area are evident and that achievement motivation will vary with
age and social changes. Other studies suggest that this motivation
construct differs between females and males. However, these
studies conflict with Farmer's in that they detect other types of
gender differences. As yet, a comprehensive model that explains
achievement motivation for women and men does not exist. But the
models we do have for women's career achievement motivation
suggest that they can serve as bases for changing women's
positions in the job market and their attitudes about achievement in
the career world.

4 **Page numbering.** APA style requires that pages be numbered with Arabic numerals, starting with 1 on the title page and continuing throughout the paper. The page number appears in the upper right corner, five spaces after the page header.

5 **Format.** APA recommends double-spacing between all lines in a paper. Margins should be one and one half inches at the top, bottom, right, and left of each page. Lines are not justified on the right side, nor are hyphenated words permitted at the end of a line. No more than twenty-five lines of text should appear on a page, excluding the running title and page number. Paragraphs are indented five spaces.

6 **Introduction and thesis.** Biagi opens the paper by presenting her thesis and the particular problem under study. Although the thesis should appear near the beginning of the paper, it need not be the first sentence. By placing the thesis here, Biagi immediately establishes the nature of her analysis and what she intends to accomplish in the paper.

7 **In-text documentation.** Biagi follows APA documentation style. When the author's name is not given within the text itself, a parenthetical reference includes the name and page number. Commas separate the elements in the reference. The publication date is *always* cited, and "p." or "pp." accompanies the page number or numbers. No title appears in the text reference unless the author is unknown.

8 **Date reference.** Because Biagi cites more than one publication by Farmer in the paper, each time she cites Farmer's name she includes in parentheses the publication date of the material cited.

9 **Developing the analysis.** As is appropriate in a study in the social sciences, Biagi begins a review of previously published research on the topic.

4

5   Career Achievement Motivation in Women

6   By identifying the factors that influence career achievement
motivation in women, we can recognize, understand, and perhaps
change the current position of women in the job market and
women's attitudes about achievement in the career world. Do men
and women differ in their career orientations? And, if they do, why
do these differences occur and what factors contribute to the
disparities? "Psychologists have generally viewed the need for
achievement [achievement motivation] as a learned motive, with
parents playing a major role in shaping their children's later

7   strivings" (Benner, 1985, p. 12). However, this single motive cannot
easily explain the historical differences between and changes within
women's and men's career orientations.

8   Farmer (1987) proposes one such model for explaining gender
differences in achievement motivation, basing the model on social
learning theory (Bandura, 1987) and on a sociocultural perspective
(Maehr, 1974, 1984). The model incorporates the idea of reciprocal

9   determinism, i.e., through interaction, the behavioral, cognitive, and
environmental factors influence one another. Farmer (1987) further
presents three constructs that both interact among themselves and
influence achievement motivation: personal, environmental, and
background. Academic self-esteem, expressiveness, independence,
ability attributes, and intrinsic values comprise the personal factors.
Environmental elements include support from parents and teachers
and support for working women, while the components of the
background construct are sex, special status, school location, race, age,

10 **Paragraph and essay development.** Biagi, following Farmer, enumerates the dimensions that have a significant influence on career motivations. This enumeration not only develops this paragraph but also provides the organizational framework for the next several paragraphs.

11 **Citing a work by two or more authors.** When citing a source with two or more authors outside of parenthetical citation, use the word "and" as Biagi does; however, if citing the source *within parentheses,* use an ampersand (&) in place of the word "and."

12 **Paraphrasing.** Biagi paraphrases relevant research to present information economically (Farmer, Kaufman and Richardson, Ireson, and Lueptow), but she documents her sources just as she would if she had quoted them directly. (See Section 45a-2 on paraphrasing.)

verbal ability, and math ability. Yet each of these dimensions has a significant influence on the career motivation of both women and men.

10   Additionally, according to Farmer, "Motivation is represented by three different but related dimensions: Aspiration, Mastery, and Career" (1987, p. 5). Aspiration motivation refers to the level of education and occupation a person hopes to attain, while mastery motivation concerns the desire to achieve a challenging task until one masters the task. Finally, career motivation becomes the commitment to the long-range prospects of a career. Farmer provides us a model, then, which we can compare to current studies of the vocational development of women.

Examining the achievement motivations individually reveals that the aspiration motivation in adolescence is not a reliable predictor of achievement in adulthood (Farmer, 1985). In particular, highly achievement-motivated female adolescents did not attain (as adults) careers comparable to their previously desired goals.

11   Likewise, Kaufman and Richardson (1982) noted a study that found that occupational aspirations of girls change over time from equal to boys at the beginning of high school to lower than boys by the end of senior year (Ireson, 1978). If the female adolescent's aspirations to achieve diminish over time, she will undoubtedly lack the motivation necessary to develop a career corresponding to her initial aspiration

12   level. Nevertheless, Lueptow (1984) concluded that adolescent girls have higher levels of achievement value orientation and academic achievement than males. He offered two suggestions for these surprising results:

13 **Block quotation.** APA guidelines require the indentation of a block quotation five spaces from the left margin. Place the period at the end of the last sentence of the quotation but before the citation. The right margin of the quotation is the same as that of the rest of the paper. In APA style, quotations of forty or more words should appear in block format with quotation marks omitted. Note that Biagi uses a lead-in sentence to prepare her audience for the quotation.

14 **Transition.** Here, and at other places in the paper, Biagi uses transitional words and phrases such as *furthermore, additionally, finally,* and *on the other hand* to achieve coherence.

15 **Developing the analysis.** As is often the case in reviewing research materials, Biagi notes a conflict between two sources and reports it. She then presents a practical application that originates from the second source cited in the paragraph, which reveals her stance in the conflict.

13   First, on the basis of these results it is likely that achievement
orientation is actually a component of the female sex role, and
not the male. Second, the author urges that a distinction be
made between achievement based on excellence and
accomplishment, which is the focus of the female achievement
orientation, and achievement through assertion and aggressive
competition, which are the achievement themes favored by
males. (Lapsley & Quintana, 1985, p. 255)

Unifying the study's results is the common discovery that adolescent
girls differ from adolescent boys on the achievement issue. Whether
one sex achieves and the other does not or whether the sexes
achieve in different realms remains unclear.

14   Furthermore, turning to mastery motivation, Farmer (1985)
found that men score higher than women on this construct and that
environmental factors have a stronger influence on women's mastery

15 motivation than on men's. These findings conflict with Lueptow's
(1984), whose results suggest that a part of the female ideal of
achievement consists of "excellence and accomplishment,"
mastering the work. The results show that women do have some
desire to achieve mastery; however, the magnitude of this
motivation is debatable. Because environmental factors such as
ethnic identification, regional location, religion, and the educational
and occupational history of family members have a relatively strong
impact on women's mastery motivation, a vocational counselor may
use this knowledge by offering support and encouragement to
female clients on the high school and collegiate levels as well as in
public and private agencies.

16   **Paraphrase and personal opinion.**   Note here how Biagi obtains a balanced blend of paraphrase and opinion. She paraphrases five different sources in this paragraph and adds her personal reflection and opinion.

17   **Audience.**   Thinking of her audience, Biagi incorporates several examples into this paragraph, which benefits the reader by making specific the theoretical concerns she presents in the paper.

16   Finally, on the career motivation construct, adolescent girls score higher than adolescent boys (Farmer, 1985). But earlier research by Rooney (1983) shows that in adulthood women score lower than men in career motivation, reflected, in part, by the positions these women hold in the job market. At the present time, young women expect to work outside the home, and data show that women are a major part of the occupational economy (Kaufman & Richardson, 1982). However, they work mainly in service and support jobs (Lueptow, 1984). Kaufman and Richardson point out that women experience difficulty gaining executive and managerial positions because of their limited access to the power centers of the professions and because of socialization that has encouraged them to be deferential to men. In addition to the socialization factor, Farmer (1987) finds that for those who have responsibilities at home, homemaking has a negative influence on career commitment for women. She suggests that conflicting role priorities may reduce women's career commitment. Several self-imposed and societal factors might hinder women from achieving as men do. Many women have refused promotions that require them to relocate away from their families or work longer hours. Others have welcomed the opportunity. The self-imposed factors may be then, partially, a product of socialization. The complex interaction between personal development and socialization makes measuring an individual's career motivation a delicate task.

17   On the other hand, the role of women in society is not static. Women, except in some third-world countries, have become

18 **Reference to a table.** At the close of this paragraph, Biagi refers to a study that she did in an earlier course. She places the table summarizing the study at the end of the paper. According to APA guidelines, she presents only the table's *highlights* in the text, not all of its details. Biagi properly identifies the author of the table by including a surname and the date in parentheses.

19 **Table signal.** Biagi, following APA guidelines, signals the placement of the table in the text. The table, however, actually appears at the end of her paper, in keeping with the wishes of her instructor. Short tables may appear on pages that contain text; longer tables appear on a separate page immediately after the page on which they are mentioned. If the paper were to be published, an editor would insert the table in the text in place of the signal.

increasingly more independent and well educated. Compared to women in the Victorian era, who were socialized to remain unemployed outside the home, women today are much more career-oriented. In particular, within the past twenty years, economic necessity, the recognition of what women can accomplish, and the feminist movement, coupled with the readiness of the culture to accept them, have resulted in drastic changes in the social mores and patterns of thought concerning women. Young children read stories about policewomen and male nurses. Adolescent girls, reversing a long-standing trend, enroll in classes in advanced math and the pure sciences. Adult women are entering the professions of law, medicine, accounting, and the professoriate in greater numbers and are slowly attaining high-ranking positions. Recently, Congress approved the right of women pilots to fly into combat situations after exemplary performances were observed during the Persian Gulf War.

18 Additionally, a preliminary study of career-oriented women showed that college-aged students rated a situation in which the woman works at home as more common than that in which the woman works in the business world. However, these same students asserted that when the woman remains at home it causes more strain on a marriage and is less fair than when the woman works outside of the home (Biagi, 1990).

19 Insert Table 1 about here

As social and cultural values change, women push for the opening of more career opportunities. If it were possible to measure women's

20 **Conclusion.** Biagi presents a conclusion in accordance with APA guidelines. She indicates how her analysis and research contribute to resolving the original problem posed in the thesis. Her conclusion is clear, direct, and unambiguous.

21 **Format of references.** The alphabetized bibliography at the end of a paper following APA style is titled "References." Center the word "References" on a separate, consecutively numbered page, and include all the works cited in your paper. Although APA style does not call for it, if Biagi's instructor suggested that she list her background reading as well, she would have titled her list "Bibliography."

22 **Edited book.** Use the abbreviation "Eds." for "editors" or "Ed." for "editor" within parentheses when referring to an edited book, as shown in Biagi's reference list. However, if the reference is to a chapter or article within an edited book, the author of the chapter or article appears first with the reference formatted as follows:

Author, A., Author, B., & Author, C. (1976). Can the chimpanzee think? In T. Regan & P. Singer (Eds.), <u>Animal rights and human obligations</u> (pp. 15-20). Englewood Cliffs, NJ: Prentice-Hall.

career motivation over the past one hundred years, it would most likely reflect this increase in women's interest in the career world. As personal and societal values change over time, women's career motivation will most likely vary with them.

20   Farmer's (1987) model for explaining career achievement motivation in women is at odds with other research on the topic. Although achievement motivation in high schools does not constitute a valuable predictor of adult career achievement, women's ideal of achievement may differ from men's and these differences must be incorporated into measurements of achievement motivation and models for prediction of career achievement. Environmental factors do influence women's mastery and career motivations. As social and cultural values change and we acknowledge economic necessity, women's desire to have careers increases along with an influx of women into the work force. These studies show that career achievement motivation in women fluctuates. Women have the power to develop it in themselves, and vocational counselors have the ability to nurture its growth through support and encouragement of female clients from the very earliest stages onward.

21   References

Bandura, A. (1978). The self system in reciprocal determinism. American psychologist, 33, 344-358.

22   Benner, D. G. (1985). Need for achievement. In D. G. Benner (Ed.), Baker encyclopedia of psychology. Grand Rapids: Baker Book House.

23 **Journal article from a full-text database.** The word *Online* is inserted in brackets after the name of the journal to indicate that the article was downloaded from an electronic source, which is cited at the end of the entry, along with the date of access (in brackets). Two other articles in this list of references—by Maehr and Rooney—were also accessed through the InfoTrac database; the electronic source is cited in the entries.

24 **Review of a book.** Because the review lacks a title, the information that describes it takes the place of the title, and Biagi places it in brackets to show that it is not the title. If the review had a title, this material would follow it, in brackets. Note also that by APA style, all publication dates appear in parentheses followed by a period.

25 **Publisher's name.** The name of a university press is spelled out in full form, but the name of a commercial publisher may be abbreviated: Macmillan Publishing Company, for example, becomes simply Macmillan.

26 **Journal article.** The volume number, underlined, follows the name of the journal and a comma. A comma also follows the volume number. The underline extends to the comma that follows the volume numbers. Pages are indicated here without the abbreviations "p." or "pp." but the abbreviations are used in referring to articles or chapters in an edited book and to articles in popular magazines and newspapers.

Farmer, H. (1985). Model of career and achievement motivation for women and men. Journal of counseling psychology, 32 (3), 663-676.

23   Farmer, H. (1987). A multivariate model for explaining gender differences in career and achievement motivation. Educational researcher, 16 [Online], 5-9. Available: InfoTrac: Expanded Academic ASAP. [1996, March 6].

Ireson, C. (1978). Girls' socialization for work. In A. Stromberg & S. Harkess (Eds.), Women working (pp. 128-139). Palo Alto: Mayfield.

Kaufman, D. R., & Richardson, B. L. (1982). Achievement and women. New York: Free Press.

24   Lapsley, D. K., & Quintana, S. M. (1985). (Review of Adolescent sex roles and social change). Sex roles, 12, 252-255.

Lueptow, L. B. (1984). Adolescent sex roles and social change. New
25   York: Columbia University Press.

26   Maehr, M. (1974). Culture and achievement motivation. American psychologist, 29, [Online], 887-896. Available: InfoTrac: Expanded Academic ASAP [1996, March 3].

Maehr, M. (1984). On doing well in science: Why Johnny no longer excels: Why Sarah never did. In S. Paris, G. Olson, & H. Stephenson (Eds.), Learning and motivation in the classroom (pp. 179-210). Hillsdale, NJ: Lawrence Erlbaum.

Rooney, G. (1983). Distinguishing characteristics of the life roles of worker, student, and homemaker for young adults. Journal of vocational behavior, 22, [Online], 324-342. Available: InfoTrac: Expanded Academic ASAP [1996, March 3].

27   **Table location.**   Tables should be placed on a separate numbered page after your references. Explain all abbreviations in the
table *except* those that are standard statistical abbreviations, as is
the case here.

28   **Note.**   Follow each table with a note, double-spaced, as Biagi
does, and place it beneath the table. Cite the author and the
copyright holder. In this case, the table comes from a paper that
Biagi wrote a few semesters earlier. Even though it is her own
work, it must be cited when used in another paper.

27

Table 1

Means, Standard Deviations, and Univariate Analyses Results
for the Gender Role Main Effect

Variable	Women work at home		Women work outside of home		F	p
	M	SD	M	SD		
Common	4.29	.65	2.92	1.05	45.73	.000*
Strain	3.75	.67	3.27	.96	7.35	.009*
Fair	3.17	.79	3.62	.99	5.40	.024*

28

Note. From "How Typical and Atypical Gender Roles Are
Valued: A Pilot Study" by E. B. Biagi, 1990. Unpublished
manuscript, University of Notre Dame, Department of
Psychology, Notre Dame. Copyright 1990 by E. B. Biagi.
Adapted by permission.

*p < .05

Part

ACADEMIC AND BUSINESS WRITING

Good writing is not confined to your English composition class. The processes that you undertake to produce an essay in a composition course are the same for all courses in any discipline in your college career and beyond. This section introduces you to the variety of writing assignments you might encounter: essays in the humanities and about literature; field research reports in the social sciences; lab reports in the natural sciences; technical reports in the applied sciences; essay examinations; and business memos, letters, faxes, and the resume. Academic writing and business writing should be clear, concise, and correct. Attention must also be given to purpose or focus, audience, and certain conventions of form.

49   Writing in the Humanities and about Literature

Disciplines in the humanities include communication arts, history, language and literature, philosophy, religion and theology, women's (gender) studies, and, in many instances, the fine and performing arts: painting and sculpture, music, dance, and theater. When you write in the humanities, you concern yourself with human values as you focus on an individual work or collection of works within one of these disciplines (for example, on a poem, a novel, a drama, a painting, or a symphony). Your writing will most likely address *what* the author, artist, or composer communicates; *how* it is communicated; *where* it fits into or adjusts the tradition of which it is a part; and how you—the reader, viewer, or listener—*react* to it. Writing in the humanities, then, incorporates subjective information because you are reacting to or interpreting a work. Much of it relies on objective data as well, however, because you will use the work itself and perhaps outside sources to support your interpretation.

In the humanities you will encounter different types of writing that either *explain* (exposition) or *persuade* (argument). (See Section 4b on the expository patterns of development and Section 6a on writing an argument.) The types of papers that you will be asked to write can take several forms. A **reaction paper** is one in which you record your thoughts, feelings, and ideas about a work, as in your reactions of pity and sorrow to Blake's poem "The Chimney Sweeper." An **interpretive paper** is one in which you discuss what the author or artist is communicating, as in writing about the feelings of loneliness and isolation in Picasso's painting *The Tragedy* from his blue period. An interpretive paper can also reflect what a work means to you. Or you might write a review of a book, film, art work, ballet, or concert. An **analysis paper,** or a **review paper,** is one in which you discuss the relationship of the parts of a work to the whole (see Sections 4c-7 and 4c-8 on analysis): for example, how each individual composition performed during a concert contributes to or detracts from the success of the concert itself. In your college career, the type of analysis paper you will most likely encounter is literary analysis, which is discussed in the following section.

49a Writing about Literature

Writing about literature is a specialized type of writing within the humanities. It involves careful reading of texts, critical thinking (see Chapter 5), and your response to the literature, whether a reaction, an interpretation, or a review.

1   Reading critically

Writing about literature begins with careful reading and *rereading* of the literature, whether works of fiction, poetry, or drama. As you read, be certain that you know the meaning of each word you encounter; if you don't, look it up. Constantly ask questions as you read: who? what? where? when? why? how? Who is the main character? What options are open to all of the characters? Where is the action occurring? When does the action take place? Why do the characters behave as they do? How do the characters solve their problems? You may not find all the answers, but keep asking the questions. Underline striking words or phrases as in this line from a sonnet by Hopkins:

It gathers to a greatness, like the <u>ooze of oil.</u>

Take notes and record your reactions to what you read in the margins or in a notebook. Use your imagination. Put yourself in the character's place: How would you react to particular situations? Then record your insights. The truths that we encounter in literature are universal truths that engage us by appealing to our imagination and intellect. However, these truths are not always obvious or transparent. We need to look for clues to find the truths the characters and their actions reveal. For example, what does Hester Prynne's confession of guilt in Hawthorne's novel *The Scarlet Letter* reveal? Thus, when you are reading, you will need to look for patterns, such as recurrences in the character's behavior, responses to adversity, or the use of dialect. You will want to be alert to symbols and the meanings that lie beneath them, as in the phrase *two roads* in Frost's "The Road Not Taken." Look for images, the pictures created by the use of figurative language (similes, metaphors, personification), such as the simile *like a thunderbolt* in Tennyson's poem "The Eagle." Be certain to think critically about and analyze the characters, the plot, the form of the text, the climax and crisis, and the resolution of the action. The topics listed in the "Literary Topics" checklist that follows can help guide you on what to be attuned to when reading. And, of course, remember that writing about literature is possible only with *careful* and *close* reading and rereading of literary texts.

2　Finding a topic

If your instructor has not given you a general topic to write about, you will need to find your own. In either case, avoid topics that are too broad, such as Captain Ahab's preoccupation with vengeance in Melville's *Moby Dick,* because you cannot write about every implication related to the topic in a literary selection. Instead, you will need to devise a limited topic such as Ahab's lapses from sanity, as revealed in some of his interactions with other characters in the novel. Use the notations you wrote in the margins and the underlined words and phrases in your text as starting points for prewriting (see Section 1a). Be certain that your prewriting (whether freewriting, clustering, journal writing, brainstorming, or questioning) centers on the literary work. Most readers have personal reactions to literature, but few instructors want you to use the literary work solely as a springboard for your personal feelings. When prewriting and then writing about a literary text, examine the aspects of it listed on the next page. Any one of these possibilities can serve as a topic for a paper.

Also, think carefully about your prewriting, the literary text, class notes, and any study aids distributed in class. Use them to posit a preliminary thesis and a working outline, which will eventually lead you to a more focused thesis. (See Sections 2a and 2b.)

3　Developing the topic

Once you have decided on a topic or thesis, you need to develop it. Like most papers written in the humanities, papers about literature involve reaction to and interpretation of the work. To develop your topic, you will analyze the text and argue your response or reaction to the literary work, using it and perhaps other sources as support.

When you write about literature, the literary work is considered the **primary source,** and many writers of essays about literature confine themselves to working with the primary source. Other writers, by choice or necessity, investigate **secondary sources**—books, reviews, and journal articles written about the primary source—and write their papers citing these secondary sources, as the author of the student paper in Section 49b does. You can, of course, consult secondary sources to discover a topic; you can also consult these sources to find support for your interpretations. You would then cite the sources to provide evidence for your analysis or argument and to avoid plagiarism.

You can develop your thesis by using the following options for structuring a literary analysis.

1. **Textual analysis.** Consider the literary work in and for itself independent of any biographical, environmental, temporal, or other influence.

2. **Canon analysis.** Consider the literary work in relation to other works by the same or another author.

3. **Biographical analysis.** Consider the literary work in relation to one or more aspects of its author's biography.

4. **Theoretical analysis.** Consider the literary work in relation to a particular theory of literature.

5. **Artifactual analysis.** Consider the literary work in relation to the historical era in which it was written.

6. **Literary tradition analysis.** Consider the literary work in relation to the tradition of which it is a part.

7. **Literary process analysis.** Consider the literary work as a whole in relation to the parts of which it is composed, and analyze how the parts relate to one another.

8. **Character analysis.** Consider the literary work in relation to the development and interaction of characters. Ask yourself why they behave as they do.

9. **Combinations of the above.**

LITERARY TOPICS

Subject	What the poem, story, novel, or drama is about
Theme	The main idea or message about the subject
Characterization	How you come to know the characters; how they are presented
Plot	The chain of cause and effect that takes the narrative from its beginning to its end
Setting	The actual or imagined place where the action occurs
Point of view	The viewpoint from which the story is told: first or third person, author's voice
Tone	The attitude toward the subject matter, the reader, or both
Devices of sound	End rhyme, internal rhyme, slant rhyme, alliteration, consonance, assonance
Images	Pictures evoked by figurative language
Figurative language	Personification, simile, metaphor, oxymoron, symbols
Symbolism	Use of a word to represent more than one idea or thing
Meter	Patterns of rhythm: iamb, anapest, and so forth

Regardless of the option you select, you can develop it by using one or more of several methods: definition, comparison, contrast, classification, analysis, and so on. (See Section 4c.) Always arrange the ideas that support your topic and thesis in a meaningful sequence. Develop the body of your paper using only your own thoughts, or incorporate appropriate secondary sources into your discussion with proper documentation. Organize your presentation to reflect an analysis (see Section 4c-7) or an argument (see Chapter 6) to show how your thesis contributes to understanding, interpreting, or reacting to a literary work. In your conclusion, restate the main points of your thesis. And always reread your writing to ensure that you do not lose sight of your purpose: to present an exposition or argument that abides by your thesis.

4   Avoiding plot summary

Bear in mind that you are writing for an audience. Assume that your readers have read the literary work, and avoid using excessive, nonrelevant plot summaries of fiction or paraphrases of poetry in place of genuine analysis or interpretation. Instead of summarizing plot, look for patterns in the behavior, speeches, and actions of the characters or sequences of events that relate to your topic. Note how these and the choices that characters make support your interpretation, and back your ideas up with relevant passages from the primary source. Remember to document such passages accurately.

5   Presenting the topic

As best you can, incorporate the vocabulary of literary criticism into your paper to be exact. Avoid writing *story* when you mean *narrative, short story, novel,* or *plot*. Avoid referring to a character as "that guy" or "that woman"; instead, name the character. Use the present tense when referring to the author and the literary work.

Not "As Chaucer wrote" **but** "as Chaucer writes"

Not "when Huck addressed Jim" **but** "when Huck addresses Jim"

When writing your first references to an author, use her or his full name: Katherine Anne Porter. In subsequent references use only the author's surname: Porter, without any titles such as Ms., Mr., or Dr.

Enclose the titles of short stories, essays, and shorter poems in quotation marks (for example, "Noon Wine," "A Modest Proposal," "Stopping by Woods"). See Section 34d. Underline the titles of novels, dramas, nonfiction books, and longer poems to indicate italics (for example, <u>Tom Jones</u>, <u>Death of a Salesman</u>, <u>The Idea of a University</u>, and <u>Beowulf</u>). See Chapter 36.

Accurately refer to subdivisions in literary works by using specific references instead of phrases like "the place where." Specifically refer to "Chapter 7" or "the third stanza." Refer to subdivisions in drama in this order: act number, scene number, and line number (if the latter two exist), separated by periods: for example, "The last sound heard in *The Cherry Orchard* is that of an ax against a tree" (4) and "In despair, King Lear tears off his clothes" (3.4.115).

When quoting from literary texts, always check your accuracy. See Sections 34a and 34b on formatting direct and block quotations.

Select a title for your essay that relates to the content of the paper. In your introduction, include the name of the literary work, its date, the author, your thesis, the necessary background material relating to your thesis, and your approach to the topic. (See the sample literary paper in the following section.)

Follow the MLA documentation style (see Chapter 46) when writing and documenting your essay unless your instructor expects another format. As in all writing, carefully document all quotations, paraphrases, and summaries (see Section 45a) to acknowledge properly all primary and secondary sources and to avoid plagiarism (see Section 45f).

49b Sample Literary Analysis

Following is an essay that analyzes a short story, written by Mindy Thomas in an introduction to literature class. Thomas arrived at her topic after a class discussion of the themes in the story "The Lottery" by Shirley Jackson. From her critical reading of the story, Thomas thought that Jackson's portrayal of the townspeople comments on the way humans blindly follow traditional ceremonies and rituals. To develop this interpretation, Thomas looked at what a number of literary critics had to say about the meaning of the story, especially about the significance of the scapegoat theme. Her analysis of this idea includes her own reactions and interpretations as well as evidence from both the story and the criticism that she read.

Note that Thomas uses the MLA style format and that the essay has been annotated in the left margin to show how her presentation develops and how she uses primary and secondary sources in support of her views.

Thomas 1

Mindy K. Thomas

English 102

April 3, 2000

Student
identification

Title

The Evils of Ignorance:

Shirley Jackson's "The Lottery"

Human beings have always feared the

Background
leading to
thesis

unknown. In order to explain our existence, people
create gods. And, to insure the happiness of these
gods and thus the continuation of human life,
people devise rituals to follow in their worship. In
many ancient civilizations human sacrifice was an
integral part of this worship. Often the gods were
appeased through the performance of scapegoat
rituals requiring that one person be sacrificed to

Secondary
source to
support thesis

atone for the sins of the whole society. Professor
Helen Nebeker observes that "those chosen for
sacrifice were not victims but saviors who would
propitiate the gods, enticing them to bring rebirth,
renewal, and thanking them with their blood"
(104). These practices, rich with symbolic meaning,
were an essential part of the culture. In "The

Thesis

Lottery" Shirley Jackson shows us such a ritual but
one in which the essential meaning has long ago
been lost.

Jackson's lottery is set in the present, but the ceremony is obviously one that has been performed for so long that no one can even remember its significance. The blackness of the box represents the evil of a community kept in darkness by its own ignorance. Nebeker explains the significance of the box this way:

First major claim

> Jackson certainly suggests the body of tradition [. . .] which the dead hand of the past codified in religion, mores, government, and the rest of culture, and passed from generation to generation, letting it grow ever more cumbersome, meaningless, and indefensible. (103-04)

Support from secondary source

Jackson tells us that the box "grew shabbier each year [. . .] and in some places was faded and stained" (73). This deterioration of the box mirrors the moral degeneration of people who perform murder for reasons they can no longer remember.

Support from primary source

Restatement of claim

This savagery, Jackson shows us, is inherent in all people and is hidden just beneath the surface of our seemingly civilized exteriors. The duality of human nature is exhibited through the characterization and actions of the villagers. As Cleanth Brooks and Robert Penn Warren note, "The cruel stoning is carried out by 'decent' citizens who in many other respects show themselves kind and thoughtful" (75). When it was time for the

Second major claim

Secondary source support

Primary
source
support

scapegoat to be murdered, Mrs. Delacroix, who earlier had made neighborly conversation with Tessie, "selected a stone so large she had to pick it up with both hands" (77). Another villager, Mr. Adams, who had previously mentioned that people in another village were "talking of giving up the lottery," was standing "in the front of the crowd" ready to attack as Mr. Warner urged the others to "come on" and begin the slaughter (75, 77). Critic Shyamal Bagchee rightly says of the townspeople

More
secondary
support

that "The spectacle of death does not cause any radical rethinking among the living" (8). And James Gibson concurs, observing that their world "has no moral rules, for the lottery has rendered them meaningless" (195).

Concession

Although the depiction of human nature in this story is a grim one, there is a small glimmer of hope. "Some places have already quit [the]

Primary
support

lotteries" (75), indicating that while human beings do have a deeply rooted fear of change, change is at least possible. Nebeker comments on this need for change:

Secondary
support

> Until enough [people] are touched strongly
> enough by the horror of their ritualistic,
> irrational actions to reject the long-perverted
> ritual, to destroy the box completely--or to
> make, if necessary, a new one reflective of
> their own conditions and needs of life--they

will never free themselves from their primitive nature [. . .]. (107)

Conclusion—restating and amplifying the thesis

Jackson's powerful story is a plea for tolerance, for compassion for others, and for progression toward a future in which the practices of society reflect a healthy social conscience. She wants us to see that we can rid ourselves of the evil that ignorance perpetuates by examining the practices we repeat out of unquestioning tradition.

Works Cited

Bagchee, Shyamal. "Design of Darkness in Shirley Jackson's 'The Lottery.'" Notes on Contemporary Literature 9.4 (1979):8-9.

Brooks, Cleanth, and Robert Penn Warren. Understanding Fiction. New York: Appleton, 1959.

Gibson, James R. "An Old Testament Analogue for 'The Lottery.'" Journal of American Literature 2.1 (1984):193-95. InfoTrac: Expanded Academic ASAP. CD-ROM. Information Access. Dec. 1990.

Jackson, Shirley. "The Lottery." Literature and the Writing Process. Elizabeth McMahan, Susan X Day, and Robert Funk. 5th ed. Upper Saddle River, NJ: Prentice, 1999. 74-79.

Nebeker, Helen E. "'The Lottery': Symbolic Tour de Force." American Literature 46 (1974): 100-07.

50 Writing in the Social, Natural, and Applied Sciences

50a Writing in the Social Sciences

Disciplines in the social sciences include anthropology, economics, government, political science, psychology, social services, and sociology, and their focus is often group behavior. Writing in the social sciences can cover, for example, the causes and effects of diverse social phenomena, the values and traditions shared by different social groups, and hypotheses and theories that explain particular types of behaviors in population groups. Research in the social sciences is ongoing. Social scientists react to new theories by carefully examining the **databases** (the raw material on which a theory is based, such as a tally of city dwellers' preferences for waste disposal) and the **methodologies** that were used to obtain the data (for example, interviews or mail-in questionnaires) to judge the validity of the results. Other social scientists study how these new theories alter or advance previous research. Social scientists rely on either quantitative or qualitative data. **Quantitative data** are statistical or numerical measures—the results of surveys, tests, or experiments. **Qualitative data** are descriptive rather than numerical and include interviews, oral histories, and descriptions of people, their cultures, and their experiences. Writing in the social sciences tends to be objective, based on fact and observation, rather than subjective, based on personal impressions, emotions, and reactions, and it takes the form of field research reports, summaries, reviews of research, case analyses, or research papers.

1 The field research report

One of the most commonly used types of writing in the social sciences is the **field research report.** This type of report involves observing human behavior or obtaining information on attitudes or opinions, which then serve as databases. You might find it helpful to consider your field research report as an exercise in problem solving. You might seek a solution, for example, to the problem of New Jersey's waste disposal now that the midwestern states are refusing to accept its garbage because of a landfill shortage. The information you gather through various methods, such as questionnaires or interviews (see Section 44b-4), leads you to some sort of solution. Writing a field research report often involves the use of statistical data in table or chart form or as figures. As in most scientific writing, writing field research reports requires objectivity. Before you begin your field research, you will find it helpful to plan specifically how you will obtain the data you need (a *methodology*) and the order in which you will seek it (*randomly* or in a *planned sequence*).

Each part of your report, other than the title, consists of complete sentences; is subject to the processes of prewriting, revision, and proofreading; and has a thesis, topic sentences, and a recognizable developmental pattern. The field research report contains the following parts:

- **Title.** The title consists of a descriptive phrase, preferably short, that summarizes the purpose or results of the report. Humorous titles are considered inappropriate.
- **Running head.** The running head is an abbreviated title that is typed in the upper right corner of each page of the paper or report, including the title page. (See the model APA paper, Section 48b.) The student authors of the report "Would You Choose This College Again?" (Section 50a-2) might use "College Choice" as their running head.
- **Abstract.** The abstract is a brief 100- to 150-word summary that provides an overview of the problem investigated, the method used, and the results.
- **Introduction.** In the introduction, you report why you did this particular research (the problem), explain why you consider it important, and offer any background information nec-

essary for understanding the problem. What results did you *expect* to obtain? Many introductions contain references to source materials used to define a problem and provide a rationale for conducting the research.

■ **Methodology.** In the methodology section, you report how you gathered the data. Examples of your methodology, such as a questionnaire or a copy of your interview questions, should appear in an appendix. Identify the number of participants, and note their age, sex, race, religion, socio-economic status, and other appropriate identifying characteristics. Also list any other sources you consulted, such as computer data banks, Census Bureau figures, and printed sources. If you use a computer in tallying your results, identify the software and hardware.

■ **Results.** The expression of your results (the solution to the problem) will usually be a mixture of prose and statistical information accompanied by tables and figures. But do not allow the statistical information to become an end in itself. What is its significance? What exactly did you discover? The answers separate the results from raw data.

■ **Conclusion.** In the conclusion, provide *your own* interpretation of the results. If you incorporate or compare and contrast other studies with your results, be certain to provide accurate citations.

■ **Appendices.** The appendices are the support and documentation for your methodology. Begin each appendix on a new page and head it "Appendix." Use identifying capital letters, as in "Appendix A," "B," or "C," if you include more than one appendix. Double-space the text.

■ **References.** See the section on documentation that follows.

2 Documenting your field research report

Most writers in the social sciences use the APA documentation style covered in Chapter 47 or the *Chicago Manual of Style* (see Section 47d). Document all methodology used, including computer software programs and any printed or nonprint sources that you quote, summarize, or paraphrase. Do this both in text (see Section 47c) and in your list of references (see Section 47c). Finally, be careful to avoid plagiarism (Section 45f); check the accuracy and format of each of your citations.

See Section 48b for a sample research paper in APA style for a social science course. Following is the introduction to a field research report that two students, working as a team, wrote for an introductory sociology course.

Would You Choose This College Again?

Introduction

In April, 1992, 512 students participated in a survey designed and administered by the authors and mailed to all graduating seniors. Our purpose was to ascertain how many of these graduating students would or would not select this college again in light of the experience and knowledge they now possess. Our survey covered three main areas in the undergraduate experience: (1) relationship to one's major department of study (availability of desired courses, quality of teaching, accessibility of faculty, responsiveness of departmental administration, quality of the writing courses in this department); (2) support services (library holdings, hours, and quality of service; availability of computer services; bookstore; placement office; housing office; and financial aid office); and (3) extracurricular activities (cultural and recreational).

Of our respondents, 51.8% received the Bachelor of Arts degree and 44.6% the Bachelor of Science degree. Sixty-five percent of the respondents were men, 33% women. Only 3% of the total were married. In terms of ethnic diversity, 3% were Asian-American, 7% Hispanic, 14% African-American, and 76% other. Eighty-eight percent of responding students received financial aid from sources as follows: 45% partial tuition scholarships, 21% student-work assistantships, and 50% guaranteed loans. A number of students received financial support from more than one source.

We anticipated that a very high percentage of students, 90% or more, would select this college again. Our expectations were too optimistic.

50b Writing in the Natural Sciences

Disciplines in the natural sciences include biology, the health professions, chemistry, earth sciences, mathematics, and physics. Writing in these areas is concerned with the natural world, particularly the causes and effects of natural phenomena, and related laboratory experiments. Researchers in the natural sciences follow the **scientific method:** (1) formulating a **hypothesis,** which is an initial attempt to explain phenomena; (2) presenting information, including previously published research, to support the hypothesis; (3) planning the investigation or experiment; (4) performing the experiment, carefully observing and recording the procedures and results; and (5) analyzing the results and providing conclusions that may or may not support the hypothesis. Scientists use only **empirical evidence,** or objective data, to support the hypothesis, and this evidence, gathered from observing natural events, is quantitative (based on numbers and statistics) rather than qualitative (based on subjective data such as ideas and emotions). Successful scientific writing is also based on empirical validation (another scientist, using the same materials and methodologies, should be able to achieve your results).

1 Lab reports

The **lab report** is the most common type of writing students do in the natural sciences. Lab reports are written after you complete an experiment or project and document not only your results but also the procedure leading to your results. You will, then, need to keep careful notes in a lab notebook. This notebook is very important. If you overlook something while taking the notes, you might have to redo the experiment. The notes will serve as the raw material from which you fashion the lab report. When preparing the lab report, write preliminary and final drafts for each part of the report. Be sure that the report is well written and that you proofread all parts. As much as possible, try to avoid using the passive voice (see Section 12b-3).

In formatting the lab report, label all parts and use complete sentences, except in the title. Each part of the report should have a recognizable organization and include a topic sentence and a developmental pattern. Process analysis and cause-and-effect analysis are most common (see Sections 4c-7 and 4c-8). The standard parts of a lab report are as follows:

- **Abstract.** The abstract should not exceed 250 words in length and should be composed of complete sentences. It summarizes the purpose of the report, the nature of the experiment, and the results.
- **Title.** The title usually consists of one or a few words that are related to the experiment. Humor in the title is inappropriate.
- **Introduction.** The introduction provides the background information (a summary of previous research on the problem), introduces the hypothesis or problem that the experiment addresses, and states what is relevant about the problem as well the objectives of the experiment. The introduction should also explain the experiment's organization.

- **Methods and materials.** The methods and materials section provides the theory that underlies the solution to the problem and then enumerates all the steps followed in the experiment. It includes a list of the apparatus and materials used, employing graphics and details of assembly, if appropriate. If you used computer programs, present detailed information on the software and hardware. You must present the steps of the experiment in the proper order; your instructor might require a flowchart.
- **Results.** In the results section, you record and discuss the results of your experiment. Since the results serve as the solution to the problem, be certain to discuss their significance. If any discrepancies occurred during the experiment, you must report and, if possible, account for them.
- **References cited.** See the documentation section that follows.

2 Documenting your lab report

Some scientists use the style and documentation formats that are specifically designed for their disciplines (see Section 47d for a listing of style manuals for use in the sciences). Others use the APA format, which is explained in Chapter 47. Ask your instructor which is preferred. The format will determine what to name the final part of your lab report: "References," "Works Cited," or "Bibliography." Here you will list the lab manual and your course textbook, as appropriate, and all journal articles, books, and reference materials you consulted. Successful lab reports not only conform to the methodologies of the scientific disciplines but also present accurate, precise documentation. Plagiarism (see Section 45f) should be avoided through careful documentation. Following are an abstract and portions of the methods and materials section of a lab report:

S. Reike
Chemistry 329
28 April 2000

Gas-Liquid Chromatography

Abstract

In this experiment, the author used gas-liquid chromatography to evaluate the individual components of a two-component system, a technique based on the speed with which the individual components move through the column in the chromatograph. A detector evaluates the retention time and the relative concentrations of each component. Four individual components were used and the retention times noted. Six two-component systems were then run and the components determined by matching the retention times of the individual components with the retention times for the four single systems; hence, the individual components in the two-component system could be determined. The components of the six systems studied are:

System A:	2 and 3	System D:	did not separate
System B:	did not separate	System E:	2 or 4 and 3
System C:	3 and 2 or 4	System F:	3 and 4

Methods and Materials

In gas-liquid chromatography, one injects a sample into the apparatus with a microsyringe. I used 2-microliter samples. The sample was introduced into an inert mobile phase of helium. The mobile phase carries the sample to the column, which contains the stationary phase. Once the sample encounters the stationary, it may be retained. Since the sample can move only in the mobile phase, the amount of time it spends in the two different phases determines the rate at which the sample moves through the column. The more time it spends in the mobile phase, the faster it moves throughout the detector. Mixtures separate based on the different times they spend in each phase. Once the sample reaches the detector, the detector responds according to the concentration of the component. A higher concentration creates a large area under the corresponding curve.

50c Writing in the Applied Sciences

The applied sciences include all branches of engineering, including aerospace, architectural, biotechnical, chemical, civil, computer science, electrical, marine, petroleum and mining, and pollution control. The type of writing used is called **technical writing.** It includes program reports, proposals, investigative reports, and technical reports.

1 The technical report

The **technical report** is composed of data collected, analyzed, and presented in an organized form that responds to the needs of a specific audience. Write the report objectively (using quantitative data such as statistics and numbers) and include visuals such as graphs, charts, maps, and tables that offer support for the conclusions or recommendations presented. Divide your technical report into sections, each beginning on a new page, with the following headings:

- **Title page.** Include a title page that briefly and clearly presents the title of the report, your name, and the date, centered on the page. Humor in a title is inappropriate.

- **Table of contents.** The table of contents functions as the outline for the report and consists of the report's headings and the related page numbers. If you devise any subheadings for your report, indent them.
- **List of tables, charts, figures.** If applicable, present the list of tables (or charts, maps, figures) on a separate page and include in it the captions of the tables and their page numbers. Number the tables consecutively with Arabic numerals: for example, "Table 1."
- **Abstract.** The abstract, which should not exceed 250 words, summarizes the nature of the report; the procedures followed; and the results, conclusions, and/or recommendations.
- **Introduction.** The introduction provides an overview of the report and whatever background information the audience may need (a summary of research related to the subject and description of the topic). Explain the purpose, scope, and function of the report, including who commissioned it, if appropriate. Present the plan and organization of the report, define appropriate terminology, and include the materials and methodology used.
- **Body.** In the body, include a detailed account of the methodology used, a description of equipment as appropriate, a statement of the results, and your analysis of the results.
- **Conclusion and recommendations.** Your conclusions will describe the results of your project, include recommendations that derive from the evidence, and suggest possible future applications of the project. If you have more than one conclusion or recommendation, list them numerically in order of importance.
- **References.** See the following documentation section.

2 Documenting your technical report

All sources and references used in a technical report must be accurately documented with in-text and end-of-text citations.

The various branches of the applied sciences use different documentation styles. The manuals for some of these appear in Section 47d; ask your instructor if you are uncertain which style to use. Your report may include appropriately numbered footnotes or endnotes (see Section 46d) and may close with either a bibliography or list of works cited. Check your citations, and carefully document your sources to avoid plagiarism (see Section 45f).

Following is the introduction from a technical report entitled "Computer-Implemented 'Concentration'" that a team of four students collaborated on for an electrical engineering course.

Introduction

"Concentration" is a game that tests a person's ability to retain information. Playing the game requires cards similar to a regular deck of playing cards except that symbols or pictures are used instead of numbers. Exactly one pair of cards exists for every different symbol in the deck. At the beginning of a game all the cards are laid out face down. A player's turn consists of trying to match two cards face up. If a player makes a match, he or she claims the two cards and plays again. If no match is made, the next player receives a turn. At the end of the game, the player with the most cards is the winner.

Our team built a computer implementation of the concentration game for two reasons. First, building this particular digital system would provide us with valuable experience in hardware design, system software development, and assembler design. Second, the end result of our efforts would be a game that is both challenging and enjoyable. Specifically, our team's objective was to implement the concentration game on a system memory card inserted into an IBM personal computer (PC). Since the size of the memory card is finite, our goal was to keep the hardware simple. We used the IBM PC monitor to simulate output comparable to the actual card game.

We developed a flowchart for our system code, defined an instruction set, and created a new flowchart that generated the AHPL code, implemented and successfully simulated the AHPL code, and completed the hardware design, which includes four different XILINX chips, the application source code, and the two-pass assembler. We then designed the printed circuit board layout for the game.

51 Writing Essay Examinations

An **essay examination** gives you the opportunity to show what you have learned in a course and gives your instructor an effective way to examine your grasp of the material studied. Essay examinations tend to be more demanding than multiple-choice tests because you are called on to recall information, analyze and evaluate it, and draw up a well-reasoned and well-written essay under time restrictions. Essay tests can be administered in any course of study but are most common in the humanities. Whatever the course, this chapter will help you to prepare for and then take essay examinations.

51a Preparing for the Examination

To write a successful essay examination, begin by studying. Reread your course notes, textbooks, and any assigned readings. Mark the important points in the texts by underlining or highlighting them. Review all of this material several times until you believe you know it. Try outlining to familiarize yourself with key points. Then try testing yourself by anticipating possible test questions—compare and contrast, analyze, define and exemplify, show cause and effect, classify—and then actually writing responses. Time yourself, and try to simulate realistic examination conditions as best you can. If your instructor is able to provide old examinations, take them. The more practice you get at thinking through the subject matter and writing about it, the better prepared you will be for the actual examination. And most important: give yourself enough time to prepare. If you can, begin a week before the test; at the very least, start three or four days before. Cramming, especially for essay examinations, is rarely effective.

51b Evaluating the Question and Timing Yourself

When writing an essay examination, you must respond to the question that is asked. The first thing to do, then, is to read the question all the way through to get a general sense of what is being asked. Then read the question again and evaluate it. Underline the key words. Pay particular attention to the verbs, especially such words as *analyze, argue, classify, compare, contrast, defend, describe, develop, evaluate, enumerate, exemplify, explain, identify, judge, justify, list, persuade, refute,* and *trace.* These words will give you clues for organizing your response. For example, in a literature examination, you might be asked to "*classify, define,* and *exemplify*" the character types in Katherine Anne Porter's short story "Noon Wine." Will you need to write an argumentative essay or construct a response with some crucial facts? Pay particular attention to the nouns in the question to determine what you are expected to write about (*reason* or *reasons, cause* or *causes*) as well as the adjectives (*main, intermediate, principal, contributing, relevant, succinct*). Keeping these key words in mind will help you to write relevant responses. If you're ever unsure about a question, be sure to ask your instructor for clarification.

When evaluating examination questions, think about how much you will need to write. After you have determined what you are expected to write in the examination, plan how much time to devote to the process of writing the response. Many college examinations require you to respond to more than one essay question. Timing yourself, then, becomes very important to ensure enough time to answer all questions fully. How much total time is to be devoted to the question: a full class period or twenty-five minutes? An incomplete essay response that results from your running out of time is rarely given full credit, no matter how accurate or well written it is. Remember to bring a watch to the examination, and use it to pace yourself. Try to allow some time for prewriting and drafting to help you generate and organize ideas. Also allot time for revision and editing. For example, if you have twenty minutes, you might allow five minutes for prewriting, twelve for producing a draft, and three for editing and proofreading.

51c Deciding on a Response Strategy

Essay examination responses can be classified as objective, subjective, or a blend of the two, depending on the question that is asked. When you write an objective response, you present factual data that can be verified. When you write a subjective response, you interpret or react to something. But subjective responses do not give you total liberty to write whatever comes into your mind; you respond to the question that is asked. Careful evaluation of the question will indicate whether an objective, subjective, or combined response strategy is best. For example, a question that reads "list the main causes for X" will require an objective strategy; "explain the effects of the causes of X on Y" will call for a subjective strategy; and "list, classify, and explain the effects of X on Y" will call for a combination objective/ subjective strategy.

51d Planning and Prewriting

To write a final draft that is clear and logical, do some planning and prewriting before you actually begin writing your response. Make notations or draw up a scratch outline on the inside cover of the examination booklet, on a separate sheet of paper, or in the margins. As you jot down ideas, ask yourself these questions: What is my thesis? What will my main points be? How will I organize them? What type of supporting examples or information will I use? How will I begin? Which patterns of paragraph development will best suit the response I have planned? How will I conclude the essay? Sketching out a blueprint of your response is a useful tactic.

51e Drafting Your Response

Having done some prewriting, look for logical relationships in the material and draw arrows or make other notations to impose order. Write a first draft if time permits; otherwise, proceed with the final draft. Be sure to state your thesis at the outset and to support it with examples and other information. Essay examination responses are often analytical and subjective in nature, but you should incorporate appropriate objective data into your response as relevant: dates, accurate citation of lines of poetry, or excerpts from well-known writings or speeches. After all, your examination response should show your instructor that you know your topic. But your essay response should not be a hodgepodge of facts. Strive to achieve an appropriate blend of analysis and fact. Also, be sure to check the logic of your response. Does the essay support your thesis? Did you avoid digressions? Are transitions used effectively? Refer to your out-line or prewriting to keep yourself on track. Also, read your re-sponse as you go along. Check each paragraph. Is there a topic sentence? Does everything within the paragraph flow logically? Are you answering the question effectively? Try to evaluate your response as you write it.

51f Revising

Although it is a good idea to read and evaluate your response as you write, you will certainly want to allow yourself some time to proofread the final copy of your response before you turn it in. Is your prose clear and precise? Is it grammatically and mechani-cally correct? Have you responded to the question asked? Essay responses that are filled with fragments, spelling errors, punctua-tion errors, illogical sequencing, faulty evidence, and digressions do not impress readers. Admittedly, instructors are aware that writing under time constraints produces anxieties and that your prose might not be as polished as it is in papers that are written more leisurely. However, do take time to revise. To make this process easier, skip lines between sentences so you have room to make changes. If your instructor will allow it, write your essay in pencil so you can erase. This way your revisions will be neater.

51g Sample Essay Examination Response

Following are an essay examination question for an abnor-mal psychology course and the student's effective response:

Question
Discuss the behaviors that indicate that a person is an alcoholic (30 minutes).

Response
See student response on the following page.

STUDENT RESPONSE

Thesis responds to the question

A person who is alcohol-dependent will be subject to varying behaviors which act alone and in combinations to signal departures from the norm. These include difficulties with personal relationships (complaints from spouse and children or friends about drinking), with employment (frequent absenteeism due to hangovers), with the law (more than one DUI offense), with social situations (isolating oneself in order to drink), and with spirituality (turning further away from God and more to drinking for strength).

Types and examples of behavior

Other types of behavior and examples act as supporting evidence

These specified behaviors accompany other types of behavior that become routine to the alcohol-addicted person. The addict is often preoccupied with the thought of drinking and has regularized the time of day at which drinking begins, a time which is approached with anticipation and oftentimes anxiety. Once drinking, many addicts undergo personality changes: the mild-mannered suddenly become loud and boisterous. Blackouts, not to be confused with fainting spells or deep sleep, occur more frequently. There are periods of memory lapse when the drinker does not remember where or when or other circumstances surrounding the drinking and constitute a middle stage of the affliction.

Conclusion— note reference to thesis

Denial is the behavioral defense mechanism the addict uses when confronted with any of the behavioral patterns of his or her drinking. Any of these behaviors, singly or in combination, are indications that a person is or might become alcohol dependent.

EXERCISE 51-1

Evaluate the preceding essay response. React to the thesis. How is it supported? What patterns of development are used? Circle all transition words. Would you organize your response differently?

STRATEGIES FOR TAKING ESSAY EXAMINATIONS

1. Begin preparing for the examination in advance.

2. Study by rereading your texts and class notes.

3. Anticipate possible exam questions and practice writing responses.

4. At the test, read the question carefully and evaluate it. Underline the key words to determine what you are being asked to do.

5. Note your time limitations. Allot time for prewriting, drafting, proofreading, and editing. Bring a watch to the test so that you can pace yourself.

6. Decide on your response strategy. Do some planning and prewriting, and begin drafting your response once you have an idea of what you want to say.

7. Proofread the essay before turning it in. Check your thesis, supporting evidence, grammar, and punctuation.

52 Writing for Business

Like all good writing, business writing should be clear, concise, and correct. In addition, writers in a business setting must meet certain conventions of form, record information accurately for later referral (sometimes with legal implications), and pay special attention to the needs of their readers.

52a The Memo

The most common form of communication in business is the memo. A **memo** addresses one or many readers within an organization or company. It is generally short (no more than a page or two), focuses on a single topic, is clearly directed to its audience, and, to a noticeable degree, follows conventions or formulas in form and content. A memo can be sent on paper or electronically through mail systems that link company offices.

1 The parts of a memo

The memo has two parts: heading and message. The memo **heading** is often printed on company memo sheets and looks something like this:

Date:

To:

From:

Subject:

The writer fills in these elements to record vital information for the file and to inform the reader directly about the message to come.

In writing the **message,** the memo writer focuses on a single topic. Short paragraphs and company abbreviations that are clear to readers are used. For example, the abbreviations for Emergency Services (ES) and Intensive Care Unit (ICU) are used in the following sample memo. Important information is highlighted in headings and lists, and these items are kept parallel. Further, drawings and diagrams often accompany the memo to support its purpose and message and to avoid lengthy discussion. The following sample is a good example of a typical business memo.

2   Sample memo

Date:	23 March 2000
To:	All Employees, Emergency Services
From:	Demetrius Jones
	Director, Patient Services
Subject:	New Procedure for Patient Admission to ICU

Effective April 15, new procedures will be implemented in the Patient Records Office to ensure that patient admissions from ES to ICU will be handled quickly.

After that date, ES personnel must complete the new Form ES-27 for any patient transferred to ICU. A copy of this form should be sent to ICU and to Patient Records.

All ES employees are asked to cooperate with this new procedure. Address any questions to me at ext. 8887.

cc: Patient Records Office

52b The Business Letter

A **business letter** is appropriate when you write to an organization or when you write on behalf of an organization to customers or clients. The letter is more formal than the memo and thus also may be used for recording important matters of policy or confidential personnel decisions within an organization.

1 Business letter formats

Business letters generally follow one of three formats: the block format, a modified block format (sometimes with indented paragraphs), and a simplified format. Check with your company to see which format is preferred. Each format is shown in a model business letter on pages 565–568.

If you use a typewriter or computer, type or print the business letter on 8½" × 11" white or off-white bond paper (erasable paper is not popular because it tends to smudge). Center the text vertically on the paper, and use wide margins. The text of the letter must be neat; messy erasures, cross-outs, and ink corrections are unacceptable. Single-space each part of the business letter, and double-space between parts.

2 The parts of a business letter

A typical business letter has these parts: heading, inside address, salutation, subject line, body, closing, notations, and an addressed envelope in which the letter is mailed. Your computer program may be able to help you format these parts automatically.

Heading

The **heading** includes the sender's address and the date of the letter. If you use letterhead stationery, you need only add the date. Otherwise, write your address (*without* your name).

Inside address

The **inside address** is simply the name and address of the reader to whom the letter will be sent. Readers are often pleased to be identified by their names, so when you write your job application letters, try to use the *names* of the persons responsible for new employee hirings. If you are unable to obtain the reader's name, then address the appropriate office or person by job title. For example:

Personnel Department

Director of Personnel

Customer Service

Write out the full name of the company—do not abbreviate. Spell all names correctly; if you are unsure of a spelling, check it. Do not guess.

Salutation

The conventional salutation, or greeting, is "Dear [Mr./Ms.] Last name:" (the formal greeting ends with a colon). If you are unsure of the gender of the reader—for example, if you are responding to a letter signed "S. H. Assad"—then write "Dear S. H. Assad." However, when gender is unknown or you are not writing to a particular individual, you may use "Dear Sir or Madam" or the name of the company, "Dear Major Corporation." Another option is to omit the salutation entirely, as is frequently done in the simplified letter format (see page 568).

Subject line

Although subject lines are common in memos, they are used less often in business letters. They may occasionally be seen in sequential letters about a project or in routine correspondence concerning orders and responses to orders. Subject lines such as the following also appear in sales letters:

YOU MAY HAVE ALREADY WON!

Body

The **body** of the letter conveys your message and should be brief and arranged in relatively short paragraphs for easy reading. The text is single-spaced with double-spacing between paragraphs. Begin the first sentence of each paragraph at the left margin if you are using the block format (see the sample letter on pages 565–566). If instead you are using the modified block format, use indented paragraphs with the first sentence of each paragraph indented five spaces (see page 567). Conclude the body with an action statement or a request for information, depending on your intent. (See the model on page 566.)

Closing

The **closing** consists of the complimentary close and the writer's signature. The most common closing phrases are "Sincerely," "Sincerely yours," and "Yours truly." The phrase "Respectfully yours" shows a bit more deference and respect, whereas "Cordially" and "Best regards" are more informal. Note that the second word in a complimentary close is not capitalized and that the entire closing phrase is followed by a comma. Type your name about four spaces below the complimentary close, leaving enough space for your signature (see pages 566 and 567 for samples of two closings). You may also type the company name, your job title, or both below your typed name. And although you type your full name, you may sign your letter with a nickname if your relationship with the reader warrants it.

In the simplified format, the closing is omitted if you have also omitted the salutation (see the sample letter of complaint in the simplified block format on page 568). In the modified block format, the closing is indented (see page 567), whereas in the block format it is positioned at the left margin (see page 566).

Notations

Beneath the closing and flush with the left margin you may include **notations,** such as "Enclosures" (sometimes abbreviated "enc." or "encl."), to direct the reader to items enclosed with the letter. Typing "EAK:fb" indicates the initials of the writer (EAK) and typist or secretary (fb), and adding "cc:" (concurrent copy) notes circulation of copies ("pc:" for photocopy) followed by the names of the recipients of the copies.

Envelope

Type your name and address in block form in the upper left corner of the envelope, unless of course the return address is already printed there. The recipient's name and address should be typed in block form exactly as they appear in the letter beginning at the middle of the envelope, as shown.

Sample business letter envelope

Return address ⟶ Samantha H. Phillips
96 Forest Ave.
Portland, ME 04103

Attention line is always placed above the firm's name ⟶ R. H. Dawson
Director of Personnel
The Big Company
800 N. French St.
Wilmington, DE 19801

↑ Reserve last line for city, state, and ZIP code

3 Writing the business letter

As you write a business letter, imagine that you are the letter's reader. What would you, as the reader, need to know? How would you react to the letter?

When you write a letter to complain or to claim an adjustment for some error in service or for a faulty product, think about the remedy you seek and about the information the reader will need to meet your claim. Present yourself as someone credible, rational, deserving of the requested adjustment. Do not attack the reader. Announce your claim and then provide a narrative of the error. For a product, include such information as the product's name, model, serial number, and warranty information. Describe the requested action (e.g., specify whether you are requesting a refund, repair, or replacement). The model letter on page 567 requests information. Note how the letter encourages a response through its specific questions and pleasant tone. A response letter in any situation should be written with the letter of request in hand.

4 Sample business letters

Job application letter in block format

96 Forest Ave.
Portland, ME 04103   ⎤— Heading
25 March 1996

R. H. Dawson
Director of Personnel
The Big Company   ⎤— Inside address
800 N. French St.
Wilmington, DE 19801

Single-spaced
text

Dear Mr. Dawson: ⎤— Salutation

Paragraphs
are not   From both Professor Lucia Gomez at the University of Southern
indented   Maine and your advertisement in the 15 March issue of the

<u>Wilmington News Journal</u>, I have learned of your opening for an entry-level accountant. I am writing to apply for that position.

As my resume shows, I will receive a degree in accounting in June. My course work has concentrated on the financial management of large multinationals like The Big Company. Each course required extensive case analyses and practical problem solving. My high grade point average indicates my strengths in those skills necessary to do well in your position.

In addition, through my work with POM Recoveries and the Publisher's Clearing House, I have gained experience in the day-to-day operation of a small and a large operation. For much of my work I was given an assignment that I completed largely on my own. I also learned and demonstrated skills with computerized accounting systems. Thus, I am confident that I can be the "knowledgeable self-starter" your advertisement seeks. A position with The Big Company especially interests me because of your recent acquisition of Steitman AG and the potential for learning about German accounting practices as I apply my knowledge of the German language and culture.

[Double-space between paragraphs]

I will be visiting Delaware during my spring break, 17-22 April, and will gladly meet with you any time during that period for an interview. If these dates are not suitable, please let me know and I'll make other arrangements for a time convenient to The Big Company.

I look forward to talking with you.

Sincerely,

S. Phillips

Samantha H. Phillips

Enc.

Body —

Closing

Notation

Letter requesting information in modified block format

Notice how the writer of this sample letter requests information, provides as much specific detail as possible, and ends the body of the letter with a summary request for information.

1111 Carriage House Drive, Apt. 27
Tallahassee, FL 32306
September 14, 2000

Indented heading

Angelo Piscatelli
Department of Entomology
Florida State University
Tallahassee, FL 32306

Dear Professor Piscatelli:

I saw a strange-looking insect in my garden yesterday. It was slender but large for an insect—about an inch long. It was a rather violent green, had greenish gossamer wings, and a tiny head with prominent black eyes. It appeared to be able to turn its head in a complete circle. As I watched the creature, it rose on its hind legs and folded its front legs. Could you identify it from this description?

Paragraphs indented 5 spaces

1. What is the name of the insect?
2. Is it destructive to plants?
3. If so, which plants?
4. What kind of spray should I use to destroy it, if necessary?

I would appreciate any information you can send me.

Indented closing lined up with heading

Sincerely yours,

Harvey Bergman

Harvey Bergman

Letter of complaint in the simplified format

Box 101D
Obden, PA 18102
May 18, 2000

Customer Service
Get Mugged, Inc.
12 Washington Lane
Crystal Keys, MA 02161

← Salutation omitted

I am writing about a problem with a recent order.

On May 1, I ordered 6 "Bunnies in Heaven" mugs from your catalog. The stock number is 45–66–77; the mugs appeared on page 10 of the catalog. On May 15, I received a package from you marked "½ dozen bunnies in heaven"; it contained, however, a combination of bunny mugs and "Moose in Maine" mugs. Moreover, the count was inaccurate. The case contained a total of 8 mugs: 4 bunnies and 4 moose.

In accordance with your guarantee, I am returning the moose mugs from the improperly packaged case to you. Please reimburse me for the postage costs and send me two more "Bunnies in Heaven" mugs. Thank you.

← Closing phrase omitted

Graziella Lopez

Graziella Lopez

52c   The Facsimile Transaction

A **facsimile transaction,** or **fax,** enables you to transmit written documents, photographs, drawings, and the like over telephone lines from a source (the sending machine) to a destination (the receiving machine) within minutes. The speed with which materials can be sent and received accounts for the wide use of faxes in the workplace.

To fax documents, whether memos, letters, or reports, prepare them as you would for mailing. The main difference will be the attachment of a facsimile cover sheet for the first page of the document. This cover sheet will contain important information including the date, the number of pages sent (this total should include your cover sheet), the name, address, and fax number of the recipient and then identical information for you, the sender. The format of cover sheets varies from business to business; for example, some cover sheets include an area for comments or messages, but all should contain the basic information just outlined.

52d The Resume

Your resume presents you as a potential employee. It must be concise, accurate, easy to read, and well designed. And it must be correct.

Start by making an inventory of your skills, education, and relevant experience. Note all of the jobs you have held, including their dates and responsibilities, as well as all paid positions, internships, and volunteer work. Also list major courses, academic achievements, and activities, especially offices held and leadership roles. Then select and arrange this information to provide a profile of yourself. Although the form of the resume may vary to suit individual tastes, most resumes conform to conventions in content and design.

1 The parts of a resume

The typical resume of a college student contains a stated objective, personal data, educational background, work experience, references, and other miscellaneous information. It is usually accompanied by a letter of application.

Objective

Although not all resumes include a statement of **objective,** some employers look for this indication of your career goal. The objective can serve as a thesis supported by the evidence that is presented later in the resume. Avoid using a generic statement to cover several objectives. Instead, tailor the objective to be specific enough to state the position you are seeking.

Personal data

The **personal data** should include your name, address (home and school, if different), and phone number.

Educational background

The **education** section should list the schools you have attended since high school, starting with the most recent (reverse chronological order) and including dates of attendance and degrees received or expected. Major and minor fields of study should also be identified.

Work experience

In the **work experience** section, you should list the jobs you have held, starting with the most recent. For each job, note the dates of employment, the title of your position, and the name and address of the company. Briefly describe your responsibilities. Avoid full sentences in the description; instead, use fragments beginning with action verbs, as in the model at the end of this chapter. Quantify your work wherever possible. Show independent work or a progression of responsibilities if that occurred.

References

Most prospective employers will expect you to provide **references:** the names of people who can vouch for you. You may keep a file of letters of reference at your college placement office; if so, note that on the resume. Because you might wish to select different references for different positions while keeping one resume for several possibilities, and because of a need to save space, you may elect not to name the references directly on the resume. Instead you may write, "References available on request."

Other information

Include mention of scholarships, awards, and athletic or other extracurricular activities, if you feel such information provides a better view of you as a potential employee. Such information also gives an interviewer a good opener for an interview. It is *your* resume. Just be brief and honest.

2 Formatting your resume

The format and appearance of your resume are almost as important as its content. The resume should be typed or printed on good-quality 8½" × 11" bond paper and should be limited to one page. Consider preparing your resume on a computer, which allows you to experiment with various formats as well as font types and sizes and the use of boldface and italics for emphasis. However, do not get carried away with your options in type fonts. Computers can also help you to tailor your resume. For example, you can easily devise and insert different specific objective statements to match the different jobs you seek. Finally, *proofread* the resume many times. One spelling error might very well send your resume to the reader's wastebasket. The following models show two successful resume formats:

Sample resume

SAMANTHA H. PHILLIPS

COLLEGE ADDRESS:
96 Forest Avenue
Portland, ME 04103
(207) 555-1155
(until June 1, 2000)

PERMANENT ADDRESS:
210 Waverly St.
Jericho, NY 11753
(513) 555-9655

OBJECTIVE:
A position in internal auditing with a large multinational organization in which I can combine my accounting skills with my knowledge of different language and cultures.

EDUCATION:
B.S. in accounting, University of Southern Maine, expected in 2000. Courses in managerial accounting, cost accounting, business law, finance, operations management, marketing. Earned 75% of college expenses.

ACTIVITIES:
German Club, intramural soccer, and baseball

PERSONAL:
Have traveled widely in the United States and Europe. Willing to relocate.

EMPLOYMENT EXPERIENCE

Summer 1999
POM Recoveries, Syosset, NY. Posted financial statements on a computer.

Spring 1999
Publisher's Clearing House, Port Washington, NY. Sorted checks, processed magazine orders, validated contest entry forms.

Summers 1996-98
Camp Thistle, Rabbit Lake, NY. Organized games, taught swimming, supervised campers.

REFERENCES:
Available upon request.

CARMEN J. BALLIE

PRESENT ADDRESS
101 West Standish, #2
DeKalb, IL 60142
309/555-1226

PERMANENT ADDRESS
469 Brainard Drive
West Point, IL 60090
708/555-0351

CAREER OBJECTIVE

To obtain a challenging position where my organizational abilities, time-management skills, and communication background can be utilized within a progressive environment.

EDUCATION

May 2000   Bachelor of Science in Public Relations, Northern Illinois University (NIU), DeKalb, IL   Minor: Business Administration   Major GPA: 3.0/4.0

PROFESSIONAL EXPERIENCE

Spring 2000   NIU Student Body Board of Directors, DeKalb, IL
Internship—One semester, 9 hours per week
Assisting the Director with various activities involving student/town liaison including planning and coordinating the Student United Way campaign.

Fall 1998   Occupational Development Center, Sycamore, IL
Internship—one semester, 9 hours per week
Composed and edited the quarterly newsletter; served on the fundraising committee; helped with initial planning for the spring fundraiser.

WORK EXPERIENCE

The following part-time positions have been held during summers and school holidays from 1993 to 1998. Besides providing money to continue my education, this employment has taught me how to be a team player, how to work effectively with the public, and how to perform efficiently and responsibly in varied work environments.

Waitress, Chi Chi's Mexican Restaurant, Deerfield, IL
Sales Associate, Compagnie International Express, Prospect Heights, IL
Lifeguard, Lincoln Club Property and McGill Management
Receptionist, Tom Todd Chevrolet, Wheeling IL

ACTIVITIES

Aug. 1996–present   Chi Omega Sorority
Editor and coordinator of alumni/parent newsletter, Spring 1999
Community service committee member
Career development committee member
Home Sweet Home volunteer (prepared and served food to the homeless)
Captain, field hockey intramural team

REFERENCES AVAILABLE UPON REQUEST

Glossary of Usage

The items in this glossary reflect current usage among experienced writers. Use the glossary to check the appropriateness of your word choices.

A, An Use the article *a* before a consonant sound; use *an* before a vowel sound.

a receipt	a history	a one-liner	a unit	a B
an idea	an hour	an officer	an umbrella	an F

Accept, Except *Accept* means "to receive"; *except* means "with the exclusion of."

> She will **accept** the award on Friday.
>
> We all went to the ceremony **except** Lola.

Allusion, Illusion An *allusion* is an indirect or casual reference to something. An *illusion* is a false or misleading perception or concept.

> The poem is filled with many **allusions** to the Bible.
>
> Five years in the theater stripped him of his **illusions** about the glamour of an actor's life.

A Lot Always write *a lot* as two words, not as *alot*. In general, avoid using *a lot* in formal writing.

A.M., P.M. or AM, PM or a.m., p.m. Use these abbreviations only with figures.

> **NOT:** The lecture ends at eleven in the **A.M.**
>
> **BUT:** The lecture ends at **11:00 A.M.**

Among, Between Use *among* with three or more people or objects. Use *between* with only two.

According to the will, the funds were to be divided equally **between** the two children.

He decided to leave his entire estate to his eldest son, rather than divide it **among** his six children.

Amount, Number   *Amount* refers to mass or quantity. It is followed by the preposition *of* and a singular noun. *Number* refers to things that can be counted. It is followed by *of* and a plural noun.

The **amount** of time he spent completing the job was far greater than the reward he derived from it.

The **number** of domestic animals that have contracted rabies is alarming.

An   *See* **a.**

And Etc.   The abbreviation *etc.* means "and other things" or "and so forth." Therefore, *and etc.* is redundant.

Anxious, Eager   *Anxious* means "worried, uneasy, uncertain." In formal writing, do not use *anxious* for *eager,* which means "expectant" or "desirous" but carries no implication of apprehension.

The doctor was **anxious** about her patient's condition.

Since we have heard so many good things about them, we are **eager** to meet our new neighbors.

Anyone, Any One   *Anyone* means "any person at all." It refers indefinitely to any person whatsoever. *Any one* refers to a specific, though unidentified, person or thing within a group. Similar cases are *everyone, every one* and *someone, some one.*

Anyone willing to work hard can get good grades.

Any one of these plans is acceptable.

Anyplace   *Anywhere* is preferred.

Anyways   *Anyway* is preferred.

Anywheres   *Anywhere* is preferred.

Arguement   This word is a variant British spelling of **argument.** *Argument* is the preferred form in the United States.

As   In general, use the stronger and clearer conjunctions *because, since,* and *while.*

> **NOT:** We could no longer see the river from our terrace, **as** the new building blocked our view.

> **BUT:** We could no longer see the river from our terrace **because** the new building blocked our view.

As, Like   *See* **like.**

Assure, Insure, Ensure   Although these three words have similar meanings, their usage varies. *Assure* is used in the sense of "to set the mind at ease." *Ensure* and *insure* are not used interchangeably in formal writing; *insure* is used to mean "to guarantee persons or property against risk"; and *ensure* is used to mean "to make sure."

Awful   In general, use a more specific adjective such as *shocking, ugly, appalling,* or *great.* In formal writing, do not use *awfully* or *awful* as an intensifier meaning "very."

Awhile, A While   *Awhile* is an adverb meaning "for a short time." It is not preceded by the preposition *for. A while* is an article plus a noun. It is usually preceded by *for.*

> We asked our guests to stay **awhile.**

> They could stay for **a while** longer.

Bad, Badly   Use the adjective *bad* before nouns and after linking verbs. Use the adverb *badly* to modify verbs or adjectives.

> Several **bad** strawberries were hidden under the good ones.

> The students felt **bad** about the loss.

> The dancer performed **badly.**

> The book was **badly** written.

Being As, Being That   Use the more formal *because* or *since.*

> **NOT:** **Being as** the sketch was signed, it was valuable.

> **BUT:** **Because** the sketch was signed, it was valuable.

> **NOT:** **Being that** they desperately needed money, they took a second mortgage on their home.

> **BUT:** **Because** they desperately needed money, they took a second mortgage on their home.

Beside, Besides   *Beside* is a preposition that means "next to." When used as a preposition, *besides* means "in addition to" or "except for." When used as an adverb, *besides* means "in addition" or "furthermore."

> She was buried **beside** her husband.
>
> **Besides** mathematics, there are no required courses.
>
> To keep warm, she wore a coat, a hat, and gloves—and a muffler **besides.**

Between   *See* **among.**

Between You and I   A common grammatical mistake. Write *between you and me*. (*You* and *me* are objects of the preposition *between*.)

Bring, Take   Use *bring* when you mean movement from a farther person or place toward a nearer one. Use *take* when you mean movement away from a nearer person or place toward a farther one.

> **Bring** me the book I left in the bedroom.
>
> **Take** this package to the post office.

Bunch   Do not use *bunch* to refer to a group of people.

Burst, Bursted, Bust, Busted   *Burst* is a verb that means "to come apart suddenly." Its past and past participle forms are both *burst,* not *bursted. Bust,* a verb meaning "to come apart suddenly" or "to break," is considered slang. Do not use it or its past form, *busted,* in formal writing.

Can, May   In formal writing, use *can* to indicate ability and *may* to indicate permission. In informal writing, you may use them interchangeably.

> **Can** the defendant answer the question? (Is he or she able to?)
>
> **May** the defendant answer the question? (Does he or she have permission to do so?)

Can't   In formal writing, avoid using *can't,* which is a contraction of *cannot.*

Can't Hardly, Can't Scarcely   Avoid these double negatives. Use *can hardly* and *can scarcely* instead.

Center Around   Use *center on* instead.

Climactic, Climatic   *Climactic* refers to the climax, or highest point of intensity. *Climatic* refers to the climate, or characteristic weather conditions.

Compare To, Compare With   Use *compare to* when referring to the similarities between essentially unlike things. Use *compare with* when referring to the similarities and differences between things of the same type.

> Hart Crane **compares** the sound of rain **to** "gently pitying laughter."
>
> The professor **compared** a poem by Hart Crane **with** one by Edna St. Vincent Millay.

Contemptible, Contemptuous   *Contemptible* means "deserving contempt." *Contemptuous* means "feeling contempt."

> She claimed that efforts to cut back funds for food programs for the poor were **contemptible.**
>
> She was **contemptuous** of people who ignored the suffering of others.

Continual, Continuous   *Continual* means "recurring regularly." *Continuous* means "occurring without interruption."

> He was kept awake by the **continual** dripping of the faucet.
>
> The nation was experiencing a period of **continuous** growth.

Convince, Persuade   *Convince,* which is often used with *of,* means "to cause to believe." *Persuade,* which is often used with an infinitive, means "to cause to do."

> The physicist **convinced** his colleague **of** the correctness of his methods.
>
> The doctor **persuaded** her patient **to undergo** therapy.

Could Of   Nonstandard. Use *could have.*

Criteria, Data, Phenomena   These words are plural and in formal writing take plural verbs. The singular forms are *criterion, datum,* and *phenomenon.*

Deal   When used to mean "agreement," "bargain," or "business transaction," this word is informal and overused, as in "a done deal." It is also considered informal when used to mean (1) "a certain amount of," as in *a great deal of noise,* (2) "important, impressive," as in "*a big deal*" and "*to make a big deal (out) of,*" and (3) "cope," as in "*I can't deal with this.*"

Disinterested, Uninterested   *Disinterested* means "impartial." *Uninterested* means "indifferent" or "not interested."

> The jury paid special attention to the testimony of one **disinterested** witness.
>
> She did not finish the book because she was **uninterested** in the subject.

Done   *Done* is the past participle of *do.* Do not use *done* as the past tense.

> **NOT:**   He always read the last page of a mystery first to find out who **done** it.
>
> **BUT:**   He always read the last page of a mystery first to find out who **did** it.

Don't   Avoid using *don't,* which is a contraction of *do not,* in formal writing. Never use *don't* as a contraction of *does not.*

Due To   In formal writing, avoid using *due to* to mean *because of.*

> **NOT:**   The shipment was delayed **due to** the bad weather.
>
> **BUT:**   The shipment was delayed **because of** the bad weather.
>
> **OR:**   The delay in the shipment **was due to** the bad weather.

Eager   *See* **anxious.**

Ensure   *See* **assure.**

Enthused   In formal writing, use *enthusiastic.*

Etc.   *See* **and etc.**

Everyday, Every Day   Use *every day* as an adverb. Use *everyday* as an adjective.

> During training, he took vitamins **every day.**
>
> He needed an **everyday** suit.

Everyone, Every One   *See* **anyone.**

Everywheres   Nonstandard. Use *everywhere*.

Exam   In formal writing, use *examination*.

Except   *See* **accept**.

Expect   In formal writing, do not use *expect* to mean "to presume or suppose."

> **NOT:**   I **expect** the performance went well.
>
> **BUT:**   I **suppose** the performance went well.

Explicit, Implicit   *Explicit* means "stated forthrightly." *Implicit* means "implied" or "suggested."

> The warning was **explicit:** Beware of the dog.
>
> Although he never said a word, his threat was **implicit** in his action.

Farther, Further   In formal writing, use *farther* to refer to geographical distance. Use *further* to refer to time, quantity, or degree.

> We were **farther** from home than we had imagined.
>
> The court demanded **further** documentation of his expenses.

Fewer, Less   Use *fewer* to refer to things that can be counted. Use *less* to refer to a collective quantity that cannot be counted.

> This year **fewer** commuters are driving their cars to work.
>
> In general, smaller cars use **less** fuel than larger cars.

Finalize   *Finalize* is an example of bureaucratic language. Do not use it in place of *complete, conclude,* or *make final*.

Fine   *Fine* is informal and weak when used for the words *very well*. In formal writing, use a more exact word.

Firstly, Secondly, Etc.   Use *first, second,* etc., instead.

Fix   In formal writing, avoid using *fix* to mean "predicament."

Flunk   *Flunk* is informal. In formal writing, use *fail*.

Folks   In formal writing, avoid using the informal word *folks* for *parents, relatives,* or *family*.

Former, Latter   *Former* means "the first mentioned of two." When three or more are mentioned, refer to the first mentioned as *first*. *Latter* means "the second mentioned of two." When three or more are mentioned, refer to the last mentioned as *last*.

> Anita and Jayne are athletes: the **former** is a gymnast, the **latter** a tennis player.
>
> The judges sampled four pies—apple, plum, rhubarb, and apricot—and gave the prize to the **last.**

Funny   In formal writing, avoid using *funny* for *odd* or *peculiar*.

Further   *See* **farther.**

Get   In formal writing, avoid using slang expressions beginning with *get: get even, get going, get on with it,* etc.

Good, Well   *Good* is an adjective. *Well* is usually an adverb, but it can also be used as an adjective meaning "healthy."

> She looks **good** in that color.
>
> They work **well** together.
>
> The baby looks **well** today.

Great   In formal writing, do not use *great* to mean "wonderful."

Had Ought, Hadn't Ought   Use *ought* and *ought not* instead.

Hanged, Hung   Use *hanged* as the past and past participle form when referring to a method of execution. Otherwise, use *hung*.

> In the Old West, horse thieves were **hanged.**
>
> The clothing was **hung** out to dry.

Has Got, Have Got   In formal writing, use simply *has* or *have*.

Herself, Himself   *See* **myself.**

Hisself   Nonstandard. Use *himself*.

Hopefully   *Hopefully* means "in a hopeful manner." Avoid using *hopefully* to mean "it is hoped" or "let us hope."

> **NOT:**   **Hopefully** it will not rain again this weekend.
>
> **BUT:**   **Let us hope** it will not rain again this weekend.

Illusion   *See* **allusion.**

Implicit   *See* **explicit.**

Imply, Infer   *Imply* means "to suggest or hint." *Infer* means "to draw a conclusion." A writer or speaker implies something; a reader or listener *infers* it.

He **implied** that he knew someone had cheated.

From his remark I **inferred** that he is worried about her.

In, Into   *In* indicates position. *Into* indicates direction of movement.

When the sergeant came **into** the barracks, she found several of the new recruits still **in** bed.

Infer   *See* **imply.**

In Regards To   Use *in regard to* or *regarding* or *as regards.*

Insure   *See* **assure.**

Interesting   Because it is overused, *interesting* has so many meanings that it has become an ambiguous word. In formal writing, explain why something is interesting rather than using the word.

Into   *See* **in.**

Irregardless   Nonstandard. Use *regardless.*

Is When, Is Where   Do not use these constructions in giving definitions.

> **NOT:**   Improvisation **is when** actors perform without preparation.
>
> **BUT:**   Improvisation **occurs when** actors perform without preparation.
>
> **OR:**   Improvisation **is** a performance by actors without preparation.
>
> **NOT:**   An aviary **is where** a large number of birds are housed.
>
> **BUT:**   An aviary **is a place where** a large number of birds are housed.
>
> **OR:**   An aviary **is** a house for a large number of birds.

Its, It's   *Its* is the possessive case of the pronoun *it. It's* is a contraction of *it is* or *it has.* Avoid the contraction *it's* in formal writing.

The cat was cleaning **its** paws.

It's too late to submit an application.

Judgement   This word is a variant British spelling of **judgment.** *Judgment* is the preferred spelling in the United States.

Kind Of, Sort Of   In formal writing, avoid using *kind of* and *sort of* as adverbs. Use instead the more formal words *rather* and *somewhat.*

NOT: His description was **kind of** sketchy.

BUT: His description was **rather** sketchy.

NOT: She left **sort of** abruptly.

BUT: She left **somewhat** abruptly.

Kind Of A, Sort Of A   When using these expressions to mean "type of," delete the *a*.

What **kind of** fabric is this?

What **sort of** person was he?

Lay   *See* **lie.**

Lead, Led   *Lead* is the present infinitive form of the verb. *Led* is the past tense and past participle form.

Learn, Teach   *Learn* means "to receive knowledge." *Teach* means "to give knowledge."

We can **learn** from the mistakes of history.

History can **teach** us many lessons.

Leave, Let   In formal writing, use the verb *leave* to mean "to depart (from)." Use the verb *let* to mean "to allow to."

Paul Simon wrote about the many ways to **leave** a lover.

The natives would not **let** themselves be photographed.

Less   *See* **fewer.**

Let   *See* **leave.**

Liable   *See* **likely.**

Lie, Lay   *Lie* is an intransitive verb that means "to recline." Its past and past participle forms are *lay* and *lain*. *Lay* is a transitive verb that means "to place." Its past and past participle forms are both *laid*. (See also Section 12c-1.)

Although he **lay** in bed for hours, he could not sleep.

Please **lay** the book on the table.

Then let it **lie** there.

Like   In formal writing, do not use *like* as a conjunction. Instead use *as, as if,* or *as though*.

NOT: The headlines claim that it looks **like** peace is at hand.

BUT: The headlines claim that it looks **as if** peace is at hand.

Likely, Liable   *Likely* indicates probability. *Liable* indicates responsibility or obligation.

Moscow asserted that changes in the makeup of the government were not **likely** to lead to changes in U.S.–Russian relations.

The court determined that the driver of the truck was **liable** for all damages.

Lose, Loose   *Lose* is a verb. *Loose* is an adjective.

In what year did Nixon **lose** the election to Kennedy?

Loose talk can cause much trouble.

Lot   *See* **a lot.**

Lot Of, Lots Of   In formal writing, use *much, plenty of,* or *many* instead.

May   *See* **can.**

May Be, Maybe   *May be* is a verb phrase. *Maybe* is an adverb meaning "perhaps."

His findings **may be** accurate.

Maybe they will find a solution.

May Of, Might Of, Must Of   Use *may have, might have,* or *must have* instead.

More Importantly, Most Importantly   Use *more important* and *most important* instead.

Most   In formal writing, avoid using *most* to mean "almost."

NOT: The survey predicted that **most** everyone would vote.

BUT: The survey predicted that **almost** everyone would vote.

Myself, Yourself, Himself, Herself, Etc.   Pronouns ending in *-self* or *-selves* are reflexive or intensive. In formal writing, do not use them in place of *I, me, you, he, her,* and so on.

NOT: My friend and **myself** are campaigning actively.

BUT: My friend and **I** are campaigning actively.

No One   *No one* is a singular indefinite pronoun and therefore requires a singular verb.

> **No one** of the students **is** able to go today.

Nice   In formal writing, replace this weak word with a more exact one—*attractive, appealing, kind,* and so forth.

Not Hardly   Avoid this double negative. Use *hardly* instead.

Nowhere Near Enough   Colloquial. In formal writing, use *not nearly enough* instead.

> **NOT:**   The concessions the company made its employees were **nowhere near enough** to prevent a strike.
>
> **BUT:**   The concessions the company made its employees were **not nearly enough** to prevent a strike.

Nowheres   Nonstandard. Use *nowhere.*

Number   *See* **amount.**

Off Of   Use *off* without *of.*

> **NOT:**   During the tremor the paintings fell **off of** the wall.
>
> **BUT:**   During the tremor the paintings fell **off** the wall.

OK, O.K., Okay   Avoid these expressions in formal writing.

Old Fashion   This phrase is a shortened form of *old fashioned;* avoid using it in formal writing.

People, Persons   Use *people* to refer to a large group collectively. Use *persons* to emphasize the individuals within the group.

> The committee is investigating ways in which **people** avoid paying their full taxes.
>
> The group thought it was near agreement when several **persons** raised objections.

Percent, Percentage   Use *percent* after a specific number. Use *percentage* after a general adjective indicating size.

> The poll showed that 75 **percent** of Americans supported the President's foreign policy.
>
> The poll showed that a large **percentage** of Americans supported the President's foreign policy.

Persuade   *See* **convince.**

Phenomena   *See* **criteria.**

P.M.   *See* **A.M.**

Principal, Principle   *Principal* is a noun meaning "chief officer" or, in finance, "capital sum." As an adjective it means "major" or "main." *Principle* is used only as a noun and means "rule" or "fundamental truth."

> The **principal** spoke to all of the teachers today.
>
> The **principal** reason for doing so is not clear.
>
> She adheres to **principles** that are admirable.

Quote, Quotation   *Quote* is a verb. *Quotation* is a noun.

> During her speech she **quoted** from one of Blake's poems.
>
> She began her speech with a **quotation** from one of Blake's poems.

Raise, Rise   *Raise* is a transitive verb meaning "to lift." Its past and past participle forms are both *raised*. *Rise* is an intransitive verb meaning "to go up." Its past and past participle are *rose* and *risen*. (See also Section 12c-3.)

> Inflation is **raising** the cost of living.
>
> The cost of living is **rising.**

Real, Really   *Real* is an adjective. *Really* is an adverb or qualifier.

> What is the **real** value of the dollar?
>
> Mortgage rates are **really** high this year.

Reason Is Because   Use *that* instead of *because* or rewrite the sentence.

> **NOT:**   The **reason** for the patient's lethargy **is because** his diet is inadequate.
>
> **BUT:**   The **reason** for the patient's lethargy **is that** his diet is inadequate.
>
> **OR:**   The **reason** for the patient's lethargy **is** an inadequate diet.
>
> **OR:**   The patient is lethargic because of an inadequate diet.

Respectably, Respectfully, Respectively   *Respectably* means "in a manner deserving respect." *Respectfully* means "in a manner showing respect." *Respectively* means "in the order given."

The tenor performed his aria **respectably,** but his voice cracked during the duet.

The defendant **respectfully** asked permission to address the court.

Baghdad and Damascus are the capitals of Iraq and Syria, **respectively.**

Rise   *See* **raise.**

Sensual, Sensuous   Both of these adjectives mean "appealing to the senses," but *sensual* describes something that arouses physical appetites, while *sensuous* describes something that leads to aesthetic enjoyment.

The censors claimed that the dancing was too **sensual.**

The painter was praised for the **sensuous** quality of his still lifes.

Set, Sit   *Set* is a transitive verb that means "to put or place." Its past and past participle forms are both *set. Sit* is an intransitive verb that means "to be seated." Its past and past participle forms are both *sat.* (See also Section 12c-2.)

The stagehands **set** the chairs on a raised platform.

The actors will **sit** in the chairs during the rehearsal.

Shall, Will   At one time it was standard to use *shall* with first-person subjects to express simple futurity and *will* with second- and third-person subjects.

SIMPLE FUTURITY

I **shall** see you at the theater.

Mark **will** meet us at the theater.

But *will* is commonly used with all persons now. Some speakers and writers still use *shall* in the first-person to express determination or resolve and in first-person questions that ask for an opinion or seek consent.

We **shall** not fail.

Shall we begin?

Should Of   Nonstandard. Use *should have.*

Sit   *See* **set.**

Someone, Some One   *See* **anyone.**
Sometime, Some Time   Use *sometime* as an adverb to mean "at an indefinite or unnamed time." Use *some time* after a preposition.

> The announcement will be made **sometime** next month.

> He has been retired for **some time** now.

Sort Of   *See* **kind of.**
Sort Of A   *See* **kind of a.**
Suppose To   *See* **use to.**
Sure, Surely   *Sure* is an adjective that means "certain." *Surely* is an adverb that means "undoubtedly" or "certainly."

> The expedition was **sure** to succeed.

> The expedition was **surely** a success.

Sure And, Try And   In formal writing, use *sure to* and *try to* instead.

> **NOT:** Be **sure and** pay attention to the speaker's body language.

> **BUT:** Be **sure to** pay attention to the speaker's body language.

Teach   *See* **learn.**
That, Which   Use *that* to introduce a restrictive clause. Use *which* to introduce either a restrictive or a nonrestrictive clause. (In order to maintain a clearer distinction between *which* and *that,* some writers use *which* to introduce only a nonrestrictive clause.)

> Is this the manuscript **that** he submitted yesterday?

> This contract, **which** is no longer valid, called for a 30 percent royalty.

Theirself, Theirselves   Nonstandard. Use *themselves.*
These Kind, Those Kind; These Sort, Those Sort   Since *kind* and *sort* are singular, use singular adjectives: *this kind, that kind, this sort, that sort.* For the plural use *these kinds, those kinds, these sorts, those sorts.*
Thusly   Use *thus.*
Try And   *See* **sure and.**
Uninterested   *See* **disinterested.**

Unique   The word *unique* means "unequaled" or "unparalleled," a quality that is not capable of comparison.

NOT: He has the **most unique** sense of humor I have encountered.

BUT: His sense of humor is **unique.**

Use To, Suppose To   The correct forms are use**d** to and suppose**d** to.

NOT: In *My Dinner with André,* Wally **use to** be a Latin teacher.

BUT: In *My Dinner with André,* Wally **used to** be a Latin teacher.

Wait For, Wait On   Use *wait for* to mean "await" or "attend to." Use *wait on* to mean "serve."

Many young actors **wait on** tables while they **wait for** the right role.

Ways   Use *way* to mean "distance."

NOT: He lives only a short **ways** from London.

BUT: He lives only a short **way** from London.

Well   *See* **good.**

When, Where   *See* **is when, is where.**

Where   Do not use *where* for *that.*

NOT: I read in the magazine **where** flood victims were receiving federal aid.

BUT: I read in the magazine **that** flood victims were receiving federal aid.

Do not use *where* for *in which.*

NOT: It is an agreement **where** everyone is happy.

BUT: It is an agreement **in which** everyone is happy.

Which, Who   Use *which* to refer to objects. Use *who* to refer to people. (*That* usually refers to objects but at times may be used to refer to people.)

The book, **which** was written by Nat Hentoff, is called *Jazz Is.*

Nat Hentoff, **who** wrote *Jazz Is,* contributes articles to many magazines.

Will   *See* **shall.**

-wise   Avoid using *-wise* as a noun suffix—*budgetwise, career-wise, marketwise.*

Without   Do not use *without* for *unless.*

> **NOT:**   The director could not act **without** the committee approved.
>
> **BUT:**   The director could not act **unless** the committee approved.
>
> **OR:**   The director could not act **without** the committee's approval.

Yourself   *See* **myself.**

Glossary of Grammatical Terms

Absolute Phrase   A group of words containing a noun and a nonfinite, or incomplete, verb. It modifies the entire clause to which it is attached, instead of an individual word within the clause. (See also Sections 9b and 23a.)

> **His energy depleted,** the fighter conceded the bout.

Abstract Noun   *See* **noun.**

Acronym   A kind of abbreviation that creates a word from parts of words or initials without periods: *radar, CARE, ROM.*

Active Voice   *See* **voice.**

Adjective   A word that modifies, or describes, a noun or pronoun. (See also Section 8d and Chapter 16.)

> In his **latest** novel, this **prodigious** writer uses several **historical** studies to create a **realistic** portrait of the man often considered our **greatest** president—Abraham Lincoln.

Adjective Clause   A dependent clause that acts as an adjective and modifies a noun or pronoun. Usually, an adjective clause begins with a relative pronoun (*who, whose, whom, that,* or *which*). (See also Sections 9d-1 and 21b.)

> The king of England **who broke with the Catholic Church** was Henry VIII.

Adverb   A word that modifies, or limits the meaning of, a verb. An adverb tells *when, where, to what extent,* or *how.* (See also Section 8e and Chapter 16.)

591

This absorbing book reports **successfully** the way computers **efficiently** function and **how** they will **most probably** affect our lives in the future.

Adverb Clause   A dependent clause that begins with a subordinating conjunction (*although, because, while,* etc.) and acts as an adverb in the sentence. (See also Sections 9d-2 and 21b.)

The museum was closed **because it was being renovated.**

Agreement   The correspondence in form between a verb and its subject or a pronoun and its antecedent to indicate person, number, and gender. (See also Chapter 13 and Section 14a.)

Each of these women **makes her** position understood.

Antecedent   The word or words to which a pronoun refers. A pronoun must agree with its antecedent in number and gender. (See also Sections 8f and 14a.)

Jack pledged **his** support for the project.

Appositive   A noun or group of words acting as a noun that renames, identifies, or gives additional information about the preceding noun or pronoun. (See also Sections 23a-2 and 28d.)

Typhoid Mary, **the notorious carrier of typhoid fever,** died in 1938.

Article   The indefinite articles are *a* and *an;* the definite article is *the.* (See also Section 8g.)

Auxiliary Verb   A form of *be* or *have* used to form perfect tenses, progressive forms of tenses, and the passive voice. (See also Section 8b.)

I **am** leaving.

They **have** left.

The money **had been** left in the safe.

Case   The structural function of a noun or a pronoun in a sentence. English has three cases—subjective, objective, and possessive. The subjective case indicates the subject of a verb or a subject complement.

The **umpire** called a strike.

The **umpire** was **he.**

The objective case indicates the direct or indirect object of a verb or the object of a preposition.

      DO   OP
Sampras returned the **serve** to Agassi. He returned it to **him.**

    IO   DO   DO
Montana gave **me** an autographed **football.** I gave **it** to my

 OP
nephew.

The possessive case indicates possession, description, or origin.

The **team's** overall performance was disappointing. **Their** overall performance was disappointing.

Nouns and some pronouns have the same form in the subjective and the objective cases; an apostrophe and *s* or an apostrophe alone is added to form the possessive case: *investor's, investors', anybody's.* The pronouns *it* and *you* have special possessive forms: *its, your,* and *yours.* The following pronouns have different forms in all three cases:

 SUBJECTIVE: I, he, she, we, they, who

 OBJECTIVE: me, him, her, us, them, whom

 POSSESSIVE: my, mine; his; her, hers; our, ours; their, theirs; whose

(See also Sections 8a and 8f, Chapter 15, and Section 37a.)

Clause A group of words with a subject and a predicate. A clause may be independent or dependent. An independent (main) clause is structurally independent and can stand by itself as a simple sentence.

The President honored the Unknown Soldier.

A dependent (subordinate) clause is not structurally independent and cannot stand by itself as a simple sentence. Therefore it must be joined to or be part of an independent clause.

> **Although newspapers strive for accuracy,** they sometimes make mistakes.

Dependent clauses, which can function as adjectives, adverbs, or nouns, usually begin with a subordinating conjunction or a relative pronoun. (See also Chapter 9.)

Collective Noun   *See* **noun.**

Comma Splice   An error that occurs when a comma is used to separate two independent clauses not joined by a conjunction. (See also Section 11a.)

Common Noun   *See* **noun.**

Comparative, Superlative   Forms of adjectives and adverbs used to make comparisons. The comparative form is used to compare two things; the superlative form is used to compare more than two. The comparative and superlative of most one-syllable adjectives and adverbs are formed by adding *-er* and *-est* to the base, or positive, form: *long, longer, longest.* The comparative and superlative of most longer adjectives and adverbs are formed by placing the words *more* and *most* before the positive form: *beautiful, more beautiful, most beautiful.* (See also Sections 8d, 8e, and 16c.)

Complement   A word or group of words that completes the meaning of a verb. The four types of complements are direct objects, indirect objects, object complements, and subject complements. (See also Sections 7c and 7d.)

Complete Predicate   *See* **predicate.**

Complete Sentence   *See* **sentence.**

Complete Subject   *See* **subject.**

Complex Sentence   *See* **sentence.**

Compound   A word or group of words that is made up of two or more parts but functions as a unit. Compound words consist of two or more words that may be written as one word, as a hyphenated word, or as separate words but that function as a single part of speech: *hairbrush, well-to-do, toaster oven.* A compound subject consists of two or more nouns or noun substitutes that take the same predicate.

> **Chemistry** and **physics** were required courses.

A compound verb consists of two or more verbs that have the same subject.

> The doctor **analyzed** the results of the tests and **made** a diagnosis.

(See also Sections 8a, 13a, and 28e and Chapter 38.)

Compound–Complex Sentence   *See* **sentence.**

Compound Sentence   *See* **sentence.**

Compound Subject   *See* **subject.**

Concrete Noun   *See* **noun.**

Conjunction   A word or set of words that joins or relates other words, phrases, clauses, or sentences. There are three types of conjunctions: coordinating conjunctions, correlative conjunctions, and subordinating conjunctions. Coordinating conjunctions (*and, but, for, nor, or, so,* and *yet*) join elements that have equal grammatical rank. Correlative conjunctions (*both . . . and, either . . . or, neither . . . nor, not only . . . but also, whether . . . or, just as . . . so*) function as coordinating conjunctions but are always used in pairs. Subordinating conjunctions (*after, as long as, because, if, since, so that, unless, until, while,* etc.) join subordinate, or dependent, clauses to main, or independent, clauses. (See also Section 8j.)

Conjunctive Adverb   An adverb that provides transition between independent clauses. (See also Section 8j.)

> The movie received many excellent reviews; **consequently,** people across the country lined up to see it.

Coordinating Conjunction   *See* **conjunction.**

Correlative Conjunction   *See* **conjunction.**

Dangling Modifier   An introductory phrase that does not clearly and sensibly modify the noun or pronoun that follows it. (See also Section 18a.)

Degrees of Modifiers   *See* **comparative, superlative.**

Demonstrative Pronoun   *See* **pronoun.**

Dependent Clause   *See* **clause.**

Determiner   One of the structure-class words, a marker of nouns. Determiners include articles (*a, the*); possessives (e.g.,

Chuck's, his, my); demonstrative pronouns (*this, that*); quantifiers (e.g., *many, several*); indefinite pronouns (e.g., *each, every*); and numbers.

Direct Object   *See* **object.**

Double Negative   A construction, considered unacceptable in standard modern English, that uses two negative words to make a negative statement. (See also Section 16d.)

Elliptical Clause   A clause in which a word is omitted but understood. (See also Chapter 15.)

> He works harder than his partner **[does].**

Expletive   The word *there, here,* or *it* when used to fill the position before a verb of being but not to add meaning to the sentence. (See also Sections 7b, 8k, and 22a.)

> **There** are several excellent reasons for taking this course. **Here** is one of them. **It** is wise to register early.

Faulty Parallelism   *See* **parallelism.**

Faulty Predication   *See* **predicate.**

Form Classes   The large, open classes of words that provide the lexical content of the language: nouns, verbs, adjectives, and adverbs. Each class has characteristic changes of form that define its membership. (See Section 8a–e.)

Fragment   *See* **sentence fragment.**

Fused Sentence   Two independent clauses written without a coordinating conjunction or a punctuation mark between them. It is not the same as a comma splice. (See also Section 11b.)

Gender   The classification of nouns and pronouns as masculine (*man, he*), feminine (*woman, she*), or neuter (*skillet, it*). (See also Sections 8f and 14a.)

Gerund   *See* **verbal.**

Gerund Phrase   *See* **phrase.**

Imperative   *See* **mood.**

Indefinite Pronoun   *See* **pronoun.**

Independent Clause   *See* **clause.**

Indicative   *See* **mood.**

Indirect Object   *See* **object.**
Infinitive   *See* **verbal.**
Infinitive Phrase   *See* **phrase.**
Intensive Pronoun   *See* **pronoun.**
Interrogative Pronoun   *See* **pronoun.**
Intransitive Verb   *See* **verb.**
Inverted Word Order   A change in the normal English word order of subject-verb-complement. (See also Sections 7b and 13h.)

Sub.

In the doorway stood **Tom.**

Irregular Verb   A verb that does not form its past tense and past participle according to the regular pattern of adding *-ed* or *-d* to the present infinitive: *begin, began, begun; draw, drew, drawn; put, put, put.* (See Chapter 12.)
Linking Verb   *See* **verb.**
Main Clause   *See* **clause.**
Misplaced Modifier   A modifier placed so that it seems to refer to a word other than the one intended. (See also Section 18b.)
Modal   A verb form used with a main verb to ask a question, to help express negation, to show future time, to emphasize, or to express such conditions as possibility, certainty, or obligation. The following words are modals: *do, does, did; can, could; may, might, must; will, shall; would, should,* and *ought to.* (See also Section 8b.)
Modifier   A word or group of words that limits the meaning of or makes more specific another word or group of words. The two kinds of modifiers are adjectives and adverbs. (See also Sections 8d and 8e.)
Mood   The aspect of a verb that indicates the writer's attitude toward the action or condition expressed by the verb. In English, there are three moods: the indicative, the imperative, and the subjunctive. The indicative expresses a factual statement or a question.

The weather **is** fine today. **Will** it **rain** tomorrow?

The imperative indicates a command or a request.

> **Buy** your tickets today.
>
> Please **be** quiet.

The subjunctive indicates a wish, an assumption, a recommendation, or something contrary to fact.

> She wished she **were** home.
>
> If she **were** mayor, she would eliminate waste from the city budget.

(See also Sections 8b and 17c.)

Nominative Case   Another name for the subjective case.

Nonessential Element   A modifying phrase or clause that does not limit, qualify, or identify the noun it modifies. Since a nonessential element is not necessary to the meaning of the clause in which it appears, it is set off with commas. (See also Section 28d.)

> *Hurlyburly,* **which was written by David Rabe,** conveys the confusion and aimlessness of modern American life.

Noun   A word that names a person, place, object, or idea. Proper nouns name particular people, places, objects, or ideas: *Gertrude Stein, Spain, Corvettes, Puritanism.* Common nouns name people, places, objects, and ideas in general, not in particular: *poet, country, cars, religion.* Concrete nouns name things that can be seen, touched, heard, smelled, or tasted: *portrait, mansion, chorus, garlic.* Abstract nouns name concepts, ideas, beliefs, and qualities: *honesty, consideration, fascism, monotheism.* Collective nouns refer to groups of people or things as though the group were a single unit: *committee, choir, navy, team.* (See also Sections 8a, 13c, and 26b.)

Noun Clause   A dependent clause that acts as a noun in a sentence. It functions as a subject, an object, or a predicate nominative. (See also Section 9d-3.)

> **That an agreement would be reached before the strike deadline** seemed unlikely.

Noun Substitute   A pronoun, gerund, clause, or other group of words that functions as a noun in a sentence. (See also Sections 8a, 8f, 9b, and 9d.)

Number   The quality of being singular or plural. (See Sections 8a, 8b, 8f, and especially Chapters 13 and 14.)

Object   A noun or noun substitute that completes the meaning of or is affected by a transitive verb or a preposition. A direct object specifies the person, place, object, or idea that directly receives the action of a transitive verb.

The three heads of state *signed* the **treaty.**

An indirect object tells to whom or what or for whom or what the action of a transitive verb is performed.

They *gave* the **refugees** food and clothing.

An object of a preposition is the noun or noun substitute that the preposition relates to another part of the sentence.

The cat is sleeping *under* the **table.**

(See also Sections 7b–d, 8i, and 9c and Chapter 15.)

Object Complement   A noun or adjective that completes the action of a transitive verb by modifying or renaming that verb's object. (See also Section 7d.)

Delilah cut his *hair* **short.**

History calls *Thomas More* a **martyr.**

Objective Case   *See* **case.**

Parallelism   The quality that characterizes sentence elements that have the same grammatical structure. (See also Section 21c.)

They enjoy fish**ing,** hunt**ing,** and swimm**ing.**

Parenthetical Expression   An expression that comments on or gives additional information about the main part of a sentence. Since a parenthetical expression interrupts the thought of the sentence, it is set off by commas. (See also Section 28d.)

Music, **I believe,** is good for the soul.

Participial phrase   *See* **phrase.**
Participle   *See* **verbal.**
Parts of Speech   The eight groups into which words are traditionally classified based on their function in a sentence.
Passive Voice   *See* **voice.**
Past Participle   *See* **verbal.**
Personal Pronoun   *See* **pronoun.**
Phrase   A group of words that lacks a subject and predicate and often functions as a single part of speech. (See also Chapter 9.)
Positive Degree   *See* **comparative, superlative.**
Possessive Case   *See* **case.**
Predicate   The part of a sentence that tells what the subject does or is. The simple predicate is the main verb, including any auxiliaries or modals.

> The rice **was** lightly **flavored** with vinegar.

The complete predicate consists of the simple predicate and all the words that modify and complement it:

> The rice **was lightly flavored with vinegar.**

(See also Section 7c.)
Predicate Adjective   An adjective that follows a linking verb and describes the subject of the verb. (See also Section 7d-4.)

> Lestrade's solution was too **simplistic.**

Predicate Nominative   A noun or noun substitute that follows a linking verb and renames the subject of the verb. (See also Section 7d-4.)

> The model for Nora Charles was **Lillian Hellman.**

Preposition   A function word used to show the relationship of a noun or pronoun to another part of the sentence. (See also Section 8i.)
Prepositional Phrase   A phrase consisting of a preposition, the object of the preposition, and all the words modifying this object. (See also Section 9a.)

The narrator **of the story** is a young man who lived **with the writer** and assisted him **in his work.**

Present Infinitive   *See* **verbal.**

Principle Parts   *See* **verb.**

Pronoun   A word that stands for or takes the place of one or more nouns. A personal pronoun takes the place of a noun that names a person or thing: *I, me, my, mine; you, your, yours; he, him, his; she, her, hers; it, its; we, us, our, ours; they, them, their, theirs.* A demonstrative pronoun points to someone or something: *this, that, these, those.* An indefinite pronoun does not take the place of a particular noun. It carries the idea of "all," "some," "any," or "none": *everyone, everything, somebody, many, anyone, anything, no one, nobody.* An interrogative pronoun is used to ask a question: *who, whom, whose, what, which.* A relative pronoun is used to form an adjective clause or a noun clause: *who, whose, whom, which, that, what, whoever, whomever, whichever, whatever.* An intensive pronoun is used for emphasis. It is formed by adding *-self* or *-selves* to the end of a personal pronoun. A reflexive pronoun, which has the same form as an intensive pronoun, is used to show that the subject is acting upon itself. (See also Section 8f and Chapters 14 and 15.)

Proper Adjective   An adjective formed from a proper noun. (See also Chapter 41.)

Machiavellian scheme, **Byronic** disposition, **Parisian** dress

Proper Noun   *See* **noun.**

Qualifier   A structure-class word that qualifies or intensifies an adjective or adverb.

You seem **rather** sad.

She runs **very** swiftly down the track.

(See also Section 8h.)

Reflexive Pronoun   *See* **pronoun.**

Regular Verb   A verb whose past tense and past participle are formed by adding *-d* or *-ed* to the present infinitive: *analyze, analyzed, analyzed; detain, detained, detained.* (See also Section 8b and Chapter 12.)

Relative Pronoun   *See* **pronoun.**

Restrictive Element   A modifying phrase or clause that limits, identifies, or qualifies the idea expressed by the noun it modifies. Since a restrictive element is necessary to the basic meaning of the clause in which it appears, it is not set off with commas. (See also Section 28d.)

> The woman **wearing the blue suit** just received a promotion.

Run-On Sentence   Two or more complete sentences that are incorrectly written as though they were one sentence. (See also Chapter 11.)

Sentence   A group of words with a subject and a predicate that expresses a complete thought. Sentences can be classified into four basic groups according to the number and kinds of clauses they contain. A simple sentence contains only one independent clause and no dependent clause.

> The relationship between the United States and Iraq needs to be improved.

A compound sentence contains two or more independent clauses but no dependent clause.

> The senator worked hard for passage of the bill, but his efforts proved futile.

A complex sentence contains one independent clause and one or more dependent clauses.

> Although the two nations were technically at peace, their secret services were fighting a covert war.

A compound–complex sentence contains two or more independent clauses and one or more dependent clauses.

> Voter confidence in the administration grew as interest rates went down; however, it quickly faded when interest rates started to rise.

(See also Chapter 7 and Section 9e.)

Sentence Fragment   An incomplete sentence written as a complete sentence. (See also Chapter 10.)
Simple Predicate   *See* **predicate.**
Simple Sentence   *See* **sentence.**
Simple Subject   *See* **subject.**
Split Infinitive   Infinitive phrase in which a modifier, usually an adverb, has been inserted between the two elements. Avoid splitting infinitives in formal writing.

> He began **to excitedly speak.**

(See also Sections 9b and 18b.)
Squinting Modifier   A modifier that, because of its placement, could refer to either the preceding or the following element in a sentence, resulting in ambiguity. (See also Section 18c.)
Structure Classes   The small, closed classes of words that explain the grammatical or structural relationships of the form classes: determiners, qualifiers, pronouns, prepositions, conjunctions, and expletives. (See Sections 8f–k.)
Style   The way in which words are arranged in written language, as distinct from the ideas that the words express.
Subject   The part of a sentence that answers the question "who?" or "what?" in regard to the predicate, or verb. The simple subject is the main noun or noun substitute in the subject.

> Women's **fashions** from the 1950s are becoming popular again.

The complete subject is the simple subject together with all the words that modify it.

> **Women's fashions from the 1950s** are becoming popular again.

A compound subject consists of two or more words that take the same predicate.

> Women's **fashions** and **hairstyles** from the 1950s are becoming popular again.

(See also Sections 7b and 13a.)
Subject Complement   *See* **complement.**
Subjective Case   *See* **case.**

Subjunctive   *See* **mood.**
Subordinate Clause   *See* **clause.**
Subordinating Conjunction   *See* **conjunction.**
Superlative Degree   *See* **comparative, superlative.**
Tense   The time expressed by the form of the verb. There are six tenses: (simple) present, present perfect, (simple) past, past perfect, (simple) future, and future perfect. Each of the tenses has a progressive form that indicates continuing action. The present tense is used to write about events or conditions that are happening or existing now.

She **writes** a column for the local newspaper.

The present tense is also used to write about natural or scientific laws, timeless truths, events in literature, habitual action, and (with an adverbial word or phrase) future time. The present perfect tense is used to write about events that occurred at some unspecified time in the past and about events and continued actions that began in the past and may still be continuing in the present.

She **has written** a series of articles about child abuse.

The past tense is used to write about events that occurred and conditions that existed at a definite time in the past and do not extend into the present.

The researcher **studied** voting trends in this district.

The past perfect tense is used to write about a past event or condition that ended before another past event or condition began.

They **had studied** the effects of television on voting trends before they made their proposals.

The future tense is used to write about events or conditions that have not yet begun.

They **will consider** her proposal.

The future perfect tense is used to write about a future event or condition that will end before another future event or condition begins or before a specified time in the future.

By next month, they **will have considered** all the proposals.

(See also Section 8b and Chapter 12.)

Transitive Verb   *See* **verb.**

Verb   A word that expresses action or a state of being and has four principal parts or forms: present infinitive, past tense, past participle, and present participle. (See also Sections 8b and 8c.) An action verb expresses action.

The ballerina **danced** beautifully.

A linking verb expresses a state of being or a condition. It connects the subject of the sentence to a word that identifies or describes it.

Vitamin C **may be** *effective* against the common cold.

A transitive verb is an action verb that takes an object.

The fleet **secures** the *coasts* against invasion.

An intransitive verb is any verb that does not take an object.

After deregulation of the industry, prices **soared.**

(See also Section 8b.)

Verb Phrase   A phrase made up of the infinitive, the present participle, or the past participle, plus one or more auxiliaries or modals.

The candidate **will make** a speech tomorrow.

Jesse Jackson **had proved** himself an effective negotiator.

The gymnasts **have been practicing** regularly.

(See also Section 8b and Chapter 12.)

Verbal   A grammatical form that is based on a verb but that functions as a noun, an adjective, or an adverb instead of as a verb, in a sentence. There are three types of verbals: participles, gerunds, and infinitives. The present participle and the past participle of most verbs can function as adjectives.

One of the most memorable figures in *Alice in Wonderland* is the **grinning** Cheshire cat.

The lawyer demanded a **written** contract.

A gerund is a verb form spelled the same way as the present participle but used as a noun in a sentence.

Walking is good for your health.

The present infinitive and the present perfect infinitive form of a verb can function as a noun, as an adjective, or as an adverb.

In *A Chorus Line,* the overriding ambition of each of the characters is **to dance.** Cassie was glad **to have gotten** the part.

(See also Section 8c.)

Verbal Phrase   A phrase consisting of a verbal and all its *complements* and *modifiers.* There are three types of verbal phrases: *participial phrases, gerund phrases,* and *infinitive phrases.* A participial phrase functions as an adjective in a sentence.

The image of a garden **filled with poisonous flowers** dominates "Rappaccini's Daughter."

A gerund phrase functions as a noun in a sentence.

Exercising in the noonday sun can be dangerous.

An infinitive phrase functions as a noun, an adjective, or an adverb.

To make the world safe for democracy was one of Wilson's goals.

(See also Section 9b.)

Voice   The indication of whether the subject performs or receives the action of the verb. If the subject performs the action, the verb and the clause are in the *active voice.*

Herman Melville **wrote** "Bartleby the Scrivener."

If the subject receives the action or is acted upon, the verb and the clause are in the *passive voice.*

"Bartleby the Scrivener" **was written** by Herman Melville.

(See also Sections 8b, 12b, and 17c.)

The User's Self-Help Section

This section contains a self-administering set of "diagnostic tests." You can use these to help yourself identify any areas in which your habitual patterns of word usage or sentence structure might need extra attention. If your scores don't satisfy you or your errors seem excessive, the answer keys will direct you to the exact topics and patterns on which you might need redirection and indicate where in this book you can find help.

First try your hand at rewriting the sentences in these diagnostic tests—in all of which you need to make some corrections. Then check the corrected sentence examples in the answer key at the end. The corrected sentences there will identify the topic at issue in the incorrect sentence and the section of this book where you can find a detailed explanation of correct usage. You can also work on the exercises in the section in the text to which the answer key has directed you. At the same time, knowing which topics give you the most problems, you can efficiently seek help in a writing lab or learning center, fully aware of where you need to concentrate your efforts. If your percentages of correct answers on these tests consistently fall below 70 percent, you are probably in need of some thoughtful redirection of your writing habits in certain areas. Of course, you should also talk to your instructor about where and how to obtain extra help.

Diagnostic Test for Grammar

Each sentence below contains a grammatical error. Correct the sentences on a separate sheet.

1. Each man in attendance will get their turn.
2. She likes to drink beer when it is hot.
3. Juanita and me are friends.
4. To who did you send the package?
5. He quietly snuck up the stairs at midnight.
6. I like to lay on the sofa.
7. If I was a bird, I could fly.
8. I should think that you are wealthy.
9. Deciding how to do it and when are big questions.
10. Either a present or a cash gift are acceptable.
11. A few of the band members also sings in the choir.
12. Latitia is the elder of three children.
13. Running on the sidewalk, my shirt got wet.
14. If I was rich, I'd loan you some money.
15. Three weeks seems like a short time now.
16. I plan to perhaps see you in December.
17. Between you and I, who will get the best grade?
18. To go or staying were difficult choices.
19. Whoever did it to you.
20. My dad gave gifts to my mother and I.

Diagnostic Test for Punctuation and Mechanics

Each sentence below contains a punctuation error. Correct the sentences on a separate sheet.

1. "no," he answered, "we will not go there."

2. Most teachers belong to the national education association.

3. Wordsworth wrote "Let Nature be your teacher."

4. My brother is in school, I am staying home.

5. We shall nevertheless do as you ask.

6. The rain as I started to wash the car began to fall.

7. The program was interesting since we had not seen it before.

8. He visited us on Monday March 17, 1996.

9. Demetrius did you go to lunch today?

10. The woman over there . . . . directs the choir.

11. She excitedly exclaimed, "Stop."

12. Lola grows roses which smell sweet, marigolds which keep bugs away, and petunias which require very little care.

13. The flag - red, white, and blue - shone in the sun.

14. Our club president said "we can raise the money.

15. Horses, dogs and a camel appeared in the parade.

16. Its nearly time to go.

17. The cat ate it's food quickly.

18. The cake was two and one-half inches high.

19. 333 students attended the rally.

20. Reverend Bill Gallanto recited the prayer of Saint Francis.

Diagnostic Test for Syntax

Each sentence contains an error in syntax except one sentence, which contains two errors. After analyzing the sentences, write them in corrected form on a separate sheet.

1. Because they do exercise. Then they eat better.

2. The very shyly pretty girl smiled.

3. I like to sing and dancing.

4. Bring the books to my brother and myself.

5. Why she gave to me the gift is a mystery to me.

6. She do pretend to be a scholar.

7. I am gone home.

8. Father being away we just didn't know how to fix it.

9. The ball was hit by the young girl.

10. There are many reasons to oppose the new tax.

11. We will depart at noon, however, we should still arrive on time.

12. Our college has a fine library, this is a strong point.

13. The train arrived late we were not very happy.

14. Most restaurants now ban smoking some people still smoke there.

15. Because we were on the bus is the reason the luggage was placed on the curb.

Diagnostic Test for Diction

Identify the inappropriate use of diction in each sentence below. After analyzing the sentences, rewrite them in appropriate ways on a separate sheet.

1. Everytime we meet, she disses me.

2. Nevertheless, we decided to make a deal.

3. The lovely speaker graced the dais while beatifically smiling at those assembled at her feet.

4. To reconcile a hard drive to its default's settings on an on-going basis, run RevRdisk after each user has logged out.

5. Our high school has men's and girls' basketball teams.

6. The senator appeared childish when visiting the prison.

7. Sandra was hired as a salesman by the insurance company.

8. Nobody likes to have a failing grade on his record.

9. The border towns are full of Mexicans who can't speak English.

10. Dr. Lola Cipia was named chairman of our department.

11. Nowhere near enough people volunteered to go.

12. His car is kind of old looking.

13. The court determined that he was likely for all damages.

14. She looked everywhere for her hair brush.

15. Be sure and pay attention to the speaker.

Self-Help Answer Keys to Diagnostic Tests

Diagnostic Test for Grammar (Key)

Give yourself a 5 percent score for each correct answer, and follow the section references for explanations of correct answers.

1. Each man in attendance will get his turn.
   (See Section 14a on pronoun agreement.)

2. She likes to drink beer when the weather is hot.
   (See Section 14b on vague pronoun reference.)

3. Juanita and I are friends.
   (See Section 15a on pronoun case.)

4. To whom did you send the package?
   (See Section 15a on pronoun case.)

5. He quietly sneaked up the stairs at midnight.
   (See Section 12c on troublesome verb forms.)

6. I like to lie on the sofa.
   (See Section 8b on transitive-intransitive verbs.)

7. If I were a bird, I could fly.
   (See Section 12b on the subjunctive mood.)

8. I would think that you are wealthy.
   (See Section 8b on modal verbs.)

9. Deciding how to do it and when is a big question.
   (See Section 13a on subject-verb agreement.)

10. Either a present or a cash gift is acceptable.
    (See Section 14a on pronoun agreement.)

11. A few of the band members also sing in the choir.
    (See Section 14a on pronoun agreement.)

12. Latitia is the eldest of three children.
    (See Section 16c on comparisons.)

13. While I was running on the sidewalk, my shirt got wet. *Or:* My shirt got wet when I was running on the sidewalk. (See Section 18a on dangling modifiers.)

14. If I were rich, I'd loan you some money. (See Section 12b on the subjunctive mood.)

15. Three weeks seem like a short time now. (See Section 13d on subject-verb agreement.)

16. I plan to see you perhaps in December. (See Section 18b on split infinitives.)

17. Between you and me, who will get the best grade? (See Section 15a on pronoun case.)

18. To go or to stay was a difficult choice. (See Section 21c on parallelism and Section 13a on compound subjects and verb agreements.)

19. Whoever did it to you was not a nice person. (See Section 10b on sentence fragments.)

20. My dad gave gifts to my mother and me. (See Section 15a on pronoun case.)

Diagnostic Test for Punctuation and Mechanics (Key)

Give yourself a 5 percent score for each correct answer, and follow the section references for explanations of correct answers.

1. "No," he answered, "We will not go there." (See Chapter 41 on capitalization.)

2. Most teachers belong to the National Education Association. (See Chapter 41 on capitalization.)

3. Wordsworth wrote: "Let Nature be your teacher." (See Section 30a on the colon.)

4. My brother is in school; I am staying home. (See Section 29a on the semicolon.)

5. We shall, nevertheless, do as you ask.
   (See Section 28d on the comma.)

6. The rain, as I started to wash the car, began to fall.
   (See Section 28d on the comma.)

7. The program was interesting, since we had not seen it before.
   (See Section 28c on the comma.)

8. He visited us on Monday, March 17, 1996.
   (See Section 28d on the comma.)

9. Demetrius, did you go to lunch today?
   (See Section 28d on the comma.)

10. The woman over there [. . .] directs the choir.
    (See Chapter 35 on ellipsis points.)

11. She excitedly exclaimed, "Stop!"
    (See Section 27c on the exclamation point.)

12. Lola grows roses, which smell sweet; marigolds, which keep bugs away; and petunias, which require very little care.
    (See Section 29b on the semicolon.)

13. The flag--red, white, and blue--shone in the sun.
    (See Section 31b on the dash.)

14. Our club president said, "We can raise the money."
    (See Section 34a on direct quotations.)

15. Horses, dogs, and a camel appeared in the parade.
    (See Section 28a on the comma.)

16. It's nearly time to go.
    (See Section 37d on the apostrophe.)

17. The cat ate its food quickly.
    (See Section 37d on the apostrophe.)

18. The cake was 2½ inches high.
    (See Chapter 40 on numbers as fractions.)

19. Three hundred and thirty-three students attended the rally.
    (See Chapter 40 on writing numbers.)

20. Rev. Bill Gallanto recited the prayer of St. Francis.
    (See Chapter 39 on abbreviations.)

Diagnostic Test for Syntax (Key)

Give yourself a 6.6 percent score for each correct answer, and follow the section references for explanations of correct answers.

1. Because they do exercise every day, they eat better.
   (See Section 10d on sentence fragments.)

2. The very pretty girl smiled shyly.
   (See Sections 8e and 16b on adverbs.)

3. I like to sing and to dance.
   (See Section 21c on parallelism.)

4. Bring the books to my brother and me.
   (See Section 15a on pronoun case.)

5. Why she gave me the gift is a mystery to me.
   (See Section 7d on indirect objects.)

6. She does pretend to be a scholar.
   (See Sections 8b and 12b on verb tense.)

7. I am going home.
   (See Sections 8b and 12b on verb tense.)

8. Father being away, we just didn't know how to fix it.
   (See Section 9b on absolute phrases.)

9. The young girl hit the ball.
   (See Sections 8b and 12b on the passive voice.)

10. Many reasons exist to oppose the new tax.
    (See Sections 7b and 8k on expletives as subjects.)

11. We will depart at noon; however, we should still arrive on time.
    (See Section 11a on the comma splice.)

12. Our college has a fine library, which is a strong point. *Or:* Our college has a fine library. This is a strong point.
    (See Section 11a on the comma splice.)

13. The train arrived late. We were not very happy. *Or:* The train arrived late and we were not very happy.
    (See Section 11b on fused sentences.)

14. Most restaurants now ban smoking. Some people still smoke there. *Or:* Most restaurants have banned smoking, but some people still smoke there.
    (See Section 11b on fused sentences.)

15. Because we were on the bus, someone placed the luggage on the curb.
    (See Section 17i on avoiding adverb clauses as subjects and Sections 8b and 12b on the passive voice.)

Diagnostic Test for Diction (Key)

Give yourself a 6.6 percent score for each correct answer, and follow the section references for explanations of correct answers.

1. Every time we meet, she acts disrespectful toward me.
   (See Section 24a on slang.)

2. Nevertheless, we decided to agree.
   (See Section 24b on colloquialisms.)

3. The speaker on the dais smiled at the audience.
   (See Section 22b on flowery language.)

4. To return the computer's hard drive to its original settings, run the RevRdisk program after each user finishes using the machine.
   (See Section 24c on jargon.)

5. Our high school has men's and women's basketball teams.
   (See Section 25a on sexist language.)

6. The senator appeared childlike when visiting the prison.
   (See Section 26d on denotation and connotation.)

7. Sandra was hired as a salesperson by the insurance company.
   (See Section 25a on sexist language.)

8. Nobody likes to have a failing grade on his or her record.
   (See Section 25a on sexist language.)

9. The border towns are full of people who can't speak English.
   (See Section 25b on biased language.)

10. Dr. Lola Cipia was named chairperson of our department.
    (See Section 25a on sexist language.)

11. Not enough people volunteered to go.
    (See Glossary of Usage.)

12. His car looks old.
    (See Glossary of Usage.)

13. The court determined that he was liable for all damages.
    (See Glossary of Usage.)

14. She looked everywhere for her hairbrush.
    (See Glossary of Usage.)

15. Pay attention to the speaker.
    (See Glossary of Usage.)

Acknowledgments

Paula Gunn Allen, "The Sacred Hoop: Recovering the Feminine in American Indian Traditions" (excerpt) from *The Sacred Hoop: Recovering the Feminine Side in American Indian Traditions*. Copyright © 1986 by Paula Gunn Allen. Reprinted with the permission of Beacon Press, Boston.

AltaVista, screen print of search results from "kwanzaa." Reprinted with the permission of Digital Equipment Corporation.

American Heritage Dictionary, entries for "doubt" and "doubtful" from *The American Heritage Dictionary, Second College Edition*. Copyright © 1985 by Houghton Mifflin Company. Reprinted with the permission of the publisher.

American Psychological Association, paraphrase of "Abstract" section from *The Publication Manual of the American Psychological Association, Third Edition*. Copyright © 1983 by The American Psychological Association. Reprinted with the permission of the publisher.

Eileen Biagi, "Career Achievement in Women." Reprinted with the permission of the author.

Kit Hoffman, "Swim For Your Life." Reprinted with the permission of the author.

John Michael Jansen, "Comparable Worth: Equal Pay for Work Judged to Be of Equal Value." Reprinted with the permission of the author.

"John Adams' Opinion of Benjamin Franklin" from *America: History and Life*. Reprinted with the permission of ABC-CLIO, Inc.

Alison Jolly, excerpts from "A New Science That Sees Animals as Conscious Beings" from *Smithsonian Magazine* (March 1983). Reprinted with the permission of the author.

John McPhee, "Oranges" (excerpt) from *Oranges*. Copyright © 1966, 1967 by John McPhee. Reprinted with the permission of Farrar, Straus & Giroux, Inc.

Index

Index

V

CONTENTS